THE AMERICAN EXPERIENCE
A Radical Reader

THE AMERICAN EXPERIENCE
A Radical Reader

edited by Harold Jaffe LONG ISLAND UNIVERSITY

John Tytell QUEENS COLLEGE

Harper & Row, Publishers New York • Evanston • London

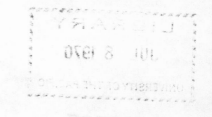

THE AMERICAN EXPERIENCE: A Radical Reader
Copyright © 1970 by Harold Jaffe and John Tytell

Library of Congress catalog card number: 74-98195

For M'Ellen and Jan

CONTENTS

Whither 433

PREFACE

The American Experience *is a "radical" reader in this sense: it employs a variety of unconventional forms (manifestoes, speeches, interviews, a symposium, poetry, rock-lyrics, and scenarios), in addition to the essay, to speak directly to—not down to—students about life in contemporary America. Why this emphasis on form and manner of presentation in a college reader? The question should rather be, Why has such a method of compilation not been used before?*

The cultural figures whom students respect most, those who have probed to the roots of our society ("radical" derives from radix, *Latin for "root") are not our essayists, nor are they primarily our writers. As Marshall McLuhan and others have observed, the written word is not nearly so essential as it once was. Young people perceive differently because they have been nurtured by singular—though sinister—foster parents: nuclear energy, computerized technology, and mass media. Naturally, they respond to the visual, the aural, the tactile, and the kinetic more readily than to the "rationally" organized essay, based as it is on traditional attitudes which often do not seem especially relevant. Moreover, America is a country in conflict, and students have engaged themselves with the real issues confronting this society. Clearly their actions—strikes, sit-ins, marches, free universities, street theater, and so on—point to their dedication and to their spiritual separation from the generations of students that preceded them.*

With these prospective readers in mind, we have attempted to adhere to two principles in compiling our anthology. First, we have collected the best writing we could find on the contemporary American experience, not excluding material previously deemed unsuitable—or, at least, unsuitable for college students. Some of this material we have culled from "underground" publications, some from more accessible sources, and in a few instances authors have written pieces specifically for this volume. Second, we have tried to narrow the gap that necessarily exists between an issue and the response to this issue by the reader. That is, instead of relying exclusively on essays that explore the implications of rock music, happenings, and obscenity, for instance, we have included the examples themselves: rock-lyrics, scenarios, and a monologue by Lenny Bruce called "The Dirty-Word Concept."

This last selection deserves special mention. Something is considered obscene only when it violates a certified taboo—which in our society has most notably meant sexuality or words suggesting sexuality. As Lenny

Bruce puts it, we have long considered it sinful to look at a healthy
naked body of the opposite sex, but not in the least sinful to view the
same body after a horrible accident, maimed and suffering. There are
indications now that our burdensome Puritan legacy has in many quarters finally been expended: the Broadway musical Hair, with its innocent nudity and occasional use of four letter words, has been successfully
touring the United States, while the Vietnam War has been losing
favor throughout the country. Which of these, after all, is intrinsically
obscene?

The American Experience is radical also in that most of our selections
suggest remedies which include significant alterations—even transformations—of certain aspects of our society so as to aid in bridging the
chasm between the reality of present-day America and the "American
Dream." We live in a land that is puzzled by the contradictions it
contains: individuality threatened by encroaching bureaucracies, affluence
surrounded by poverty, preachments about equality in the face of racial
turmoil. Perhaps there is not much time left in which to change, but
there is no time for despair. We must explore viable alternatives—most
of the writers in this volume insist that there are still some left.

The first section, "Legacy of the Beat Generation," points to the past
and to the future. Allen Ginsberg's "America," the first selection, is
spiritual heir to the visions of Anne Hutchinson, Roger Williams,
Emerson, Whitman, and Hart Crane; and Ginsberg himself is guru to a
whole generation of disenfranchised young people throughout the world.
Mailer's "The White Negro" examines the "beat" white youth's identification with the culture of the Negro, a phenomenon that encourages
Eldridge Cleaver in his otherwise despairing essay on race relations from
Soul on Ice, which begins the "Black Consciousness" section. James
Baldwin, Malcolm X, Stokely Carmichael, and LeRoi Jones, also
represented, have influenced and enlightened men of conscience every-
where, especially American university students, as the section "New
Politics and the University" clearly indicates.

In addition to stimulating political responses within and outside the
"system," the protest against dehumanization has engendered entirely
new ways of perceiving experience—new ways of coping, as it were.
Included in the section "New Life Styles" are some of the most provocative and cogent writings on mysticism, Zen, drugs, and touch-therapy.
Section five, "New Directions in the Arts," demonstrates responses
in the various arts to the American experience, with writings on
experimental music, Pop art, cinema, drama, "happenings," and rock

music. *Section six contains a monologue by Lenny Bruce, rock-lyrics, poetry, fiction, and a one-act play. The final section, "Whither," looks to the future: Tom Hayden, Paul Goodman, Gary Snyder, and the late Martin Luther King, Jr., agree upon the unhealthy condition of our culture but offer different possibilities for regeneration.*

The American Experience attempts to document the conflicts of the 1960s while anticipating the directions of the 1970s. Because our anthology is exceptionally readable, as well as uncompromisingly relevant, we like to think of it as a paracollege reader intended primarily, though not exclusively, for the college student, since anyone interested in understanding contemporary America would benefit from reading the selections.

HAROLD JAFFE
JOHN TYTELL

ACKNOWLEDGMENTS

We are grateful to those who aided in the compilation of this volume: James Goldman, Christina Katz, M'Ellen Tytell, and Jan Grisingher. We would also like to thank the editors of Freedomways, Irving Davis *of SNCC, and Alan Douglas of Douglas International.*

LEGACY
OF THE BEAT
GENERATION

Much of the current impetus for social change can be traced to the defiant moral thrust of a group of writers who began to criticize American materialism after World War II. Calling themselves the Beat (for beatific) Generation, these writers—Jack Kerouac, Allen Ginsberg, Lawrence Ferlinghetti, Gary Snyder, and others—chose to dissociate themselves from conventional patterns of existence. Rejecting the stultifying possibilities of positions in industry and comforts in suburbia, they "dug" jazz, experimented with drugs and various exotic disciplines such as Zen Buddhism. They excoriated our society for betraying the "American Dream" of Walt Whitman, as Allen Ginsberg does in his poem "America"; like Whitman, they attempted to revivify their own lives by identifying with outcast groups such as the Mexicans, the Indians, and the American Negroes. Norman Mailer's essay, "The White Negro," shows how the two cultures— white and black—were merged by the alienated beat sensibility into the new life style of the hipster.

America

America I've given you all and now I'm nothing.
America two dollars and twentyseven cents January 17, 1956.
I can't stand my own mind.
America when will we end the human war?
Go fuck yourself with your atom bomb.
I don't feel good don't bother me.
I won't write my poem till I'm in my right mind.
America when will you be angelic?
When will you take off your clothes?
When will you look at yourself through the grave?
When will you be worthy of your million Trotskyites?
America why are your libraries full of tears?
America when will you send your eggs to India?
When can I go into the supermarket and buy what I need with my
    good looks?
America after all it is you and I who are perfect not the next world.
Your machinery is too much for me.
You made me want to be a saint.
There must be some other way to settle this argument.
Burroughs is in Tangiers I don't think he'll come back it's sinister.
Are you being sinister or is this some form of practical joke?
I'm trying to come to the point.
I refuse to give up my obsession.
America stop pushing I know what I'm doing.
America the plum blossoms are falling.
I haven't read the newspapers for months, everybody goes on trial for
    murder.
America I feel sentimental about the Wobblies.
America I used to be a communist when I was a kid I'm not sorry.
I smoke marijuana every chance I get.
I sit in my house for days on end and stare at the roses in the closet.
When I go to Chinatown I get drunk and never get laid.
My mind is made up there's going to be trouble.
You should have seen me reading Marx.
My psychoanalyst thinks I'm perfectly right.
I won't say the Lord's Prayer.
I have mystical visions and cosmic vibrations.
America I still haven't told you what you did to Uncle Max after he
    came over from Russia.

I'm addressing you.
Are you going to let your emotional life be run by Time Magazine?
I'm obsessed by Time Magazine.
I read it every week.
Its cover stares at me every time I slink past the corner candystore.
I read it in the basement of the Berkeley Public Library.
It's always telling me about responsibility. Businessmen are serious.
    Movie producers are serious. Everybody's serious but me.
It occurs to me that I am America.
I am talking to myself again.

Asia is rising against me.
I haven't got a chinaman's chance.
I'd better consider my national resources.
My national resources consist of two joints of marijuana millions of
    genitals an unpublishable private literature that goes 1400 miles an
    hour and twentyfive-thousand mental institutions.
I say nothing about my prisons nor the millions of underprivileged who
    live in my flowerpots under the light of five hundred suns.
I have abolished the whorehouses of France, Tangiers is the next to go.
My ambition is to be President despite the fact that I'm a Catholic.

America how can I write a holy litany in your silly mood?
I will continue like Henry Ford my strophes are as individual as
    his automobiles more so they're all different sexes.
America I will sell you strophes $2500 apiece $500 down on your
    old strophe
America free Tom Mooney
America save the Spanish Loyalists
America Sacco & Vanzetti must not die
America I am the Scottsboro boys.
America when I was seven momma took me to Communist Cell meetings
    they sold us garbanzos a handful per ticket a ticket costs a nickel
    and the speeches were free everybody was angelic and sentimental
    about the workers it was all so sincere you have no idea what a
    good thing the party was in 1835 Scott Nearing was a grand old
    man a real mensch Mother Bloor made me cry I once saw Israel
    Amter plain. Everybody must have been a spy.
America you don't really want to go to war.
America it's them bad Russians.
Them Russians them Russians and them Chinamen. And them
    Russians.
The Russia wants to eat us alive. The Russia's power mad. She wants
    to take our cars from out our garages.
Her wants to grab Chicago. Her needs a Red Readers' Digest. Her

wants our auto plants in Siberia. Him big bureaucracy running our
fillingstations.
That no good. Ugh. Him make Indians learn read. Him need big black
niggers. Hah. Her make us all work sixteen hours a day, Help.
America this is quite serious.
America this is the impression I get from looking in the television set.
America is this correct?
I'd better get right down to the job.
It's true I don't want to join the Army or turn lathes in precision parts
factories, I'm nearsighted and psychopathic anyway.
America I'm putting my queer shoulder to the wheel.

The White Negro

Superficial Reflections on the Hipster

Our search for the rebels of the generation led us to the hipster. The hipster is an enfant terrible turned inside out. In character with his time, he is trying to get back at the conformists by lying low . . . You can't interview a hipster because his main goal is to keep out of a society which, he thinks, is trying to make everyone over in its own image. He takes marijuana because it supplies him with experiences that can't be shared with "squares." He may affect a broad-brimmed hat or a zoot suit, but usually he prefers to skulk unmarked. The hipster may be a jazz musician; he is rarely an artist, almost never a writer. He may earn his living as a petty criminal, a hobo, a carnival roustabout or a free-lance moving man in Greenwich Village, but some hipsters have found a safe refuge in the upper income brackets as television comics or movie actors. (The late James Dean, for one, was a hipster hero.) . . . It is tempting to describe the hipster in psychiatric terms as infantile, but the style of his infantilism is a sign of the times. He does not try to enforce his will on others, Napoleon-fashion, but contents himself with a magical omnipotence never disproved because never tested. . . . As the only extreme nonconformist of his generation, he exercises a powerful if underground appeal for conformists, through newspaper accounts of his delinquencies, his structureless jazz, and his emotive grunt words. —CAROLINE BIRD: "Born 1930: The Unlost Generation," *Harper's Bazaar*, Feb. 1957.

Probably, we will never be able to determine the psychic havoc of the concentration camps and the atom bomb upon the unconscious mind of almost everyone alive in these years. For the first time in civilized history, perhaps for the first time in all of history, we have been forced to live with the suppressed knowledge that the smallest facets of our personality or the most minor projection of our ideas, or indeed the absence of ideas and the absence of personality could mean equally well that we might still be doomed to die as a cipher in some vast statistical operation in which our teeth would be counted, and our hair would be saved, but our death itself would be unknown, unhonored, and unremarked, a death which could not follow with dignity as a possible consequence to serious actions we had chosen, but rather a death by *deus ex machina* in a gas chamber or a radioactive city; and so if in the midst of civilization—that civilization founded upon the Faustian urge to dominate nature by mastering time, mastering the links of social cause and effect—in the middle of an economic civilization founded upon the confidence that time could indeed be subjected to our will, our psyche was subjected itself to the intolerable anxiety that death being causeless, life was causeless as well, and time deprived of cause and effect had come to a stop.

The Second World War presented a mirror to the human condition which blinded anyone who looked into it. For if tens of millions were killed in concentration camps out of the inexorable agonies and contractions of super-states founded upon the always insoluble contradictions of injustice, one was then obliged also to see that no matter how crippled and perverted an image of man was the society he had created, it was nonetheless his creation, his collective creation (at least his collective creation from the past) and if society was so murderous, then who could ignore the most hideous of questions about his own nature?

Worse. One could hardly maintain the courage to be individual, to speak one's own voice, for the years in which one could complacently accept oneself as part of an elite by being a radical were forever gone. A man knew that when he dissented, he gave a note upon his life which could be called in any year of overt crisis. No wonder then that these have been the years of conformity and depression. A stench of fear has come out of every pore of American life, and we suffer from a collective failure of nerve. The only courage, with rare exceptions, that we have been witness to, has been the isolated courage of isolated people.

2

It is on this bleak scene that a phenomenon has appeared: the American existentialist—the hipster, the man who knows that if our collective condition is to live with instant death by atomic war, relatively quick death by the State as *l'univers concentrationnaire*, or with a slow death by conformity with every creative and rebellious instinct stifled (at what damage to the mind and the heart and the liver and the nerves no research foundation for cancer will discover in a hurry), if the fate of twentieth-century man is to live with death from adolescence to premature senescence, why then the only life-giving answer is to accept the terms of death, to live with death as immediate danger, to divorce oneself from society, to exist without roots, to set out on that uncharted journey into the rebellious imperatives of the self. In short, whether the life is criminal or not, the decision is to encourage the psychopath in oneself, to explore that domain of experience where security is boredom and therefore sickness, and one exists in the present, in that enormous present which is without past or future, memory or planned intention, the life where a man must go until he is beat, where he must gamble with his energies through all those small or large crises of courage and unforeseen situations which beset his day, where he must be with it or doomed not to swing. The unstated essence of Hip, its psychopathic brilliance, quivers with the knowledge that new kinds of victories increase one's power for new kinds of perception; and defeats, the wrong kind of defeats, attack the body and imprison one's energy until one is jailed in the prison air of other people's habits, other people's defeats, boredom, quiet desperation, and muted icy self-destroying rage. One is Hip or one is Square (the alternative which each new generation coming into American life is beginning to feel), one is a rebel or one conforms, one is a frontiersman in the Wild West of American night life, or else a Square cell, trapped in the totalitarian tissues of American society, doomed willy-nilly to conform if one is to succeed.

A totalitarian society makes enormous demands on the courage of men, and a partially totalitarian society makes even greater demands, for the general anxiety is greater. Indeed if one is to be a man, almost any kind of unconventional action often takes disproportionate courage. So it is no accident that the source of Hip is the Negro for he has been living on the margin between totalitarianism and democracy for two centuries. But the presence of Hip as a working philosophy in the sub-worlds of American life is probably due to jazz, and its knifelike entrance into culture, its subtle but so penetrating influence on an avant-garde generation—that postwar generation of adventurers who (some consciously, some by osmosis) had absorbed the lessons of disillusionment and digust of the twenties, the depression, and the war. Sharing a collective disbelief in the words of men who had too much money and controlled too many things, they knew almost as powerful a disbelief in the socially monolithic ideas of the single mate, the solid family, and the respectable love life. If the intellectual antecedents of this generation can be traced to such separate influences as D. H. Lawrence, Henry Miller, and Wilhelm Reich, the viable philosophy of Hemingway fit most of their facts: in a bad world, as he was to say over and over again (while taking time out from his parvenu snobbery and dedicated gourmandize), in a bad world there is no love nor mercy nor charity nor justice unless a man can keep his courage, and this indeed fitted some of the facts. What fitted the need of the adventurer even more precisely was Hemingway's categorical imperative that what made him feel good became therefore The Good.

So no wonder that in certain cities of America, in New York of course, and New Orleans, in Chicago and San Francisco and Los Angeles, in such American cities as Paris and Mexico, D.F., this particular part of a generation was attracted to what the Negro had to offer. In such places as Greenwich Village, a ménage-à-trois was completed—the bohemian and the juvenile delinquent came face-to-face with the Negro, and the hipster was a fact in American life. If marijuana was the wedding ring, the child was the language of Hip for its argot gave expression to abstract states of feeling which all could share, at least all who were Hip. And in this wedding of the white and the black it was the Negro who brought the cultural dowry. Any Negro who wishes to live must live with danger from his first day, and no experience can ever be casual to him, no Negro can saunter down a street with any real certainty that violence will not visit him on his walk. The cameos of security for the average white: mother and the home, job and the family, are not even a mockery to millions of Negroes; they are impossible. The Negro has the simplest of alternatives: live a life of constant humility or ever-threatening danger. In such a pass where paranoia is as vital to survival as blood, the Negro had stayed alive and begun to grow by following the need of his body where he could. Knowing in the cells of his existence that life was war, nothing but war, the Negro (all exceptions admitted) could rarely afford the sophisticated inhibitions of civilization, and so he kept for his survival the art of the primitive, he lived in the enormous present, he subsisted for his Saturday night kicks, relinquishing the pleasures of the mind for the more obligatory pleasures of the body, and in his music he gave voice to the character and quality of his existence, to his rage and the infinite variations of joy, lust, languor, growl, cramp, pinch, scream, and despair of his orgasm. For jazz is orgasm, it is the music of orgasm, good orgasm and bad, and so it spoke across a nation, it had the communication of art even where it was watered, perverted, corrupted, and almost killed, it spoke in no matter what laundered popular way of instantaneous existential states to which some whites could respond, it was indeed a communication by art because it said, "I feel this, and now you do too."

So there was a new breed of adventurers, urban adventurers who drifted out at night looking for action with a black man's code to fit their facts. The hipster had absorbed the existentialist synapses of the Negro, and for practical purposes could be considered a white Negro.

To be an existentialist, one must be able to feel oneself—one must know one's desires, one's rages, one's anguish, one must be aware of the character of one's frustration and know what would satisfy it. The over-civilized man can be an existentialist only if it is chic, and deserts it quickly for the next chic. To be a real existentialist (Sartre admittedly to the contrary) one must be religious, one must have one's sense of the "purpose"—whatever the purpose may be—but a life which is directed by one's faith in the necessity of action is a life committed to the notion that the substratum of existence is the search, the end meaningful but mysterious; it is impossible to live such a life unless one's emotions provide their profound conviction. Only the French, alienated beyond alienation from their unconscious could welcome an existential philosophy without ever feeling it at all; indeed only a Frenchman by declaring that the unconscious did not exist could then proceed to explore the delicate involutions of consciousness, the microscopically sensuous and all but ineffable *frissons* of mental becoming, in order finally to create the theology of atheism and so submit that in a world of absurdities the existential absurdity is most coherent.

In the dialogue between the atheist and the mystic, the atheist is on the side of life, rational life, undialectical life—since he conceives of death as emptiness, he can, no matter how weary or despairing, wish for nothing but more life; his pride is that he does not transpose his weakness and spiritual fatigue into a romantic longing for death, for such appreciation of death is then all too capable of being elaborated by his imagination into a universe of meaningful structure and moral orchestration.

Yet this masculine argument can mean very little for the mystic. The mystic can accept the atheist's description of his weakness, he can agree that his mysticism was a response to despair. And yet . . . and yet his argument is that he, the mystic, is the one finally who has chosen to live with death, and so death is his experience and not the atheist's, and the atheist by eschewing the limitless dimensions of profound despair has rendered himself incapable to judge the experience. The real argument which the mystic must always advance is the very intensity of his private vision—his argument depends from the vision precisely because what was felt in the vision is so extraordinary that no rational argument, no hypotheses of "oceanic feelings" and certainly no skeptical reductions can explain away what has become for him the reality more real than the reality of closely reasoned logic. His inner experience of the possibilities within death is his logic. So, too, for the existentialist. And the psychopath. And the saint and the bullfighter and the lover. The common denominator for all of them is their burning consciousness of the present, exactly that incandescent consciousness which the possibilities within death has opened for them. There is a depth of desperation to the condition which enables one to remain in life only by engaging death, but the reward is their knowledge that what is happening at each instant of the electric present is good or bad for them, good or bad for their cause, their love, their action, their need.

It is this knowledge which provides the curious community of feeling in the world of the hipster, a muted cool religious revival to be sure, but the element which is exciting, disturbing, nightmarish perhaps, is that incompatibles have come to bed, the inner life and the violent life, the orgy and the dream of love, the desire to murder and the desire to create, a dialectical conception of existence with a lust for power, a dark, romantic, and yet undeniably dynamic view of existence for it sees every man and woman as moving individually through each moment of life forward into growth or backward into death.

3

It may be fruitful to consider the hipster a philosophical psychopath, a man interested not only in the dangerous imperatives of his psychopathy but in codifying, at least for himself, the suppositions on which his inner universe is constructed. By this premise the hipster is a psychopath, and yet not a psychopath but the negation of the psychopath, for he possesses the narcissistic detachment of the philosopher, that absorption in the recessive nuances of one's own motive which is so alien to the unreasoning drive of the psychopath. In this country where new millions of psychopaths are developed each year, stamped with the mint of our contradictory popular culture (where sex is sin and yet sex is paradise), it is as if there has been room already for the development of the antithetical psychopath who extrapolates from his own condition, from the inner certainty that his rebellion is just, a radical vision of the universe which thus separates him from the general ignorance, reactionary prejudice, and self-doubt of the more conventional psychopath. Having converted his unconscious experience into much conscious knowledge, the hipster has shifted the focus of his desire from immediate gratification toward that wider passion for future power which is the mark of civilized man. Yet with an irreducible difference. For Hip is the sophistication of the wise primitive in a giant jungle, and so its appeal is still beyond the civilized man. If there are ten million Amercans who are more or less psychopathic (and the figure is most modest), there are probably not more than one hundred thousand men and women who consciously see themselves as hipsters, but their importance is that they are an elite with the potential ruthlessness of an elite, and a language most adolescents can understand instinctively, for the hipster's intense view of existence matches their experience and their desire to rebel.

Before one can say more about the hipster, there is obviously much to be said about the psychopathic personality. Now, for reasons which may be more curious than the similarity of the words, even many people with a psychoanalytical orientation often confuse the psychopath with the psychotic. Yet the terms are polar. The psychotic is legally insane, the psychopath is not; the psychotic is almost always incapable of discharging in physical acts the rage of his frustration, while the psychopath at his extreme is virtually as incapable of restraining his violence. The psychotic lives in so misty a world that what is happening at each moment of his life is not very real to him whereas the psychopath seldom knows any reality greater than the face, the voice, the being of the particular people among whom he may find himself at any moment. Sheldon and Eleanor Glueck describe him as follows:

> The psychopath . . . can be distinguished from the person sliding into or clambering out of a "true psychotic" state by the long tough persistence of his anti-social attitude and behaviour and the absence of hallucinations, delusions, manic flight of ideas, confusion, disorientation, and other dramatic signs of psychosis.

The late Robert Lindner, one of the few experts on the subject, in his book *Rebel Without a Cause—The Hypnoanalysis of a Criminal Psychopath* presented part of his definition in this way:

> . . . the psychopath is a rebel without a cause, an agitator without a slogan, a revolutionary without a program: in other words, his rebelliousness is aimed to achieve goals satisfactory to himself alone; he is incapable of exertions for the sake of others. All his efforts, hidden under no matter what disguise, represent investments designed to satisfy his immediate wishes and desires. . . . The psychopath, like the child, cannot delay the pleasures of gratification; and this trait is one of his underlying, universal characteristics. He cannot wait upon erotic gratification which convention demands should be preceded by the chase before the kill: he must rape. He cannot wait upon the development of prestige in society: his egoistic ambitions lead him to leap into headlines by daring performances. Like a red thread the predominance of this mechanism for immediate satisfaction runs through the history of every psychopath. It explains not only his behaviour but also the violent nature of his acts.

Yet even Linder who was the most imaginative and most sympathetic of the psychoanalysts who have studied the psychopathic personality was not ready to project himself into the essential sympathy—which is that the psychopath may indeed be the perverted and dangerous front-runner of a new kind of personality which could become the central expression of human nature before the twentieth century is over. For the psychopath is better adapted to dominate those mutually contradictory inhibitions upon violence and love which civilization has exacted of us, and if it be remembered that not every psychopath is an extreme case, and that the condition of psychopathy is present in a host of people including many politicians, professional soldiers, newspaper columnists, entertainers, artists, jazz musicians, callgirls, promiscuous homosexuals and half the executives of Hollywood, television, and advertising, it can be seen that there are aspects of psychopathy which already exert considerable cultural influence.

What characterizes almost every psychopath and part-psychopath is that they are trying to create a new nervous system for themselves. Generally we are obliged to act with a nervous system which has been formed from infancy, and which carries in the style of its circuits the very contradictions of our parents and our early milieu. Therefore, we are obliged, most of us, to meet the tempo of the present and the future with reflexes and rhythms which come from the past. It is not only the "dead weight of the institutions of the past" but indeed the inefficient and often antiquated nervous circuits of the past which strangle our potentiality for responding to new possibilities which might be exciting for our individual growth.

Through most of modern history, "sublimation" was possible: at the expense of expressing only a small portion of oneself, that small portion could be expressed intensely. But sublimation depends on a reasonable tempo to history. If the collective life of a generation has moved too quickly, the "past" by which particular men and women of that generation may function is not, let us say, thirty years old, but relatively a hundred or two hundred years old. And so the nervous system is overstressed beyond the possibility of such compromises as sublimation, especially since the stable middle-class values so prerequisite to sublimation have been virtually destroyed in our time, at least as nourishing values free of confusion or doubt. In such a crisis of accelerated historical tempo and deteriorated values, neurosis tends to be replaced by psychopathy, and the success of psychoanalysis (which even ten years ago gave promise of becoming a direct major force) diminishes because of its inbuilt and characteristic incapacity to handle patients more complex, more experienced, or more adventurous than the analyst himself. In practice, psychoanalysis has by now become all too often no more than a psychic blood-letting. The patient is not so much changed as aged, and the infantile fantasies which he is encouraged to express are condemned to exhaust themselves against the analyst's nonresponsive reactions.

The result for all too many patients is a diminution, a "tranquilizing" of their most interesting qualities and vices. The patient is indeed not so much altered as worn out—less bad, less good, less bright, less willful, less destructive, less creative. He is thus able to conform to that contradictory and unbearable society which first created his neurosis. He can conform to what he loathes because he no longer has the passion to feel loathing so intensely.

The psychopath is notoriously difficult to analyze because the fundamental decision of his nature is to try to live the infantile fantasy, and in this decision (given the dreary alternative of psychoanalysis) there may be a certain instinctive wisdom. For there is a dialectic to changing one's nature, the dialectic which underlies all psychoanalytic method: it is the knowledge that if one is to change one's habits, one must go back to the source of their creation, and so the psychopath exploring backward along the road of the homosexual, the orgiast, the drug-addict, the rapist, the robber, and the murderer seeks to find those violent parallels to the violent and often hopeless contradictions he knew as an infant and as a child. For if he has the courage to meet the parallel situation at the moment when he is ready, then he has a chance to act as he never acted before, and in satisfying the frustration—if he can succeed—he may then pass by symbolic substitute through the locks of incest. In thus giving expression to the buried infant in himself, he can lessen the tension of those infantile desires and so free himself to remake a bit of his nervous system. Like the neurotic he is looking for the opportunity to grow up a second time, but the psychopath knows instinctively that to express a forbidden impulse actively is far more beneficial to him than merely to confess the desire in the safety of a doctor's room. The psychopath is ordinately ambitious, too ambitious ever to trade his warped brilliant conception of his possible victories in life for the grim if peaceful attrition of the analyst's couch. So his associational journey into the past is lived out in the theatre of the present, and he exists for those charged situations where his senses are so alive that he can be aware actively (as the analysand is aware passively) of what his habits are, and how he can change them. The strength of the psychopath is that he knows (where most of us can only guess) what is good for him and what is bad for him at exactly those instants when an old crippling habit has become so attacked by experience that the potentiality exists to change it, to replace a negative and empty fear with an outward action, even if—and here I obey the logic of the extreme psychopath— even if the fear is of himself, and the action is to murder. The psychopath murders—if he has the courage—out of the necessity to purge his violence, for if he cannot empty his hatred then he cannot love, his being is frozen with implacable self-hatred for his cowardice. (It can of course be suggested that it takes little courage for two strong eighteen-year-old hoodlums, let us say, to beat in the brains of a candy-store keeper, and indeed the act—even by the logic of the psychopath—is not likely to prove very therapeutic, for the victim is not an immediate equal. Still, courage of a sort is necessary, for one murders not only a weak fifty-year-old man but an institution as well, one violates private property, one enters into a new relation with the police and introduces a dangerous element into one's life. The hoodlum is therefore daring the unknown, and so no matter how brutal the act, it is not altogether cowardly.)

At bottom, the drama of the psychopath is that he seeks love. Not love as the search for a mate, but love as the search for an orgasm more apocalyptic than the one which preceded it. Orgasm is his therapy—he knows at the seed of his being that good orgasm opens his possibilities and bad orgasm imprisons him. But in this search, the psychopath becomes an embodiment of the extreme contradictions of the society which formed his character, and the apocalyptic orgasm often remains as remote as the Holy Grail, for there are clusters and nests and ambushes of violence in his own necessities and in the imperatives and retaliations of the men and women among whom he lives his life, so that even as he drains his hatred in one act or another, so the conditions of his life create it anew in him until the drama of his movements bears a sardonic resemblance to the frog who climbed a few feet in the well only to drop back again.

Yet there is this to be said for the search after the good orgasm: when one lives in a civilized world, and still can enjoy none of the cultural nectar of such a world because the paradoxes on which civilization is built demand that there remain a cultureless and alienated bottom of exploitable human material, then the logic of becoming a sexual outlaw (if one's psychological roots are bedded in the bottom) is that one has at least a running competitive chance to be physically healthy so long as one stays alive. It is therefore no accident that psychopathy is most prevalent with the Negro. Hated from outside and therefore hating himself, the Negro was forced into the position of exploring all those moral wildernesses of civilized life which the Square automatically condemns as delinquent or evil or immature or morbid or self-destructive or corrupt. (Actually the terms have equal weight. Depending on the telescope of the cultural clique from which the Square surveys the universe, "evil" or "immature" are equally strong terms of condemnation.) But the Negro, not being privileged to gratify his self-esteem with the heady satisfactions of categorical condemnation, chose to move instead in that other direction where all situations are equally valid, and in the worst of perversion, promiscuity, pimpery, drug addiction, rape, razor-slash, bottle-break, what-have-you, the Negro discovered and elaborated a morality of the bottom, an ethical differentiation between the good and the bad in every human activity from the go-getter pimp (as opposed to the lazy one) to the relatively dependable pusher or prostitute. Add to this, the cunning of their language, the abstract ambiguous alternatives in which from the danger of their oppression they learned to speak ("Well, now, man, like I'm looking for a cat to turn me on . . ."), add even more the profound sensitivity of the Negro jazzman who was the cultural mentor of a people, and it is not too difficult to believe that the language of Hip which evolved was an artful language, tested and shaped by an intense experience and therefore different in kind from white slang, as different as the special obscenity of the soldier, which in its emphasis upon "ass" as the soul and "shit" as circumstance, was able to express the existential states of the enlisted man. What makes Hip a special language is that it cannot really be taught—if one shares none of the experiences of elation and exhaustion which it is equipped to describe, then it seems merely arch or vulgar or irritating. It is a pictorial language, but pictorial like non-objective art, imbued with the dialectic of small but intense change, a language for the microcosm, in this case, man, for it takes the immediate experiences of any passing man and magnifies the dynamic of his movements, not specifically but abstractly so that he is seen more as a vector in a network of forces than as a static character in a crystallized field. (Which latter is the practical view of the snob.) For example, there is real difficulty in trying to find a Hip substitute for "stubborn." The best possibility I can come up with is: "That cat will never come off his groove, dad." But groove implies movement, narrow movement but motion nonetheless. There is really no way to describe someone who does not move at all. Even a creep does move—if at a pace exasperatingly more slow than the pace of the cool cats.

4

Like children, hipsters are fighting for the sweet, and their language is a set of subtle indications of their success or failure in the competition for pleasure. Unstated but obvious is the social sense that there is not nearly enough sweet for everyone. And so the sweet goes only to the victor, the best, the most, the man who knows the most about how to find his energy and how not to lose it. The emphasis is on energy because the psychopath and the hipster are nothing without it since they do not have the protection of a position or a class to rely on when they have overextended themselves. So the language of Hip is a language of energy, how it is found, how it is lost.

But let us see. I have jotted down perhaps a dozen words, the Hip perhaps most in use and most likely to last with the minimum of variation. The words are man, go, put down, make, beat, cool, swing, with it, crazy, dig, flip, creep, hip, square. They serve a variety of purposes and the nuance of the voice uses the nuance of the situation to convey the subtle contextual difference. If the hipster moves through his life on a constant search with glimpses of Mecca in many a turn of his experience (Mecca being the apocalyptic orgasm) and if everyone in the civilized world is at least in some small degree a sexual cripple, the hipster lives with the knowledge of how he is sexually crippled and where he is sexually alive, and the faces of experience which life presents to him each day are engaged, dismissed, or avoided as his need directs and his lifemanship makes possible. For life is a contest between people in which the victor generally recuperates quickly and the loser takes long to mend, a perpetual competition of colliding explorers in which one must grow or else pay more for remaining the same (pay in sickness, or depression, or anguish for the lost opportunity), but pay or grow.

Therefore one finds words like go, and make it, and with it, and swing: "Go" with its sense that after hours or days or months or years of monotony, boredom, and depression one has finally had one's chance, one has amassed enough energy to meet an exciting opportunity with all one's present talents for the flip (up or down) and so one is ready to go, ready to gamble. Movement is always to be preferred to inaction. In motion a man has a chance, his body is warm, his instincts are quick, and when the crisis comes, whether of love or violence, he can make it, he can win, he can release a little more energy for himself since he hates himself a little less, he can make a little better nervous system, make it a little more possible to go again, to go faster next time and so make more and thus find more people with whom he can swing. For to swing is to communicate, is to convey the rhythms of one's own being to a lover, a friend, or an audience, and—equally necessary— be able to feel the rhythms of their response. To swing with the rhythms of another is to enrich oneself—the conception of the learning process as dug by Hip is that one cannot really learn until one contains within oneself the implicit rhythm of the subject or the person. As an example,

I remember once hearing a Negro friend have an intellectual discussion at a party for half an hour with a white girl who was a few years out of college. The Negro literally could not read or write, but he had an extraordinary ear and a fine sense of mimicry. So as the girl spoke, he would detect the particular formal uncertainties in her argument, and in a pleasant (if slightly Southern) English accent, he would respond to one or another facet of her doubts. When she would finish what she felt was a particularly well-articulated idea, he would smile privately and say, "Other-direction . . . do you really believe in that?"

"Well . . . No," the girl would stammer, "now that you get down to it, there is something disgusting about it to me," and she would go off again for five more minutes.

Of course the Negro was not learning anything about the merits and demerits of the argument, but he was learning a great deal about a type of girl he had never met before, and that was what he wanted. Being unable to read or write, he could hardly be interested in ideas nearly as much as in lifemanship, and so he eschewed any attempt to obey the precision or lack of precision in the girl's language, and instead sensed her character (and the values of her social type) by swinging with the nuances of her voice.

So to swing is to be able to learn, and by learning take a step toward making it, toward creating. What is to be created is not nearly so important as the hipster's belief that when he really makes it, he will be able to turn his hand to anything, even to self-discipline. What he must do before that is find his courage at the moment of violence, or equally make it in the act of love, find a little more between his woman and himself, or indeed between his mate and himself (since many hipsters are bisexual), but paramount, imperative, is the necessity to make it because in making it, one is making the new habit, unearthing the new talent which the old frustration denied.

Whereas if you goof (the ugliest word in Hip), if you lapse back into being a frightened stupid child, or if you flip, if you lose your control, reveal the buried weaker more feminine part of your nature, then it is more difficult to swing the next time, your ear is less alive, your bad and energy-wasting habits are further confirmed, you are farther away from being with it. But to be with it is to have grace, is to be closer to the secrets of that inner unconscious life which will nourish you if you can hear it, for you are then nearer to that God which every hipster believes is located in the senses of his body, that trapped, mutilated and nonetheless megalomaniacal God who is It, who is energy, life, sex, force, the Yoga's *prana*, the Reichian's orgone,

Lawrence's "blood," Hemingway's "good," the Shavian life-force; "It"; God; not the God of the churches but the unachievable whisper of mystery within the sex, the paradise of limitless energy and perception just beyond the next wave of the next orgasm.

To which a cool cat might reply, "Crazy, man!"

Because, after all, what I have offered above is an hypothesis, no more, and there is not the hipster alive who is not absorbed in his own tumultuous hypothesis. Mine is interesting, mine is way out (on the avenue of the mystery along the road to "It") but still I am just one cat in a world of cool cats, and everything interesting is crazy, or at least so the Squares who do not know how to swing would say.

(And yet crazy is also the self-protective irony of the hipster. Living with questions and not with answers, he is so different in his isolation and in the far reach of his imagination from almost everyone with whom he deals in the outer world of the Square, and meets generally so much enmity, competition, and hatred in the world of Hip, that his isolation is always in danger of turning upon itself, and leaving him indeed just that, crazy.)

If, however, you agree with my hypothesis, if you as a cat are way out too, and we are in the same groove (the universe now being glimpsed as a series of ever-extending radii from the center), why then you say simply, "I dig," because neither knowledge nor imagination comes easily, it is buried in the pain of one's forgotten experience, and so one must work to find it, one must occasionally exhaust oneself by digging into the self in order to perceive the outside. And indeed it is essential to dig the most, for if you do not dig you lose your superiority over the Square, and so you are less likely to be cool (to be in control of a situation because you have swung where the Square has not, or because you have allowed to come to consciousness a pain, a guilt, a shame or a desire which the other has not had the courage to face). To be cool is to be equipped, and if you are equipped it is more difficult for the next cat who comes along to put you down. And of course one can hardly afford to be put down too often, or one is beat, one has lost one's confidence, one has lost one's will, one is impotent in the world of action and so closer to the demeaning flip of becoming a queer, or indeed closer to dying, and therefore it is even more difficult to recover enough energy to try to make it again, because once a cat is beat he has nothing to give, and no one is interested any longer in making it with him. This is the terror of the hipster—to be beat— because once the sweet of sex has deserted him, he still cannot give up the search. It is not granted to the hipster to grow old gracefully—

he has been captured too early by the oldest dream of power, the gold fountain of Ponce de León, the fountain of youth where the gold is in the orgasm.

To be beat is therefore a flip, it is a situation beyond one's experience, impossible to anticipate—which indeed in the circular vocabulary of Hip is still another meaning for flip, but then I have given just a few of the connotations of these words. Like most primitive vocabularies each word is a prime symbol and serves a dozen or a hundred functions of communication in the instinctive dialectic through which the hipster perceives his experience, that dialectic of the instantaneous differentials of existence in which one is forever moving forward into more or retreating into less.

5

It is impossible to conceive a new philosophy until one creates a new language, but a new popular language (while it must implicitly contain a new philosophy) does not necessarily present its philosophy overtly. It can be asked then what really is unique in the life-view of Hip which raises its argot above the passing verbal whimsies of the bohemian or the lumpenproletariat.

The answer would be in the psychopathic element of Hip which has almost no interest in viewing human nature, or better, in judging human nature, from a set of standards conceived a priori to the experience, standards inherited from the past. Since Hip sees every answer as posing immediately a new alternative, a new question, its emphasis is on complexity rather than simplicity (such complexity that its language without the illumination of the voice and the articulation of the face and body remains hopelessly incommunicative). Given its emphasis on complexity, Hip abdicates from any conventional moral responsibility because it would argue that the results of our actions are unforeseeable, and so we cannot know if we do good or bad, we cannot even know (in the Joycean sense of the good and the bad) whether we have given energy to another, and indeed if we could, there would still be no idea of what ultimately the other would do with it.

Therefore, men are not seen as good or bad (that they are good-and-bad is taken for granted) but rather each man is glimpsed as a collection of possibilities, some more possible than others (the view of character implicit in Hip) and some humans are considered more capable than others of reaching more possibilities within themselves in less time, provided, and this is the dynamic, provided the particular character can swing at the right time. And here arises the sense of context which differentiates Hip from a Square view of character. Hip sees the context as generally dominating the man, dominating him because his character is less significant than the context in which he must function. Since it is arbitrarily five times more demanding of one's energy to accomplish even an inconsequential action in an unfavorable context than a favorable one, man is then not only his character but his context, since the success or failure of an action in a given context reacts upon the character and therefore affects what the character will be in the next context. What dominates both character and context is the energy available at the moment of intense context.

Character being thus seen as perpetually ambivalent and dynamic enters then into an absolute relativity where there are no truths other than the isolated truths of what each observer feels at each instant of his existence. To take a perhaps unjustified metaphysical extrapolation, it is as if the universe which has usually existed conceptually as a Fact (even if the Fact were Berkeley's God) but a Fact which it was the aim of all science and philosophy to reveal, becomes instead a changing reality whose laws are remade at each instant by everything living, but most particularly man, man raised to a neo-medieval summit where the truth is not what one has felt yesterday or what one expects to feel tomorrow but rather truth is no more nor less than what one feels at each instant in the perpetual climax of the present.

What is consequent therefore is the divorce of man from his values, the liberation of the self from the Super-Ego of society. The only Hip morality (but of course it is an ever-present morality) is to do what one feels whenever and wherever it is possible, and—this is how the war of the Hip and the Square begins—to be engaged in one primal battle: to open the limits of the possible for oneself, for oneself alone, because that is one's need. Yet in widening the arena of the possible, one widens it reciprocally for others as well, so that the nihilistic fulfillment of each man's desire contains its antithesis of human co-operation.

If the ethic reduces to Know Thyself and Be Thyself, what makes it radically different from Socratic moderation with its stern conservative respect for the experience of the past is that the Hip ethic is immoderation, childlike in its adoration of the present (and indeed to respect the past means that one must also respect such ugly consequences of the past as the collective murders of the State). It is this adoration of the present which contains the affirmation of Hip, because its ultimate logic surpasses even the unforgettable solution of the

Marquis de Sade to sex, private property, and the family, that all men and women have absolute but temporary rights over the bodies of all other men and women—the nihilism of Hip proposes as its final tendency that every social restraint and category be removed, and the affirmation implicit in the proposal is that man would prove to be more creative than murderous and so would not destroy himself. Which is exactly what separates Hip from the authoritarian philosophies which now appeal to the conservative and liberal temper—what haunts the middle of the twentieth century is that faith in man has been lost, and the appeal of authority has been that it would restrain us from ourselves. Hip, which would return us to ourselves, at no matter what price in individual violence, is the affirmation of the barbarian, for it requires a primitive passion about human nature to believe that individual acts of violence are always to be preferred to the collective violence of the State; it takes literal faith in the creative possibilities of the human being to envisage acts of violence as the catharsis which prepares growth.

Whether the hipster's desire for absolute sexual freedom contains any genuinely radical conception of a different world is of course another matter, and it is possible, since the hipster lives with his hatred, that many of them are the material for an elite of storm troopers ready to follow the first truly magnetic leader whose view of mass murder is phrased in a language which reaches their emotions. But given the desperation of his condition as a psychic outlaw, the hipster is equally a candidate for the most reactionary and most radical of movements, and so it is just as possible that many hipsters will come— if the crisis deepens—to a radical comprehension of the horror of society, for even as the radical has had his incommunicable dissent confirmed in his experience by precisely the frustration, the denied opportunities, and the bitter years which his ideas have cost him, so the sexual adventurer deflected from his goal by the implacable animosity of a society constructed to deny the sexual radical as well, may yet come to an equally bitter comprehension of the slow relentless inhumanity of the conservative power which controls him from without and from within. And in being so controlled, denied, and starved into the attrition of conformity, indeed the hipster may come to see that his condition is no more than an exaggeration of the human condition, and if he would be free, then everyone must be free. Yet, this is possible too, for the heart of Hip is its emphasis upon courage at the moment of crisis, and it is pleasant to think that courage contains within itself (as the explanation of its existence) some glimpse of the necessity of life to become more than it has been.

It is obviously not very possible to speculate with sharp focus on the future of the hipster. Certain possibilities must be evident, however, and the most central is that the organic growth of Hip depends on whether the Negro emerges as a dominating force in American life. Since the Negro knows more about the ugliness and danger of life than the white, it is probable that if the Negro can win his equality, he will possess a potential superiority, a superiority so feared that the fear itself has become the underground drama of domestic policies. Like all conservative political fear it is the fear of unforeseeable consequences, for the Negro's equality would tear a profound shift into the psychology, the sexuality, and the moral imagination of every white alive.

With this possible emergence of the Negro, Hip may erupt as a psychically armed rebellion whose sexual impetus may rebound against the antisexual foundation of every organized power in America, and bring into the air such animosities, antipathies, and new conflicts of interest that the mean empty hypocrisies of mass conformity will no longer work. A time of violence, new hysteria, confusion, and rebellion will then be likely to replace the time of conformity. At that time, if the liberal should prove realistic in his belief that there is peaceful room for every tendency in American life, then Hip would end by being absorbed as a colorful figure in the tapestry. But if this is not the reality, and the economic, the social, the psychological, and finally the moral crises accompanying the rise of the Negro should prove insupportable, then a time is coming when every political guidepost will be gone, and millions of liberals will be faced with political dilemmas they have so far succeeded in evading, and with a view of human nature they do not wish to accept. To take the desegregation of the schools in the South as an example, it is quite likely that the reactionary sees the reality more closely than the liberal when he argues that the deeper issue is not desegregation but miscegenation. (As a radical I am of course facing in the opposite direction from the White Citizen's Councils—obviously I believe it is the absolute human right of the Negro to mate with the white, and matings there will undoubtedly be, for there will be Negro high school boys brave enough to chance their lives.) But for the average liberal whose mind has been dulled by the committee-ish cant of the professional liberal, miscegenation is not an issue because he has been told that the Negro does not desire it. So, when it comes, miscegenation will be a terror, comparable perhaps to the derangement of the American Communists when the icons to Stalin came tumbling down. The average American Communist held to the myth of Stalin for reasons which had little to do with the political evidence and everything to do with their psychic necessities. In this sense it is equally a psychic necessity for the liberal to believe that the Negro and even the reactionary Southern white are eventually and fundamentally people like himself, capable of becoming good liberals too if only they can be reached by good liberal reason. What the liberal cannot bear to admit is the hatred beneath the skin of a society so unjust that the amount of collective violence buried in the people is perhaps incapable of being contained, and therefore if one wants a better world one does well to hold one's breath, for a worse world is bound to come first, and the dilemma may well be this: given such hatred, it must either vent itself nihilistically or become turned into the cold murderous liquidations of the totalitarian state.

6

No matter what its horrors the twentieth century is a vastly exciting century for its tendency is to reduce all of life to its ultimate alternatives. One can well wonder if the last war of them all will be between the blacks and the whites, or between the women and the men, or between the beautiful and ugly, the pillagers and managers, or the rebels and the regulators. Which of course is carrying speculation beyond the point where speculation is still serious, and yet despair at the monotony and bleakness of the future have become so engrained in the radical temper that the radical is in danger of abdicating from all imagination. What a man feels is the impulse for his creative effort, and if an alien but nonetheless passionate instinct about the meaning of life has come so unexpectedly from a virtually illiterate people, come out of the most intense conditions of exploitation, cruelty, violence, frustration, and lust, and yet has succeeded as an instinct in keeping this tortured people alive, then it is perhaps possible that the Negro holds more of the tail of the expanding elephant of truth than the radical, and if this is so, the radical humanist could do worse than to brood upon the phenomenon. For if a revolutionary time should come again, there would be a crucial difference if someone had already delineated a neo-Marxian calculus aimed at comprehending every circuit and process of society from ukase to kiss as the communications of human energy—a calculus capable of translating the economic relations of man into his psychological relations and then back again, his productive relations thereby embracing his sexual relations as well, until the crises of capitalism in the twentieth century would yet be understood as the unconscious adaptations of a society to solve its economic imbalance at the expense of a new mass psychological imbalance. It is almost beyond the imagination to conceive of a work in which the drama of human energy is engaged, and a theory of its social currents and dissipations, its imprisonments, expressions, and tragic wastes are fitted into some gigantic synthesis of human action where the body of Marxist thought, and particularly the epic grandeur of *Das Kapital* (that first of the major *psychologies* to approach the mystery of social cruelty so simply and practically as to say that we are a collective body of humans whose life-energy is wasted, displaced, and procedurally stolen as it passes from one of us to another)—where particularly the epic grandeur of *Das Kapital* would find its place in an even more God-like view of human justice and injustice, in some more excruciating vision of those intimate and institutional processes which lead to our creations and disasters, our growth, our attrition, and our rebellion.

BLACK
CONSCIOUSNESS

In "The White Negro," Norman Mailer *proclaimed that "hipness"* *as a form of consciousness would spread only in proportion to Amer-* *ica's emotional awareness of its black people.* One hundred years after the American Civil War, black Americans throughout the country began to realize that their peonage had not been terminated, that no end to second-class citizenship was in sight. *The Civil Rights Movement of the early 1960s, a coalition of determined black stu-* *dents and young white "radicals" from the North, gained publicity but little actual progress: the buoyant illusion of equality in America had been punctured, but the struggle had only begun.*

Suddenly, in the past few years, black leaders commenced to articulate the plight of their people with an unprecedented vigor and urgency. Confronting the resistance of those who were wary of yielding privileges, the black movement became more self-conscious, more aggressive, less compromising. The stale liberal plea for patience could no longer be tolerated. Blacks, particularly the young, wanted all they felt they deserved as citizens of a "free" country, and they were willing to risk anything—including their own lives—in order to achieve it.

In this section, some of the most respected voices in the black community describe the difficulties of living in white America, and point to the paths which would lead to total equality for the Negro. James Baldwin, in an interview with Dr. Kenneth Clark, anticipates more violent responses in his admission that the black moderate approach has largely failed to heal the racial wounds in our society. Eldridge Cleaver and Dr. Lloyd Delany, a psychologist, attack the illusion of white supremacy by revealing the severe disorders in the white psyche. Malcolm X and Stokely Carmichael are less inclined to psychologize than to explore immediate courses of action for the black man. LeRoi Jones attempts to demonstrate how theater can be used to provoke "necessary" violence in the black viewer. The selections from La Vida *and* Down These Mean Streets *dramatize the problem of being Puerto Rican in America. Abbie Hoffman, formerly a worker for the Student Nonviolent Coordinating Com-* *mittee (SNCC), and more recently an originator of the "yippies," demonstrates how the white hipster shares the persecution of the black man.*

James Baldwin: An Interview

The following interview with James Baldwin occurred under extraordinary circumstances. We were scheduled to be at the television studio at 5:00 P.M. on Friday, May 24, 1963, the day of the well-publicized meeting between Attorney General Robert Kennedy and James Baldwin and some of his friends. The meeting had aroused in all of us an intense level of emotions. The seeming inability to communicate the passionate insistence of Mr. Baldwin that the Attorney General had to understand the sense of urgency of the Negro people, and the need of the Attorney General to protect the image of liberal concern within the context of political realism had contributed to an excruciating sense of impasse. The meeting continued for nearly three hours, and resulted in Mr. Baldwin's and my being an hour and a half late for the taping of the interview. On the way to the studio, it was clear that the emotionality and general sense of frustration resulting from the meeting with the Attorney General would be carried over into the interview. Indeed, many times in the taxicab, Baldwin said that he was not sure that he would be able to go through with the interview. He stated repeatedly, "Kenneth, all I need is a drink. Can't we stop at the nearest bar? I must decompress."

Literally, there was no time either to prepare questions or to discuss generally what course the interview would take. When we reached the studio the cameraman and technicians were understandably impatient. We were placed immediately in our chairs while they set up the camera for proper angles, lighting, and determined the voice levels. During this brief interval, Baldwin and I merely had time to reassure each other that we did not know exactly what we were going to talk about. The interview which follows is purely spontaneous, and in the trite words of television, "completely (but completely) unrehearsed." In fact, neither Baldwin nor I was quite sure of what we had actually said during the interview immediately afterward or in the following weeks. We were unable to recall either specific questions and answers, or general trends. We were sure only of the mood and the fact that the interview was in someway dominated by our earlier experience with the Attorney General. We thought that we had probably devoted the entire interview to a rehashing of that meeting.

Kenneth B. Clark, "James Baldwin—An Interview." Originally appeared under the title "James Baldwin Talks with Kenneth B. Clark" in *The Negro Protest*. Reprinted by permission of the Beacon Press. Copyright © 1963 by Kenneth B. Clark.

James Baldwin is a little man, physically, with tremendous emotional and intellectual power. He radiates a nervous, sensitive involvement with all aspects of his environment. One has the impression that he speaks with his entire body. His ideas, his feelings, and his words appear to form a complete unity. In his conversations he is the essence of spontaneity and one has the impression that he is incapable of communicating anything other than the total truth which he feels and thinks at that particular time. I began our interview by asking Baldwin about his childhood, and given the circumstances it is not surprising that he replied:

What a funny question! My mind is some place else, really; but to think back on it—I was born in Harlem, Harlem Hospital, and grew up—the first house I remember was on Park Avenue, which is not the American Park Avenue, or maybe it *is* the American Park Avenue.

CLARK Uptown Park Avenue.

BALDWIN Uptown Park Avenue, where the railroad tracks are. We used to play on the roof and in the—I can't call it an alley—but near the river—it was a kind of dump, a garbage dump. That was the first—those were the first scenes I remember. I remember my father had trouble keeping us alive; there were nine of us. And I was the oldest so I took care of the kids and dealt with Daddy. I understand him much better now. Part of his problem was he couldn't feed his kids, but I was a kid and I didn't know that. And he was very religious and very rigid. He kept us together, I must say. And when I look back on it—after all it was nearly forty years ago that I was born—when I think back on my growing up and walk that same block today, because it's still there, and think of the kids on that block now, I'm aware that something terrible has happened which is very hard to describe. I am, in all but in technical fact, a Southerner. My father was born in the South—no, my mother was born in the South, and if they had waited two more seconds I might have been born in the South. But that means I was raised by families whose roots were essentially rural——

CLARK Southern rural.

BALDWIN Southern rural and whose relationship to the church was very direct because it was the only means they had of expressing their pain and their despair. But twenty years later the moral authority which was present in the Negro Northern community when I was growing up has vanished. And people talk about progress, and I look at Harlem which I really knew—I know it like I know my hand—and it is much worse there today than it was when I was growing up.

CLARK Would you say this is true of the schools too?

BALDWIN It is much worse in the schools.

CLARK What school did you go to?

BALDWIN I went to P.S. 24 and I went to P.S. 139.

CLARK We are fellow alumni. I went to 139.

BALDWIN I didn't like a lot of my teachers, but I had a couple of teachers who were very nice to me; one was a Negro teacher. And I remember—you ask me these questions and I'm trying to answer you—I remember coming home from school, you can guess how young I must have been, and my mother asked me if my teacher was colored or white, and I said she was a little bit colored and a little bit white, but she was about your color. And as a matter of fact I was right. That's part of the dilemma of being an American Negro; that one is a little bit colored and a little bit white, and not only in physical terms but in the head and in the heart, and there are days—this is one of them—when you wonder what your role is in this country and what your future is in it; how precisely you are going to reconcile it to your situation here and how you are going to communicate to the vast heedless, unthinking, cruel white majority, that you are here. And to be here means that you can't be anywhere else. I could, my own person, leave this country and go to Africa, I could go to China, I could go to Russia, I could go to Cuba, but I'm an American and that is a *fact*.

CLARK Yes. Jim——

BALDWIN Am I going ahead?

CLARK No, these are certainly some of the things that we are after, but as I read your writings and know that you came out of P.S. 24 and my alma mater, Junior High School 139, I see that no one could write with the feeling and with the skill with which you write if you did not get, in P.S. 24 and 139, a certain type of education. Now I'd like to go back to the point that you made that the Harlem you knew when you were growing up is not the Harlem now and see if we can relate this also even to the school.

BALDWIN Let's see. Let's see if we can. It was probably very important for me—I haven't thought of this for a long time—it was important at the point I was going to P.S. 24—the only Negro school principal as far as I know in the entire history of New York was the principal— a woman named Mrs. Ayer, and she liked me. And in a way I guess she proved to me that I didn't have to be entirely defined by my circumstances, because you know that every Negro child knows what his circumstances are though he can't articulate them, because he is born into a republic which assures him in as many ways as it knows how, and has got great force, that he has a certain place and he can never rise above it. And what has happened in Harlem since is that that generation has passed away.

CLARK Mrs. Ayer was a sort of a model in a sense.

BALDWIN She was a proof. She was a living proof that I was not necessarily what the country said I was.

CLARK Then it is significant, Jim, that we do not have a single Negro principal in the New York public school system today.

BALDWIN And it is *not* because "there ain't nobody around who can do it," you know. One's involved in a very curious and a very serious battle concerning which I think the time has come to be as explicit as one can possibly be. The great victims in this country of an institution called segregation (it is not a southern custom but has been for a hundred years a national way of life) the great victims are white people, the white man's children. Lorraine Hansberry said this afternoon—we were talking about the problem of being a Negro in this society—Lorraine said she wasn't too concerned really about Negro manhood since they had managed to endure and to even transcend some fantastic things, but she was very worried about a civilization which could produce those five policemen standing on the Negro woman's neck in Birmingham or wherever it was, and I am too. I'm terrified at the moral apathy, the death of the heart, which is happening in my country. These people have deluded themselves for so long that they really don't think I'm human. I base this on their conduct, not on what they say, and this means that they have become in themselves moral monsters. It's a terrible indictment. I mean every word I say.

CLARK Well, we are confronted with the racial confrontation in America today. I think the picture of dogs in the hands of human beings attacking other human beings——

BALDWIN In a free country—in the middle of the twentieth century.

CLARK This Birmingham is clearly not restricted to Birmingham as you so eloquently pointed out. What do you think can be done to change, to use your term, the moral fiber of America?

BALDWIN I think that one has got to find some way of putting the present administration of this country on the spot. One has got to force, somehow, from Washington, a moral commitment, not to the Negro people, but to the life of this country. It doesn't matter any longer—and I'm speaking for myself, Jimmy Baldwin, and I think I'm speaking for a great many other Negroes too—it doesn't matter any longer what you do to me; you can put me in jail, you can kill me. By the time I was seventeen, you'd done everything that you could do to me. The problem now is how are you going to save yourself? It was a great shock to me—I want to say this on the air—the Attorney General did not know——

CLARK You mean the Attorney General of the United States?

BALDWIN Mister Robert Kennedy—didn't know that I would have trouble convincing my nephew to go to Cuba, for example, to liberate the Cubans in defense of a government which now says it is doing everything it can do, which cannot liberate me. Now, there are twenty million Negroes in this country, and you can't put them all in jail. I know how my nephew feels, I know how I feel, I know how the cats in the barbershop feel. A boy last week, he was sixteen, in San Francisco told me on television—thank God, we got him to talk, maybe somebody else ought to listen—he said, "I got no country. I got no flag." Now, he's only sixteen years old, and I couldn't say, "You do." I don't have any evidence to prove that he does. They were tearing down his house, because San Francisco is engaging, as most Northern cities now are engaged, in something called urban renewal, which means moving Negroes out; it means Negro removal, that is what it means. And the federal government is an accomplice to this fact. Now, we are talking about human beings; there's not such a thing as a monolithic wall or some abstraction called the Negro problem; these are Negro boys and girls, who at sixteen and seventeen don't believe the country means anything that it says and don't feel they have any place here on the basis of the performance of the entire country.

CLARK But now, Jim——

BALDWIN Am I exaggerating?

CLARK No, I certainly could not say that you are exaggerating, but there is this picture of a group of young Negro college students in the South coming from colleges where the whole system seems to conspire to keep them from having courage, integrity, clarity and the willingness to take the risks which they have been taking for these last three or four years. Could you react to the student non-violent movement which has made such an impact on America, which has affected both Negroes and whites and seems to have jolted them out of the lethargy of tokenism and moderation? How do you account for this, Jim?

BALDWIN Well, of course, one of the things I think that happened, Ken, really, is that in the first place, the Negro has never been as docile as white Americans wanted to believe. That was a myth. We were not singing and dancing down on the levee. We were trying to keep alive; we were trying to survive a very brutal system. The Negro has never been happy in "his" place. What those kids first of all proved—first of all they proved *that*. They come from a long line of fighters. And what they also prove—I want to get to your point, really—what they also prove is not that the Negro has changed, but that the country has arrived at a place where he can no longer contain the revolt. He can no longer, as he could do once—let's say I was a Negro college president, and I needed a new chemistry lab., so I was a Negro leader. I was a Negro leader because the white man said I was, and I came to get a new chemistry lab., "Please, suh," and the tacit price I paid for the chemistry lab. was controlled by the people I represented. And now I can't do that. When the boy said this afternoon—we were talking to a Negro student this afternoon who had been through it all, who's half dead and only about twenty-five. Jerome Smith. That's an awful lot to ask a person to bear. The country has sat back in admiration of all those kids for three or four or five years and has not lifted a finger to help them. Now, we all knew. I know you knew and I knew, too, that a moment was coming when we couldn't guarantee, that no one can guarantee, that he won't reach the breaking point. You can only survive so many beatings, so much humiliation, so much despair, so many broken promises, before something gives. Human beings are not by nature non-violent. Those children had to pay a terrible price in discipline, moral discipline, an interior effort of courage which the country cannot imagine, because it still thinks Gary Cooper, for example, was a man. I mean his image—I have nothing against him, you know, *him*.

CLARK You said something, that you cannot expect them to remain constantly non-violent.

BALDWIN No, you can't! You can't! And, furthermore, they were always, these students that we are talking about, a minority—the students we are talking about, not in Tallahassee. There were some students protesting, but there were many, many, many, many more students who had given up, who were desperate and whom Malcolm X can reach, for example, much more easily than I can.

CLARK What do you mean?

BALDWIN Well, Malcolm tells them—what Malcolm tells them, in effect, is that they should be proud of being black, and God knows that they should be. That is a very important thing to hear in a country which assures you that you should be ashamed of it. Of course, in order to do this, what he does is destroy a truth and invent a history. What he does is say, "You're better *because* you're black." Well, of course that isn't true. That's the trouble.

CLARK Do you think this is an appealing approach and that the Black Muslims in preaching black supremacy seem to exploit the frustration of the Negro?

BALDWIN I don't think, to put it as simply as I can, and without trying now to investigate whatever the motives of any given Muslim leader may be. It is the only movement in the country that you can call grass roots. I hate to say that, but it's true. Because it is the only— when Malcolm talks or the Muslim ministers talk, they articulate for all the Negro people who hear them, who listen to them. They articulate their suffering, the suffering which has been in this country so long denied. That's Malcolm's great authority over any of his audiences. He corroborates their reality; he tells them that they really exist.

CLARK Jim, do you think that this is a more effective appeal than the appeal of Martin Luther King?

BALDWIN It is much more sinister because it is much more effective. It is much more effective, because it is, after all, comparatively easy to invest a population with false morale by giving them a false sense of superiority, and it will always break down in a crisis. That's the history of Europe simply; it's one of the reasons that we are in this terrible place. It is one of the reasons that we have five cops standing on the black woman's neck in Birmingham, because at some point they believed, they were taught and they *believed* that they were better than other people because they were white. It leads to moral bankruptcy. It is inevitable, it cannot but lead there. But my point here is that the country is for the first time worried about the Muslim movement. It shouldn't be worried about the Muslim movement, that's not the problem. The problem is to eliminate the conditions which breed the Muslim movement.

CLARK I'd like to come back to get some of your thoughts about the relationship between Martin Luther King's appeal, that is, effectively, non-violence and his philosophy of disciplined love for the oppressor. What is the relationship between this and the reality of the Negro masses?

BALDWIN Well, to leave Martin out of it for a moment. Martin's a very rare, a very great man. Martin's rare for two reasons: probably just because he *is*; and because he's a real Christian. He really believes in non-violence. He has arrived at something in himself which permits him—allows him to do it, and he still has great moral authority in the South. He has none whatever in the North. Poor Martin has gone through God knows what kind of hell to awaken the American conscience, but Martin has reached the end of his rope. There are some things Martin can't do; Martin's only one man. Martin can't solve the nation's central problem by himself. There are lots of people, lots of black people I mean, now, who "don't go to church no more" and don't listen to Martin, you know, and who anyway are themselves produced by a civilization which has always glorified violence unless the Negro has the gun so that Martin is undercut by the performance of the country. The country is only concerned about non-violence if it seems as if I'm going to get violent, because I worry about non-violence if it's some Alabama sheriff.

CLARK Jim, what do you see deep in the recesses of your own mind as the future of our nation, and I ask that question in that way because I think the future of the Negro and the future of the nation are linked.

BALDWIN They're insoluble.

CLARK Now, how—what do you see? Are you essentially optimistic or pessimistic? And I don't really want to put words in your mouth because what I really want to find out is what you really believe.

BALDWIN I'm both glad and sorry you asked me that question, but I'll do my best to answer it. I can't be a pessimist because I'm alive. To be a pessimist means that you have agreed that human life is an academic matter, so I'm forced to be an optimist; I'm forced to believe that we can survive whatever we must survive. But the future of the Negro in this country is precisely as bright or as dark as the future of the country. It is entirely up to the American people and our representatives, it is entirely up to the American people whether or not they are going to face and deal with and embrace the stranger whom they maligned so long. What white people have to do is try to find out in their own hearts why it was necessary to have a nigger in the first place. Because I'm not a nigger, I am a man, but if you think I'm a nigger, it means you need it. The question you got to ask yourself—the white population has got to ask itself, North and South, because it's one country and for a Negro there's no difference between the North and South; there's just a difference in the way they castrate you, but the fact of the castration is the American fact. If I'm not the nigger here and if you invented him—you, the white people, invented him, then you've got to find out why. And the future of the country depends on that. Whether or not it's able to ask that question.

CLARK As a Negro and an American, I can only hope that America has the strength——

BALDWIN Moral strength.

CLARK ——and the capacity to ask and answer that question——

BALDWIN To *face* that question, to *face* that question!

CLARK ——in an affirmative and constructive way.

The White Race and Its Heroes

White people cannot, in the generality, be taken as models of how to live. Rather, the white man is himself in sore need of new standards, which will release him from his confusion and place him once again in fruitful communion with the depths of his own being. —JAMES BALDWIN, *The Fire Next Time*

Right from the go, let me make one thing absolutely clear: I am not now, nor have I ever been, a white man. Nor, I hasten to add, am I now a Black Muslim—although I used to be. But I *am* an Ofay Watcher, a member of that unchartered, amorphous league which has members on all continents and the islands of the seas. Ofay Watchers Anonymous, we might be called, because we exist concealed in the shadows wherever colored people have known oppression by whites, by white enslavers, colonizers, imperialists, and neo-colonialists.

Did it irritate you, compatriot, for me to string those epithets out like that? Tolerate me. My intention was not necessarily to sprinkle salt over anyone's wounds. I did it primarily to relieve a certain pressure on my brain. Do you cop that? If not, then we're in trouble, because we Ofay Watchers have a pronounced tendency to slip into that mood. If it is bothersome to you, it is quite a task for me because not too long ago it was my way of life to preach, as ardently as I could, that the white race is a race of devils, created by their maker to do evil, and make evil appear as good; that the white race is the natural, unchangeable enemy of the black man, who is the original man, owner, maker, cream of the planet Earth; that the white race was soon to be destroyed by Allah, and that the black man would then inherit the earth, which has always, in fact, been his.

I have, so to speak, washed my hands in the blood of the martyr, Malcolm X, whose retreat from the precipice of madness created new room for others to turn about in, and I am now caught up in that tiny space, attempting a maneuver of my own. Having renounced the teachings of Elijah Muhammad, I find that a rebirth does not follow automatically, of its own accord, that a void is left in one's vision, and this void seeks constantly to obliterate itself by pulling one back to one's former outlook. I have tried a tentative compromise by adopting a select vocabulary, so that now when I see the whites of *their* eyes, instead of saying "devil" or "beast" I say "imperialist" or "colonialist," and everyone seems to be happier.

In silence, we have spent our years watching the ofays, trying to understand them, on the principle that you have a better chance coping with the known than with the unknown. Some of us have been, and some still are, interested in learning whether it is *ultimately* possible to live in the same territory with people who seem so disagreeable to live with; still others want to get as far away from ofays as possible. What we share in common is the desire to break the ofays' power over us.

At times of fundamental social change, such as the era in which we live, it is easy to be deceived by the onrush of events, beguiled by the craving for social stability into mistaking transitory phenomena for enduring reality. The strength and permanence of "white backlash" in America is just such an illusion. However much this rear-guard action might seem to grow in strength, the initiative, and the future, rest with those whites and blacks who have liberated themselves from the master/slave syndrome. And these are to be found mainly among the youth.

Over the past twelve years there has surfaced a political conflict between the generations that is deeper, even, than the struggle between the races. Its first dramatic manifestation was within the ranks of the Negro people, when college students in the South, fed up with Uncle Tom's hat-in-hand approach to revolution, threw off the yoke of the NAACP. When these students initiated the first sit-ins, their spirit spread like a raging fire across the nation, and the technique of non-violent direct action, constantly refined and honed into a sharp cutting tool, swiftly matured. The older Negro "leaders," who are now all die-hard advocates of this tactic, scolded the students for sitting-in. The students rained down contempt upon their hoary heads. In the pre-sit-in days, these conservative leaders had always succeeded in putting down insurgent elements among the Negro people. (A measure of their power, prior to the students' rebellion, is shown by their success in isolating such great black men as the late W. E. B. DuBois and Paul Robeson, when these stalwarts, refusing to bite their tongues, lost favor with the U.S. government by their unstinting efforts to link up the Negro revolution with national liberation movements around the world.)

The "Negro leaders," and the whites who depended upon them to control their people, were outraged by the impudence of the students.

Calling for a moratorium on student initiative, they were greeted instead by an encore of sit-ins, and retired to their ivory towers to contemplate the new phenomenon. Others, less prudent because held on a tighter leash by the whites, had their careers brought to an abrupt end because they thought they could lead a black/white backlash against the students, only to find themselves in a kind of Bay of Pigs. Negro college presidents, who expelled students from all-Negro colleges in an attempt to quash the demonstrations, ended up losing their jobs; the victorious students would no longer allow them to preside over the campuses. The spontaneous protests on southern campuses over the repressive measures of their college administrations were an earnest of the Free Speech upheaval which years later was to shake the UC campus at Berkeley. In countless ways, the rebellion of the black students served as catalyst for the brewing revolt of the whites.

What has suddenly happened is that the white race has lost it heroes. Worse, its heroes have been revealed as villains and its greatest heroes as the arch-villains. The new generations of whites, appalled by the sanguine and despicable record carved over the face of the globe by their race in the last five hundred years, are rejecting the panoply of white heroes, whose heroism consisted in erecting the inglorious edifice of colonialism and imperialism; heroes whose careers rested on a system of foreign and domestic exploitation, rooted in the myth of white supremacy and the manifest destiny of the white race. The emerging shape of a new world order, and the requisites for survival in such a world, are fostering in young whites a new outlook. They recoil in shame from the spectacle of cowboys and pioneers—their heoric forefathers whose exploits filled earlier generations with pride—galloping across a movie screen shooting down Indians like Coke bottles. Even Winston Churchill, who is looked upon by older whites as perhaps the greatest hero of the twentieth century—even he, because of the system of which he was a creature and which he served, is an arch-villain in the eyes of the young white rebels.

At the close of World War Two, national liberation movements in the colonized world picked up new momentum and audacity, seeking to cash in on the democratic promises made by the Allies during the war. The Atlantic Charter, signed by President Roosevelt and Prime Minister Churchill in 1941, affirming "the right of all people to choose the form of government under which they may live," established the principle, although it took years of postwar struggle to give this piece of rhetoric even the appearance of reality. And just as world revolution has prompted the oppressed to re-evaluate their self-image in terms of the changing conditions, to slough off the servile attitudes inculcated by long years of subordination, the same dynamics of change have prompted the white people of the world to re-evaluate their self-image as well, to disabuse themselves of the Master Race psychology developed over centuries of imperial hegemony.

It is among the white youth of the world that the greatest change is taking place. It is they who are experiencing the great psychic pain of waking into consciousness to find their inherited heroes turned by events into villains. Communication and understanding between the older and younger generations of whites has entered a crisis. The elders, who, in the tradition of privileged classes or races, genuinely do not understand the youth, trapped by old ways of thinking and blind to the future, have only just begun to be vexed—because the youth have only just begun to rebel. So thoroughgoing is the revolution in the psyches of white youth that the traditional tolerance which every older generation has found it necessary to display is quickly exhausted, leaving a gulf of fear, hostility, mutual misunderstanding, and contempt.

The rebellion of the oppressed peoples of the world, along with the Negro revolution in America, have opened the way to a new evaluation of history, a re-examination of the role played by the white race since the beginning of European expansion. The positive achievements are also there in the record, and future generations will applaud them. But there can be no applause now, not while the master still holds the whip in his hand! Not even the master's own children can find it possible to applaud him—he cannot even applaud himself! The negative rings too loudly. Slave-catchers, slaveowners, murderers, butchers, invaders, oppressors—the white heroes have acquired new names. The great white statesmen whom school children are taught to revere are revealed as the architects of systems of human exploitation and slavery. Religious leaders are exposed as condoners and justifiers of all these evil deeds. Schoolteachers and college professors are seen as a clique of brainwashers and whitewashers.

The white youth of today are coming to see, intuitively, that to escape the onus of the history their fathers made they must face and admit the moral truth concerning the works of their fathers. That such venerated figures as George Washington and Thomas Jefferson owned hundreds of black slaves, that all of the Presidents up to Lincoln presided over a slave state, and that every President since Lincoln connived politically and cynically with the issues affecting the human rights and general welfare of the broad masses of the American people—these facts weigh heavily upon the hearts of these young people.

The elders do not like to give these youngsters credit for being able to understand what is going on and what has gone on. When speaking of juvenile delinquency, or the rebellious attitude of today's youth, the elders employ a glib rhetoric. They speak of the "alienation of youth," the desire of the young to be independent, the problems of "the father image" and "the mother image" and their effect upon growing children who lack sound models upon which to pattern themselves. But they consider it bad form to connect the problems of the youth with the central event of our era—the national liberation movements abroad and the Negro revolution at home. The foundations of authority have been blasted to bits in America because the whole society has been indicted, tried, and convicted of injustice. To the youth, the elders are Ugly Americans; to the elders, the youth have gone mad.

The rebellion of the white youth has gone through four broadly discernible stages. First there was an initial recoiling away, a rejection of the conformity which America expected, and had always received, sooner or later, from its youth. The disaffected youth were refusing to participate in the system, having discovered that America, far from helping the underdog, was up to its ears in the mud trying to hold the dog down. Because of the publicity and self-advertisements of the more vocal rebels, this period has come to be known as the beatnik era, although not all of the youth affected by these changes thought of themselves as beatniks. The howl of the beatniks and their scathing, outraged denunciation of the system—characterized by Ginsberg as Moloch, a bloodthirsty Semitic deity to which the ancient tribes sacrificed their firstborn children—was a serious, irrevocable declaration of war. It is revealing that the elders looked upon the beatniks as mere obscene misfits who were too lazy to take baths and too stingy to buy a haircut. The elders had eyes but couldn't see, ears but couldn't hear—not even when the message came through as clearly as in this remarkable passage from Jack Kerouac's *On the Road*:

At lilac evening I walked with every muscle aching among the lights of 27th and Welton in the Denver colored section, wishing I were a Negro, feeling that the best the white world had offered was not enough ecstasy for me, not enough life, joy, kicks, darkness, music, not enough night. I wished I were a Denver Mexican, or even a poor overworked Jap, anything but what I so drearily was, a "white man" disillusioned. All my life I'd had white ambitions. . . . I passed the dark porches of Mexican and Negro homes; soft voices were there, occasionally the dusky knee of some sensuous gal; the dark faces of the men behind rose arbors. Little children sat like sages in ancient rocking chairs.

The second stage arrived when these young people, having decided emphatically that the world, and particularly the U.S.A., was unacceptable to them in its present form, began an active search for roles they could play in changing the society. If many of these young people were content to lay up in their cool beat pads, smoking pot and listening to jazz in a perpetual orgy of esoteric bliss, there were others, less crushed by the system, who recognized the need for positive action. Moloch could not ask for anything more than to have its disaffected victims withdraw into safe, passive, apolitical little nonparticipatory islands, in an economy less and less able to provide jobs for the growing pool of unemployed. If all the unemployed had followed the lead of the beatniks, Moloch would gladly have legalized the use of euphoric drugs and marijuana, passed out free jazz albums and sleeping bags, to all those willing to sign affidavits promising to remain "beat." The non-beat disenchanted white youth were attracted magnetically to the Negro revolution, which had begun to take on a mass, insurrectionary tone. But they had difficulty understanding their relationship to the Negro, and what role "whites" could play in a "Negro revolution." For the time being they watched the Negro activists from afar.

The third stage, which is rapidly drawing to a close, emerged when white youth started joining Negro demonstrations in large numbers. The presence of whites among the demonstrators emboldened the Negro leaders and allowed them to use tactics they never would have been able to employ with all-black troops. The racist conscience of America is such that murder does not register as murder, really, unless the victim is white. And it was only when the newspapers and magazines started carrying pictures and stories of white demonstrators being beaten and maimed by mobs and police that the public began to protest. Negroes have become so used to this double standard that they, too, react differently to the death of a white. When white freedom riders were brutalized along with blacks, a sigh of relief went up from the black masses, because the blacks knew that white blood is the coin of freedom in a land where for four hundred years black blood has been shed unremarked and with impunity. America has never truly been outraged by the murder of a black man, woman, or child. White politicians may, if Negroes are aroused by a particular murder, say with their lips what they know with their minds they should feel with their hearts— but don't.

It is a measure of what the Negro feels that when the two white and one black civil rights workers were murdered in Mississippi in 1964, the event was welcomed by Negroes on a level of understanding beyond and deeper than the grief they felt for the victims and their families. This welcoming of violence and death to whites can almost be heard— indeed it can be heard—in the inevitable words, oft repeated by Negroes, that those whites, and blacks, do not die in vain. So it was with Mrs. Viola Liuzzo. And much of the anger which Negroes felt toward Martin Luther King during the Battle of Selma stemmed from the fact that he denied history a great moment, never to be recaptured, when he turned tail on the Edmund Pettus Bridge and refused to all those whites behind him what they had traveled thousands of miles to receive. If the police had turned them back by force, all those nuns, priests, rabbis, preachers, and distinguished ladies and gentlemen old and young—as they had done the Negroes a week earlier—the violence and brutality of the system would have been ruthlessly exposed. Or if, seeing King determined to lead them on to Montgomery, the troopers had stepped aside to avoid precisely the confrontation that Washington would not have tolerated, it would have signaled the capitulation of the militant white South. As it turned out, the March on Montgomery was a show of somewhat dim luster, stage-managed by the Establishment. But by this time the young whites were already active participants in the Negro revolution. In fact they had begun to transform it into something broader, with the potential of encompassing the whole of America in a radical reordering of society.

The fourth stage, now in its infancy, sees these white youth taking the initiative, using techniques learned in the Negro struggle to attack problems in the general society. The classic example of this new energy in action was the student battle on the UC campus at Berkeley, California—the Free Speech Movement. Leading the revolt were veterans of the civil rights movement, some of whom spent time on the firing line in the wilderness of Mississippi/Alabama. Flowing from the same momentum were student demonstrations against U.S. interference in the internal affairs of Vietnam, Cuba, the Dominican Republic, and the Congo and U.S. aid to apartheid in South Africa. The students even aroused the intellectual community to actions and positions unthinkable a few years ago: witness the teach-ins. But their revolt is deeper than single-issue protest. The characteristics of the white rebels which most alarm their elders—the long hair, the new dances, their love for Negro music, their use of marijuana, their mystical attitude toward sex—are all tools of their rebellion. They have turned these tools against the totalitarian fabric of American society—and they mean to change it.

From the beginning, America has been a schizophrenic nation. Its two conflicting images of itself were never reconciled, because never before has the survival of its most cherished myths made a reconciliation mandatory. Once before, during the bitter struggle between North and South climaxed by the Civil War, the two images of America came into conflict, although whites North and South scarcely understood it. The image of America held by its most alienated citizens was advanced neither by the North nor by the South; it was perhaps best expressed by Frederick Douglass, who was born into slavery in 1817, escaped to the North, and became the greatest leader-spokesman for the blacks of his era. In words that can still, years later, arouse an audience of black Americans, Frederick Douglass delivered, in 1852, a scorching indictment in his Fourth of July oration in Rochester:

> What to the American slave is your Fourth of July? I answer: a day that reveals to him, more than all other days in the year, the gross injustice and cruelty to which he is the constant victim. To him your celebration is a sham; your boasted liberty, an unholy license; your national greatness, swelling vanity; your sounds of rejoicing are empty and heartless; your denunciation of tyrants, brass-fronted impudence; your shouts of liberty and equality, hollow mockery; your prayers and hymns, your sermons and thanksgivings, with all your religious parade and solemnity, are, to him, more bombast, fraud, deception, impiety and hypocrisy—a thin veil to cover up crimes which would disgrace a nation of savages. . . .
>
> You boast of your love of liberty, your superior civilization, and your pure Christianity, while the whole political power of the nation (as embodied in the two great political parties) is solemnly pledged to support and perpetuate the enslavement of three millions of your countrymen. You hurl your anathemas at the crown-headed tyrants of Russia and Austria and pride yourselves on your democratic institutions, while you yourselves consent to be the mere *tools* and *bodyguards* of the tyrants of Virginia and Carolina.
>
> You invite to your shores fugitives of oppression from abroad, honor them with banquets, greet them with ovations, cheer them, toast them, salute them, protect them, and pour out your money to them like water; but the fugitive from your own land you advertise, hunt, arrest, shoot, and kill. You glory in your refinement and your universal education; yet you maintain a system as barbarous and dreadful as ever stained the character of a nation— a system begun in avarice, supported in pride, and perpetuated in cruelty.
>
> You shed tears over fallen Hungary, and make the sad story of her wrongs the theme of your poets, statesmen and orators, till your gallant sons are ready to fly to arms to vindicate her cause against the oppressor; but, in regard to the ten thousand wrongs of the American slave, you would enforce the strictest silence, and would hail him as an enemy of the nation who dares to make these wrongs the subject of public discourse!

This most alienated view of America was preached by the Abolitionists, and by Harriet Beecher Stowe in her *Uncle Tom's Cabin.*

But such a view of America was too distasteful to receive wide attention, and serious debate about America's image and her reality was engaged in only on the fringes of society. Even when confronted with overwhelming evidence to the contrary, most white Americans have found it possible, after steadying their rattled nerves, to settle comfortably back into their vaunted belief that America is dedicated to the proposition that all men are created equal and endowed by their Creator with certain inalienable rights—life, liberty, and the pursuit of happiness. With the Constitution for a rudder and the Declaration of Independence as its guiding star, the ship of state is sailing always toward a brighter vision of freedom and justice for all.

Because there is no common ground between these two contradictory images of America, they had to be kept apart. But the moment the blacks were let into the white world—let out of the voiceless and faceless cages of their ghettos, singing, walking, talking, dancing, writing, and orating *their* image of America and of Americans—the white world was suddenly challenged to match its practice to its preachments. And this is why those whites who abandon the *white* image of America and adopt the *black* are greeted with such unmitigated hostility by their elders.

For all these years whites have been taught to believe in the myth they preached, while Negroes have had to face the bitter reality of what America practiced. But without the lies and distortions, white Americans would not have been able to do the things they have done. When whites are forced to look honestly upon the objective proof of their deeds, the cement of mendacity holding white society together swiftly disintegrates. On the other hand, the core of the black world's vision remains intact, and in fact begins to expand and spread into the psychological territory vacated by the non-viable white lies, i.e., into the minds of young whites. It is remarkable how the system worked for so many years, how the majority of whites remained effectively unaware of any contradiction between their view of the world and that world itself. The mechanism by which this was rendered possible requires examination at this point.

Let us recall that the white man, in order to justify slavery and, later on, to justify segregation, elaborated a complex, all-pervasive myth which at one time classified the black man as a subhuman beast of burden. The myth was progressively modified, gradually elevating the blacks on the scale of evolution, following their slowly changing status, until the plateau of separate-but-equal was reached at the close of the nineteenth century. During slavery, the black was seen as a mindless

Supermasculine Menial. Forced to do the backbreaking work, he was conceived in terms of his ability to do such work—"field niggers," etc. The white man administered the plantation, doing all the thinking, exercising omnipotent power over the slaves. He had little difficulty dissociating himself from the black slaves, and he could not conceive of their positions being reversed or even reversible.

Blacks and whites being conceived as mutually exclusive types, those attributes imputed to the blacks could not also be imputed to the whites—at least not in equal degree—without blurring the line separating the races. These images were based upon the social function of the two races, the work they performed. The ideal white man was one who knew how to use his head, who knew how to manage and control things and get things done. Those whites who were not in a position to perform these fuctions nevertheless aspired to them. The ideal black man was one who did exactly as he was told, and did it efficiently and cheerfully. "Slaves," said Frederick Douglass, "are generally expected to sing as well as to work." As the black man's position and function became more varied, the images of white and black, having become stereotypes, lagged behind.

The separate-but-equal doctrine was promulgated by the Supreme Court in 1896. It had the same purpose domestically as the Open Door Policy toward China in the international arena: to stabilize a situation and subordinate a non-white population so that racist exploiters could manipulate those people according to their own selfish interests. These doctrines were foisted off as *the epitome of enlightened justice, the highest expression of morality*. Sanctified by religion, justified by philosophy and legalized by the Supreme Court, separate-but-equal was enforced by day by agencies of the law, and by the KKK & Co. under cover of night. Booker T. Washington, the Martin Luther King of his day, accepted separate-but-equal in the name of all Negroes. W. E. B. DuBois denounced it.

Separate-but-equal marked the last stage of the white man's flight into cultural neurosis, and the beginning of the black man's frantic striving to assert his humanity and equalize his position with the white. Blacks ventured into all fields of endeavor to which they could gain entrance. Their goal was to present in all fields a performance that would equal or surpass that of the whites. It was long axiomatic among blacks that a black had to be twice as competent as a white in any field in order to win grudging recognition from the whites. This produced a pathological motivation in the blacks to equal or surpass the whites, and a pathological motivation in the whites to maintain a distance from the blacks. This is the rack on which black and white Americans receive their delicious torture! At first there was the color bar, flatly denying the blacks entrance to certain spheres of activity. When this no longer worked, and blacks invaded sector after sector of American life and economy, the whites evolved other methods of keeping their distance. The illusion of the Negro's inferior nature had to be maintained.

One device evolved by the whites was to tab whatever the blacks did with the prefix "Negro." We had *Negro* literature, *Negro* athletes, *Negro* music, *Negro* doctors, *Negro* politicians, *Negro* workers. The malignant ingeniousness of this device is that although it accurately describes an objective biological fact—or, at least, a sociological fact in America—it concealed the paramount psychological fact: that to the white mind, prefixing anything with "Negro" automatically consigned it to an inferior category. A well-known example of the white necessity to deny due credit to blacks is in the realm of music. White musicians were famous for going to Harlem and other Negro cultural centers literally to steal the black man's music, carrying it back across the color line into the Great White World and passing off the watered-down loot as their own original creations. Blacks, meanwhile, were ridiculed as *Negro* musicians playing inferior coon music.

The Negro revolution at home and national liberation movements abroad have unceremoniously shattered the world of fantasy in which the whites have been living. It is painful that many do not yet see that their fantasy world has been rendered uninhabitable in the last half of the twentieth century. But it is away from this world that the white youth of today are turning. The "paper tiger" hero, James Bond, offering the whites a triumphant image of themselves, is saying what many whites want desperately to hear reaffirmed: *I am still the White Man, lord of the land, licensed to kill, and the world is still an empire at my feet.* James Bond feeds on that secret little anxiety, the psychological white backlash, felt in some degree by most whites alive. It is exasperating to see little brown men and little yellow men from the mysterious Orient, and the opaque black men of Africa (to say nothing of these impudent American Negroes!) who come to the UN and talk smart to us, who are scurrying all over *our* globe in their strange modes of dress—much as if they were new, unpleasant arrivals from another planet. Many whites believe in their ulcers that it is only a matter of time before the Marines get the signal to round up these truants and put them back securely in their cages. But it is away from this fantasy world that the white youth of today are turning.

In the world revolution now under way, the initiative rests with people of color. That growing numbers of white youth are repudiating their heritage of blood and taking people of color as their heroes and models is a tribute not only to their insight but to the resilience of the human spirit. For today the heroes of the initiative are people not usually thought of as white: Fidel Castro, Che Guevara, Kwame Nkrumah, Mao Tse-tung, Gamal Abdel Nasser, Robert F. Williams, Malcolm X, Ben Bella, John Lewis, Martin Luther King, Jr., Robert Parris Moses, Ho Chi Minh, Stokeley Carmichael, W. E. B. DuBois, James Forman, Chou En-lai.

The white youth of today have begun to react to the fact that the "American Way of Life" is a fossil of history. What do they care if their old baldheaded and crew-cut elders don't dig their caveman mops? They couldn't care less about the old, stiffassed honkies who don't like their new dances: Frug, Monkey, Jerk, Swim, Watusi. All they know is that it feels good to swing to way-out body-rhythms instead of drag-assing across the dance floor like zombies to the dead beat of mind-smothered Mickey Mouse music. Is it any wonder that the youth have lost all respect for their elders, for law and order, when for as long as they can remember all they've witnessed is a monumental bickering over the Negro's place in American society and the right of people around the world to be left alone by outside powers? They have witnessed the law, both domestic and international, being spat upon by those who do not like its terms. Is it any wonder, then, that they feel justified, by sitting-in and freedom riding, in breaking laws made by lawless men? Old funny-styled, zipper-mouthed political night riders know nothing but to haul out an investigating committee *to look into the disturbance* to find the cause of the unrest among the youth. Look into a mirror! The cause is you, Mr. and Mrs. Yesterday, you with your forked tongues.

A young white today cannot help but recoil from the base deeds of his people. On every side, on every continent, he sees racial arrogance, savage brutality toward the conquered and subjugated people, genocide; he sees the human cargo of the slave trade; he sees the systematic extermination of American Indians; he sees the civilized nations of Europe fighting in imperial depravity over the lands of other people—and over possession of the very people themselves. There seems to be no end to the ghastly deeds of which his people are guilty. GUILTY. The slaughter of the Jews by the Germans, the dropping of atomic bombs on the Japanese people—these deeds weigh heavily upon the prostrate souls and tumultuous consciences of the white youth. The white heroes, their hands dripping with blood, are dead.

The young whites know that the colored people of the world, Afro-

Americans included, do not seek revenge for their suffering. They seek the same things the white rebel wants: an end to war and exploitation. Black and white, the young rebels are free people, free in a way that Americans have never been before in the history of their country. And they are outraged.

There is in America today a generation of white youth that is truly worthy of a black man's respect, and this is a rare event in the foul annals of American history. From the beginning of the contact between blacks and whites, there has been very little reason for a black man to respect a white, with such exceptions as John Brown and others lesser known. But respect commands itself and it can neither be given nor withheld when it is due. If a man like Malcolm X could change and repudiate racism, if I myself and other former Muslims can change, if young whites can change, then there is hope for America. It was certainly strange to find myself, while steeped in the doctrine that all whites were devils by nature, commanded by the heart to applaud and acknowledge respect for these young whites—despite the fact that they are descendants of the masters and I the descendant of slave. The sins of the fathers are visited upon the heads of the children—but only if the children continue in the evil deeds of the fathers.

LLOYD T. DELANY

The White American Psyche—Exploration of Racism

Ye specious worthies who scoff at me
Whence thrives your politics
As long as ye have ruled the world?
From dagger thrust and murder! —CHARLES DE COSTER: *Ulenspiegel*

On April 29, 1968, Thomas A. Johnson, a black reporter for the *New York Times*, reported the following conversation: "A German in Vietnam asked a Negro civilian if he was aware of how some American whites talked about Negroes when they were alone. The Negro said he was.

" 'Do you know that they call you animals,' the German said, 'that they say you have tails and that they seem especially anxious that foreigners—myself and the Vietnamese—hear this?'

" 'I know,' the Negro said.

" 'What's wrong with them?' the German said.

" 'They're white Americans,' he was told. 'A strange breed of people.' "

Much has been written about the impact of bigotry on the psychology of the black American. However, very little in the literature deals with the psychodynamics of white racism. This imbalance is crucial, for the continual harping on what impact white racism has on blacks still maintains the myth that it is "a black problem." The imbalance fosters the distortion that whites are mainly bystanders in this illness while in fact they are both creators and victims of the sickness of racism.

It is important that the black American have some understanding of the pathology of white racism so that he may deal with it more appropriately. It is consequently necessary to examine some of the psychodynamic aspects of white racism and what accounts for "this strange breed of people" and their racism.

The historical base of racism rests on the Anglo-Dutch attitudes and sentiments which stemmed from their original ignorance of blacks. The tenets of Protestantism and capitalism, a form of economy that requires the perpetuation of an exploitable group, compounded the development of racism. From these three main roots slavery emerged and was maintained. However, certain psychological mechanisms also accompanied this development, enabling the American racist to deny his barbarity and exploitation.

Lloyd T. Delany, "The White American Psyche—Exploration of Racism." From *Freedomways (Magazine): A Quarterly Review of the Freedom Movement*, Vol. 8, No. 3, Summer, 1968. Reprinted by permission.

If an individual were to walk into a psychiatrist's or a psychologist's office exhibiting the symptoms that are so typical of the racist, there isn't a clinician of any competence that would not immediately diagnose him as grossly pathological. Yet when the society at large employs these mechanisms they are overlooked. Part of the explanation for overlooking this rests with the obvious fact that the very people who would diagnose the pathology are themselves racists and consequently unable and unwilling to view their behavior as sick. Moreover, the endemic nature of racism makes it easier to ignore its pathology. It is as if everyone in the society has the flu perpetually; under such circumstances it would take some careful analysis to recognize that, despite its prevalence, to have the flu is to be sick. Too often people are wont to mistake the prevalence of a form of behavior as testimony to its normalcy. The man who kills one man on a street corner with a knife is considered a murderer; the man who drops an atom bomb, killing fifty thousand humans, is a hero because he is merely one of many. What is common soon comes to be regarded as normal. Hence, the commonness of racism enables most in the society to ignore its pathological nature. Yet even the prevalence of racism would not enable the racist to be unknowing of his illness unless he employed the usual devices employed by all sick people to avoid confrontation with their pathology.

The Process of Depersonalization

The underlying psychodynamic basis of racism is the process of depersonalization, a psychological process which is an aberration and manifested by stark denial of reality. The racist denies the reality that he is interacting with other humans. The energy necessary to maintain this pervasive denial of reality is extraordinary; it drains the racist to a considerable extent, crippling him and his society in serious ways.

The process of depersonalization utilized by the racist is sustained by many mental operations. These specific mechanisms employed by the racist are important to recognize. They are modeled in many ways after the specific mechanisms present in all emotionally disturbed people.

Evasion and Avoidance

Evasion and avoidance are a disturbed mental process known to all clinicians. This is a pathological mechanism in which the person avoids or evades confronting, facing, recognizing anything that would be a source of tension, anxiety or fear. The utilization of avoidance and evasion in the white racist is quite clear though its form is sometimes misunderstood by blacks.

Many blacks have had the experience of walking in the white section of town and being passed in the street by a white who they know quite well. This is sometimes misinterpreted by the black man to mean the white who walks past him without indicating recognition is unwilling to greet his black friend in public. This may, in some instances, be an accurate appraisal; it is most often not so. What is more usually the case is that most white Americans, until very recently, did not look at or see blacks. This is one way to avoid having to face the reality that there are blacks and that if there are blacks one must deal with them. Avoidance and evasion are an unconscious process, unrecognized by the person employing it. To test this, the next time it occurs simply tap your white acquaintance on the shoulder and he'll be quite delighted to see you. Whites do not see blacks, wishing unconsciously they were not there.

A contemporary consequence of this evasion and avoidance is manifested in the shock and surprise about what is now called the rise of black militance and nationalism. The white American is only now being awakened to the fact that he has been living for four hundred years with blacks. Rap Brown, Stokely Carmichael, Ron Karenga and other nationalists can easily reach the headlines of any paper today by merely uttering a sentence whether it has much virtue or not because of this new found black awareness in the white press.

What is not known by most whites is that the militance of blacks today is neither new nor unique. A cogent illustration of this is in a poem written by the late Langston Hughes. The poem is entitled *Roland Hayes Beaten* and was written in 1942.

> *Negroes*
> *Sweet and docile*
> *Meek, humble, and kind;*
> *Beware the day*
> *They change their minds!*
>
> *Wind*
> *In the cotton fields,*
> *Gentle breezes*
> *Beware the hour*
> *It uproots the trees!*

Though white historians are aware of it, most white Americans are completely unaware of the fact that Marcus Garvey in the 1920's was able to amass the greatest support among black people any movement in this nation has ever achieved. And the stridency of Garvey has not been exceeded by any contemporary black militant.

The increasing new awareness of the black man occasioned by the early civil rights demonstrations and later the more militant direct action programs has shaken somewhat the utilization of the mechanism of evasion and avoidance, but other pathological devices used by the white racist still exist.

Acting Out and Projection

The acting out and projection of white racists frequently confound, frustrate and sometimes even amuse blacks.

Acting out is a neurotic mechanism in which a person is unable to contain his own feelings, therefore he translates his feelings directly into some form of overt behavior. Usually these are feelings that are destructive. The hatred of the white racist is commonly acted out in his overt violence. The testimony to white violence goes back a long time.

Acting out, however, is commonly combined with projection, another mechanism employed by the white racist. This is also a neurotic defense. The individuals who are projecting ascribe to others behavior, thoughts, feelings, attitudes, and sentiments that they have themselves but which they find unacceptable and hence attribute to others.

The fear and panic that periodically sweep across the nation are living testimony to the pathological use of both acting out and projection. In an article appearing in the *Wall Street Journal* on April 23, 1968, headlined "White Racism: Ghetto Violence Brings Hardening of Attitudes Towards Negro Groups," the following item appears: "A recent visit to the gun shop in Allan Park tells a good deal about the climate of fear in many parts of the metropolitan area.

"The clerk, a balding paunchy man, has the rapt attention of several customers when he says, 'The word is out that if there's any trouble this summer and you see a black man in your neighborhood, shoot to kill and ask questions later. They [Negroes] are gonna send carloads of firebombs into the suburbs to suck the police out of the city.'"

By projecting his own hatred and violence onto this mythical "black horde invading his suburb," the "paunchy man" can act out this violence while disowning the responsibility of it. By creating a myth that blacks are violent, he can justify himself and his killing of innocent blacks. When he is unable to personally accomplish this, he utilizes his police force to carry out what he is not able to do himself.

The projection of his hatred and violence on the black man requires a certain amount of reality denial; for well this "paunchy man" knows that the so-called riots have all occurred within the black communities, that invariably, just as in the past, the so-called riots take a far greater toll of black lives than of whites. The so-called riots of today, as the riots of the past, invariably end with many more blacks being killed than whites and most of them innocent of even the so-called crimes of looting and arson.

The National Advisory Commission's Report on Civil Disorders (as they refer to them) is replete with instances of innocent black people being slain during these so-called disorders. There was the 10-year-old child slain in his father's car, the family entirely uninvolved and unaware that a so-called civil disorder was going on. There is Rebecca Brown, shot in the back through her apartment window after she rushed to grasp her two-year-old from the window so that he would not be harmed. There was the man sitting in a rocking chair on his porch slain by National Guardsmen, and many more. But this balding, paunchy white racist can ignore the murder of these innocents. And by this process of projection can justify the continuation of his doing the same things he and his forefathers before him have always done.

Projection is not only limited to such things as white violence; white sexuality is also projected. The recent Pulitzer Prize-winning novel of William Styron is a good example of white lechery projected. Once again blacks are subjected in this best-selling novel to the fantasies and projections of a white racist who, under the guise of sympathy for blacks, projects his own sexual preoccupation onto his twisted fictionalized version of the black revolutionary Nat Turner. Styron's projection of his sexuality into the character of Nat Turner required not only a distortion of history but an emasculation of this revolutionary figure. He ends up depicted, in Styron's portrayal, as puking over the fact that he has killed a callow, white adolescent girl, a pure fantasy of Styron's sick Southern imagination.

The white southerner who decries most the sanctity of white womanhood is also the most preoccupied with raping and violating black womanhood. Southerners have been able to do this without fully confronting the meaning of their acts by projecting their sexual and and aggressive feelings onto the black man, creating the fantasy of black sexuality and aggression, then acting as if the fantasy they have created is a reality. Thus, projection is manifested in any number of ways covering the deep seated violence, sexuality, and inferiority of the white racist.

No one has more aptly pointed out how whites project their feelings of inferiority than James Baldwin in his essay *The Fire Next Time*. In this essay Baldwin comments extensively on how the projection of inferiority feelings on the part of the white racist occurs. And he sums this up when he points out that the white racist needs the "nigger" because it is the "nigger" in him that he cannot tolerate.

Eldridge Cleaver in his book of essays *Soul on Ice* discusses in some detail the often thinly disguised admiration whites have of blacks and how recently whites have increasingly modeled themselves after blacks. The white campus revolts are but one illustration of this.

Jack Kerouac is the least restrained in his admiration of the black man when he has the hero of his novel *On the Road* saying, "I walked . . . wishing I were a Negro, feeling that the best the white world had offered was not enough ecstasy for me, not enough life, joy, kicks, darkness, music, not enough night."

Too often black psychologists and other black social scientists have in their stress of the impact of racism on black people minimized the psychological need of the white racist to create an inferior being. It is this need that reflects the basic sense of inferiority and inadequacy on the part of the white racist, masking often his admiration for the black man. He needs an inferior and he projects his inadequacies, his failing, relying on the pathetic device of skin color to establish his "superiority." So sad this fragile, frantic need that hinges on the irrelevance of skin color, a fact not even within the control of the white man. Yet it is this desperation to find something or someone on which he can heap his profound sense of inadequacy and inferiority that the "nigger" had to be created and perpetuated in the minds of the white racists.

Indeed too much emphasis has been placed on the inferiority feeling engendered in blacks without the concomitant recognition on the part of blacks that whites also have these deep-seated inadequate feelings and frequently they project their inferiority feelings. The white women spitting at six- and seven-year-olds in New Orleans are the victims of their bottomless feelings of failure and frustration. The helpless black children become the easy prey for these emotionally disturbed women.

A segment of the black militant movement makes a similar error as do the social scientists mentioned above by constantly haranguing about the superiority of blackness, failing to recognize that the need to state over and over their blackness in the terms and contexts in which they do is still playing the game according to the white racists. The man who experiences his worth and adequacy does not have to proclaim it, he knows it. Some forms of black nationalism mask feelings of deprivation, frustration about not having been given the things they wanted from "the white massa." Like the two-year-old having a tantrum, sulking in the corner, feeling hurt and injured but covering up this hurt and injury by screaming, the black militant sulks, feels hurt, and substitutes rhetoric for screaming. The black militants who proclaim the desire for separation in effect isolating themselves are often unwilling to face that they too have bought the white racist's message that they are indeed inferior.

It is understandable why black separatists exist in the black community. It is also well to recognize that in joining hands with the white separatists, the black segregationist may be masking his fear of confronting and competing with whites. Black separatism stems from despair and anger about white racism but it also serves a secondary purpose, in effect complementing and complying with the aims of the white racist. The black separatists should examine carefully what is wrong when they find their cause supported by the same people who enslaved their grandparents and raped their mothers.

Attempted Justification

This is a mechanism in which the sick individual attempts to apply a reasonable explanation to cover the unconscious impulses, thoughts, and feelings that would be quite distressful if they were aware of them. The racist's behavior is replete with examples of this defense operation. For example, the continual harping on the obviously fallacious notion that blacks not having achieved equality in the society is the responsibility of blacks, is one of the common utilizations of attempted justification. In spite of the endless issuing of reports, facts and figures to demonstrate both historical and current reasons for the inequity that exists in the society, white racists continue to act as if this mass of information were unknown to them. This is not merely a political device, although it has manipulative political advantages; it is a psychological device as well. For example, it enables the racist living in the suburbs to talk about his unwillingness to hand out federal monies for slum clearance while ignoring the fact that the home in which he lives is supported and subsidized by federal funds, usually obtained through Veteran Administration or Federal Housing Administration loans. It enables the racist to ignore the fact that only 800,000 units have been constructed in the thirty-one-year history of subsidized federal housing in ghetto communities, but 10 *million* units have been constructed in middle and upper income communities utilizing federal subsidies.

The white racist, riding to his suburban home with a bumper sticker "I fight poverty, I work," attempts to justify his behavior while ignoring the fact that he refuses to hire any black people in his place of business or that he works in a place which discriminates against blacks of equal capacity and skill. In one breath he talks of the fact that blacks like living in the slums and the next moment he attends a committee meeting to protest a black family moving into the community and failing in that, he throws a brick through their window.

Throughout the summer of so-called riots, white TV men, radio reporters and newspaper reporters roamed freely through the black communities emerging unharmed. In fact their greatest threat came not from the black community but from the white police force who sometimes either deliberately or mistakenly attacked them. Yet throughout all of this they were able to comment and write or report their stories about "the black violence" ignoring the fact that they were standing in the midst of this so-called black violence unharmed.

The white racist continues to draw invidious parallels between the gains of such immigrant groups as the Italians, Irish and Jews and the blacks, citing this as proof of black inferiority. In his attempted justification of his racism he ignores the fact that none of these groups were subjected to enslavement, none was the victim of federal, state, and local government policies to keep him in subservience and therefore there is no parallel.

In his attempted justification, he explains away the fact that the Irish, Italians and Jews were not brought to this country against their will, their families were not broken up deliberately, nor were they perpetually subjected to all manners of barbarities and cruelties to keep them in a state of slavery and subjugation. All history and all present reality are ignored as the white racist, in his pathological attempt to justify himself, relies on these devices.

Implications for Black Response

Crucial then to the welfare of black people is the recognition that we live in a society of whites that is pathological and that many of the members of society are profoundly sick people. Their pathology is expressed in their overt behavior and in the utilization of all the devices and mechanisms that are recognized as pathological by people who daily treat sick people. They disassociate, transfer blame, deny reality, they use avoidance and evasion, they act out feelings of hatred, grandiosity and perverse sexuality, they rationalize and attempt to justify their irrational acts.

As one would not walk into a ward of violent, emotionally disturbed people unprepared for what consequences may eventuate by ignoring their pathology, the black man must come to recognize that he is living in the midst of grossly pathological people. The pathology of racism has had not only direct impact on the racist's life and mind but on the black man's life and mind as well. Baldwin says this in another way in his essay *The Fire Next Time*: "White people cannot, in the generality, be taken as models of how to live. Rather, the white man is himself in sore need of new standards, which will release him from his confusion and place him once again in fruitful communication with the depths of his own being."

Black Identity

Yet the black man must come to realize that he need neither emulate nor completely disassociate himself from the society in which he is now a member. To simply withdraw in the presence of the mania in which one lives is, in a sense, to feed that mania. On the other hand to emulate it is to destroy oneself.

Blacks are in the midst of an identity crisis. Its origins are in the historical roots of the racist nature of this society. That identity cannot be established, however, by either ignoring the pathology of the white racist with whom blacks live or by merely denouncing every aspect of the society and acting as if it is possible to go into some separate reclusive state of isolation. Such withdrawal becomes itself pathological. The identity crisis for the black man is centered in his seeking a way in which he neither has to disown those aspects of the society which are important, constructive and instrumental in providing him a full rich life nor by passively accepting those aspects of the society which would prevent him from doing so. An essential aspect of recognizing who you are is to recognize who are others.

It is important that the black man pay more attention to who he really is, to reject the myths and fantasies that the pathological racist society has crowned him with but it is also important that the black man recognize the nature of the white man with whom he is living.

The noted and eminent late sociologist E. Franklin Frazier, in his brilliant but scathing account of the black bourgeoisie, decried the black middle class imitation of the vacuous white middle class behavior and values. Accurate as this analysis is, it seems to overlook the important factor that to want a good life, to want to have the comforts, assets and advantages that this country offers, is not in itself to be criticized. But such striving must not be merely imitative of a sick model. This is the pitfall blacks must avoid. The desire to aspire, to be educated, to be affluent, is not to be white—it is to be human. To be human is something many whites in this society know little about.

The Ballot or the Bullet

Ten days after Malcolm X's declaration of independence, the Muslim Mosque, Inc., held the first of a series of four Sunday night public rallies in Harlem, at which Malcolm began the job of formulating the ideology and philosophy of a new movement. In the opinion of many who heard these talks, they were the best he ever gave. Unfortunately, taped recordings of these meetings were not available in the preparation of this book. Simultaneously, however, Malcolm began to accept speaking engagements outside of New York—at Chester, Pennsylvania; Boston; Cleveland; Detroit; etc.—and tapes of some of these were available.

In the Cleveland talk, given at Cory Methodist Church on April 3, 1964, Malcolm presented many of the themes he had been developing in the Harlem rallies. The meeting, sponsored by the Cleveland chapter of the Congress of Racial Equality, took the form of a symposium entitled "The Negro Revolt—What Comes Next?" The first speaker was Louis E. Lomax, whose talk was in line with CORE doctrine and was well received by the large, predominantly Negro audience. Malcolm's talk got even more applause, although it differed in fundamental respects from anything ever said at a CORE meeting.

"The Ballot or the Bullet," Malcolm's own title for his speech, was notable, among other things, for its statement that elements of black nationalism were present and growing in such organizations as the NAACP and CORE. For various reasons, the black nationalist convention, which in this talk he projected for August, 1964, was not held.

Mr. Moderator, Brother Lomax, brothers and sisters, friends and enemies; I just can't believe everyone in here is a friend and I don't want to leave anybody out. The question tonight, as I understand it, is "The Negro Revolt, and Where Do We Go From Here?" or "What Next?" In my little humble way of understanding it, it points toward either the ballot or the bullet.

Before we try and explain what is meant by the ballot or the bullet, I would like to clarify something concerning myself. I'm still a Muslim, my religion is still Islam. That's my personal belief. Just as Adam Clayton Powell is a Christian minister who heads the Abyssinian Baptist Church in New York, but at the same time takes part in the political struggles to try and bring about rights to the black people in this country; and Dr. Martin Luther King is a Christian minister down in Atlanta, Georgia, who heads another organization fighting for the civil rights of black people in this country; and Rev. Galamison, I guess you've heard of him, is another Christian minister in New York who has been deeply involved in the school boycotts to eliminate segregated education; well, I myself am a minister, not a Christian minister, but a Muslim minister; and I believe in action on all fronts by whatever means necessary.

Although I'm still a Muslim, I'm not here tonight to discuss my religion. I'm not here to try and change your religion. I'm not here to argue or discuss anything that we differ about, because it's time for us to submerge our differences and realize that it is best for us to first see that we have the same problem, a common problem—a problem that will make you catch hell whether you're a Baptist, or a Methodist, or a Muslim, or a nationalist. Whether you're educated or illiterate, whether you live on the boulevard or in the alley, you're going to catch hell just like I am. We're all in the same boat and we all are going to catch the same hell from the same man. He just happens to be a white man. All of us have suffered here, in this country, political oppression at the hands of the white man, economic exploitation at the hands of the white man, and social degradation at the hands of the white man.

Now in speaking like this, it doesn't mean that we're anti-white, but it does mean we're anti-exploitation, we're anti-degradation, we're anti-oppression. And if the white man doesn't want us to be anti-him, let him stop oppressing and exploiting and degrading us. Whether we are Christians or Muslims or nationalists or agnostics or atheists, we must first learn to forget our differences. If we have differences, let us differ in the closet; when we come out in front, let us not have anything to argue about until we get finished arguing with the man. If the late President Kennedy could get together with Khrushchev and exchange some wheat, we certainly have more in common with each other than Kennedy and Khrushchev had with each other.

If we don't do something real soon, I think you'll have to agree that we're going to be forced either to use the ballot or the bullet. It's one or the other in 1964. It isn't that time is running out—time has run out! 1964 threatens to be the most explosive year America has ever witnessed. The most explosive year. Why? It's also a political year. It's the year when all of the white politicians will be back in the so-called Negro community jiving you and me for some votes. The year when all of the white political crooks will be right back in your and my community with their false promises, building up our hopes for a letdown, with their trickery and their treachery, with their false promises which they don't intend to keep. As they nourish these dissatisfactions, it can only lead to one thing, an explosion; and now we have the type of black man on the scene in America today—I'm sorry, Brother Lomax—who just doesn't intend to turn the other cheek any longer.

Don't let anybody tell you anything about the odds are against you. If they draft you, they send you to Korea and make you face 800 million Chinese. If you can be brave over there, you can be brave right here. These odds aren't as great as those odds. And if you fight here, you will at least know what you're fighting for.

I'm not a politician, not even a student of politics; in fact, I'm not a student of much of anything. I'm not a Democrat, I'm not a Republican, and I don't even consider myself an American. If you and I were Americans, there'd be no problem. Those Hunkies that just got off the boat, they're already Americans; Polacks are already Americans; the Italian refugees are already Americans. Everything that came out of Europe, every blue-eyed thing, is already an American. And as long as you and I have been over here, we aren't Americans yet.

Well, I am one who doesn't believe in deluding myself. I'm not going to sit at your table and watch you eat, with nothing on my plate, and call myself a diner. Sitting at the table doesn't make you a diner, unless you eat some of what's on that plate. Being here in America doesn't make you an American. Being born here in America doesn't make you an American. Why, if birth made you American, you wouldn't need any legislation, you wouldn't need any amendments to the Constitution, you wouldn't be faced with civil-rights filibustering in Washington, D.C., right now. They don't have to pass civil-rights legislation to make a Polack an American.

No, I'm not an American. I'm one of the 22 million black people who are the victims of Americanism. One of the 22 million black people who are the victims of democracy, nothing but disguised hypocrisy. So, I'm not standing here speaking to you as an American, or a patriot, or a flag-saluter, or a flag-waver—no, not I. I'm speaking as a victim of this American system. And I see America through the eyes of the victim. I don't see any American dream; I see an American nightmare.

These 22 million victims are waking up. Their eyes are coming open. They're beginning to see what they used to only look at. They're becoming politically mature. They are realizing that there are new political trends from coast to coast. As they see these new political trends, it's possible for them to see that every time there's an election the races are so close that they have to have a recount. They had to recount in Massachusetts to see who was going to be governor, it was so close. It was the same way in Rhode Island, in Minnesota, and in many other parts of the country. And the same with Kennedy and Nixon when they ran for president. It was so close they had to count all over again. Well, what does this mean? It means that when white people are evenly divided; and black people have a bloc of votes of their own, it is left up to them to determine who's going to sit in the White House and who's going to be in the dog house.

It was the black man's vote that put the present administration in Washington, D.C. Your vote, your dumb vote, your ignorant vote, your wasted vote put in an administration in Washington, D.C., that has seen fit to pass every kind of legislation imaginable, saving you until last, then filibustering on top of that. And your and my leaders have the audacity to run around clapping their hands and talk about how much progress we're making. And what a good president we have. If he wasn't good in Texas, he sure can't be good in Washington, D.C. Because Texas is a lynch state. It is in the same breath as Mississippi, no different; only they lynch you in Texas with a Texas accent and lynch you in Mississippi with a Mississippi accent. And these Negro leaders have the audacity to go and have some coffee in the White House with a Texan, a Southern cracker—that's all he is—and then come out and tell you and me that he's going to be better for us because, since he's from the South, he knows how to deal with the Southerners. What kind of logic is that? Let Eastland be president, he's from the South too. He should be better able to deal with them than Johnson.

In this present administration they have in the House of Representatives 257 Democrats to only 177 Republicans. They control two-thirds of the House vote. Why can't they pass something that will help you and me? In the Senate, there are 67 senators who are of the Democratic Party. Only 33 of them are Republicans. Why, the Democrats have got the government sewed up, and you're the one who sewed it up for them. And what have they given you for it? Four years in office, and just now getting around to some civil-rights legislation. Just now, after everything else is gone, out of the way, they're going to sit down now and play with you all summer long—the same old giant con game that they call filibuster. All those are in cahoots together. Don't you ever think they're not in cahoots together, for the man that is heading the civil-rights filibuster is a man from Georgia named Richard Russell. When Johnson became president, the first man he asked for when he got back to Washington, D.C., was "Dicky"—that's how tight they are. That's his boy, that's his pal, that's his buddy. But they're playing that old con game. One of them makes believe he's for you, and he's got it fixed where the other one is so tight against you, he never has to keep his promise.

So it's time in 1964 to wake up. And when you see them coming up with that kind of conspiracy, let them know your eyes are open. And let them know you got something else that's wide open too. It's got to be the ballot or the bullet. The ballot or the bullet. If you're afraid to use an expression like that, you should get on out of the country, you should get back in the cotton patch, you should get back in the alley. They get all the Negro vote, and after they get it, the Negro gets nothing in return. All they did when they got to Washington was give a few big jobs. Those big Negroes didn't need big jobs, they already had jobs. That's camouflage, that's trickery, that's treachery, window-dressing. I'm not trying to knock out the Democrats for the Republicans, we'll get to them in a minute. But it is true—you put the Democrats first and the Democrats put you last.

Look at it the way it is. What alibis do they use, since they control Congress and the Senate? What alibi do they use when you and I ask, "Well, when are you going to keep your promise?" They blame the Dixiecrats. What is a Dixiecrat? A Democrat. A Dixiecrat is nothing but a Democrat in disguise. The titular head of the Democrats is also the head of the Dixiecrats, because the Dixiecrats are a part of the Democratic Party. The Democrats have never kicked the Dixiecrats out of the party. The Dixiecrats bolted themselves once, but the Democrats didn't put them out. Imagine, these lowdown Southern segregationists put the Northern Democrats down. But the Northern Democrats have never put the Dixiecrats down. No, look at that thing the way it is. They have got a con game going on, a political con game, and you and I are in the middle. It's time for you and me to wake up and start looking at it like it is, and trying to understand it like it is; and then we can deal with it like it is.

The Dixiecrats in Washington, D.C., control the key committees that run the government. The only reason the Dixiecrats control these committees is because they have seniority. The only reason they have seniority is because they come from states where Negroes can't vote. This is not even a government that's based on democracy. It is not a government that is made up of representatives of the people. Half of the people in the South can't even vote. Eastland is not even supposed to be in Washington. Half of the senators and congressmen who occupy these key positions in Washington, D.C., are there illegally, are there unconstitutionally.

I was in Washington, D.C., a week ago Thursday, when they were debating whether or not they should let the bill come onto the floor. And in the back of the room where the Senate meets, there's a huge map of the United States, and on that map it shows the location of Negroes throughout the country. And it shows that the Southern section of the country, the states that are most heavily concentrated with Negroes, are the ones that have senators and congressmen standing up filibustering and doing all other kinds of trickery to keep the Negro from being able to vote. This is pitiful. But it's not pitiful for us any longer; it's actually pitiful for the white man, because soon now, as the Negro awakens a little more and sees the vise that he's in, sees the bag that he's in, sees the real game that he's in, then the Negro's going to develop a new tactic.

These senators and congressmen actually violate the constitutional amendments that guarantee the people of that particular state or county the right to vote. And the Constitution itself has within it the machinery to expel any representative from a state where the voting rights of the people are violated. You don't even need new legislation. Any person in Congress right now, who is there from a state or a district where the voting rights of the people are violated, that particular person should be expelled from Congress. And when you expel him, you've removed one of the obstacles in the path of any real meaningful legislation in this country. In fact, when you expel them, you don't need new legislation, because they will be replaced by black representatives from counties and districts where the black man is in the majority, not in the minority.

If the black man in these Southern states had his full voting rights, the key Dixiecrats in Washington, D.C., which means the key Democrats in Washington D.C., would lose their seats. The Democratic Party itself would lose its power. It would cease to be powerful as a party. When you see the amount of power that would be lost by the Democratic Party if it were to lose the Dixiecrat wing, or branch, or element, you can see where it's against the interests of the Democrats to give voting rights to Negroes in states where the Democrats have been in complete power and authority ever since the Civil War. You just can't belong to that party without analyzing it.

I say again, I'm not anti-Democrat, I'm not anti-Republican, I'm not anti-anything. I'm just questioning their sincerity, and some of the strategy that they've been using on our people by promising them promises that they don't intend to keep. When you keep the Democrats in power, you're keeping the Dixiecrats in power. I doubt that my good Brother Lomax will deny that. A vote for a Democrat is a vote for a

Dixiecrat. That's why, in 1964, it's time now for you and me to become more politically mature and realize what the ballot is for; what we're supposed to get when we cast a ballot; and that if we don't cast a ballot, it's going to end up in a situation where we're going to have to cast a bullet. It's either a ballot or a bullet.

In the North, they do it a different way. They have a system that's known as gerrymandering, whatever that means. It means when Negroes become too heavily concentrated in a certain area, and begin to gain too much political power, the white man comes along and changes the district lines. You may say, "Why do you keep saying white man?" Because it's the white man who does it. I haven't ever seen any Negro changing any lines. They don't let him get near the line. It's the white man who does this. And usually, it's the white man who grins at you the most, and pats you on the back, and is supposed to be your friend. He may be friendly, but he's not your friend.

So, what I'm trying to impress upon you, in essence, is this: You and I in America are faced not with a segregationist conspiracy, we're faced with a government conspiracy. Everyone who's filibustering is a senator —that's the government. Everyone who's finagling in Washington, D.C., is a congressman—that's the government. You don't have anybody putting blocks in your path but people who are a part of the government. The same government that you go abroad to fight for and die for is the government that is in a conspiracy to deprive you of your voting rights, deprive you of your economic opportunities, deprive you of decent housing, deprive you of decent education. You don't need to go to the employer alone, it is the government itself, the government of America, that is responsible for the oppression and exploitation and degradation of black people in this country. And you should drop it in their lap. This government has failed the Negro. This so-called democracy has failed the Negro. And all these white liberals have definitely failed the Negro.

So, where do we go from here? First, we need some friends. We need some new allies. The entire civil-rights struggle needs a new interpretation, a broader interpretation. We need to look at this civil-rights thing from another angle—from the inside as well as from the outside. To those of us whose philosophy is black nationalism, the only way you can get involved in the civil-rights struggle is give it a new interpretation. That old interpretation excluded us. It kept us out. So, we're giving a new interpretation to the civil-rights struggle, an interpretation that will enable us to come into it, take part in it. And these handkerchief-heads who have been dillydallying and pussyfooting and compromising—we don't intend to let them pussyfoot and dillydally and compromise any longer.

How can you thank a man for giving you what's already yours? How then can you thank him for giving you only part of what's already yours? You haven't even made progress, if what's being given to you, you should have had already. That's not progress. And I love my Brother Lomax, the way he pointed out we're right back where we were in 1954. We're not even as far up as we were in 1954. We're behind where we were in 1954. There's more segregation now than there was in 1954. There's more racial animosity, more racial hatred, more racial violence today in 1964, than there was in 1954. Where is the progress?

And now you're facing a situation where the young Negro's coming up. They don't want to hear that "turn-the-other-cheek" stuff, no. In Jacksonville, those were teenagers, they were throwing Molotov cocktails. Negroes have never done that before. But it shows you there's a new deal coming in. There's new thinking coming in. There's new strategy coming in. It'll be Molotov cocktails this month, hand grenades next month, and something else next month. It'll be ballots, or it'll be bullets. It'll be liberty, or it will be death. The only difference about this kind of death—it'll be reciprocal. You know what is meant by "reciprocal"? That's one of Brother Lomax's words, I stole it from him. I don't usually deal with those big words because I don't usually deal with big people. I deal with small people. I find you can get a whole lot of small people and whip hell out of a whole lot of big people. They haven't got anything to lose, and they've got everything to gain. And they'll let you know in a minute: "It takes two to tango; when I go, you go."

The black nationalists, those whose philosophy is black nationalism, in bringing about this new interpretation of the entire meaning of civil rights, look upon it as meaning, as Brother Lomax has pointed out, equality of opportunity. Well, we're justified in seeking civil rights, if it means equality of opportunity, because all we're doing there is trying to collect for our investment. Our mothers and fathers invested sweat and blood. Three hundred and ten years we worked in this country without a dime in return—I mean without a *dime* in return. You let the white man walk around here talking how rich this country is, but you never stop to think how it got rich so quick. It got rich because you made it rich.

You take the people who are in this audience right now. They're poor, we're all poor as individuals. Our weekly salary individually amounts to hardly anything. But if you take the salary of everyone in here collectively it'll fill up a whole lot of baskets. It's a lot of wealth. If you can collect the wages of just these people right here for a year, you'll be rich —richer than rich. When you look at it like that, think how rich Uncle Sam had to become, not with this handful, but millions of black people. Your and my mother and father, who didn't work an eight-hour shift, but worked from "can't see" in the morning until "can't see" at night, and worked for nothing, making the white man rich, making Uncle Sam rich.

This is our investment. This is our contribution—our blood. Not only did we give of our free labor, we gave of our blood. Every time he had a call to arms, we were the first ones in uniform. We died on every battlefield the white man had. We have made a greater sacrifice than anybody who's standing up in America today. We have made a greater contribution and have collected less. Civil rights, for those of us whose philosophy is black nationalism, means: "Give it to us now. Don't wait for next year. Give it to us yesterday, and that's not fast enough."

I might stop right here to point out one thing. Whenever you're going after something that belongs to you, anyone who's depriving you of the right to have it is a criminal. Understand that. Whenever you are going after something that is yours, you are within your legal rights to lay claim to it. And anyone who puts forth any effort to deprive you of that which is yours, is breaking the law, is a criminal. And this was pointed out by the Supreme Court decision. It outlawed segregation. Which means segregation is against the law. Which means a segregationist is breaking the law. A segregationist is a criminal. You can't label him as anything other than that. And when you demonstrate against segregation, the law is on your side. The Supreme Court is on your side.

Now, who is it that opposes you in carrying out the law? The police department itself. With police dogs and clubs. Whenever you demonstrate against segregation, whether it is segregated education, segregated housing, or anything else, the law is on your side, and anyone who stands in the way is not the law any longer. They are breaking the law, they are not representatives of the law. Any time you demonstrate against segregation and a man has the audacity to put a police dog on you, kill that dog, kill him, I'm telling you, kill that dog. I say it, if they put me in jail tomorrow, kill—that—dog. Then you'll put a stop to it. Now, if these white people in here don't want to see that kind of action, get down and tell the mayor to tell the police department to pull the dogs in. That's all you have to do. If you don't do it, someone else will.

If you don't take this kind of stand, your little children will grow up and look at you and think "shame." If you don't take an uncompromising stand—I don't mean go out and get violent; but at the same time you should never be nonviolent unless you run into some nonviolence. I'm nonviolent with those who are nonviolent with me. But when you drop that violence on me, you've made me go insane, and I'm not responsible for what I do. And that's the way every Negro should get. Any time you know you're within the law, within your legal rights, within your moral rights, in accord with justice, then die for what you believe in. But don't die alone. Let your dying be reciprocal. This is what is meant by equality. What's good for the goose is good for the gander.

When we begin to get in this area, we need new friends, we need new allies. We need to expand the civil-rights struggle to a higher level—to the level of human rights. Whenever you are in a civil-rights struggle, whether you know it or not, you are confining yourself to the jurisdiction of Uncle Sam. No one from the outside world can speak out in your behalf as long as your struggle is a civil-rights struggle. Civil rights comes within the domestic affairs of this country. All of our African brothers and our Asian brothers and our Latin-American brothers cannot open their mouths and interfere in the domestic affairs of the United States. And as long as it's civil rights, this comes under the jurisdiction of Uncle Sam.

But the United Nations has what's known as the charter of human rights, it has a committee that deals in human rights. You may wonder why all of the atrocities that have been committed in Africa, and in Hungary and in Asia and in Latin America are brought before the UN, and the Negro problem is never brought before the UN. This is part of the conspiracy. This old, tricky, blue-eyed liberal who is supposed to be your and my friend, supposed to be in our corner, supposed to be subsidizing our struggle, and supposed to be acting in the capacity of an adviser, never tells you anything about human rights. They keep you wrapped up in civil rights. And you spend so much time barking up the civil-rights tree, you don't even know there's a human-rights tree on the same floor.

When you expand the civil-rights struggle to the level of human rights, you can then take the case of the black man in this country before the nations in the UN. You can take it before the General Assembly. You can take Uncle Sam before a world court. But the only level you can do it on is the level of human rights. Civil rights keeps you under his restrictions, under his jurisdiction. Civil rights keeps you in his pocket. Civil rights means you're asking Uncle Sam to treat you right. Human rights are something you were born with. Human rights are your God-given rights. Human rights are the rights that are recognized by all nations of this earth. And any time any one violates your human rights, you can take them to the world court. Uncle Sam's hands are dripping with blood, dripping with the blood of the black man in this country. He's the earth's number-one hypocrite. He has the audacity —yes, he has—imagine him posing as the leader of the free world. The free world!—and you over here singing "We Shall Overcome." Expand the civil-rights struggle to the level of human rights, take it into the United Nations, where our African brothers can throw their weight on our side, where our Asian brothers can throw their weight on our side, where our Latin-American brothers can throw their weight on our side, and where 800 million Chinamen are sitting there waiting to throw their weight on our side.

Let the world know how bloody his hands are. Let the world know the hyprocrisy that's practiced over here. Let it be the ballot or the bullet. Let him know that it must be the ballot or the bullet.

When you take your case to Washington, D.C., you're taking it to the criminal who's responsible; it's like running from the wolf to the fox. They're all in cahoots together. They all work political chicanery and make you look like a chump before the eyes of the world. Here you are walking around in America, getting ready to be drafted and sent abroad, like a tin soldier, and when you get over there, people ask you what are you fighting for, and you have to stick your tongue in your check. No, take Uncle Sam to court, take him before the world.

By ballot I only mean freedom. Don't you know—I disagree with Lomax on this issue—that the ballot is more important than the dollar? Can I prove it? Yes. Look in the UN. There are poor nations in the UN; yet those poor nations can get together with their voting power and keep the rich nations from making a move. They have one nation—one vote, everyone has an equal vote. And when those brothers from Asia, and Africa and the darker parts of this earth get together, their voting power is sufficient to hold Sam in check. Or Russia in check. Or some other section of the earth in check. So, the ballot is most important.

Right now, in this country, if you and I, 22 million African-Americans—that's what we are—Africans who are in America. You're nothing but Africans. Nothing but Africans. In fact, you'd get farther calling yourself African instead of Negro. Africans don't catch hell. You're the only one catching hell. They don't have to pass civil-rights bills for Africans. An African can go anywhere he wants right now. All you've got to do is tie your head up. That's right, go anywhere you want. Just stop being a Negro. Change your name to Hoogagagooba. That'll show you how silly the white man is. You're dealing with a silly man. A friend of mine who's very dark put a turban on his head and went into a restaurant in Atlanta before they called themselves desegregated. He went into a white restaurant, he sat down, they served him, and he said, "What would happen if a Negro came in here?" And there he's sitting, black as night, but because he had his head wrapped up the waitress looked back at him and says, "Why, there wouldn't no nigger dare come in here."

So, you're dealing with a man whose bias and prejudice are making him lose his mind, his intelligence, every day. He's frightened. He looks around and sees what's taking place on this earth, and he sees that the pendulum of time is swinging in your direction. The dark people are waking up. They're losing their fear of the white man. No place where he's fighting right now is he winning. Everywhere he's fighting, he's fighting someone your and my complexion. And they're beating him. He can't win any more. He's won his last battle. He failed to win the Korean War. He couldn't win it. He had to sign a truce. That's a loss. Any time Uncle Sam, with all his machinery for warfare, is held to a draw by some rice-eaters, he's lost the battle. He had to sign a truce. America's not supposed to sign a truce. She's supposed to be bad. But she's not bad any more. She's bad as long as she can use her hydrogen bomb, but she can't use hers for fear Russia might use hers. Russia can't use hers, for fear that Sam might use his. So, both of them are weaponless. They can't use the weapon because each's weapon nullifies the other's. So the only place where action can take place is on the ground. And the white man can't win another war fighting on the ground. Those days are over. The black man knows it, the brown man knows it, the red man knows it, and the yellow man knows it. So they engage him in guerrilla warfare. That's not his style. You've got to have heart to be a guerrilla warrior, and he hasn't got any heart. I'm telling you now.

I just want to give you a little briefing on guerrilla warfare because, before you know it, before you know it—it takes heart to be a guerrilla warrior because you're on your own. In conventional warfare you have tanks and a whole lot of other people with you to back you up, planes over your head and all that kind of stuff. But a guerrilla is on his own. All you have is a rifle, some sneakers and a bowl of rice, and that's all you need—and a lot of heart. The Japanese on some of those islands in the Pacific, when the American soldiers landed, one Japanese sometimes could hold the whole army off, He'd just wait until the sun went down, and when the sun went down they were all equal. He would take his little blade and slip from bush to bush, and from American to American.

The white soldiers couldn't cope with that. Whenever you see a white soldier that fought in the Pacific, he has the shakes, he has a nervous condition, because they scared him to death.

The same thing happened to the French up in French Indochina. People who just a few years previously were rice farmers got together and ran the heavily-mechanized French army out of Indochina. You don't need it—modern warfare today won't work. This is the day of the guerrilla. They did the same thing in Algeria. Algerians, who were nothing but Bedouins, took a rifle and sneaked off to the hills, and de Gaulle and all of his highfalutin' war machinery couldn't defeat those guerrillas. Nowhere on this earth does the white man win in a guerrilla warfare. It's not his speed. Just as guerrilla warfare is prevailing in Asia and in parts of Africa and in parts of Latin America, you've got to be mighty naive, or you've got to play the black man cheap, if you don't think some day he's going to wake up and find that it's got to be the ballot or the bullet.

I would like to say, in closing, a few things concerning the Muslim Mosque, Inc., which we established recently in New York City. It's true we're Muslims and our religion is Islam, but we don't mix our religion with our politics and our economics and our social and civil activities—not any more. We keep our religion in our mosque. After our religious services are over, then as Muslims we become involved in political action, economic action and social and civic action. We become involved with anybody, anywhere, any time and in any manner that's designed to eliminate the evils, the political, economic and social evils that are afflicting the people of our community.

The political philosophy of black nationalism means that the black man should control the politics and the politicians in his own community; no more. The black man in the black community has to be re-educated into the science of politics so he will know what politics is supposed to bring him in return. Don't be throwing out any ballots. A ballot is like a bullet. You don't throw your ballots until you see a target, and if that target is not within your reach, keep your ballot in your pocket. The political philosophy of black nationalism is being taught in the Christian church. It's being taught in the NAACP. It's being taught in CORE meetings. It's being taught in SNCC [Student Nonviolent Coordinating Committee] meetings. It's being taught in Muslim meetings. It's being taught where nothing but atheists and agnostics come together. It's being taught everywhere. Black people are fed up with the dillydallying, pussyfooting, compromising approach that we've been using toward getting our freedom. We want freedom *now*, but we're not going to get it saying "We Shall Overcome." We've got to fight until we overcome.

The economic philosophy of black nationalism is pure and simple. It only means that we should control the economy of our community. Why should white people be running all the stores in our community? Why should white people be running the banks of our community? Why should the economy of our community be in the hands of the white man? Why? If a black man can't move his store into a white community, you tell me why a white man should move his store into a black community. The philosophy of black nationalism involves a re-education program in the black community in regards to economics. Our people have to be made to see that any time you take your dollar out of your community and spend it in a community where you don't live, the community where you live will get poorer and poorer, and the community where you spend your money will get richer and richer. Then you wonder why where you live is always a ghetto or a slum area. And where you and I are concerned, not only do we lose it when we spend it out of the community, but the white man has got all our stores in the community tied up; so that though we spend it in the community, at sundown the man who runs the store takes it over across town somewhere. He's got us in a vise.

So the economic philosophy of black nationalism means in every church, in every civic organization, in every fraternal order, it's time now for our people to become conscious of the importance of controlling the economy of our community. If we own the stores, if we operate the businesses, if we try and establish some industry in our own community, then we're developing to the position where we are creating employment for our own kind. Once you gain control of the economy of your own community, then you don't have to picket and boycott and beg some cracker downtown for a job in his business.

The social philosophy of black nationalism only means that we have to get together and remove the evils, the vices, alcoholism, drug addiction, and other evils that are destroying the moral fiber of our community. We ourselves have to lift the level of our community, the standard of our community to a higher level, make our own society beautiful so that we will be satisfied in our own social circles and won't be running around here trying to knock our way into a social circle where we're not wanted.

So I say, in spreading a gospel such as black nationalism, it is not designed to make the black man re-evaluate the white man—you know him already—but to make the black man re-evaluate himself. Don't change the white man's mind—you can't change his mind, and that whole thing about appealing to the moral conscience of America—America's conscience is bankrupt. She lost all conscience a long time ago. Uncle Sam has no conscience. They don't know what morals are. They don't try and eliminate an evil because it's evil, or because it's illegal, or because it's immoral; they eliminate it only when it threatens their existence. So you're wasting your time appealing to the moral conscience of a bankrupt man like Uncle Sam. If he had a conscience, he'd straighten this thing out with no more pressure being put upon him. So it is not necessary to change the white man's mind. We have to change our own mind. You can't change his mind about us. We've got to change our own minds about each other. We have to see each other with new eyes. We have to see each other as brothers and sisters. We have to come together with warmth so we can develop unity and harmony that's necessary to get this problem solved ourselves. How can we do this? How can we avoid jealousy? How can we avoid the suspicion and the divisions that exist in the community? I'll tell you how.

I have watched how Billy Graham comes into a city, spreading what he calls the gospel of Christ, which is only white nationalism. That's what he is. Billy Graham is a white nationalist; I'm a black nationalist. But since it's the natural tendency for leaders to be jealous and look upon a powerful figure like Graham with suspicion and envy, how is it possible for him to come into a city and get all the cooperation of the church leaders? Don't think because they're church leaders that they don't have weaknesses that make them envious and jealous—no, everybody's got it. It's not an accident that when they want to choose a cardinal [as Pope] over there in Rome, they get in a closet so you can't hear them cussing and fighting and carrying on.

Billy Graham comes in preaching the gospel of Christ, he evangelizes the gospel, he stirs everybody up, but he never tries to start a church. If he came in trying to start a church, all the churches would be against him. So, he just comes in talking about Christ and tells everybody who gets Christ to go to any church where Christ is; and in this way the church cooperates with him. So we're going to take a page from his book.

Our gospel is black nationalism. We're not trying to threaten the existence of any organization, but we're spreading the gospel of black nationalism. Anywhere there's a church that is also preaching and practicing the gospel of black nationalism, join that church. If the NAACP is preaching and practicing the gospel of black nationalism, join the

NAACP. If CORE is spreading and practicing the gospel of black nationalism, join CORE. Join any organization that has a gospel that's for the uplift of the black man. And when you get into it and see them pussyfooting or compromising, pull out of it because that's not black nationalism. We'll find another one.

And in this manner, the organizations will increase in number and in quantity and in quality, and by August, it is then our intention to have a black nationalist convention which will consist of delegates from all over the country who are interested in the political, economic and social philosophy of black nationalism. After these delegates convene, we will hold a seminar, we will hold discussions, we will listen to everyone. We want to hear new ideas and new solutions and new answers. And at that time, if we see fit then to form a black nationalist party, we'll form a black nationalist party. If it's necessary to form a black nationalist army, we'll form a black nationalist army. It'll be the ballot or the bullet. It'll be liberty or it'll be death.

It's time for you and me to stop sitting in this country, letting some cracker senators, Northern crackers and Southern crackers, sit there in Washington, D.C., and come to a conclusion in their mind that you and I are supposed to have civil rights. There's no white man going to tell me anything about *my* rights. Brothers and sisters, always remember, if it doesn't take senators and congressmen and presidential proclamations to give freedom to the white man, it is not necessary for legislation or proclamation or Supreme Court decisions to give freedom to the black man. You let that white man know, if this is a country of freedom, let it be a country of freedom; and if it's not a country of freedom, change it.

We will work with anybody, anywhere, at any time, who is genuinely interested in tackling the problem head-on, nonviolently as long as the enemy is nonviolent, but violent when the enemy gets violent. We'll work with you on the voter-registration drive, we'll work with you on rent strikes, we'll work with you on school boycotts—I don't believe in any kind of integration; I'm not even worried about it because I know you're not going to get it anyway; you're not going to get it because you're afraid to die; you've got to be ready to die if you try and force yourself on the white man, because he'll get just as violent as those crackers in Mississippi, right here in Cleveland. But we will still work with you on the school boycotts because we're against a segregated school system. A segregated school system produces children who, when they graduate, graduate with crippled minds. But this does not mean that a school is segregated because it's all black. A segregated school means a school that is controlled by people who have no real interest in it whatsoever.

Let me explain what I mean. A segregated district or community is a community in which people live, but outsiders control the politics and the economy of that community. They never refer to the white section as a segregated community. It's the all-Negro section that's a segregated community. Why? The white man controls his own school, his own bank, his own economy, his own politics, his own everything, his own community—but he also controls yours. When you're under someone else's control, you're segregated. They'll always give you the lowest or the worst that there is to offer, but it doesn't mean you're segregated just because you have your own. You've got to *control* your own. Just like the white man has control of his, you need to control yours.

You know the best way to get rid of segregation? The white man is more afraid of separation than he is of integration. Segregation means that he puts you away from him, but not far enough for you to be out of his jurisdiction; separation means you're gone. And the white man will integrate faster than he'll let you separate. So we will work with you against the segregated school system because it's criminal, because it is absolutely destructive, in every way imaginable, to the minds of the children who have to be exposed to that type of crippling education.

Last but not least, I must say this concerning the great controversy over rifles and shotguns. The only thing that I've ever said is that in areas where the government has proven itself either unwilling or unable to defend the lives and the property of Negroes, it's time for Negroes to defend themselves. Article number two of the constitutional amendments provides you and me the right to own a rifle or a shotgun. It is constitutionally legal to own a shotgun or a rifle. This doesn't mean you're going to get a rifle and form battalions and go out looking for white folks, although you'd be within your rights—I mean, you'd be justified; but that would be illegal and we don't do anything illegal. If the white man doesn't want the black man buying rifles and shotguns, then let the government do its job. That's all. And don't let the white man come to you and ask you what you think about what Malcolm says—why, you old Uncle Tom. He would never ask you if he thought you were going to say, "Amen!" No, he is making a Tom out of you.

So, this doesn't mean forming rifle clubs and going out looking for people, but it is time, in 1964, if you are a man, to let that man know. If he's not going to do his job in running the government and providing you and me with the protection that our taxes are supposed to be for, since he spends all those billions for his defense budget, he certainly can't begrudge you and me spending $12 or $15 for a single-shot, or double-action. I hope you understand. Don't go out shooting people, but any time, brothers and sisters, and especially the men in this audience—some of you wearing Congressional Medals of Honor, with shoulders this wide, chests this big, muscles that big—any time you and I sit around and read where they bomb a church and murder in cold blood, not some grownups, but four little girls while they were praying to the same god the white man taught them to pray to, and you and I see the government go down and can't find who did it.

Why, this man—he can find Eichmann hiding down in Argentina somewhere. Let two or three American soldiers, who are minding somebody else's business way over in South Vietnam, get killed, and he'll send battleships, sticking his nose in their business. He wanted to send troops down to Cuba and make them have what he calls free elections— this old cracker who doesn't have free elections in his own country. No, if you never see me another time in your life, if I die in the morning, I'll die saying one thing: the ballot or the bullet, the ballot or the bullet.

If a Negro in 1964 has to sit around and wait for some cracker senator to filibuster when it comes to the rights of black people, why, you and I should hang our heads in shame. You talk about a march on Washington in 1963, you haven't seen anything. There's some more going down in '64. And this time they're not going like they went last year. They're not going singing "We Shall Overcome." They're not going with placards already painted for them. They're not going with round-trip tickets. They're going with one-way tickets.

And if they don't want that non-nonviolent army going down there, tell them to bring the filibuster to a halt. The black nationalists aren't going to wait. Lyndon B. Johnson is the head of the Democratic Party. If he's for civil rights, let him go in there right now and declare himself. Let him go in there right now and take a moral stand—right now, not later. Tell him, don't wait until election time. If he waits too long, brothers and sisters, he will be responsible for letting a condition develop in this country which will create a climate that will bring seeds up out of the ground with vegetation on the end of them looking like something these people never dreamed of. In 1964, it's the ballot or the bullet. Thank you.

What We Want

One of the tragedies of the struggle against racism is that up to now there has been no national organization which could speak to the growing militancy of young black people in the urban ghetto. There has been only a civil rights movement, whose tone of voice was adapted to an audience of liberal whites. It served as a sort of buffer zone between them and angry young blacks.

None of its so-called leaders could go into a rioting community and be listened to. In a sense, I blame ourselves—together with the mass media—for what has happened in Watts, Harlem, Chicago, Cleveland, Omaha. Each time the people in those cities saw Martin Luther King get slapped, they became angry; when they saw four little black girls bombed to death, they were angrier; and when nothing happened, they were steaming. We had nothing to offer that they could see, except to go out and be beaten again. We helped to build their frustration.

For too many years, black Americans marched and had their heads broken and got shot. They were saying to the country, "Look, you guys are supposed to be nice guys and we are only going to do what we are supposed to do—why do you beat us up, why don't you give us what we ask, why don't you straighten yourselves out?" After years of this, we are at almost the same point—because we demonstrated from a position of weakness. We cannot be expected any longer to march and have our heads broken in order to say to whites: come on, you're nice guys. For you are not nice guys. We have found you out.

An organization which claims to speak for the needs of a community —as does the Student Nonviolent Coordinating Committee—must speak in the tone of that community, not as somebody else's buffer zone. This is the significance of black power as a slogan. For once, black people are going to use the words they want to use—not just the words whites want to hear. And they will do this no matter how often the press tries to stop the use of the slogan by equating it with racism or separatism.

An organization which claims to be working for the needs of a community—as SNCC does—must work to provide that community with a position of strength from which to make its voice heard. This is the significance of black power beyond the slogan.

Black power can be clearly defined for those who do not attach the fears of white America to their questions about it. We should begin with the basic fact that black Americans have two problems: they are poor and they are black. All other problems arise from this two-sided reality: lack of education, the so-called apathy of black men. Any program to end racism must address itself to that double reality.

Almost from its beginning, SNCC sought to address itself to both conditions with a program aimed at winning political power for impoverished Southern blacks. We had to begin with politics because black Americans are a propertyless people in a country where property is valued above all. We had to work for power, because this country does not function by morality, love, and nonviolence, but by power. Thus we determined to win political power, with the idea of moving on from there into activity that would have economic effects. With power, the masses could *make or participate in making* the decisions which govern their destinies, and thus create basic change in their day-to-day lives

But if political power seemed to be the key to self-determination, it was also obvious that the key had been thrown down a deep well many years earlier. Disenfranchisement, maintained by racist terror, made it impossible to talk about organizing for political power in 1960. The right to vote had to be won, and SNCC workers devoted their energies to this from 1961 to 1965. They set up voter registration drives in the Deep South. They created pressure for the vote by holding mock elections in Mississippi in 1963 and by helping to establish the Mississippi Freedom Democratic Party (MFDP) in 1964. That struggle was eased, though not won, with the passage of the 1965 Voting Rights Act. SNCC workers could then address themselves to the question: "Who can we vote for, to have our needs met—how do we make our vote meaningful?"

SNCC had already gone to Atlantic City for recognition of the Mississippi Freedom Democratic Party by the Democratic convention and been rejected; it had gone with the MFDP to Washington for recognition by Congress and been rejected. In Arkansas, SNCC helped thirty Negroes to run for School Board elections; all but one were defeated, and there was evidence of fraud and intimidation sufficient to cause their defeat. In Atlanta, Julian Bond ran for the state legislature and was elected—twice—and unseated—twice. In several states, black farmers ran in elections for agricultural committees which make crucial decisions concerning land use, loans, etc. Although they won places on a number of committees, they never gained the majorities needed to control them.

All of the efforts were attempts to win black power. Then, in Alabama, the opportunity came to see how blacks could be organized on an independent party basis. An unusual Alabama law provides that any group of citizens can nominate candidates for county office and, if they win 20 per cent of the vote, may be recognized as a county political party. The same then applies on a state level. SNCC went to organize in several counties such as Lowndes, where black people—who form 80 per cent of the population and have an average annual income of $943 —felt they could accomplish nothing within the framework of the Alabama Democratic Party because of its racism and because the qualifying fee for this year's elections was raised from $50 to $500 in order to prevent most Negroes from becoming candidates. On May 3, five new county "freedom organizations" convened and nominated candidates for the offices of sheriff, tax assessor, members of the school boards. These men and women are up for election in November—if they live until then. Their ballot symbol is the black panther: a bold, beautiful animal, representing the strength and dignity of black demands today. A man needs a black panther on his side when he and his family must endure— as hundreds of Alabamians have endured—loss of job, eviction, starvation, and sometimes death, for political activity. He may also need a gun and SNCC reaffirms the right of black men everywhere to defend themselves when threatened or attacked. As for initiating the use of violence, we hope that such programs as ours will make that unnecessary; but it is not for us to tell black communities whether they can or cannot use any particular form of action to resolve their problems. Responsibility for the use of violence by black men, whether in self-defense or initiated by them, lies with the white community.

This is the specific historical experience from which SNCC's call for "black power" emerged on the Mississippi march last July. But the concept of "black power" is not a recent or isolated phenomenon: It has grown out of the ferment of agitation and activity by different people and organizations in many black communities over the years. Our last year of work in Alabama added a new concrete possibility. In Lowndes county, for example, black power will mean that if a Negro is elected sheriff, he can end police brutality. If a black man is elected tax assessor, he can collect and channel funds for the building of better roads and schools serving black people—thus advancing the move from political power into the economic arena. In such areas as Lowndes, where black men have a majority, they will attempt to use it to exercise control. This is what they seek: control. Where Negroes lack a majority, black power means proper representation and sharing of control. It means the creation of power bases from which black people can work to change state-wide or nationwide patterns of oppression through pressure from strength —instead of weakness. Politically, black power means what it has always meant to SNCC: the coming-together of black people to elect representatives and *to force those representatives to speak to their needs.* It does not mean merely putting black faces into office. A man or woman who is black and from the slums cannot be automatically expected to speak to the needs of black people. Most of the black politicians we see around the country today are not what SNCC means by black power. The power must be that of a community, and emanate from there.

SNCC today is working in both North and South on programs of voter registration and independent political organizing. In some places, such as Alabama, Los Angeles, New York, Philadelphia, and New Jersey, independent organizing under the black panther symbol is in progress. The creation of a national "black panther party" must come about; it will take time to build, and it is much too early to predict its success. We have no infallible master plan and we make no claim to exclusive knowledge of how to end racism; different groups will work in their own different ways. SNCC cannot spell out the full logistics of self-determination but it can address itself to the problem by helping black communities define their needs, realize their strength, and go into action along a variety of lines which they must choose for themselves. Without knowing all the answers, it can address itself to the basic problem of poverty; to that fact that in Lowndes County, 86 white families own 90 per cent of the land. What are black people in that county going to do for jobs, where are they going to get money? There must be reallocation of land, of money.

Ultimately, the economic foundations of this country must be shaken if black people are to control their lives. The colonies of the United States—and this includes the black ghettos within its borders, north and south—must be liberated. For a century, this nation has been like an octopus of exploitation, its tenacles stretching from Mississippi and Harlem to South America, the Middle East, southern Africa, and Vietnam; the form of exploitation varies from area to area but the essential result has been the same—a powerful few have been maintained and enriched at the expense of the poor and voiceless colored masses. This pattern must be broken. As its grip loosens here and there around the world, the hopes of black Americans become more realistic. For racism to die, a totally different America must be born.

This is what the white society does not wish to face; this is why that society prefers to talk about integration. But integration speaks not at all to the problem of poverty, only to the problem of blackness. Integration today means the man who "makes it," leaving his black brothers behind in the ghetto as fast as his new sports car will take him. It has no relevance to the Harlem wino or to the cottonpicker making three dollars a day. As a lady I know in Alabama once said, "the food that Ralph Bunche eats doesn't fill my stomach."

Integration, moreover, speaks to the problem of blackness in a despicable way. As a goal, it has been based on complete acceptance of the fact that *in order to have* a decent house or education, blacks must move into a white neighborhood or send their children to a white school. This reinforces, among both black and white, the idea that "white" is automatically better and "black" is by definition inferior. This is why integration is a subterfuge for the maintenance of white supremacy. It allows the nation to focus on a handful of Southern children who get into white schools, at great price, and to ignore the 95 per cent who are left behind in unimproved all-black schools. Such situations will not change until black people have power—to control their own school boards, in this case. Then Negroes become equal in a way that means something, and integration ceases to be a one-way street. Then integration doesn't mean draining skills and energies from the ghetto into white neighborhoods; then it can mean white people moving from Beverly Hills into Watts, white people joining the Lowndes County Freedom Organization. Then integration becomes relevant.

Last April, before the furor over black power, Christopher Jencks wrote in a *New Republic* article on white Mississippi's manipulation of the anti-poverty program:

> The war on poverty has been predicated on the notion that there is such a thing as *a community* which can be defined geographically and mobilized for a collective effort to help the poor. This theory has no relationship to reality in the Deep South. In every Mississippi county there are *two* communities. Despite all the pious platitudes of the moderates on both sides, these two communities habitually see their interests in terms of conflict rather than cooperation. Only when the Negro community can muster enough political, economic and professional strength to compete on somewhat equal terms, will Negroes believe in the possibility of true cooperation and whites accept its necessity. En route to integration, the Negro community needs to develop greater independence—a chance to run its own affairs and not cave in whenever "the man" barks . . . Or so it seems to me, and to most of the knowledgeable people with whom I talked in Mississippi. To OEO, this judgment may sound like black nationalism . . .

Mr. Jencks, a white reporter, perceived the reason why America's anti-poverty program has been a sick farce in both North and South. In the South, it is clearly racism which prevents the poor from running their own programs; in the North, it more often seems to be politicking and bureaucracy. But the results are not so different: In the North, non-whites make up 42 per cent of all families in metropolitan "poverty areas" and only 6 per cent of families in areas classified as not poor. SNCC has been working with local residents in Arkansas, Alabama, and Mississippi to achieve control by the poor of the program and its funds; it has also been working with groups in the North, and the struggle is no less difficult. Behind it all is a federal government which cares far more about winning the war on the Vietnamese than the war on poverty; which has put the poverty program in the hands of self-serving politicians and bureaucrats rather than the poor themselves; which is unwilling to curb the misuse of white power but quick to condemn black power.

To most whites, black power seems to mean that the Mau Mau are coming to the suburbs at night. The Mau Mau are coming, and whites must stop them. Articles appear about plots to "get Whitey," creating an atmosphere in which "law and order must be maintained." Once again, responsibility is shifted from the oppressor to the oppressed. Other whites chide, "Don't forget—you're only 10 per cent of the population; if you get too smart, we'll wipe you out." If they are liberals, they complain, "What about me?—don't you want my help any more?" These are people supposedly concerned about black Americans, but today they think first of themselves, of their feelings of rejection. Or they admonish, "you can't get anywhere without coalitions," without considering the problems of coalition with whom?; on what terms? (coalescing from weakness can mean absorption, betrayal); when? Or they accuse us of "polarizing the races" by our calls for black unity, when the true responsibility for polarization lies with whites who will not accept their responsibility as the majority power for making the democratic process work.

White America will not face the problem of color, the reality of it. The well-intended say: "We're all human, everybody is really decent, we must forget color." But color cannot be "forgotten" until its weight is recognized and dealt with. White America will not acknowledge that the ways in which this country sees itself are contradicted by being black —and always have been. Whereas most of the people who settled this country came here for freedom or for economic opportunity, blacks were brought here to be slaves. When the Lowndes County Freedom Organization chose the black panther as its symbol, it was christened by the press "the Black Panther Party"—but the Alabama Democratic

Party, whose symbol is a rooster, has never been called the White Cock Party. No one ever talked about "white power" because power in this country *is* white. All this adds up to more than merely identifying a group phenomenon by some catchy name or adjective. The furor over that black panther reveals the problems that white America has with color and sex; the furor over "black power" reveals how deep racism runs and the great fear which is attached to it.

Whites will not see that I, for example, as a person oppressed because of my blackness, have common cause with other blacks who are oppressed because of blackness. This is not to say that there are no white people who see things as I do, but that it is black people I must speak to first. It must be the oppressed to whom SNCC addresses itself primarily, not to friends from the oppressing group.

From birth, black people are told a set of lies about themselves. We are told that we are lazy—yet I drive through the Delta area of Mississippi and watch black people picking cotton in the hot sun for fourteen hours. We are told, "If you work hard, you'll succeed"—but if that were true, black people would own this country. We are oppressed because we are black—not because we are ignorant, not because we are lazy, not because we're stupid (and got good rhythm), but because we're black.

I remember that when I was a boy, I used to go to see Tarzan movies on Saturday. White Tarzan used to beat up the black natives. I would sit there yelling, "Kill the beasts, kill the savages, kill 'em!" I was saying: Kill *me*. It was as if a Jewish boy watched Nazis taking Jews off to concentration camps and cheered them on. Today, I want the chief to beat hell out of Tarzan and send him back to Europe. But it takes time to become free of the lies and their shaming effect on black minds. It takes time to reject the most important lie: that black people inherently can't do the same things white people can do, unless white people help them.

The need for psychological equality is the reason why SNCC today believes that blacks must organize in the black community. Only black people can convey the revolutionary idea that black people are able to do things themselves. Only they can help create in the community an aroused and continuing black consciousness that will provide the basis for political strength. In the past, white allies have furthered white supremacy without the whites involved realizing it—or wanting it, I think. Black people must do things for themselves; they must get poverty money they will control and spend themselves, they must conduct tutorial programs themselves so that black children can identify with black people. This is one reason Africa has such importance: The reality of black men ruling their own nations gives blacks elsewhere a sense of possibility, of power, which they do not now have.

This does not mean we don't welcome help, or friends. But we want the right to decide whether anyone is, in fact, our friend. In the past, black Americans have been almost the only people whom everybody and his momma could jump up and call their friends. We have been tokens, symbols, objects—as I was in high school to many young whites, who liked having "a Negro friend." We want to decide who is our friend, and we will not accept someone who comes to us and says: "If you do, X, Y, and Z, then I'll help you." We will not be told whom we should choose as allies. We will not be isolated from any group or nation except by our own choice. We cannot have the oppressors telling the oppressed how to rid themselves of the oppressor.

I have said that most liberal whites react to "black power" with the question, What about me?, rather than saying: Tell me what you want me to do and I'll see if I can do it. There are answers to the right question. One of the most disturbing things about almost all white supporters of the movement has been that they are afraid to go into their own communities—which is where the racism exists—and work to get rid of it. They want to run from Berkeley to tell us what to do in Mississippi; let them look instead at Berkeley. They admonish blacks to be nonviolent; let them preach nonviolence in the white community. They come to teach me Negro history; let them go to the suburbs and open up freedom schools for whites. Let them work to stop America's racist foreign policy; let them press this government to cease supporting the economy of South Africa.

There is a vital job to be done among poor whites. We hope to see, eventually, a coalition between poor blacks and poor whites. That is the only coalition which seems acceptable to us, and we see such a coalition as the major internal instrument of change in American society. SNCC has tried several times to organize poor whites; we are trying again now, with an initial training program in Tennessee. It is purely academic today to talk about bringing poor blacks and whites together, but the job of creating a poor-white power bloc must be attempted. The main responsibility for it falls upon whites. Black and white can work together in the white community where possible; it is not possible, however, to go into a poor Southern town and talk about integration. Poor whites everywhere are becoming more hostile—not less—partly because they see the nation's attention focused on black poverty and nobody coming to them. Too many young middle-class Americans, like some sort of Pepsi generation, have wanted to come alive through the black community; They've wanted to be where the action is—and the action has been the black community.

Black people do not want to "take over" this country. They don't want to "get whitey"; they just want to get him off their backs, as the saying goes. It was for example the exploitation by Jewish landlords and merchants which first created black resentment toward Jews—not Judaism. The white man is irrelevant to blacks, except as an oppressive force. Blacks want to be in his place, yes, but not in order to terrorize and lynch and starve him. They want to be in his place because that is where a decent life can be had.

But our vision is not merely of a society in which all black men have enough to buy the good things of life. When we urge that black money go into black pockets, we mean the communal pocket. We want to see money go back into the community and used to benefit it. We want to see the cooperative concept applied in business and banking. We want to see black ghetto residents demand that an exploiting landlord or storekeeper sell them, at minimal cost, a building or a shop that they will own and improve cooperatively; they can back their demand with a rent strike, or a boycott, and a community so unified behind them that no one else will move into the building or buy at the store. The society we seek to build among black people, then, is not a capitalist one. It is a society in which the spirit of community and humanistic love prevail. The word love is suspect; black expectations of what it might produce have been betrayed too often. But those were expectations of a response from the white community, which failed us. The love we seek to encourage is within the black community, the only American community where men call each other "brother" when they meet. We can build a community of love only where we have the ability and power to do so: among blacks.

As for white America, perhaps it can stop crying out against "black supremacy," "black nationalism," "racism in reverse," and begin facing reality. The reality is that this nation, from top to bottom, is racist; that racism is not primarily a problem of "human relations" but of an exploitation maintained—either actively or through silence—by the society as a whole. Camus and Sartre have asked, can a man condemn himself? Can whites, particularly liberal whites, condemn themselves? Can they stop blaming us, and blame their own system? Are they capable of the shame which might become a revolutionary emotion?

We have found that they usually cannot condemn themselves, and so we have done it. But the rebuilding of this society, if at all possible, is basically the responsibility of whites—not blacks. We won't fight to save the present society, in Vietnam or anywhere else. We are just going to work, in the way *we* see fit, and on goals *we* define, not for civil rights but for all our human rights.

The Revolutionary Theatre

The Revolutionary Theatre should force change; it should be change. (All their faces turned into the lights and you work on them black nigger magic, and cleanse them at having seen the ugliness. And if the beautiful see themselves, they will love themselves.) We are preaching virtue again, but by that to mean NOW, toward what seems the most constructive use of the world.

The Revolutionary Theatre must EXPOSE! Show up the insides of these humans, look into black skulls. White men will cower before this theatre because it hates them. Because they themselves have been trained to hate. The Revolutionary Theatre must hate them for hating. For presuming with their technology to deny the supremacy of the Spirit. They will all die because of this.

The Revolutionary Theatre must teach them their deaths. It must crack their faces open to the mad cries of the poor. It must teach them about silence and the truths lodged there. It must kill any God anyone names except Common Sense. The Revolutionary Theatre should flush the fags and murders out of Lincoln's face.

It should stagger through our universe correcting, insulting, preaching, spitting craziness—but a craziness taught to us in our most rational moments. People must be taught to trust true scientists (knowers, diggers, oddballs) and that the holiness of life is the constant possibility of widening the consciousness. And they must be incited to strike back against *any* agency that attempts to prevent this widening.

The Revolutionary Theatre must Accuse and Attack anything that can be accused and attacked. It must Accuse and Attack because it is a theatre of Victims. It looks at the sky with the victims' eyes, and moves the victims to look at the strength in their minds and their bodies.

Clay in *Dutchman*, Ray in *The Toilet*, Walker in *The Slave*, are all victims. In the Western sense they could be heroes. But the Revolutionary Theatre, even if it is Western, must be anti-Western. It must show horrible coming attractions of *The Crumbling of the West*. Even as Artaud designed *The Conquest of Mexico*, so we must design *The Conquest of White Eye*, and show the missionaries and wiggly Liberals dying under blasts of concrete. For sound effects, wild screams of joy, from all the peoples of the world.

The Revolutionary Theatre must take dreams and give them a reality.

LeRoi Jones, "The Revolutionary Theatre," from *Liberator* magazine, Vol. 5, No. 7. Copyright © 1965 by *Liberator*. Reprinted by permission.

It must isolate the ritual and historical cycles of reality. But it must be food for all those who need food, and daring propaganda for the beauty of the Human Mind. It is a political theatre, a weapon to help in the slaughter of these dim-witted fatbellied white guys who somehow believe that the rest of the world is here for them to slobber on.

This should be a theatre of World Spirit. Where the spirit can be shown to be the most competent force in the world. Force. Spirit. Feeling. The language will be anybody's, but tightened by the poet's backbone. And even the language must show what the facts are in this consciousness epic, what's happening. We will talk about the world, and the preciseness with which we are able to summon the world will be our art. Art is method. And art, "like any ashtray or senator," remains in the world. Wittgenstein said ethics and aesthetics are one. I believe this. So the Broadway theatre is a theatre of reaction whose ethics, like its aesthetics, reflect the spiritual values of this unholy society, which sends young crackers all over the world blowing off colored people's heads. (In some of these flippy Southern towns they even shoot up the immigrants' Favorite Son, be it Michael Schwerner or JFKennedy.)

The Revolutionary Theatre is shaped by the world, and moves to reshape the world, using as its force the natural force and perpetual vibrations of the mind in the world. We are history and desire, what we are, and what any experience can make us.

It is a social theatre, but all theatre is social theatre. But we will change the drawing rooms into places where real things can be said about a real world, or into smoky rooms where the destruction of Washington can be plotted. The Revolutionary Theatre must function like an incendiary pencil planted in Curtis Lemay's cap. So that when the final curtain goes down brains are splattered over the seats and the floor, and bleeding nuns must wire SOS's to Belgians with gold teeth.

Our theatre will show victims so that their brothers in the audience will be better able to understand that they are the brothers of victims, and that they themselves are victims if they are blood brothers. And what we show must cause the blood to rush, so that pre-revolutionary temperaments will be bathed in this blood, and it will cause their deepest souls to move, and they will find themselves tensed and clenched, even ready to die, at what the soul has been taught. We will scream and cry, murder, run through the streets in agony, if it means some soul will be moved, moved to actual life understanding of what the world is, and what it ought to be. We are preaching virtue and feeling, and a natural sense of the self in the world. All men live in the world, and the world ought to be a place for them to live.

What is called the imagination (from image, magi, magic, magician, etc.) is a practical vector from the soul. It stores all data, and can be called on to solve all our "problems." The imagination is the projection of ourselves past our sense of ourselves as "things." Imagination (Image) is all possibility, because from the image, the initial circumscribed energy, any use (idea) is possible. And so begins that image's use in the world. Possibility is what moves us.

The popular white man's theatre like the popular white man's novel shows tired white lives, and the problems of eating white sugar, or else it herds bigcaboosed blondes onto huge stages in rhinestones and makes believe they are dancing or singing. WHITE BUSINESSMEN OF THE WORLD, DO YOU WANT TO SEE PEOPLE REALLY DANCING AND SINGING??? ALL OF YOU GO UP TO HARLEM AND GET YOURSELF KILLED. THERE WILL BE DANCING AND SINGING, THEN, FOR REAL!! (In *The Slave*, Walker Vessels, the black revolutionary, wears an armband, which is the insignia of the attacking army—a big red-lipped minstrel, grinning like crazy.)

The liberal white man's objection to the theatre of the revolution (if he is "hip" enough) will be on aesthetic grounds. Most white Western artists do not need to be "political," since usually, whether they know it or not, they are in complete sympathy with the most repressive social forces in the world today. There are more junior birdmen fascists running around the West today disguised as Artists than there are disguised as fascists. (But then, that word, *Fascist*, and with it *Fascism*, has been made obsolete by the words *America*, and *Americanism*.) The American Artist usually turns out to be just a super-Bourgeois, because, finally, all he has to show for his sojourn through the world is "better taste" than the Bourgeois—many times not even that.

Americans will hate the Revolutionary Theatre because it will be out to destroy them and whatever they believe is real. American cops will try to close the theatres where such nakedness of the human spirit is paraded. American producers will say revolutionary plays are filth, usually because they will treat human life as if it were actually happening. American directors will say that the white guys in the plays are too abstract and cowardly ("don't get me wrong . . . I mean aesthetically . . .") and they will be right.

The force we want is of twenty million spooks storming America with furious cries and unstoppable weapons. We want actual explosions and actual brutality: AN EPIC IS CRUMBLING and we must give it the space and hugeness of its actual demise. The Revolutionary Theatre, which is now peopled with victims, will soon begin to be peopled with new kinds of heroes—not the weak Hamlets debating whether or not they are ready to die for what's on their minds, but men and women (and minds) digging out from under a thousand years of "high art" and weak-faced daliance. We must make an art that will function so as to call down the actual wrath of world spirit. We are witch doctors and assassins, but we will open a place for the true scientists to expand our consciousness. This is a theatre of assault. The play that will split the heavens for us will be called THE DESTRUCTION OF AMERICA. The heroes will be Crazy Horse, Denmark Vesey, Patrice Lumumba, and not history, not memory, not sad sentimental groping for a warmth in our despair; these will be new men, new heroes, and their enemies most of you who are reading this.

Puerto Rican Life in New York

We Puerto Ricans here in New York turn to each other for friendship. We go out on Fridays because that's the beginning of the *weekend*. A whole bunch of us Puerto Ricans go out together. Because as far as having friends of other races go, the only one I have now is an American Negro who owns *un bar*.

Lots of people here have relatives in New Jersey, Pennsylvania, well, all over. So they often spend the *weekends* out of town. Others go to dances or to the beach. That's what we mostly do for entertainment in summer, have picnics at Coney Island. A big group of Latins go together. Coney Island is full of people—all sorts mixed together. There you find white and black Americans. But many other beaches are different; they don't want Negroes or Puerto Ricans.

We have our own clubs here too. There's one that holds a meeting every Sunday over the radio. They talk about the governors, what they're like and what they have done. That club is now trying to get rid of that law of Rockefeller's, the one that says a cop can go into your house at five o'clock in the morning or any hour he pleases and open your door for no reason at all. Rockefeller is a Republican, see? And he's in power in New York, but that law is bad.

The club wants to end racial discrimination like for example in that *World's Fair* where they didn't hire Negroes or Latins. The people at the club said Negroes should work there. But the whites wouldn't allow that and neither would the governor, that Republican, Rockefeller. The land where the *Fair* was belonged to the government but the *buildings* were private property. They belonged to companies, see? And if a private company doesn't want to hire black people, it's within its rights, isn't it? Like supposing a Latin wanted someone to work in his house. He'd look for another Latin, one of his own people. He has a right to. Well, the companies have that same right. Although it's bad because we all need to work and we're all equal.

I would like to work for the equality of Negroes and whites, although I can't say that racial prejudice has really screwed me up much. But I don't agree with this business of the Negroes fighting. Many of them do it as a blind. They steal and shield themselves behind the race problem. I wouldn't get mixed up in those fights; they are Americans and understand each other. I'd let myself be drawn into something like that only if it was the Puerto Ricans who were in it. We have nothing to do with this business, so there's no need to get involved in fights.

If it were in my power to help the Puerto Ricans any way I chose, I would choose a good education for them, for the little ones who are growing up now. I would like them to have good schools where they would be taught English, yes, but Spanish too. That's what's wrong with the system up here—they don't teach Spanish to our children. That's bad, because if a child of yours is born and brought up here and then goes back to Puerto Rico, he can't get a job. How can he, when he knows no Spanish? It's good to know English. But Spanish is for speaking to your own people. That's the problem the children of Puerto Ricans have up here. They understand Spanish but they can't speak or write it.

A good education would help them to get jobs. Because sometimes Puerto Ricans come here to get a job and they can't find one. They want to work and earn money but don't have any schooling at all. They find themselves in a tight spot and maybe they have school children to support, so they'll accept any job that comes their way, usually the worst ones. That's one cause for the delinquency there is among us.

Another thing I would like to work for is better housing. Puerto Ricans can't get good apartments here because the landlords begin raising the rent. They don't want us because they say we're dirty and messy. All pay for what a few of us do. What happens is that when a Puerto Rican rents a place he cracks the plaster on the walls by driving in nails to hang pictures. And then he paints the different rooms different colors. Americans don't like that. So if a Puerto Rican goes to look for an apartment in a pretty part of the city, he finds they charge a hundred and fifty or two hundred dollars' rent. How can we pay that? A Puerto Rican here barely earns enough to pay for rent and food.

It's easy enough for married couples without children to get apartments, but a family with three or four children has trouble. Nobody wants to rent to them. And we Puerto Ricans usually do have children. So we have to look for months and then settle for the worst, for apartments full of rats and crawling with cockroaches. The more you clean, the more they come. There are more rats than people in New York, where we Latins live, I mean.

Not me, I live well. But there are many Puerto Ricans who are much worse off than I am. Just take a look around El Barrio, the section where so many Puerto Ricans live. I went there once with my brother-in-law and Soledad, and I haven't been back since. There's too much

vice in that place; children fifteen or sixteen years old smoking marijuana right out in public, streets full of people at all hours of the day
and night, garbage cans all over the place! People throw bottles, tin
cans, all sorts of rubbish onto the street. That place is a calamity.

When they see the way we live here, many Americans get the idea
that we came over like the Italians and Jews did. They have to come
with a passport, see? They think we are the same. That and their racial
prejudice are the things that make me dislike Americans. Whites here
are full of prejudice against Latins and Negroes. In Puerto Rico it
isn't like that. You can go any place a white man can, as long as you
can pay your way. And a white man can sit down to eat at the same
table as a Negro. But not here. That's why the United States is having
so many troubles. That's why I say I don't like Americans. What I
like is their country. The life here, the way, the manner of living.

Here one lives without gossip, see? You do your work and nobody
interferes with anybody else. I also like the atmosphere here. You earn
enough money so that you can go and see pretty things. You don't
get bored, because you can afford to go to the movies or to the prize
fights. When you're broke you can always go to Forty-second Street
and look at all the pretty lights. Or you can go to Rockaway. It looks
like La Esmeralda, like the Point at Stop 10, except that the people in
Rockaway are rich.

Maybe if Puerto Rico became a state it would be like this country,
but I don't think so. It's too small to have the things they have here.
Why, Puerto Rico would fit into New York City, it's so small! Yet,
I'd like to have Puerto Rico become State Fifty-One, just to see what
would happen. Although when I left Puerto Rico, the governor was
building roads, new hotels, new houses. Well, the people of Puerto
Rico are progressing and I know that Muñoz Marín and the Popular
Party have done good work. It's a pity that he doesn't want to be
governor again next year.

But did you know that his party wants to do away with the slums?
That's bad. It means they want to get rid of everything in La Esmeralda
and in the slums at Stop 21. Now, if Ferré, the Statehood candidate,
wins, he has promised to build new houses in La Esmeralda and let
the people stay there. Ferré says that he's going to make a better Puerto
Rico, with more work, a better life, more rights. That's what he
promises but I don't know if he'll keep his word. His Republican Party
was in power once and it fell because it didn't keep its promises.

Not that it makes any difference in the way I feel. I belong to that
party because I believe in its ideals. And Nanda does too. Nanda

worked in the registration of new voters for the Party. Afterward we would go to the meetings. She'd put on a dress made from a Republican flag and pin a sign on it saying she wanted Ferré to win. We used to go to different places on the island like that, talking the whole night through.

What Republicans want is to have the United States take Puerto Rico over completely, once and for all. Because right now Puerto Rico is half Puerto Rican and half United States. It flies both the Puerto Rican and the American flags. All they have to do to make us into a state is to add one more star to the American flag.

There's another party too, the *Pipiolos*.* They want Puerto Rico to be free like Mexico, Santo Domingo, Jamaica, Venezuela, and such places. That's bad. If that happened, we would need a passport to get out of Puerto Rico. What they want is a republic, which means that if you're a bad governor they'll get you out without an election or anything, with bullets.

The trouble with republics is that they have to defend themselves because they don't have another country to help them. Cuba used to be a republic, right? And what did it have to do? Call on the Russians for help. Now it's Communist. But Castro isn't bad. When he was in the Sierra Maestra with his guerrillas, he asked the Americans for help and the Americans refused because they were on Batista's side. That's why he had to go to the Russians. If we became a republic now, Fidel Castro could take us over whenever he wanted to. All he'd have to do is send over a couple of Communist war planes.

If only Communism now were as it used to be! I don't know whether this is true or not, but I have read that Communism used to mean that if you had a plate of rice you shared it with everybody. If a man had a thousand dollars in the bank he had to share them with everybody else, and all were equal. That's what Communism used to be but it isn't like that any more. Now under Communism, what's mine is mine and what's yours belongs to you. The man who owns the most is the most respected one. If you have nothing, you're worth nothing. I don't like that kind of Communism. Why, besides all the things I've just told you, I also heard over the radio that in Russia they make children study from the time they are four months old! Besides, Russia is a military country. Do you know what that means? It means that at the age of fifteen a boy is already serving in the *Army* or the *Navy*. That's what's happening in Cuba today, people are forced to do things.

* Partido Independentista Puertorriqueño (PIP).

You can't say no, because the government gives all the orders. And you can't change the government because there's only one party, the Communists. You can't say, "I don't like this country." You *have* to like it. It's not like here, where you're free. If you don't like one thing, you can go around the corner and get another.

If Puerto Rico were a republic we would starve to death. We have to buy everything from outside. Even our ships we have to buy outside. So if we were free, we would have to call on other republics for help. Naturally, the United States would help us if we were a republic, but it would be only the kind of help they give Mexico, Venezuela, and all those places. We'd have to submit to a lot of regulations.

Lately I have heard that the priests in Puerto Rico have formed a party of their own. It is called the Christian PAC.* It belongs to Rome, to Catholic people. If they win, who is going to govern Puerto Rico? The Catholics? I'm Catholic myself so I would be allowed to live, but what about all the people who are not? Religion has nothing to do with politics. President Kennedy was a member of the Catholic Church but that did not keep him from also being a member of the Democratic Party. Tell me now, suppose PAC wins the election, what will become of Puerto Rico? Who's going to feed us? We would have to wait until ships came from Rome bringing us food. And when Rome falls, who will support us? We'll have to live on bread and wine, I guess.

Well, I live in New York and I don't meddle with what goes on here. I do see that Kennedy, the President who was killed, was pure gold. He was a Democrat and that's the same as being a *Popular* in Puerto Rico. But even so, he was good. Do you know what he fought for? For equality between Negroes and whites. For civil rights, which are the rights that belong to us, like not allowing a cop to come into your house and search it without your leave. The privacy of the home is a right that every one of us has. And he was also for your right not to be stopped and searched by a cop for no reason at all as you walk quietly down a street, minding your own business. And for Negroes' rights to get a job as well as white men. All those are civil rights. President Kennedy was in favor of all that.

Imagine, he knew Cuba was Communist but he was willing to help them in spite of that. They were the ones who said no. And then, some of Kennedy's people were jailed over in Cuba and he exchanged them for a shipful of medicines. And that's when they killed him.

Now Johnson has succeeded Kennedy. Johnson is from Texas, where

* Partido Acción Cristiana.

they killed Washington—I mean, Abraham Lincoln. There's a lot of racial prejudice in that state. Although it's so rich in oil wells and such, people have gotten scared of that place. Presidents won't dare to travel through Texas any more. Those people down there are too brutal. The way things are, Texas is having the same trouble as the Jews, one Texan killed Kennedy and now the're all paying for it.

Johnson doesn't seem to be like Kennedy, who was always talking about the Latins and looking out for them. But this one isn't like that. He's not talkative. And when he does talk it's only about politics for himself and his people. What's more, I don't think he writes his own speeches. Somebody else writes them and they give them to Johnson to read. He doesn't put ideas of his own mind into them.

I have never voted, because I wasn't old enough. I was twenty-one this year and I'd like to vote, now that I'm of age. But I won't have the chance because I didn't register. I didn't know where to go or anything. I asked around but everybody said it was somewhere in Brooklyn, they didn't know exactly where. It isn't like Puerto Rico, where someone comes to your house and asks you which party you plan to vote for and then they send you a little card.

If I could, I'd like to vote for the Republicans because my *mamá* is a Republican. But not for Rockefeller. I'd vote for some other candidate, like Kennedy's brother, for instance. Rockefeller doesn't stand up for the Latins or the Negroes. And yet, if you stop to think, you'll realize that in New York there are more Latins and Negroes than whites. But when two men apply for the same job, a white man and a Negro, they hire the white man and push us aside. They treat us like they treat the Negroes, you see. And that in spite of the fact that the Puerto Rican works hard. If he sees a box that's meant to be carried by two men, he heaves it up and carries it by himself, even if it weighs a hundred pounds. We like the toughest kind of work.

How to Be a Negro Without Really Trying

I had been away from home maybe three months, knocking around, sleeping in cold hallways, hungry a lot of the time. The fucking heart was going out of me. Maybe I should make it down to the Bowery, I thought, and lap up some sneaky pete with the rest of the bums.

No, I decided, one thing still stood out clear; one thing still made sense and counted—me. Nothing else but me—and I hadda pull outta this shit kick.

It was winter, and all I had on was a paper-weight sports jacket. The cold winds were blowing my skin against my chest. I walked into a bar at 103rd Street and Third Avenue, trying to look like I had a pound on me and was warm. In front of the jukebox was a colored guy and a big, chunky broad. The guy was beating out time and the girl was digging. Not all of her moved, just the right parts.

I smiled. "Cold, eh?" I said, and added, "My name is Piri."

"Sure is, kid," he said. "Mine's Pane, and that's my sistuh, Lorry." I followed his finger as he pointed to her.

"It's cold," I mumbled to no one in particular.

"Want a drink, kid?"

I tried not to act too anxious. "Yeah, cool man," I said casually. Pane took a bottle from his back pocket and handed it to me. "How strong can I hit it?" I asked, holding the bottle to my lips.

"Roll," he said, and I put inside me the warmth and affection of my new friends.

After half an hour a new bottle popped out and I got another long taste, and home was with me, I wasn't so lonely. The hours slipped by. I talked and Pane and his sister were one with me. Then the place was gonna close and I knew it was going to be cold again. Pane was high but not plastered. He nudged Lorry and said, "Let's go." I just sat there.

They got up and walked away. As they reached the door I saw Lorry nudge her brother and whisper something. He shook his head and looked back at me. I waved at him, hoping that the look on his face meant what I thought it did.

"Hey, kid, what's your name again?"

"Piri—some guys call me Johnny."

"Have you got a place to sleep?"

"Uh-uh," I said. I made a mental list of the places I had slept since I left home—friends' pads at the beginning, with relatives until the welcome was overdrawn, then rooftops, under the stairs, basements, stoops, parked cars.

"Well, we ain't got much room, but you're welcome to share it," Pane said. "You gotta sleep on the floor, 'cause all we got is one room for Lorry, her two kids, and me."

"Crazy, man. Thanks a lot," I said. I almost felt my luck was going to change. I tightened up against the cold and hustled down the street. A couple of blocks over, between Park and Madison, we went down the stairs into a basement. I felt the warmth from the furnace greet me and I welcomed it like a two-days-late home-relief check. Pane fumbled with the key and opened the door into a small room. I noticed that the cellar had been partioned into several rooms and one kitchen for sharing. Lorry smiled at me and said, "Honey, it ain't much, but it beats a blank."

"*Gracias.*" I smiled, and it was for real. "Thanks, Lorry."

She spread a quilt on the floor between the big bed where she and the two kids slept and a couch where Pane slept. I lay down on my back, my hands behind my head. The room was so small I could touch both the bed and the couch. I felt almost safe.

Soon Pane was sleeping hard on his whiskey. In the dim darkness I saw Lorry looking down at me. "You asleep, honey?" she asked.

"No, I ain't," I answered.

She slowly made room in her big warm bed, and just like that I climbed in and made love to her—"love" because I was grateful to her, because I wanted her body as much as she wanted mine. It was all natural, all good, all as innocent and pure as anything could be in Home, Sweet Harlem. That was that—she was my woman. No matter that I was sixteen and she was thirty-three. Her caring, her loving were as young or as old as I wanted it to be.

Months passed. I got a job—Lorry inspired that with carfare and lunch. Every week I gave her a few bucks and loved her as much as I could. Still, I had the feeling that I was in a deep nothing and had to get on. Then I lost the lousy job.

I decided I couldn't stay with Lorry any more. I had been playing around with this Puerto Rican girl who lived in one of the basement rooms. She was sure a pretty bitch, with a kid and no husband. I didn't want Lorry to cop a complex, but I couldn't dig her the way she wanted me to. One night I cut out. The Puerto Rican girl had just hustled ten bucks and she was talking about all the things it would

buy for the kid. They needed food and clothes real bad. I saw where
she put her pocketbook and waited until she was in the kitchen getting
some grits for her kid. Then I went to her room and copped the ten
bucks and made it up to the Bronx. I had a hangout up there. I gave
a street buddy five bucks and he let me share his pad for a couple of
weeks till I could cop a job.

A few days after I'd copped the ten dollars I ran into the girl. She
knew it had been me. She made a plea for her bread back, for her
kid. I didn't take it and brushed past her. I didn't have to look into
her eyes to know the hate she bore me. But it was her or me, and as
always, it had to be me. Besides, I had bought some pot with the five
left over and rolled some good-size bombers that immediately put me
in business. I had a good-o thought: soon as I was straight, I'd lay
her ten *bolos* back on her.

I looked for work, but not too hard. Then I saw this ad in a newspaper:

YOUNG MEN, 17–30
GREAT OPPORTUNITY
LEARN WHILE WORKING
EARN WHILE TRAINING
Door-to-door salesmen in household wares. Guaranteed by Good
Housekeeping. Salary and commission.
603 E. 73 St.   2nd fl.—9 a.m.

"Dig, Louie, this sounds good," I said to my boy. "Let's go over
in the morning. Hell, with our gift of *labia* we're a mother-hopping
cinch to cop a slave."

"*Chevere*, Piri, man, we got all Harlem and we know plenty people.
Bet we can earn a hundred bucks or more on commissions alone."

We went down the next day and walked into the office and a girl
handed me and Louie each a paper with a number on it and told us
to please have a seat. My number was 16 and Louie's was 17. Man,
me and Louie were sparklin'. We had our best togs on; they were
pressed like a razor and our shoes shone like a bald head with a pound
of grease on it.

"Number 16, please?" the girl called out.

I winked at Louie and he gave me the V-for-victory sign.

"Right this way, sir, through the door on your left," the girl said.

I walked into the office and there was this paddy sitting there. He looked up at me and broke out into the friendliest smile I ever saw, like I was a long-lost relative. "Come in, come right in," he said. "Have a chair—that's right, sit right there. Well, sir, you're here bright and and early. That's what our organization likes to see. Yes sir, punctuality is the first commandment in a salesman's bible. So you're interested in selling our household wares—guaranteed, of course, by *Good House-keeping*. Had any experience selling?"

"Well, not exactly, sir, but—er—when I was a kid—I mean, younger, I used to sell shopping bags in the *Marketa*."

"The what?"

"The *Marketa* on 110th Street and Park Avenue. It, er, runs all the way up to 116th Street."

"Ummm, I see."

"And my mom—er, mother, used to knit fancy things called *tapetes*. I think they're called doilies, and I used to sell them door to door, and I made out pretty good. I know how to talk to people, Mr.—er—"

"Mr. Christian, Mr. Harold Christian. See?" and he pointed a skinny finger at a piece of wood with his name carved on it. "Ha, ha, ha," he added, "just like us followers of our Lord Jesus Christ are called. Are you Christian?"

"Yes, sir."

"A good Catholic, I bet. I never miss a Sunday mass; how about you?"

"No, sir, I try not to." *Whee-eoo!* I thought. *Almost said I was Protestant.*

"Fine, fine, now let's see . . ." Good Catholic Mr. Christian took out some forms. "What's your name?"

"Piri Thomas—P-i-r-i."

"Age?"

"Er, seventeen—born September 30, 1928."

Mr. Christian counted off on the fingers of one hand . . . "twenty-eight, er, thirty-eight, forty-five—ahum, you were just seventeen this September."

"That's right. Paper said from seventeen to thirty."

"O, yes—yes, yes, that's correct. Where do you live?"

I couldn't give him the Long Island address; it was too far away. So I said, "109 East 104th Street."

"That's way uptown, isn't it?"

"Yes, sir."

"Isn't that, um, Harlem?"

"Yes, sir, it's split up in different sections, like the Italian section and Irish and Negro and the Puerto Rican section. I live in the Puerto Rican section. It's called the *Barrio*."

"The *Bar-ree-o?*"

I smiled. "Yes, sir, it's Spanish for 'the place'—er—like a community."

"Oh, I see. But you're not Puerto Rican, are you? You speak fairly good English even though once in a while you use some slang—of course, it's sort of picturesque."

"My parents are Puerto Ricans."

"Is Thomas a Puerto Rican name?"

"Er—well, my mother's family name is Montañez," I said, wondering if that would help prove I was a Puerto Rican. "There are a lot of Puerto Ricans with American names. My father told me that after Spain turned Puerto Rico over to the United States at the end of the Spanish-American War, a lot of Americans were stationed there and got married to Puerto Rican girls." *Probably fucked 'em and forgot 'em,* I thought.

"Oh, I—er, see. How about your education? High school diploma?"

"No, sir, I quit in my second year . . ."

"Tsh, tsh, that was very foolish of you. Education is a wonderful thing, Mr. Thomas. It's really the only way for one to get ahead, especially when—er, uh—why did you leave school?"

My mind shouted out, *On account of you funny paddies and your funny ideas in this funny world,* but I said, very *cara palo,* "Well, sir, we got a big family and—well, I'm the oldest and I had to help out and—well, I quit." Then, in a sincere fast breath, I added, "But I'm going to study nights. I agree with you that education is the only way to get ahead, especially when—"

"Fine, fine. What's your Social Security number?"

I said quickly: "072–20–2800.'

"By memory, eh? Good! A good salesman's second commandment should be a good memory. Got a phone?"

"Yes, sir. Lehigh 3–6050, and ask for Mr. Dandy. He's my uncle. He doesn't speak English very well, but you can leave any message for me with him."

"Very, very good, Mr. Thomas. Well, this will be all for now. We will get in touch with you."

"Uh, how soon, about, Mr. Christian? 'Cause I'd like to start work, or rather, training, as soon as possible."

"I can't definitely say, Mr. Thomas, but it will be in the near future. Right now our designated territory is fully capacitated. But we're opening another soon and we'll need good men to work it."

"You can't work the territory you want?" I asked.

"Oh, no! This is scientifically planned," he said.

"I'd like to work in Harlem," I said, "but, uh—I can make it wherever you put me to sell."

"That's the spirit!" Mr. Christian bubbled. "The third commandment of a good salesman is he faces any challenge, wherever it may be."

I took Mr. Christian's friendly outstretched hand and felt the warm, firm grip and thought, *This paddy is gonna be all right to work for.* As I walked out, I turned my head and said, "Thank you very much, sir, for the opportunity."

"Not at all, not at all. We need bright young blood for this growing organization, and those that grow with us will be headed for great things."

"Thank you. So long."

"So long, and don't forget to go to mass."

"No, sir, I sure won't!"

"What church you go to?" he asked suddenly.

"Uh"—I tried to remember the name of the Catholic Church on 106th Street—"Saint Cecilia's!" I finally burst out.

"Oh yes, that's on, er, 106th Street between Park and Lexington. Do you know Father Kresser?"

"Gee, the name sounds sort of familiar," I cooled it. "I can almost place him, but I can't say for sure."

"Well, that's all right. He probably wouldn't remember me, but I was a youngster when he had a parish farther downtown. I used to go there. Well, if you run into him, give him my regards."

"I sure will. So long, and thanks again." I closed the door carefully and walked out to where Louie was still sitting.

"Man, Piri," he said, "you was in there a beau-coup long-ass time."

"Shh, Louie, cool your language."

"Got the job? You were in there long enough for two jobs."

I smiled and made an okay face.

Louie cupped his hand to his mouth and put his head next to mine. "That cat ain't a faggot, is he?" he whispered.

I whispered back with exaggerated disgust, "Man! What a fuckin' dirty mind you got."

"Just asking, man," he said. "Sometimes these guys are *patos* and if you handle them right, you get the best breaks. Well, how'd you make out?"

"In like Flynn, Louie."

"Cool, man, hope I get the same break."

"Number 17," the girl called.

"Here I go," Louie said to me.

"*Suerte,* Louie," I said. I gave him the V-for-victory sign and watched his back disappear and dimly heard Mr. Christian's friendly "Come right in. Have a—" before the door closed behind Louie.

Jesus, I thought. *I hope Louie gets through okay. It'll be great to work in the same job. Maybe we can even work together. He'll cover one side of the street and I'll cover the other. As tight as me and Louie are, we'll pool what we make on commissions and split halfies.*

"Hey Piri," Louie said, "let's go."

"Damn, Louie, you just went in," I said. "You only been in there about five minutes or so. How'd Mr. Christian sound?"

We walked down the stairs.

"Okay, I guess. Real friendly, and he asked me questions, one-two-three."

"And?"

"And I'm in!"

"Cool breeze. What phone did you give?" I asked.

"I ain't got no phone. Hey, there's the bus!"

We started to run. "Fuck running," I said, "let's walk a while and celebrate. Man, you could've gave him Dandy's number like I did. Aw, well, they'll probably send you a telegram or special delivery letter telling you when to start work."

"What for?" Louie asked.

"So's they can tell you when the new territory is opened up and when to come in," I said. "Cause the other territory—"

"What new territory?"

I opened my mouth to answer and Louie and I knew what was shakin' at the same fuckin' time. The difference between me and Louie was he was white. "That cat Mr. Christian tell you about calling you when some new territory opens up?" Louie said in a low voice.

I nodded, "Yeah."

"Damn! That motherfucker asked me to come and start that training jazz on Monday. Gave me a whole lotta shit about working in a virgin territory that's so big us future salesmen wouldn't give each other competition or something like that." Louie dug that hate feeling in me. He tried to make me feel good by telling me that maybe they got a different program and Mr. Christian was considering me for a special kinda job.

"Let's go back," I said coldly.

"What for, Piri?"

"You see any colored cats up there?"

"Yeah, *panín*, there's a few. Why?"

"Let's wait here in front of the place."

"*Por qué?*" asked Louie.

I didn't answer. I just watched paddies come down out of that office and make it. "Louie," I said, "ask the next *blanco* that comes down how the job hiring is. There's one now."

Louie walked over to him. "Say, excuse me, Mac," he said, "Are they hiring up there—you know, salesmen?"

"Yes, they are," the guy answered. "I start Monday. Why don't you apply if you're looking for work? It's—"

"Thanks a lot, Mac," Louie said. "I might do that." He came back and started to open his mouth.

"Forget it, *amigo*," I said. "I heard the chump."

We waited some more and a colored cat came down. "Hey, bruh," I called.

"You callin' me?"

"Yeah. I dug the ad in the paper. How's the hiring? Putting guys on?"

"I don't know, man. I mean I got some highly devoted crap about getting in touch with me when a new turf opens up."

"Thanks, man," I said.

"You're welcome. Going up?"

"Naw, I changed my mind." I nodded to Louie, and he came up to me like he was down for whatever I was down for.

"Let's walk," I said. I didn't feel so much angry as I did sick, like throwing-up sick. Later, when I told this story to my buddy, a colored cat, he said, "Hell, Piri, Ah know stuff like that can sure burn a cat up, but a Negro faces that all the time."

"I know that," I said, "but I wasn't a Negro then. I was still only a Puerto Rican."

The White Niggers

You want to get a glimpse of what it feels like to be a nigger? Let your hair grow long. Longhairs, that new minority, are getting the crap kicked out of them by cops all over the country, and with the beatings and jailings comes the destruction of flower power. COPS EAT FLOWERS painted in large white letters last fall on Second Avenue and St. Marks Place signaled the end of flower power. As the kids pour back into the Lower East Side they bring with them tales of police harassment previously reserved only for blacks. Two hundred kids busted on Boston Common for "idleness." Three kids arrested for vagrancy in Nevada (even though they all had money) and held fifty days before they even had a trial. Kids arrested in Indiana get their hair cut and then are thrown out of the jail without even going to trial. In Florida a head shop was smashed by the police and the owners were told bluntly, "We don't want your kind around here. Get your ass out of town." Anyone who takes to the road going cross-country literally takes his life in his hands.

Here in enlightened New York things are not much better. The block I live on, St. Marks Place, is patrolled by no less than twenty cops at a time (one block!). Undercover agents in plain clothes slouch against the building waiting for trouble. Kids being searched and asked to produce identification is a normal occurrence. Communes are raided by the week in a massive hunt for America's young runaways.

Pot, long used as a method of busting black people, is now being used as a means of eliminating young white activists. There are, I am told, over thirty thousand people currently in prison for smoking pot. On the Lower East side pot is more common than cigarettes. Public Smoke-Ins in Tompkins Square Park last summer attracted five thousand heads each time. The police had just about thrown in the towel and concentrated on eliminating major dealers (which is difficult, since, by definition, a major dealer has already bribed the cops). That was true at least up until a month ago. Jerry Rubin is a well known activist on the Lower East Side. A confirmed radical, Jerry was active in the Berkeley Free Speech Movement, the Vietnam Day Committee, project director of October's siege at the Pentagon, a key figure in Yippie! and an architect of plans for demonstrations at the Democratic National Convention in Chicago. Detectives from the Narcotics Squad raided his apartment, ripped a poster of Castro off the wall, searched his files and phone book for information, and forced him up against the wall, demanding information on Yippie! plans for Chicago. All this was under the pretext of a pot bust. The pot, however, was not as interesting to the cops as Jerry's politics, and for not talking Jerry received a few slugs and a kick in the back which resulted in a fractured coccyx. Jerry is on trial now and could receive up to fifteen years in prison for something I'm sure we all do, namely take a puff on a harmless flower. A simple weed that grows wild and has been used by people for thousands of years seems to be causing some fuss.

I have no friend who has not been in jail. Jail for even one night can be a learning experience equal to a year in college. Did you know, for example, that you can commit suicide by stuffing cigarette filters in your mouth? Only cops could think that one up. Filters are cut off all your cigarettes in jail. Did you ever have your ass searched? I always wonder what they are looking for. Machine guns? Supreme Court decisions? Civil rights? The Supreme Court is a long way from the Ninth Precinct and the Ninth Precinct is a longer way still from the cop on the beat.

People down here are arrested for passing out leaflets, standing on the corner, handing out free food, not carrying identification, and a variety of similar offenses. Recently six armed cops arrested a longhair on charges of conspiracy. It was never explained how one person can commit conspiracy. All these cases are now being thrown out of the courts by puzzled judges, but looking out the window on St. Marks Place one wonders how long it will take before people will be put away for long terms in prison for such activities. Paranoids are prophets down here.

I was recently busted for standing on the corner of my block. In the police station a TPF (Tactical Patrol Force) cop threatened to gouge my eyes out with his fingers if I didn't stop smiling. He had assured me he was proficient at such tasks. He gave me a punch in the head just to let me know he knew some other tricks besides eye-gouging. It is this reality we are bringing to Chicago with us—the reality of our daily lives.

NEW POLITICS
AND THE UNIVERSITY

The black man's struggle for equality clearly inspired and gave impetus to the formulation of the "New Left" and to its attempts to restructure the American political system. Indeed, many of those most deeply involved in ending the Vietnam War have been equally committed to "wresting" complete freedom for the Negro. However, in the last few years, as the various black leaders consolidated their energies and filled their constituencies with Negroes, white radicals have concerned themselves primarily with ending our foreign war, which at this writing has accounted for more than a half million deaths in Vietnam.

In universities throughout the country assemblies of students and faculties formed "teach-ins" to discuss ways of stopping American participation in the war. In the parks and streets of the cities, in the nation's capital, outraged protesters marched and rallied. The war continued. Young men fled the country; many who stayed publicly burned their draft cards, risking harsh jail sentences and humiliation. Respected members of the society—clergy, writers, teachers—illegally counseled young draft-resisters, and in some instances were prosecuted. Meanwhile, the war "effort" was intensified. The spiraling costs of our military needs meant that less funds were available to alleviate poverty and to curtail the rising inflation at home. Many Americans could not but wonder whether social progress was to be systematically and indefinitely postponed because of the confused priorities of a deluded and power-mad government.

The frustrated efforts of thousands of dissenters, most of whom were of college age, created startling repercussions within the United States, and particularly on the campuses of the universities. An apathetic student body had been socially ignited: never was the gap between this country's potential and its reality so apparent. In the late sixties, universities became battlegrounds where radical alternatives to our political and social structure were not only posited—but practiced. The vast, anonymous "multiversities," where administrations worked hand in hand with war-oriented government agencies, and faculty members were caught up in the exigencies of research and publication, symbolized only too clearly the values of American society at large. The unrest began at Berkeley, then Columbia, and then spread to hundreds of colleges and universities: "radical" students demanded that the administrations sever ties with the government, demanded a greater role in policy making, demanded more democratic admissions policies, demanded the abolition of ROTC programs. . . . The results were predictable: recriminations, suspensions, policemen on the campuses, the National Guard. Where dissent was curtailed on one campus, it erupted elsewhere. Recently, Dr. Calvin H. Plimpton, President of Amherst College, suggested, in an open letter to President Nixon, that campus disorder is a reflection and not a cause of social disorder, that student agitation "will continue until you and the other political leaders of our country address more effectively, massively and persistently the major social and foreign problems of our country."

In this section, Herbert Marcuse and Abbie Hoffman recommend ways in which humans can gain precedence over the machine, even as we approach 1984. Recalling Emerson's "American Scholar" address, Dr. Timothy Leary indicts American universities for merely conditioning students to become a part of the "system," and he proclaims the need for a true discovery of self. Many professors have been in the vanguard of the protest against the dehumanizing aspects of the universities. A policy statement by the New University Conference (a recently formed association of radical professors, teachers, and graduate students) attempts a sane analysis of student demands. Martin Duberman and Louis Kampf point to various areas in which the universities have failed to fulfill the expectations of students, and they suggest remedies.

Marcuse Defines His New Left Line

Six months ago, sir, your name was almost unknown in France. It came to prominence in connection with the student revolt in Berlin, then in connection with student demonstrations in America. Next it was linked with the May demonstrations here. And now, all of a sudden, your last book has become a best-seller. How do you see your own position in relation to the student uprisings all over the world?

MARCUSE The answer is very simple. I am deeply committed to the movement of "angry students," but I am certainly not their spokesman. It is the press and publicity that have given me this title and have turned me into a rather salable piece of merchandise. I particularly object to the juxtaposition of my name and photograph with those of Che Guevara, Debray, Rudi Dutschke, etc., because these men have truly risked and are still risking their lives in the battle for a more human society, whereas I participate in this battle only through my words and my ideas. It is a fundamental difference.

Still, your words preceded the student action.

MARCUSE Oh, there are very few students who have really read me, I think. . . .

No doubt, especially in France; but there are also very few students who have chosen a doctrine for their revolt. Can we say that for these students you are the theorist?

MARCUSE If that is true, I am very happy to hear it. But it's more a case of encounter than of direct influence. . . . In my books, I have tried to make a critique of society—and not only of capitalist society—in terms that avoid all ideology. Even the Socialist ideology, even the Marxist ideology. I have tried to show that contemporary society is a repressive society in all its aspects, that even the comfort, the prosperity, the alleged political and moral freedom are utilized for oppressive ends.

I have tried to show that any change would require a total rejec-

Jean-Louis Ferrier, et al., "Marcuse Defines His New Left Line," from *The New York Times Magazine,* October 27, 1968. © 1968 by The New York Times Company. Reprinted by permission.

tion or, to speak the language of the students, a perpetual confrontation of this society. And that it is not merely a question of changing the institutions but rather, and this is more important, of totally changing human beings in their attitudes, their instincts, their goals, and their values.

This, I think, is the point of contact between my books and the worldwide student movement.

But you feel that they did not need you to arrive at these ideas, is that right?

MARCUSE One of the essential characteristics of the student movement is that the students apply to reality what has been taught them in the abstract through the work of the masters who have developed the great values of Western civilization. For example, the primacy of natural law over established law, the inalienable right to resist tyranny and all illegitimate authority. . . . They simply cannot comprehend why these great principles should remain on the level of ideas instead of being put into practice. And that is exactly what they are doing.

Do you mean that fundamentally this is a humanist movement?

MARCUSE They object to that term because according to them, humanism is a bourgeois, personal value. It is a philosophy which is inseparable from a destructive reality. But in their minds there is no point in worrying about the philosophy of a few persons; the point is to bring about a radical change in the society as a whole. So they want no part of the term "humanist."

You know, of course, that here in France we are very far from that "affluent society" whose destruction you propose and which for the moment exists, for better or worse, only in the United States.

MARCUSE I have been accused of concentrating my critique on American society, and this is quite true. I have said so myself. But this is not only because I know this country better than any other: it is because I believe or I am afraid that American society may become the model for the other capitalist countries, and maybe even for the Socialist countries. I also believe that this route can be avoided, but again, this would presuppose a fundamental change, a total break with the content of the needs and aspirations of people as they are conditioned today.

A break . . . that is, a revolution.

MARCUSE Precisely.

Do you believe in the existence of a revolutionary impulse in the industrial societies?

MARCUSE You know quite well that the student movement contains a very strong element of anarchy. Very strong. And this is really new.

Anarchy—new?

MARCUSE In the revolutionary movement of the 20th century, I believe it is new. At least on this scale, it is new. This means that the students have perceived the rigidity of the traditional political organizations, their petrification, the fact that they have stifled any revolutionary impulse. So it is outside of these organizations that the revolt spontaneously occurs.

But spontaneity is not enough. It is also necessary to have an organization. But a new, very flexible kind of organization, one that does not impose rigorous principles, one that allows for movement and initiative. An organization without the "bosses" of the old parties or political groups. This point is very important. The leaders of today are the products of publicity. In the actual movement there are no leaders as there were in the Bolshevik Revolution, for example.

In other words, it is anti-Leninist?

MARCUSE Yes. In fact, Daniel Cohn-Bendit has severely criticized Leninism-Marxism on this ground.

Does this mean that you rely on anarchism to bring about this revolution you desire?

MARCUSE No. But I do believe that the anarchist element is a very powerful and very progressive force, and that it is necessary to preserve this element as one of the factors in a larger and more structured process.

And yet you yourself are the opposite of an anarchist.

MARCUSE That may be true, but I wish you'd tell me why.

Isn't it because your work is dialectical? Your work is very carefully constructed. Do you think of yourself as an anarchist?

MARCUSE No. I am not an anarchist because I cannot imagine how one can combat a society which is mobilized and organized in its totality against any revolutionary movement, against any effective opposition; I do not see how one can combat such a society, such a concentrated force—military force, police force, etc.—without any organization. It won't work.

No, it won't work. The Communists will quote you Lenin's analysis of "leftism" which, according to him, was the manifestation of "petits bourgeois overcome with rage before the horrors of capitalism . . . a revolutionary attitude which is unstable, unproductive, and susceptible of rapidly changing into submission or apathy or going mad over some bourgeois fad or other."

MARCUSE I do not agree. Today's left is far from the reaction of *petite bourgeoisie* to a revolutionary party, as in Lenin's day. It is the reaction of a revolutionary minority to the established party which the Communist party has become, which is no longer the party of Lenin, but a social democratic party.

If anarchy doesn't work and if the Communist parties are no longer revolutionary, what do you hope for from the student unrest but a superficial disorder which only serves to stiffen the repression?

MARCUSE All militant opposition takes the risk of increasing repression. This has never been a reason to stop the opposition. Otherwise, all progress would be impossible.

No doubt. But don't you think the notion of the "progress" that might result from a revolution deserves to be better defined? You denounce the subtle restraints that weigh upon the citizens of modern societies. Wouldn't a revolution result in exchanging one series of restraints for another?

MARCUSE Of course. But there are progressive restraints and reactionary restraints. For example, restraints imposed upon the elemental aggressiveness of man, upon the instinct of destruction, the death instinct, the transformation of this elemental aggressiveness into an energy that could be used for the improvement and protection of life—such restraints would be necessary in the freest society. For example, industries would not be permitted to pollute the air, nor would the "White Citizens Council" be permitted to disseminate racism or to possess firearms, as they are in the United States today. . . . Of course there would be restraints; but they would be progressive ones.

The ones you mention are commonplace enough. The possession of firearms is forbidden in France, and in America it is a survival, not a creation of the affluent society. Let us consider freedom of expression, which means a great deal to us. In the free society which you advocate this freedom disappears, does it not?

MARCUSE I have written that I believe it is necessary not to extend freedom of the press to movements which are obviously aggressive and destructive, like the Nazi movement. But with the exception of this special case, I am not against freedom of expression. . . .

Even when this means the propagation of racist, nationalist or colonialist ideas?

MARCUSE Here my answer is no. I am not in favor of granting free expression to racist, anti-Semitic, neo-Nazi movements. Certainly not; because the interval between the word and the act is too brief today. At least in American society, the one with which I am familiar. You know the famous statement of Justice Holmes, that civil rights can be withdrawn in a single case: the case of immediate danger. Today this immediate danger exists everywhere.

Can't this formula be turned against you in connection with students, revolutionaries, or Communists?

MARCUSE It always is. And my answer is always the same. I do not believe that the Communism conceived by the great Marxist theorists is, by its very nature, aggressive and destructive; quite the contrary.

But has it not become so under certain historical circumstances? Isn't there something aggressive and destructive about the Soviet policy toward Hungary in 1956, or toward Czechoslovakia today?

MARCUSE Yes. But that isn't Communism, it is Stalinism. I would certainly use all possible restraints to oppose Stalinism, but that is not Communism.

Why do you criticize America more severely for its deviations from the democratic ideal than you do Communism for its deviations from the Communist ideal?

MARCUSE I am just as critical of these deviations in Communist countries. However, I believe that the institutions and the whole culture of the capitalism of monopolies militate against the development of a democratic socialism.

And you believe that one day we shall see an ideal Communist society?

MARCUSE Well, at least there is the theory. There is the whole Marxist theory. That exists. And there is also Cuba. There is China. There is the Communist policy during the heroic period of the Bolshevik Revolution.

Do you mean that Communist societies do these reprehensible things in spite of themselves? That the Soviet Union invaded Czechoslovakia in spite of herself?

MARCUSE In spite of the idea of Communism, not in spite of the Soviet Union. The invasion of Czechoslovakia is one of the most reprehensible acts in the history of Socialism. It is a brutal expression of the policy of power that has long been practiced by the Soviet Union in political and economic competition with capitalism. I believe that many of the reprehensible things that happen in the Communist countries are the result of competitive coexistence with capitalism, while poverty continues to reign in the Communist countries.

Here you are touching upon an important point. It does not seem possible to reduce poverty without an extremely coercive organization. So once again we find that restraint is necessary.

MARCUSE Certainly. But here, too, there can be progressive restraint.

Take a country in which poverty coexists with luxury, waste, and comfort for the privileged. . . . It is necessary to curb this waste to eliminate poverty, misery, and inequality. These are necessary restraints.

Unfortunately, there is no economic correlation. It is not the curbing of waste that eliminates poverty, it is production.

MARCUSE That's true. But my point is that the restraints that certainly exist in, say, Cuba, are not the same as those that are felt in capitalist economies.

Cuba is perhaps not a very good example of a successful Socialist economy, since the country is totally dependent on daily deliveries of Soviet petroleum. If the Soviet Union were to stop those deliveries for two weeks . . .

MARCUSE I don't know what would happen. But even under these conditions of dependence on the Soviet Union, Cuba has made tremendous progress.

In comparison with what she was that's certainly true. Have you been there?

MARCUSE No. I can't get authorization from the Americans.

Why do you despair of all progress within the framework of the American democracy?

MARCUSE Do you really think that democracy is making progress in the United States?

Compared with the period of "The Grapes of Wrath," yes.

MARCUSE I disagree. Look at the elections, the candidates for the Presidency of the United States, fabricated by the huge political machines. And who can find the differences between these candidates? If that's democracy, it's a farce. The people have said nothing and they have been asked nothing.

True. But at the same time thousands of young Americans have shown in recent months that they were against the war in Vietnam, that they were willing to work to eliminate the ghettos, to act in the political sphere.

MARCUSE This movement is encountering a more and more effective repression.

Do you feel, then, that we are witnessing a definite obstruction of American society?

MARCUSE The answer is a little more complicated than that. There is a possibility of progress toward democracy in the United States, but only through movements that are increasingly militant and radical. Not at all within the limits of the established process. This process is a game and the American students have lost interest in playing this game, they have lost confidence in this allegedly democratic process.

Do you believe in the possibility of revolution in the United States?

MARCUSE Absolutely not. Not at all.

Why not?

MARCUSE Because there is no collaboration between the students and the workers, not even on the level on which it occurred in France in May and June.

In that case, what role do you attribute to the student?

MARCUSE They are militant minorities who can articulate the needs and aspirations of the silent masses. But by themselves they are not revolutionaries, and nobody says they are. The students know that very well.

So their only role is to reveal?

MARCUSE Yes. And this is very interesting. Here as well as in the United States, the students can truly be called spokesmen.

And who will make the revolution in America, in Germany, in France, if the students do not make contact with the working class?

MARCUSE I cannot imagine. In spite of everything that has been said, I still cannot imagine a revolution without the working class.

The drawback—at least from the viewpoint of revolution—is that the working class is more interested in belonging to the affluent society than in destroying it, although it also hopes to modify certain aspects of it. At least this is the case in France. It is different in other countries?

MARCUSE You say that in France the working class is not yet integrated but that it would like to be. . . . In the United States it is integrated and it wants to be. This means that revolution postulates first of all the emergence of a new type of man with needs and aspirations that are qualitatively different from the aggressive and repressive needs and aspirations of established societies. It is true that the working class today shares in large measure the needs and aspirations of the dominant classes, and that without a break with the present content of needs, revolution is inconceivable.

So it will not happen tomorrow, it seems. It is easier to seize power than to change the needs of men. But what do you mean by aggressive needs?

MARCUSE For example, the need to continue the competitive struggle for existence—the need to buy a new car every two years, the need to buy a new television set, the need to watch television five or six hours a day. This is already a vital need for a very large share of the population, and it is an aggressive and repressive need.

Aggressive to watch television? But it would seem on the face of it to be a passive activity?

MARCUSE Are you familiar with the programs on American television? Nothing but shooting. And they always stimulate the consumption that subjects people to the capitalist mode of production.

There can be a different use of television.

MARCUSE Of course. All this is not the fault of television, the fault of the automobile, the fault of technology in general. It is the fault of the miserable use that is made of technological progress. Television could just as well be used to reeducate the population.

In what sense? To persuade people that they do not need cars or television sets or refrigerators or washing machines?

MARCUSE Yes, if this merchandise prevents the liberation of the serfs from their "voluntary servitude."

Wouldn't this create some problems for the people who work in the factories where they make cars, refrigerators, etc?

MARCUSE They will shut down for a week or two. Everyone will go to the country. And then the real work will begin, the work of abolishing poverty, the work of abolishing inequality, instead of the work of waste which is performed in the society of consumption. In the United States, for example, General Motors and Ford, instead of producing private cars, will produce cars for public transportation, so that public transportation can become human.

It will take a lot of television programs to persuade the working class to make a revolution that will reduce their wages, do away with their cars, and reduce their consumption. And in the meantime there is reason to fear that things may take a different turn, that all the people affected by the economic difficulties may potentially furnish a fascist mass. Doesn't fascism always come out of an economic crisis?

MARCUSE That's true. The revolutionary process always begins with and in an economic crisis. But this crisis would offer two possibilities: the so-called neo-fascist possibility, in which the masses turn toward a regime that is much more authoritarian and repressive, and the opposite possibility, that the masses may see an opportunity to construct a free society in which such crises would be avoidable. There are always two possibilities. One cannot, for fear of seeing the first materialize, stop hoping and working for the second through the education of the masses. And not only by words, but by actions.

For the present, aren't you afraid that these actions, especially when they are violent, will produce the opposite effect, and that the society will become even more repressive in order to defend itself?

MARCUSE Unfortunately, that is a very real possibility. But that is not sufficient reason to give up. On the contrary, we must increase the opposition, reinforce it. There will always be privileged classes which will oppose any fundamental change.

It is not the privileged classes which have manifested their opposition in France. It is the middle class and part of the working class. The privileged classes have been content to exploit the dissatisfaction.

MARCUSE Next you'll tell me that the revolutionary militants are responsible for the reaction. In Germany they are already saying that neo-Nazism is the result of student action.

In France, the result of the elections is incontestably the response of the majority of the country to the May movement, which frightened them.

MARCUSE Well, we must fight that fear!

Do you think that one can fight fear with violence?

MARCUSE Violence, I confess, is very dangerous for those who are the weakest. But first we should examine our terminology. People are always talking about violence, but they forget that there are different kinds of violence, with different functions. There is a violence of aggression and a violence of defense. There is a violence of police forces or armed forces or of the Ku Klux Klan, and there is a violence in the opposition to these aggressive manifestations of violence.

The students have said that they are opposing the violence of society, legal violence, institutionalized violence. Their violence is that of defense. They have said this, and I believe it is true.

Thanks to a kind of political linguistics, we never use the word violence to describe the actions of the police, we never use the word violence to describe the actions of the Special Forces in Vietnam. But the word is readily applied to the actions of students who defend themselves from the police, burn cars or chop down trees. This is a typical example of political linguistics, utilized as a weapon by the established society.

There has been a lot of fuss in France over the burned automobiles. But nobody gets at all excited about the enormous number of automobiles destroyed every day on the highways, not only in France but all over the world. The number of deaths in highway accidents in America is 50,000 per year.

And between 13,000 and 14,000 in France.

MARCUSE But that doesn't count. Whereas one burned automobile is terrible, it is the supreme crime against property. But the other crime doesn't count!

How do you explain this phenomenon?

MARCUSE Because the other crime has a function in production. It is profitable to society.

But people don't kill themselves to make a profit. How can you separate the society from the people who compose it? Society is not some special tribunal of people who meet in secret and say to each other: we are going to see to it that people kill themselves on the highways so that we can sell a lot of cars! Society is everyone, and everyone consents. You have a car yourself and you drive it . . . .

MARCUSE But there is a very good reason for all this. It is that this society, at the stage it is at, must mobilize our aggressive instincts to an exorbitant degree to counteract the frustrations imposed by the daily struggle for existence. The little man who works eight hours a day in the factory, who does an inhuman and stupefying work, on the weekend sits behind a huge machine much more powerful than himself, and there he can utilize all his antisocial aggressiveness. And this is absolutely necessary. If this aggressiveness were not sublimated in the speed and power of the automobile, it might be directed against the dominant powers.

This seems to be what is happening in spite of the weekend traffic!

MARCUSE No. It is only the students who are revolting and crying, "We are all German Jews!" that is, We are all oppressed.

And why do you think this diffuse oppression is more precisely experienced and formulated by the students? Why is it that the torch of revolution which seemed to be wavering, to say the least, in the industrial countries, has passed into their hands?

MARCUSE It is because they are not integrated. This is a very interesting point. In the United States, for example, there is a vast difference in behavior between the students and teachers in the social sciences and the humanities on the one hand and the natural sciences on the other. The majority comes from the first group. In France, I believe it is not the same. . . .

No, it isn't.

MARCUSE And in the study of these sciences they have learned a great deal. The nature of power, the existence of the forces behind the facts. They have also become very much aware of what goes on in societies. And this awareness is absolutely impossible for the vast majority of the population, which is, in some sense, inside the social machine. If you will, the students are playing the role of the professional members of the intelligentsia before the French Revolution.

You know that Tocqueville denounced the role of writers in the revolution of 1789, precisely because they were on the fringe of political life, lacking experience in public life, constructing arbitrary schemata.

MARCUSE Magnificent! And here is my answer to Tocqueville. I say that it is precisely *because* the students and intellectuals have no experience in what is today called politics that they are in the avant-garde. Because the political experience today is the experience of a game that is both faked and bloody.

Politics has always been a bloody game which kings and heads of state played among themselves. Do you mean that today it is faked because the people have the illusion of participating in this game?

MARCUSE Yes. Who really participates in politics? Who takes part in it? Any important decision is always made by a very small minority. Take the war in Vietnam. Who really participated in that decision? A dozen people, I would say. Afterwards the Government solicits and receives the support of the population. But in the case of Vietnam, even Congress did did not get a chance to learn the facts. No, the people do not participate in decisions. We do not participate. Only in secondary decisions.

But if the American Government stops the war tomorrow—they certainly will some day—won't it be as a result of public opinion? Of the revolt in public opinion?

MARCUSE Precisely. And who is responsible for this change in public opinion?

American television.

MARCUSE No, no! First there were the students. Opposition to the war began in the universities.

There is a slight contradiction in what you say, since you have written that this opposition is tolerated insofar as it has no power.

MARCUSE It may have the power to alter American policy, but not the system itself. The framework of society will remain the same.

And to try to destroy this society which is guilty of violence, you feel that violence is both legitimate and desirable. Does this mean that you think it impossible to evolve peacefully and within the democratic framework toward a nonrepressive, freer society?

MARCUSE The students have said it: a revolution is always just as violent as the violence it combats. I believe they are right.

But you still think it is possible, in spite of the judgment of Freud, to whom you refer frequently in "Eros and Civilization," to create a free society. Doesn't this betray a remarkable optimism?

MARCUSE I am optimistic, because I believe that never in the history of humanity have the resources necessary to create a free society existed to such a degree. I am pessimistic because I believe that the established societies—capitalist society in particular—are totally organized and mobilized against this possibility.

Perhaps because people are afraid of freedom?

MARCUSE Many people are afraid of freedom, certainly. They are conditioned to be afraid of it. They say to themselves: if people only had to work, say, five hours a week, what would they do with this freedom?

This is a condition which is not related to capitalism. The whole Judeo-Christian civilization is founded on work and is the product of work.

MARCUSE Yes and no. Look at feudal society. That was truly a Christian society and yet work was not a value in it; on the contrary.

Because there were slaves, villagers. It was very convenient for the feudal lords.

MARCUSE There were slaves, but the system of values was altogether different. And it was within this system that the culture was created. There is no such thing as bourgeois culture. Every genuine bourgeois culture is against the bourgeoisie.

In other words, we should return to the feudal system, but with machines taking the place of the slaves?

MARCUSE We must have machines in place of slaves, but without returning to the feudal system. It would be the end of work, and at the same time the end of the capitalist system. Marx saw this in that famous passage where he says that with technological progress and automation, man is separated from the instruments of production, is dissociated from material production, and acts simply as a free subject, experimenting with the material possibilities of the machines, etc. But this would also mean the end of an economy founded on exchange value. Because the product would no longer be worth anything as merchandise. And this is the specter that haunts the established society.

Do you regard work, effort, as a repressive value?

MARCUSE It all depends on its purpose. Effort is not repressive by itself. Effort in art, in every creative act, in love. . . .

Would you work if you were not obliged to do so?

MARCUSE Certainly. I work if I am not obliged to do so.

Do you consider yourself a free man?

MARCUSE Me? I believe that nobody is free in this society. Nobody.

Have you been psychoanalyzed?

MARCUSE Never. Do you think I need to be?

It's quite possible, but that's beside the point. What seems curious is that you have made such a thorough study of the work of Freud and his views on the inevitably repressive quality of all civilization without asking yourself about your own obstacles to the exercise of your personal freedom.

MARCUSE I have discussed Freud only on the level of theory, not on the level of therapy.

Don't you give European civilization any credit for being able to create its own values in reaction to American civilization while at the same time appropriating the positive element in that civilization, that is, the technical progress which you yourself have said is absolutely fundamental to the liberation of man?

MARCUSE It is almost impossible to speak of a European civilization today. Perhaps it is even impossible to speak of a Western civilization. I believe that Eastern civilization and Western civilization are assimilating each other at an ever increasing rate. And the European civilization of today has already absorbed much of American civilization. So it seems impossible to imagine a European civilization separated from the influence of America. Except, perhaps, in a few very isolated sectors of intellectual culture. Poetry, for example.

So you think the battle is lost. That we are Americans?

MARCUSE We mustn't say it is lost. It is possible to change, to utilize the possibilities of American civilization for the good of humanity. We must utilize everything that enables us to facilitate daily life, to make it more tolerable. . . . We could already, today, end air pollution, for example. The means exist.

What role do you envision for art in the free society of which you dream, since art is by definition denial, challenge?

MARCUSE I am not a prophet. In the affluent society, art is an interesting phenomenon. On the one hand, it rejects and accuses the established society; on the other hand, it is offered and sold on the market. There is not a single artistic style, however avant-garde, that does not sell. This means that the function of art is problematic, to say the least. There has been talk of the end of art, and there really is among the artists a feeling that art today has no function. There are museums, concerts, paintings in the homes of the rich, but art no longer has a function. So it wants to become an essential part of reality, to change reality.

Look at the graffiti, for example. For me, this is perhaps the most interesting aspect of the events of May, the coming together of Marx and André Breton. Imagination in power: that is truly revolutionary. It is new and revolutionary to try to translate into reality the most advanced ideas and values of the imagination. This proves that people have learned an important lesson: that truth is not only in rationality, but just as much and perhaps more in the imaginary.

The imaginary is above all the only realm where man's freedom has always been complete, where nothing has succeeded in curbing it. Dreams bear witness to this.

MARCUSE Yes. And this is why I believe that the student rebellion, whatever its immediate results, is a real turning point in the development of contemporary society.

Because the students are reintegrating the imaginary with reality?

MARCUSE Yes. There is a graffito which I like very much which goes, "Be realists, demand the impossible." That is magnificent. And another: "Watch out, ears have walls." That is realistic!

You have no desire to go back to Germany?

MARCUSE I don't think so. Only to give lectures. But I like the German students very much, they are terrific!

Have they succeeded any better than the others in making contact with the working class?

MARCUSE No. Their collaboration has been even more precarious.

Is it true that in the United States you received threats from the Ku Klux Klan?

MARCUSE They were signed Ku Klux Klan, but I don't think it was they who sent them.

Is it true that you moved out of your house following these threats?

MARCUSE Yes. Not in a panic, but I did leave. Frankly, I wasn't afraid. My students came and surrounded the house with their cars to protect me. . . . In one sense, they were right in thinking that there was a risk.

And do you feel that your life in the United States can continue, now that your notoriety has put you in the public eye?

MARCUSE I'm not sure, not at all sure. At the university there's no problem. But universities are always oases.

Do you think that the American university as it is set up now can be a model for the French university, for example?

MARCUSE One must distinguish among American universities. The large universities are always sanctuaries for free thought and a rather solid education. Take mine, for example, the University of California in San Diego. This is probably the most reactionary area in the United States—a large military base, a center of so-called defense industry, retired colonels and admirals. I have no difficulty with the university, the administration, or my colleagues. But I have a great deal of difficulty at the hands of the community, the good middle-class townspeople. No problems with the students. Relations between professors and students are, I think, much more informal than here and in Germany.

In this respect, you, know, there really is an egalitarian tradition in the United States. The sanctity of the professor does not exist. It is the American materialism that prevents it. The professor is a salaried man who has studied, who has learned certain things, and who teaches them; he is not at all a mythical personage identified with the Father, not at all. His political position depends upon his position in the university hierarchy. If you reach a permanent position it is practically impossible to fire you. My own situation is precarious, and I am very curious to find out whether I will be able to retain my position at the university.

What you say is very serious. If freedom of expression no longer exists in the United States, it will no longer exist anywhere . . . or perhaps in England?

MARCUSE Yes. England may turn out to be one of the last liberal countries. The democracy of the masses is not favorable to nonconformist
intellectuals. . . .

This is the crux of the matter. You have often been criticized for
wanting to establish a Platonic dictatorship of the elite. Is this correct?

MARCUSE There is a very interesting passage in John Stuart Mill, who
was not exactly an advocate of dictatorship. He says that in a civilized
society educated people must have political prerogatives to oppose
the emotions, attitudes and ideas of the uneducated masses.
   I have never said that it was necessary to establish a Platonic dictatorship because there is no philosopher who is capable of doing this.
But to be perfectly frank, I don't know which is worst: a dictatorship of politicians, managers and generals, or a dictatorship of intellectuals.
   Personally, if this is the choice, I would prefer the dictatorship of
the intellectuals, if there is no possibility of a genuine free democracy. Unfortunately this alternative does not exist at present.

The dictatorship of the intellectuals must first be established to educate
and reform the masses, after which, in a remote future, when people
have changed, democracy and freedom will reign. Is that it?

MARCUSE Not a true dictatorship, but a more important role for intellectuals, yes. I think that the resentment of the worker movement
against the intellectuals is one of the reasons why this movement has
stopped today.

The dictatorship of the intellectuals is rather disturbing to the extent
that intellectuals often become cruel because they are afraid of action.

MARCUSE Is that really so? There is only one example in history of a
cruel intellectual: Robespierre.

And Saint-Just.

MARCUSE We must compare the cruelty of Robespierre and Saint-Just
with the cruelty and the bureaucratized violence of an Eichmann. Or
even with the institutionalized violence of modern societies. Nazi
cruelty is cruelty as a technique of administration. The Nazis were not

intellectuals. With intellectuals, cruelty and violence are always much more immediate, shorter, less cruel. Robespierre did not use torture. Torture is not an essential aspect of the French Revolution.

You know intellectuals: they are not, or are only slightly, in touch with reality. Can you imagine a society functioning under their direct government? What effect would this have for on trains running on time, for example? Or on organizing production?

MARCUSE If you identify reality with established reality you are right. But intellectuals do not or should not identify reality with established reality. Given the imagination and rationality of true intellectuals, we can expect great things. In any case, the famous dictatorship of the intellectuals has never existed.

Perhaps because an intellectual is by his very nature an individualist. Lenin said this, too. What form of dictatorship do you prefer? One that operates directly as is the case in the Soviet Union, for example, or one that adopts the mask of democracy?

MARCUSE It is absolutely necessary not to isolate a given situation from its tendencies for development. There is a social and political repression which can foster human progress, which can lead toward a true democracy and a true freedom. And there is a repression which does the opposite. I have always said that I utterly reject Stalinian repression and the repressive policy of Communism, although I recognize that the Socialist base of these countries contains the possibility of development toward liberalization and ultimately toward a free society.

It is a question of not being too skeptical about the end . . . .

MARCUSE I am very skeptical about the end, in both cases.

Do you think that man can be free and at the same time believe in the existence of God?

MARCUSE The liberation of man depends neither on God nor on the nonexistence of God. It is not the idea of God which has been an obstacle to human liberation, but the use that has been made of the idea of God.

But why has this use been made of it?

MARCUSE From the beginning, religion has been allied with the ruling strata of society. In the case of Christianity, not from the very beginning, but still, rather early on.

In short, one must belong to the ruling strata of society! That is the sad conclusion that one could cynically draw from what you say. All the rest is adventure, more or less doomed to failure. Of course, one can prefer adventure, need adventure, and dream of being Guevara, in Paris or Berlin.

MARCUSE Guevara was not adventure; it was the alliance between adventure and revolutionary politics. If revolution does not contain an element of adventurism, it is worthless. All the rest is organization, labor unions, social democracy, the establishment. Adventure is always beyond. . . .

What you call adventurism, others call romanticism . . . .

MARCUSE Call it what you will. Adventure is transcendence of the given reality. Those who no longer wish to contain the revolution within the framework of the given reality. Call it what you will—adventurism, romanticism, imagination—it is an element necessary to all revolution.

No doubt. But it would seem that a concrete analysis of the situation in the countries in which one wants to make a revolution is also not an entirely negligible element. Provided, of course, that cne wants to bring it off, and not merely to dream. One more question. You denounce as a painful form of oppression and one from which we suffer the deprivation of solitude and silence inflicted on us by modern society. Isn't this a plague that is just as characteristic of collectivist societies?

MARCUSE First of all, we must eliminate the concept of collectivist societies. There are many modes of collectivization. There is a collectivism that is based on true human solidarity. There is a collectivism that is based on an authoritarian regime that is imposed on people. The destruction of autonomy, silence and solitude occurs in the so-called free societies as well as in the so-called collectivist societies. The decisive problem is to determine whether the limitations imposed on the individual are imposed in order to further the domination and indoctrination of the masses, or, on the contrary, in the interest of human progress.

It would be interesting to learn which noises are the progressive ones, if only so as to bear them with a smile. Sorry . . . we were being facetious.

MARCUSE So was I. There is no free society without silence, without the internal and external spaces of solitude in which individual freedom can develop. If there is neither private life, nor autonomy, nor silence, nor solitude in a Socialist society—well, it is very simple: it is not a Socialist society! Not yet.

Skulldiggery

This Digger phenomenon deserves a close examination by the peace movement—not that these jottings will necessarily make things clearer; clarity, alas, is not one of our goals. Confusion is mightier than the sword!

First it is important to distinguish between hippies and Diggers. Both are myths: that is, there is no definition, there is no organized conspiracy; both are in one sense a huge put-on. Hippies, however, are a myth created by media and as such they are forced to play certain media-oriented roles. They are media-manipulated. Diggers too are myth, but a grass-roots myth created from within. We have learned to manipulate media. Diggers are more politically oriented but at the same time bigger fuckoffs. Diggers are zenlike in that we have totally destroyed words and replaced them with "doing"—action becomes the only reality. Like Lao-tzu: *"The way to do is to be."* We cry, " no one understands us," while at the same time, winking out of the corner of our eye, recognizing that if the straight world understood all this Digger shit, it would render us impotent, because understanding is the first step to control and control is the secret to our extinction.

This reluctance to define ourselves gives us glorious freedom in which to fuck with the system. We become communist-racist-acid-headed freaks, holding flowers in one hand and bombs in the other. The Old Left says we work for the CIA. Ex-Marines stomp on us as Pinkos. Newport police jail us as smut peddlers. Newark cops arrest us as riot inciters. (These four events were all triggered by passing out free copies of the same poem.) So what the hell are we doing, you ask? We are dynamiting brain cells. We are putting people through changes. The key to the puzzle lies in theater. We are theater in the streets: total and committed. We aim to involve people and use (unlike other movements locked in ideology) any weapon (prop) we can find. The aim is not to earn the respect, admiration, and love of everybody—it's to get people to do, to participate, whether positively or negatively. All is relevant, only "the play's the thing."

. . . Stand on a street corner with 500 leaflets and explode. Give some to a sad-looking female. Tell guys that pass, "Hey, can you help her out? She can't do it by herself and her father's a communist cell leader and will beat her up if she doesn't pass them out." Recruit a person to read the leaflet aloud while all this distribution is going on. Run around tearing the leaflets, selling them, trading them. Rip one in half and give half to one person and half to another and tell them to make love. Do it all fast. Like slapstick movies. Make sure everyone has a good time. People love to laugh—it's a riot. Riot—that's an interesting word-game if you want to play it.

Don't be for or against. Riots—environmental and psychological—are Holy, so don't screw around with explanations. Theater also has some advantages. It is involving for those people that are ready for it while at the same time dismissed as nonthreatening by those that could potentially wreck the stage. It's dynamite. By allowing all: loving, cheating, anger, violence, stealing, trading, you become situation-oriented and as such become more effective. You believe in participatory democracy (especially when talking to a New Left audience), only you call it "everyone doing his thing." You let people decide, no strings attached. During the riots in Newark we smuggled in food, giving it to our underground soul brothers SNCC and NCUP (Newark Community Union Project).

"We brought a lot of canned goods, Tom, so the people can eat them or throw them at the cops."

Like many of the people in the riot, we dug the scene. Had a ball passing out food. Seven truckloads in all. And that's another key to the riddle: Dig what you're doing! Make war on paranoia. Don't be afraid. Don't get uptight. There's a war against property going on. I ask an old black woman in Newark, "What's going on?" and she tells me they stole her shoes and she's roaring with laughter. Spades and Diggers are one. Diggersareniggers. Both stand for the destruction of property. There are many ways to destroy property: to change is to destroy—give it away free. The free thing (another clue) is the most revolutionary thing in America today. Free dances, free food, free theater (constantly), free stores, free bus rides, free dope, free housing, and most important, free money. Theater will capture the attention of the country, the destruction of the monetary system will bring it to its knees. Really fuck with money. Burn it, smoke it to get high, trade with it, set up boxes of it in the streets marked "Free Money," panhandle it, steal it, throw it away.

Scene: *Washington Square Park. Actors: one very nicely dressed white liberal, one down-and-out-looking Digger. Audience: a large crowd of similar liberals, of various sexes. The title of the play: FOOD FOR NEWARK SPADES.*

DIG Sir, could you please spare a dollar for some food for Negroes in Newark?

LIB Gee, I'm sorry, I don't have much money on me.

DIG [*still pleading, hat in hand*] We're collecting food at Liberty House.*
Couldn't you buy a dollar's worth and bring it over?

LIB If I had a dollar, I certainly would.

DIG [*exploding*] I think you're full of shit. Here's ten dollars (pulling out real American money and shoving it in his face), go buy some food and bring it over to Liberty House.

LIB [*getting a bit annoyed but still wanting to be polite*] Oh no, I couldn't take money from you.

DIG [*throwing the money on the ground*] Well, there it is on the ground, do something with it.

The Digger walks away dropping clues to understanding the street drama: Liberty House, Black, Newark, Food, Free, Money.

The rumors begin to fly as rumors always do. Rumors have power. Like myths, people become involved in them, adding, subtracting, multiplying. Get them involved. Let them participate. If it's spelled out to the letter there is no room for participation. Nobody participates in ideology. Never lie—Diggers never lie. Once committed in a street drama, never turn back. Be prepared to die if it's necessary to gain your point.

!   !   !   !   !   !   !   !   !

Don't rely on words. Words are the absolute in horseshit. Rely on doing—go all the way every time. Move fast. If you spend too long on one play, it becomes boring to you and the audience. When they get bored, they are turned off. They are not receiving information. Get their attention, leave a few clues and vanish. Change your costume, use the props around you. Each morning begin naked. Destroy your name, be-

* Liberty House is what first brought me to New York. It was set up in the West Village to serve as a retail outlet for crafts made in cooperatives in Mississippi. It was a branch of the SNCC operations; some of us under the leadership of Jesse Morris formed the Poor People's Corporation and quickly trained poor blacks in craft skills and business management. We were told by all sorts of fancy economic experts that it was impossible to train these people, never mind giving them control of the businesses. The experts might be interested in knowing that the program not only has survived three years but has expanded quite successfully without help from the government and in an extremely hostile environment (Mississippi). This type of program is next best to FREE and we are developing a similar one for the Lower East Side. If readers want to order catalogues of the products, they should write to Liberty House, 313 West Pascagoula Street, Jackson, Miss.

come unlisted, go underground. Find brothers. Soul brothers. Black people, Puerto Ricans, Dropouts, Bowery Bums. Find out where they're at. Don't fuck with their thing. P.R.s dig manhood, don't play sissy. Black people dig pot, don't give them acid. Dropouts dig flowers, don't give them I. F. Stone weeklies. Bowery bums dig wine, don't give them Bibles. Become aware of the most effective props. On the Lower East Side pot is an effective prop, it is the least common denominator. It makes us all outlaws, brothers, niggers. Smoke it in public. It really has an effect on P.R.s, really challenges their concept of courage.

"Hey man, you're brave enough to kill someone, and not brave enough to smoke pot in the park!"

That kind of thing is a good deal more effective than sermons on the holiness of passive resistance. Use non-verbal props and media. Music is another denominator. Conga-Rock, get together. The Diggers and Pee Wee's gang (largest P.R. gang on New York's Lower East Side) threw a large dance at the Cheetah, a discotheque, on August 15. *Conga-Rock. Something for everybody. Do your thing. Don't give speeches. Don't have meetings. Don't have panel shows. They are all dead. Drama is anything you can get away with.* Remember that last peace demonstration? Do you recall the speeches of the Bread and Puppet Theater and Stokely yelling "Hell no, we won't go!" That was drama, not explanation. The point is nobody gives a shit anymore about troop strength, escalation, crying over napalm. A peace rally speech to me is like reading the *National Guardian* which is like watching the TV reports on Highway Fatalities which is like praying for riots to end which is like BULLSHIT! Herbert Marcuse says flower children have the answer. He smoked hashish at the big world happening in London in early August. Pray tell, what is a good Marxist to do?

Accept contradictions, that's what life is all about. Have a good time. Scrawled on the wall of the American pavilion at Expo '67 is our slogan in bright Day-glo: "It is the duty of all revolutionists to make love." Do weird things. Silly-putty sabotage and monkey warfare. John Roche, who is now intellectual-in-residence fink at the White House, once said that if Hitler had been captured in 1937, brought to Trafalgar Square, and had his pants pulled down, he could never have risen to power. Every time he tried one of those spectacular speeches the people would have just laughed at him because the image of "Mein Führer" with his pants down around his ankles would have been too much.

Think about it.

The Humanities and Inhumanities

American higher education, like any institution, lives by myths. Still feeling theatened by the seriousness of purpose shown by students during last spring's campus rebellions, the educator's myth of the moment informs us of both the practicality and the transcendent beauty of a liberal (or humanistic) education. The same noble speech is being (or has recently been) addressed to thousands of freshmen: whether at West Point, Swarthmore, the Texas College of Mines, M.I.T. or the University of Michigan hardly seems to matter. It informs them of the primacy of a liberal—rather than a specialized, or technical—education. The humanities, the speech continues, release us from irrationally held prejudices; they open our minds; they teach us to be generalists instead of specialists. In short, a liberal education transforms the narrow career-oriented youth into a free, though of course responsible, man or woman of culture.

The underlying assumption of the speech is that four years of exposure to a balanced curriculum will produce young men and women who are objective, rational, yet not without feeling; who being free of ideological blinders will be blessed with a sense of their own autonomy. Having been made intellectually independent by their study of Homer, the Renaissance, atomic particles, Wordsworth, brain waves, Pop art and total environments, they are capable of discovering the relevant past and applying it to the problems of the moment. They are prisoners neither of history nor of the imperatives of current urgencies. Consequently they are eminently capable of dealing with the insistent pressures of change. Having absorbed the best civilization has to offer, they will be able to retain their humanity though practically engulfed by inhuman events. Briefly put, they will be liberal. Certainly, they will not resort to the barbarism of riots.

I suppose there is a grain of truth at the center of this hollow rhetoric. Certainly the motives which generate such words are often decent enough. Yet I suspect that the hearts of most academics attending freshman orientation sink as they hear the noble sentiments being piled on. There is a moment when one expects the dean of freshmen either to burst into tears, to choke on his own words, or perhaps to double up with laughter. He knows that his colleagues know his words are fake; and I suggest that most of the students see us all—teachers, deans, administrators—for the frauds we are. Is it not time we forgot

Louis Kampf, "The Humanities and Inhumanities." Copyright © 1968 by *The Nation* (September 30, 1968). Reprinted by permission of *The Nation*.

about the nobility of the humanities and asked what their real function is, what social purposes they, in fact, serve?

Hardly a day passes without some representative of the industrial elite letting us know that America's corporate enterprises, not to speak of its government agencies, need managers who are not only steeped in the techniques of operations research but who are equally adept at quoting John Donne or T. S. Eliot. At M.I.T., the Sloan Fellows in Industrial Management are expected to devote a fairly substantial amount of their time to the study of literature. The exposure to literature, we are to assume, makes them better—indeed, more enlightened— managers. But who are these managers? What is their task?

> No one knows who will live in this cage in the future, or whether at the end of this tremendous development entirely new prophets will arise, or there will be a great rebirth of old ideas and ideals, or, if neither, mechanized petrification, embellished with a sort of convulsive self-importance. For the last stage of this cultural development, it might well be truly said: "Specialists without spirit, sensualists without hearts; this nullity imagines that it has attained a level of civilization never before achieved."

The melancholy words are Max Weber's. The occupants of his cage are the functionaries of the bureaucracy bequeathed us by the Protestant ethic and the spirit of capitalism. The culture he feared was one in which rationalization of the profit motive, rather than the simple urge to earn money, becomes its own end, and efficiency is pursued with religious—yet mechanical—zeal. To further such ends, traditional education is replaced by training programs for technicians and efficiency experts. M.I.T., the Harvard Business School, and their brothers and sisters were fathered by the needs of industrial capitalism.

But today such an analysis may seem naive, even simple-minded. We know that our business schools give courses in social responsibility; moreover, our industrial managers conduct seminars on the needs of the Third World and the family structure of the poor. And who would doubt that this derives from anything but the best of motives? But before we congratulate ourselves on our good luck, we might take a closer look at modern capitalism. Clearly we have moved beyond that stage of rationalization which merely involves problems in engineering. Moreover, the complexities of modern finance—the mother of industrial development—involve a subtlety of human manipulation undreamed of by Weber's contemporaries. And as the complexity insinuates itself into all areas of the social system, we reach a point where our corporations and financial institutions effectively control most public—as well as private—institutions. As Kenneth Galbraith has pointed out, in this situation the main function of the American Government is not to promote the public sector but to keep the social order stable enough for business to do its business. Its second large task is to see that America's educational institutions provide the corporate machine with enough functionaries to keep it oiled.

The function of higher education, then, is to turn out those industrial cadres, rocket engineers, researchers, planners, personnel managers and development experts needed by the economy. But not only this; our colleges and universities have also been charged with the task of shaping the more ordinary functionaries: the kind who were once not subject to a four-year grind through the educational mill. Looked at in terms of real industrial need these four years of classes, laboratories, football games, hours in the library and bull sessions seem entirely superfluous. But that is not the point. For beyond immediate mechanical requirements there are the larger social imperatives. Social order must be maintained, and the whole fabric of traditions which gives a society its continuity must be kept intact. If this proves to be impossible, then at least appearances must be kept up; patches covering up the rents must be made invisible. As ordinary mechanical tasks multiply, as more of the labor force takes on white-collar jobs and finds itself pushed into the middle class, the process of acculturation becomes increasingly difficult. Formerly, those few who climbed the social ladder learned their manners—were educated to the proper social style—by their gradual exposure to the more or less culturally advanced. This was a slow and haphazard process; many fell by the wayside and never attained the style of life appropriate to their economic station. If the production of consumer goods is to expand, the goods must be consumed. To accomplish this, the new industrial cadres must be prepared for an "enriched"—that is, a cultured—style of life. Above all, the new class must never be allowed to feel that it constitutes a new industrial proletariat.

Let me return to Weber's metaphor: the animals in the bureaucratic cage must be civilized. Yet having consciousness, the task of civilizing tends to go beyond the development of conditioned reflexes. It must concern itself with the inescapable fact of human creativity and with the reality of man's historical memory. Both are, after all, basic components of what we call culture; they are integral to man as a species. The ordinary functionary, then, must be convinced that the rationalized task he performs—his ordinary, and inexplicable, job of work—is somehow connected to traditional culture—to all those monuments, both artistic and social, which represent our historical aspirations. What had formerly been the property of an elite now also belongs to the bureaucrat; for he, after all, has become a member of that elite. Or so he thinks. In any case, he knows he has his place in the traditions of the social system—and it is good. Consequently, there is no point in directing the anger of one's frustrations, of one's secret dissatisfactions, at the system itself, for one would be turning them against oneself—against that historic culture one has attained.

And therefore the future home economist, insurance salesman, even department store floorwalker must be made to believe that these tasks are—however mysteriously—connected to Homer, the Athenians, the Judeo-Christian tradition, and the rest of our cultural baggage. The connections may not be clear, but we feel a terrible guilt if we do not perceive them.

To perform this job of acculturation requires an expanding system of colleges and universities; to run them, a force of educational functionaries whose size seems to have no limit. The opportunities for administrators, professors, research executives, even writers, painters and composers are getting better every day. If nothing else, our colleges provide a marvelous haven for Cabinet members, mayors, Presidential advisers and generals, who are temporarily out of work. They, like their fellow humanities professors, are also students of the liberal arts. But, once more, this job of training and acculturation must proceed without upsetting our traditional notion of the university's function. The educational cadres must believe that they perform the humane tasks of scholarship. So they all write articles, and monographs, and books, and reviews of books and bibliographies of these reviews. At the highest level, in our important graduate schools, they train people like themselves to train people like themselves, to train people like themselves, to train people like themselves. . . .

Far from teaching young people to become aware of their capacities, a liberal education allows them—worse, forces them—to ignore themselves. As for the nagging reality of a world desperately in need of social change, the ordinary liberal education pretends either that the need does not exist, or that it can be taken care of painlessly, as a matter of ordinary academic routine. One thing is certain: change must do no violence to the traditional humanistic values embedded in the curriculum. These foundations of a liberal education are sacred. Thus the master task of the humanities becomes one of accommodating students to the social dislocations of industrial society by hiding their painful apprenticeship—their rite of admission to an appropriate office— behind the mask of a traditional culture. Confronted by the radical transformation of roles played by the educated, the liberal arts must assure us that the *status quo* is, after all, being maintained.

An odd development. Matthew Arnold once taught us that the object of studying the best that had been thought or said is to criticize our present mode of life, to make us see the object as it really is. Instead the study of our classics seems to provide us with ideological blinders. It mystifies—to use R. D. Laing's phrase—the very basis of our experience: our way of seeing, feeling, knowing. The humanities have been the educational system's unwitting collaborators in destroying our experience—that is, our humanity. For by blinding us to social mechanisms they have made us unconscious; they have made us the victims of a myth; they have kept us from seeing things as they really are. And, to quote Laing again. "If our experience is destroyed, our behavior will be destructive." And so it is. It is so because our culture has taught us to disguise competitive aggression as social benevolence, oppression as freedom, hate as love. These marvelous transformations have been effected not only by those who control our most powerful institutions but by our educators—our experts in acculturation. The lesson concerning the relationship of culture to aggression taught us by *Civilization and Its Discontents* seems not to have sunk in. Or perhaps it has sunk in all too well. As Freud observed, we desperately stand in need of our defense mechanisms.

But perhaps we are running out of defense mechanisms. Perhaps the contradictions liberal education creates for students are beginning to turn on us; perhaps the young will make us ask those questions we have so long refused to ask.

How so? The meaning of life is in action—whether the acts be physical or mental. Fulfilled action frees us; it makes us independent. When we can relate our thoughts, our yearnings, to activity; when our vague projections issue in conscious work—then we may rightly feel that we have our lives under a measure of control. Formerly the purpose of a traditional liberal education had been to train a cultured— and humane—elite. The act of ruling, of governing and giving guidance, was the activity which gave life its meaning; it fulfilled the objectives of the education. Clearly we still have the same goals in mind for the liberal arts today. Supposedly they teach us to be creative and to act humanely. And are these not the standards we set for our elite?

But consciousness has made a fool of our objectives; for the young—or at least for some of them—the ideological fog has been cleared by the very contradictions of their education.

Precisely because we have been liberal in our education, our best students have come to understand that our deepest intellectual concerns—their very enthusiasms, their most intense involvements—cannot issue in any sort of activity which makes a claim to any social relevance beyond acculturation. And if there be no such social relevance, how can activity be fulfilling? Thus there is an almost inevitable split between thought and action. Thought may be free, but activity is controlled; stated educational objectives may be ethical, but actions immoral. The thoughts and feelings engendered by liberal education—the cultural enrichment we offer the young—become ideological masks for the politics of those who rule.

And the best of our students know this. They know that their studies are divorced from meaningful activity. They know that their courses are not intended to further their self-development; rather they become a part of the students' property, their capital. Their knowledge—technical or humanistic—makes them a product. As the material and cultural embodiments of this knowledge grow—and recall, these embodiments are products of man's self-formation, actualizations of his ideas—our practical activities, in a most ironic fashion, become ever more faintly related to our thoughts and feelings; their connection to the meaningful development of ideas and passions becomes more and more tenuous. Consciousness has once more played us for the destructive fools we are. For the object of a liberal education, we tell ourselves, is the fulfillment of individual capacities, of ideas and passions. Through such fulfillment, we assume, men can become whole, sane, peaceful and free—that is, humane.

But the split we have created in the student's life has allowed him to see his education for what it is. He knows that his studies—especially those in the humanities, he is informed by our managers—make him a more valuable piece of private property. He knows that his labor in the classroom transforms him into an object; that he makes of himself a product.

Since it is the student himself who becomes the product of his own labor, he is in tension with himself; he is split. He sells those treasures which, we have taught him, best represent his humanity—that is, his civilization, his culture, his liberal education. And so he is at war with his own being, for the battle over this piece of private property is a battle over himself. For the best of our students the study of the humanities creates a more intense consciousness of this situation. Indeed, self-knowledge creates a condition which puts that very education—the act of preparing oneself for one's role—beyond endurance. What truly liberally educated human being can bear to be a commodity with consciousness?

Such are the ends of a liberal education—or at least one of the unintended ends. In their attempt to use the traditional liberal arts to gain social consent, our managers have created a situation where students must risk their sanity in order to enact the lessons of their education; or they must turn into commodities, accommodating themselves—consciously or otherwise—to the lie on which their education is based.

In seeking alternatives, the educator's first impulse is to suggest curricular reform; jiggle the mechanism a bit, make a great-books course out of freshman composition, even have them reading Norman Mailer and Mao Tse-tung. Such reforms, we assume, will effect a fundamental change in the lives of our students. I doubt it. Changes in the curriculum—though often valuable and necessary—may have the ultimate effect of making the acculturating mechanisms more efficient. They may make the beast more cultured, but will not change its objectives. To break out of Weber's cage, to face the imperatives of fundamental change without dogma—if these are the conditions to which we hope our students will aspire, we shall need a most fundamental critique of the very social basis and function of higher education. Much academic political science will serve as an example. Aside from its more gross involvements with the CIA, the field's major object is to put government *policy*—unlike the more trivial matter of its *execution*—beyond criticism; to harden ideologies like the "national interest" into unassailable dogmas. Political science has done its job well, for it has succeeded in putting real political inquiry beyond the pale of academic respectability. This situation will not be changed by curricular reforms alone. If students are once more to ask meaningful questions about the state, and if they are to meet these questions with programs they can translate into action, the very *ends* we set for political science will have to be changed.

The objective of a liberal education, it seems to me, should be the harmonious reconciliation of philosophy (that is, our ways of thinking), action and nature (the world; what there is). This condition is possible only when we do not feel estranged from the products of our thoughts and actions, when we do not feel separated from the nature we have helped to create. Unhappily, industrial capitalism is rooted in these divisions. In our divided state philosophy (our principles of education) must not be allowed to become an integral expression of culture; it must not serve to rationalize the divisions induced by the industrial system. It can remain philosophy, rather than ideology, only as it is *critical*. And so for the humanities or liberal arts.

How is this criticism to be expressed? Most often, I suspect, in acts which appear irrational, if not deranged. On October 16, 1967, while watching nearly 300 students turning in their draft cards at Arlington Street Church in Boston, I understood—and was saddened by that understanding—that these young men were involved in a desperate act of rejecting a civilization. The moral outrage required for this heroic act is disfiguring; it warps one's sense of reality; it too makes one's view of the world partial. Yet this seemingly mad act of rejecting an illegitimate and immoral authority was really an attempt to relate thought to action; to assert that the products of one's actions are one's own; that freedom—or at least the struggle for it—is a human necessity. Saying "Hell, no, we won't go!" is one way for the student to expose the lie of his education. Exploiting the class privilege of one's college deferment is, after all, a moral fraud—a fraud to which higher education not only closes its eyes but which it encourages. Ironically, in their act of criticism, in their act of rejection in willfully separating themselves from society these draft resisters tried to assert their wholeness.

Yet what of the madness of this act? Recent studies of schizophrenics have shown that insanity may provide the morally sensitive with the only means of staying alive in a disordered world. The ordering principle imposed by insanity on destructive chaos keeps one from suicide. This is one way of relating thought to action; or, more simply, to *act*— rather than turning inward self-destructively. Yet there is an alternative to pathology. And the students who take their education seriously and resist the draft have pointed to that alternative. Our ordering principle as educators must be criticism or, going further, counteraction, resistance. This may not sound much like the detachment, the wholeness, we associate with the humanities. Indeed, we know criticism tends to induce disorder and most of its serious practitioners often act like uncivilized madmen. But consider that the only real choice may be whether to be mad (though civilized) on society's terms, or on one's own.

If resistance be madness, it is at least human madness, not the rationalized madness, not the rationalized lunacy of an abstract process.

If our students are to retain—or perhaps discover—their humanity, they will have to oppose the system of acculturation and spiritual servitude which our colleges encourage. And opposition to abstractions constantly tempts one into irrational confrontations; the bars of the cage are beyond rationality.

Surely, the truly humanistic educator must strive to create a world which does not demand of our students acts of madness as the price for spiritual wholeness. Our primary need then is not for a liberal education but for one which is actively committed to an end. If we are to break out of the empty rhetoric of liberal educational reform, scholarship may need to become allied with activism.

Activism on what front? Not on the campus alone. For one thing, the university is not the place where students and their teachers are most likely to liberate themselves from the shackles of ideology. For higher education's institutional nature has shaped it into an instrument of perpetuation for our most cherished—that is, humanistic—ideologies: the university and most of its faculty has a vested interest to protect. And if we are to take Richard Hofstadter's commencement address at Columbia as an index, that vested interest will be defended against campus activists in the name of free scholarly inquiry. For it is the student strikers, Professor Hofstadter would have us believe, who are the chief threat to the values of humane scholarship.

Those scholars concerned with liberating themselves from such academic dogma and effecting fundamental change in the role played by the liberal arts, might have to begin by performing principal groupings (such as the New University Conference) which create alliances both within and outside the university. These groupings will have to gain a sense of identity by taking clear, strong and public stances on the most important moral issues which confront our students: Vietnam, the draft, race, poverty, the nature of higher education, the uses of scholarship. Or to go deeper: American imperialism, war itself, the function of private property, sex and aggression. What is more, analyses should be complemented by meaningful political action. Such activity may, in some cases, involve divisions within the faculty. But this surely must be the first step if our philosophy is to relate to our acts. Some things cannot—and must not—be smoothed over. Surely one thing our students must learn is to take their thoughts seriously.

The special urgency and occasional violence of the students' demands for university reform derive, I think, from an intuition that the liberal arts, rather than being the property of educational establishments, should embody our civilization's highest achievements. This intuition makes the integration of the liberal arts into the students' daily lives a condition toward which they (and we) desperately yearn. Yet if we are to see the object as it is, in Matthew Arnold's sense, we must look at the liberal arts within their social context. If liberal education is to perform its proper function—to help the students see things as they are, to face them humanely and freely—then that education must be placed within an appropriate social context. Creating this context becomes, consequently, the foremost task for the liberal arts.

This involves a transformation of consciousness, a transformation which must be radical—that is, it must take hold at the root. To reach this goal, the economic and social conditions which enslave our students must also be radically transformed. Is this possible inside our educational institutions? Within the imperatives of our social system? I doubt it. Yet our society is being shaken; it changes radically in spite of ourselves, and in spite of our universities. Though we have no clear answers or directives for action, we must make the attempt. For only in the attempt will our analyses unfold, our activity become consciously meaningful.

The Student Rebellion

The New University Conference is a national membership organization of radical faculty, graduate students, independent intellectuals, and university employees. Many of us were but recently a part of the student movement; most of us have been active in the peace and civil-rights movements. We believe it is important at this time to state our position on the controversies in our universities, on the student movement, and on the responses by the authorities to that movement. We do so with the hope that the substantive issues raised by the student movement will be honestly confronted and debated, and that the thrust toward repression of that movement will be blunted and turned back.

We support the new student movement, for we believe it is the main hope of creating a movement for social change in America and within the universities. The society in which the student movement is growing is in need of radical change; it is in the context of this need that we must understand the controversies now raging about the American university.

This country is well into a crisis resulting from the failure of "liberal" and "moderate" foreign and domestic policies. Twenty years of Cold War, the Korean War, and the current genocidal war in Vietnam finds us on the brink of further wars throughout the Third World. America has become the most dangerous nation in the international community. At home the welfare state has failed to provide a decent life for the black and white poor. Lifetimes of struggle seem to have brought black people no closer to liberation and equality. Dominated by large corporations, and increasingly subordinating and sacrificing human needs to their profit requirements, our allegedly affluent society has been unable to provide working people with the social conditions for material security, tranquility, or personal meaning which are the legitimate aspirations of all men. Barbarities abroad and failure at home have given rise to an increasingly bold racism and a rightist political movement spouting chauvinism and the demand for law and order. No established political grouping is now setting forth any program which could deal with these problems.

In this context, it cannot be surprising that many young people—especially those who have taken democratic ideals most seriously—are

New University Conference, Statement on Student Rebellion. Reprinted by permission of the New University Conference.

in a revolutionary mood. Nor should it be surprising that there is special bitterness directed at those institutions and members of preceding generations who have most aggressively proclaimed their liberalism, their humaneness, their commitment to truth and social progress. For behind these claims, we have seen in our time a long series of betrayals, then political paralysis, impotence, and childishness.

The student movement arose in conjunction with the civil-rights and anti-war movements. It was a response to the racism, imperialism, lack of meaningful democratic controls and procedures, psychological and moral squalor, and irrationality which characterize our society. These characteristics are reflected in our universities and colleges. The student movement has been growing in size and intensity during the past eight years and has carried a spirit of revolt into hundreds of universities and colleges, and, recently, high schools. This spirit is clearly manifested in the scores of direct-action demonstrations which have been occurring in recent years, as well as in the less-dramatic but continuing ferment which has emerged at virtually every college and university.

The student movement includes:

- the struggle by humanist and radical white youth to end the complicity of the university with war and imperialism, with racism and domestic suppression of black and other minorities, with bureaucratic values and corporate interests;
- the struggle by black students for full cultural recognition and autonomy on white campuses, for an end to paternalistic control at black colleges, and for full community control at community colleges;
- the struggle by large groups of students for full citizenship in the university as a just end in itself, for recognition of their adult status, and for a curriculum which is useful to their search for personal meaning and social relevance rather than one which is oriented toward the needs of the corporation and the state for trained manpower.

This movement, and its allies—among whom we include ourselves—has made some advances. On some campuses, black students have won increased respect and voice. On some campuses, students have won elemental rights of free speech and press and assembly previously denied them. Rules governing social life and extracurricular activity have been liberalized, students have achieved some voice in setting university policies, there have been a few efforts to reduce university involvement with military institutions.

Moreover, the student revolt has seriously shaken the national political structure, and led some politicians to gear their rhetoric and platforms to winning the support of "youth."

But reform and respect have not been the dominant response to the student revolt. Increasingly students have found that, as their demands have probed to the heart of the authority structure of the universities, they have been met by a solidifying wall of resistance from university officials. And on many campuses even elemental demands for change have been frustrated by hostile or indifferent faculty and administrators. In the absence of citizenship rights, students have discovered that often the only actions that bring results are those involving the disruption of the routine processes of the institution—the strike, the sit-in, the seizure of buildings.

Such challenges to the authority of university managers have resulted in an increased effort to repress students: many universities have adopted rules restricting the right of students to engage in protest; hundreds of student activists have been suspended, expelled, or beaten and jailed by police with the active support of university officials; others have been threatened with loss of government financial support; many faculty members who have participated in campus protests have lost their positions.

In the coming period, as student unrest continues, we may expect new efforts to repress the movement. The banning of organizations, the screening of new students, the administration of institutional loyalty oaths as a condition of admission or employment are some of the measures now proposed in various quarters.

To justify the emerging repression, an ideological rationale is being constructed. Administrators and faculty increasingly argue that, while some student protesters may be "sincere" or "idealistic," there is also on the campus a hard core of "extremists" or "nihilists" who are "bent on destroying the university" through the use of "violence." The identity of such "nihilists" is often left vague, though Students for a Democratic Society (SDS), whose chapters have often been catalysts for campus confrontations, is increasingly being named as their organizational embodiment. The purpose of differentiating SDS and other radical groups from the mass of politically active students is, quite clearly, to lay the groundwork for the exclusion of SDS from the campus, and to fire the most militant faculty supporters.

We in the New University Conference share the basic goals and commitments of the student movement. We share with student activists the aim of constructing a grass-roots movement in this country that can have a real effect in stopping American efforts to dominate other peoples, that can win a fundamental reordering of priorities in this country so that genuine equality can become a realistic hope, that can disrupt the drift toward technologically-based authoritarianism and a garrison state, that can find new modes of political and social organization which will permit our vast resources to be shared for the benefit of all men and provide the basis for personal liberation.

We have hoped that the university could be a center of work toward these ends. That hope, however, seems increasingly illusory. We shall all come to realize that through the veil of "official neutrality" and protestations of innocence, the universities—including the "great centers of learning"—are partners with the most pernicious forces in our society.

Our experience at the university has taught us that higher education exists primarily to serve the white middle class, and only marginally to serve minority groups and working-class youth. Though covering itself with the cloak of democratic rhetoric, the university rejects democratic governance within its community in both theory and practice. The trend toward the fragmented and impersonal multiversity, existing on the largesse of the corporations and the permanent war economy, is not merely a product of social complexity. Rather, it is the institution-alization of the narrow interests of the most privileged minority of the faculty and administrators. These men serve their own interests and careers by gaining control of huge budgets, which sometimes turn them into corporate servants at yet another branch office, sometimes make their laboratories government outposts, and too often leave the whole institution financially dependent on military expenditures. With boards of trustees composed of the wealthy elite, whose interests are so often identified with the university's, or with some abstract rationale for more living space, urban universities disrupt and "develop" their surrounding communities quite without regard for the wishes of, or the human cost to, the residents of these neighborhoods.

Even if we were to abdicate all social and citizen responsibilities, and were to restrict our view of the university to the situation we are in as teachers and students, we would be forced to observe that "liberal education" has become a sham. College education has taken on the function of accrediting young men and women for personally stifling jobs which maintain the old order. This education does not even provide authentic skills or crafts—merely the styles which admit one to the great bureaucracies. University attendance today is, for most young people, a four-year socialization process which is intended to teach obedience and moderation, and a trained incapacity for creativity.

When students do not find the curriculum particularly helpful in their efforts to become fulfilled persons, or serious citizens, or engaged intellectuals, what, after all, is that last saving grace of the university?

These issues are now the subject of widespread debate on the American campus. The student movement deserves full credit for raising them, and for fundamentally challenging the university's claim to be a "neutral," "pluralist," and independent institution. In short, the activist students, through their dramatic action, and also their less-well-known but valuable research and analysis, have identified the university as an agency of established class and political interests. Our own experience tells us this analysis is fundamentally correct.

Thus, charges of nihilism, of spiteful destructiveness, of blind violence, made against the student movement divert attention from the substantive issues which students have raised. These charges arise from the fact that campus radicals are challenging power and privilege, are raising fundamental questions about authority, about the official pretensions of those who run the university, and about the legitimacy of the political system served by the university.

We share with the radical students a profound skepticism that the universities can be fundamentally reorganized prior to a transformation of the larger society. But we have seen the growth of new movements on college campuses in spite of institutional hostility. Some of us believe that it is in the power of radicals and other humanists in the university to create and hold space within it for the development of democratic values and radical social criticism, and for resistance to militarism and racism. The university may serve the worst interests and exemplify many of the most stultifying trends in our society; yet, because it is intrinsically vulnerable to critical thought, an opposition develops within it which embodies new vision and new hope for the society. Even those of us who are skeptical about the possibilities of achieving genuine structural reform believe that our movement can play a crucial role in the broader movements to transform America.

Taking these beliefs seriously requires that we forge new roles for ourselves, not as mediators between administrators and students, but as co-belligerents with all that that implies for our own security. Too often faculty members and others of good will seek to mediate campus conflicts in order to "save" the institution or prevent "busts" and severe "backlash." In general these attempts are pathetic in their feebleness, and prove to students once again that they have no allies.

Because we believe the universities are key institutions for shaping the future of our society, and because we believe that the struggle over the purposes of the university is one we are obliged to participate in, we urge our colleagues to organize for political struggle. We in the NUC believe that the main lines of that struggle should be based on the following principles, and we urge our colleagues who share our concerns to support and act on them:

1. Support the right of protest of all members of the university.

The defense of students' right of protest, including the right to disrupt institutional processes, is in all of our interests, not only theirs. When students demand "amnesty" for violating university rules and occupying university facilities, they are challenging the legitimacy of an authority structure from which they are excluded, denying its right to punish them, and asserting their right to participate directly in university government.

In certain respects, these students' claims are similar to those made by workers on strike—and in our society it is now unthinkable that workers would be held to have been justly dismissed or police called to put down industrial strikes. Of course, student demands go beyond orthodox union demands, for they justly call for basic change in the structure of authority. Ultimately, the power to disrupt is the only dependable weapon of the powerless in their defense of democratic values in this society. We dispute the right of university authorities to identify their interests with those of the university as a whole; therefore we deny the legitimacy of their use of coercive power to call the cops, fire faculty, and suspend students.

2. Support full citizenship for students in the government of the university.

Students, like any other group of citizens, should have full control over policies and rules governing their social lives, political expression, and extracurricular activity. The processes of education—including the formulation of curricula, the structure and techniques for learning, and policies concerning personnel—should be co-determined by students and faculty on the basis of equality. We believe that this is not only more democratic, but will provide a better environment for learning as well. And we hold that all university officials should be democratically responsible to faculty and students in every decision, including those (such as portfolio investment policies) which are now seen as trustees' prerogatives. Faculty radicals have a crucial role to play in working to achieve democratization of the campus and the enfranchisement of students.

3. Oppose military and corporate intrusion on the campus.

One sign of the growth of the military-industrial complex has been the control of an expanding fraction of the labor of social and natural scientists. The penetration of the universities by the military and its adjuncts has been central to this development. We oppose this penetration, not only because it is destructive to the university as an agency of truth, criticism, and free exchange, but even more importantly because it makes possible the more effective oppression of whole peoples and nations and repression of struggles for liberation. We call for the withdrawal of the university from the war against the poor and colored, abroad and at home, and an evacuation of our universities by the various military and paramilitary agencies and their functionaries. We call for the end of campus research which uses the techniques of science for espionage or the subversion and destruction of popular movements, and for the end of classified or military mission-oriented research.

The criteria determining legitimacy or illegitimacy of any project is not, of course, the funding agency, although grants from certain sponsors are inevitably suspect, but its substantive character and probable application of the results. While one cannot hold a researcher responsible for remote, exotic, and accidental applications of his work, research activity which has patent and unmistakable military or paramilitary applications must not be legitimized by universities.

We do not believe that anyone has a "right" to utilize university resources for racist, military, or imperialist activities. The notion that "academic freedom" excuses or permits such activity or research is a bizarre and disingenuous misuse of the doctrine.

As opponents of American militarism we support political movements against the power of the military-industrial complex. As educators and students as well, we will do what we can to combat their influence and their right to exist at our universities.

In the meantime we note, with some irony, that if the university's protestations of "pluralism" and "neutrality" had any basis in fact, there would be the same massive funding for aiding insurgents in the society, for producing reports for the powerless about the behavior of the powerful, as there is now for research on the powerless and insurgent to facilitate their control.

4. Oppose the class biases of the university.

We do not believe that in a society like this a genuinely egalitarian institution can be created out of the present university. But the effort to expose and work against the class biases of the university can be educative; in addition, there is a chance to win some gains for those who are now largely excluded from the system. In particular:

• the character of university governing boards ought to be widely publicized, debated, and confronted. We ought to be demanding a university governmental structure which is not dominated by white, rich, and powerful men, who have little competence to run an educational institution, but who do have an active desire to prevent the institution from serving intellectual or social functions which damage their power. In principle, the governmental structure of the university should be democratically responsible to the community.

• the class composition of student bodies ought to be challenged. Not only are black youth largely excluded, but also the youth of other racial and ethnic minorities as well as the children of white workers. We stand for a university which sees itself as responsible for providing educational opportunity for all classes and ethnic groups.

• we want to break down the caste-like elitism which pervades major universities and colleges. This means work on new curricula which transcend both vocationalist and elitist versions of higher education. It means a new academic culture, which abandons the hallowed rituals, deferences, and styles which reinforce the elite character of the "top" schools. It means new employment policies for academic and non-academic staffs which deliberately compensate for the exclusion of lower status groups. It means quick and genuine recognition of black cultural and intellectual demands.

• we want urban universities which are fully responsible to the people whose lives they affect and in whose midst they exist; this means in the first instance that communities affected by university expansion and development must possess a veto-power over such programs.

In short: if the university were a democratic institution, if it stood against racism, if it refused to serve imperialist and militarist ends, if it were genuinely diverse in the interests it served and in its internal composition, if it asserted its independence of oppressive institutions and forces, then there would be no special need for challenging it— and community might be possible on the campus. But then, too, it would have a difficult time surviving in a society such as ours.

It is now clear that the universities throughout the world will not be peaceful until there is peace in the world; that the life of reason cannot exist until societies based upon reason begin to be built; that intellectual freedom is utopian unless men everywhere are free. This reality will not be changed by efforts to repress the student revolt, nor to impose solutions by force, nor to dampen the movement through procedural reform.

We believe that the effort to create the new university—to realize the fundamental aspirations of the new movements—is a part of the effort to transform the society as a whole. Neither effort can be achieved without intense conflict, turmoil, sacrifice, and pain. SDS proclaims, "A free university in a free society."

We can settle for nothing less.

On Misunderstanding Student Rebels

The Young, it is becoming clear, are regarded with considerable hatred in our country. Resentment against them cannot be explained simply as a reaction to the style of a particular generation, for in recent years the young have been attacked on such divergent grounds that the grounds themselves take on the appearance of pretext. In the 1950s we denounced students for their inertia, their indifference to public questions, their absorption in the rituals of fraternities and football, their dutiful pursuit of "achievement." In the 1960s we condemn them for the opposite qualities: for their passion, their absorption in public questions, their disgust with the trivia of college parties and athletics, their refusal to settle for mechanical processes of education.

Since the past two college generations have been denounced with equal vehemence for opposite inclinations, it seems plausible to conclude that it is not those inclinations but the very fact of their youth that makes them the target for so much murderous abuse. This conclusion may seem to contradict the fact that American society, above all others, is known for its adoration of youth. But that itself, paradoxically, is one cause of adult hostility: our youth-obsessed elders resent the eighteen-year-old's possession of the good looks and high spirits they so desperately simulate.

Adult anger at the physical superiority of the young has usually been contained by the comforting assumption that eighteen-year-olds are at least the moral, intellectual, and emotional inferiors of their elders. College students have traditionally been viewed as apprentices, almost as supplicants. And until recently they accepted their role as dutiful petitioners for entry into the world of adult insight and skill.

As no one needs reminding, they no longer accept that role, though most of their elders continue the struggle to confine them to it. Today's eighteen-to-twenty-year-old considers himself an adult, by which he does not mean (as so many forty-year-olds unconsciously do) that he has ceased growing, but that he has grown up enough to make his own decisions. In every sense, even statistically, his case is a strong one.

The weight of recent physiological and psychological evidence establishes the student claim that today's eighteen-year-olds mature more rapidly than those of earlier generations. Physically, they are taller and heavier than their counterparts at the turn of the century. Boys reach

Martin Duberman, "On Misunderstanding Student Rebels." Reprinted from *The Atlantic Monthly*. Copyright © 1968 by Martin Duberman. Reprinted by permission of The Sterling Lord Agency.

puberty around age fourteen, and girls begin to menstruate at the average age of twelve years, nine months (in both cases almost two years earlier than in 1900).

Moreover, there is much evidence that this earlier physical maturity is matched by emotional and intellectual precocity. According to Dr. C. Keith Conners, director of the Child Development Laboratory at Massachusetts General Hospital, both emotional and intellectual growth are today largely completed by age eighteen. By this Dr. Conners means that the difficult trials of adolescence are over, the basic patterns of personality have become stabilized, and the ability to reason abstractly —to form hypotheses and make deductions—has been established. This does not mean, of course, that no further maturity is possible after age eighteen. Additional information and experience do (or at least should) provide material for continuing reassessments. But that, of course, is (or should be) true of all of us.

In terms of knowledge already possessed, moreover, the graduating high school senior of today, thanks both to the media and to the stepped-up pace of academic work, is well informed on any number of topics—the new math, say, or the physical properties of the atom—of which his elders are ignorant. And as for experience, I am not at all sure that the eighteen-year-old who has had his senses activated by early sexual relations, strobe lights, pot, soul, and rock, and his political instincts honed by Vietnam, the draft, and the civil rights movement, should not be considered more vitally alive, more instinctually sound, than the typical forty-year-old who has spent his additional twenty years glued to the tube, the routinized job, the baseball and stock statistics.

The Academic Mandarins

It is bad enough that we have refused to extend to students the rights and responsibilities which their 'maturity warrants. What is perhaps worse is that many of those who hold positions of power or prestige in our universities have learned so little from the upheavals which that refusal has produced. A recent spate of books and articles by such men demonstrates anew their uneducability; they make it clear, by their continuing patronization and belittlement, that students still have an uphill fight in their struggle to be taken seriously.

One case in point, though not the most egregious, is that of George F. Kennan. When Kennan's article "Rebels Without a Program" (aptly characterized by Richard Poirier as "a new containment policy for youth") appeared in the New York *Times* Sunday Magazine for

January 21, 1968, it drew such an unprecedented reply from students and teachers (including a letter from me) that the Atlantic Monthly Press decided to issue the article, and replies, and a lengthy rebuttal by Kennan as a separate volume, *Democracy and the Student Left*. In that rebuttal, Kennan does acknowledge that the public questions agitating the country are indeed "so harrowing" and "harbor such apocalyptic implications that it is silly to suggest," as he originally had, that college students should go about their studies as usual.

But having acknowledged that "harrowing" problems face the country, Kennan proceeds, by a curious indirection, to minimize them. He lectures student activists on their "inability to see and enjoy the element of absurdity in human behavior" (adding, gratuitously, that he suspects their love lives, no less than their politics, are "tense, anxious, defiant and joyless"), on their "social science" rhetoric, and on their indifference to "nature as a possible compensating or sustaining factor in the face of social or political frustration." Kennan fails, however, to make clear how the merit of the issues the students raise in any way depends on the "inadequate" manner in which they raise them. I, for one, cannot see how the Vietnam War or the plight of our ghetto-dwellers might become more attractive or tolerable if viewed with an awareness of "the element of absurdity in human behavior" or described in a rhetoric free of social science jargon or escaped from by periodic trips to the wilderness.

Kennan insists that the students' obliviousness to nature, *et al*, is symptomatic of their "lack of interest in the creation of any real style and distinction of personal life generally." By which he means, as he goes on to specify, their lack of "manners," their untidiness, their disinterest in "personal hygiene," their refusal to cultivate the "amenities." It is debatable that this description is either accurate or significant, as applied to the nonpolitical, drug-oriented "hippies," but it is certainly not a valid description of campus activists, the ostensible subjects of Kennan's critique.

The main point, of course, is not that the new generation lacks "any real style," but that Kennan is unable to perceive much of its distinctiveness. Kennan is a good eighteenth-century *philosophe*, distrustful of "enthusiasm," and preoccupied with the rationalist credo of restraint and temperance in all things. Since "passion" is suspect, it follows (albeit unconsciously) that no injustice warrants fervent disapproval. What the new generation believes and Kennan apparently does not is that "moderation" can itself become a form of paralysis, even of immorality—like the moderate protest of Pope Pius XII against the extermination of Jews.

If Kennan's condescension toward the different life-style of the young were peculiar to him, it could be more readily ignored. But in fact his attitude is the characteristic response of the older generation to the younger. Any number of other examples are possible, but I will mention only two of the more prominent: Sidney Hook and Jacques Barzun.

Hook has published two statements (that I know of) on the recent ferment at Columbia, a long article, "The Prospects of Academe," in *Encounter* for August, 1968, and a brief note in the *Psychiatry and Social Science Review*. It is difficult to choose between them in deciding the high point to date for gray-bearded arrogance. In the shorter piece Hook flatly states that the Columbia rebels "had no grievances," and that they were interested solely in "violence, obscenity and hysterical insult." In the longer article Hook characterizes the protesters as "callow and immature adolescents, whose dominant mood, like that of all adolescents, is "irrationalism." While denouncing students for their passion, this self-appointed defender of "reason" and of the university as the "citadel of reason" himself indulges in a rhetoric so inflamed ("Fanatics don't lack sincerity. . . . They drip with sincerity—and when they have power, with blood—other people's blood") that by comparison the most apocalyptic students seem models of sobriety. Hook even declares that "there are some things one should not be moderate about"—which is exactly what the student activists (and Barry Goldwater) have said. The students, of course, mean it is acceptable to be passionately against war and racism. Hook (and Goldwater) mean it is acceptable to be passionately against those who passionately protest war and racism.

The Case of Jacques Barzun

Hook's themes—that college students are adolescents, that the best proof of their childishness is that they are "emotional" and that emotion (in others) is bad—are to be found in their most explicit form in Jacques Barzun's new book, *The American University*. In a note in the book's preface Barzun, who was dean of faculties and provost at Columbia from 1958 to 1967, explains that the manuscript was in the hands of the publisher six weeks before the student outbreak on April 23, 1968. But lest we be tempted on that account to excuse some of the positions he adopts in his book, Barzun further adds that despite the outbreak he has "found no reason to change or add to the substance of what I had written months earlier." Among the views he has found no need to modify is his statement that Grayson Kirk has always shown himself "ready and eager for progressive changes." Barzun does not pause to define "progressive," but one can't help thinking he uses the word in its original sense to describe the reforms that preceded World War I. Certainly nothing in his attitude toward students would place him beyond the year 1915.

Barzun begins his discussion of the college population by adopting the Olympian view; they are, after all, young men, and that means "turbulence is to be expected, heightened nowadays by the presence of girls. . . ." In other words, a certain amount of inherent anger adheres to the condition of being young (it *is* a "condition," in Barzun's view), and anger must find its outlet. The nature of the outlet is almost a matter of indifference: if "the people of the town" do not provide a convenient target, well then, it might just as well be politics.

Still in the Olympian vein, Barzun further suggests—it is as close as he ever comes to implicating society—that "perhaps our lack of proper ceremonies for initiation into the tribe leaves the young to devise their own proof of manhood." Barzun loves dismissing the young with this kind of casual irony. Its elegant offhandedness is a useful device for keeping a proper distance between the generations. It is also useful—though of this Barzun seems unaware—for expressing the savagery which he likes to think is confined to the student population. Barzun claims the undergraduates would themselves welcome rites of initiation, for what they really want, he insists, is more, not less, discipline. When they speak of the impersonality of the university, they mean, it seems, "the looseness of its grip upon them." Kennan makes the same point in almost the same words: students are currently objecting to parietal rules, he asserts, because "the rules have relaxed too much rather than that they have been relaxed too little." According to both men, students are starved for structure, are desperate to be introduced to the rigors of logic. In Barzun's phrasing, they are looking for "order," for "intellectual habits"; they sense that this is the balance they need, for like all youngsters they are in a "fever and frenzy," "their mind is monopolized by their inner life."

To meet this "rage for order," Barzun and Kennan posit a properly antiseptic university, a place of "respite and meditation" whose "proper work," in Barzun's phrase, is "in the catacombs under the strife-torn crossroads." He fills this subterranean cemetery with properly lifeless figures; they are "somewhat hushed" they give pause, as at Chartres, to the "spiritual grandeur of their surroundings." Yet just as one begins to feel, in the rush of Christian imagery, that Barzun has spent so many years surrounded by campus Gothic as to have lost all sense of distinction between the university and the church, he stoutly declares that *his* catacombs will not be peopled by early Christians. He dislikes that breed; it was marked by the same distasteful qualities he associates with today's young radicals: "indifference to clothes and cleanliness, a distrust and neglect of reasoning . . . a freedom in sexuality, which is really a lowering of its intensity and value . . . and—most symptomatic—a free field given to the growth of hair."

Barzun also shares with Kennan and Hook the proposition that "emotion" has no place on campus, and that since student rebels tend to be emotional, it can be safely assumed they are also unreliable. All three men equate (and thereby confuse) "emotion" with "irrationality," and all employ a vocabulary of neat opposites—"reason" versus "emotion"—that separates what our experience combines. They see education as "the cultivation and tempering of the mind" but fail to see that "enthusiasm" is one path by which that tempering proceeds. (For an understanding of the role emotion might and should play in learning, they would do well to read a remarkable new book by George B. Leonard, *Education and Ecstasy*. Though Leonard's discussion is chiefly centered on the lower grades, almost everything he says has applicability to higher education as well, especially his remark that schools as presently structured tame the "unnamed powers" of their students—their chief effect is to "limit possibilities, narrow perceptions and bring the individual's career as a learner (changer) to an end." Leonard forsees schools where the children will not emerge as mere knowledge machines but as beings who have also learned about their bodies, emotions, and senses. He is as authentically the voice of the future as Barzun's is that of the past.)

Barzun is also huffy at other "nonsense" currently being peddled about teaching, especially the idea that teacher and student should explore together, each learning from the other. This view, he asserts, has done "immense harm to both parties. The teacher has relaxed his efforts while the student has unleashed his conceit." And of what does that "conceit" consist? Barzun is quick to tell us: the conviction that they (the students) have something to contribute. "Only rarely," he declares, with a hauteur appropriate to the century from which most of his ideas spring, does a teacher "hear from a student a fact he does not know or a thought that is original and true . . . to make believe that their knowledge and his are equal is an abdication and a lie."

And so we are back, as always in Barzun's schema, to the confinement of his starting assumption: students are children and, usually, fools. His contempt for undergraduates is pervasive. They are, very simply, not to be trusted; "student reliability is at a low ebb," he warns, and especially in that of radical students, who have but one purpose: to destroy. The evidence Barzun marshals to justify his contempt is so exasperatingly trivial (as well as suspect in its accuracy) that it demeans its compiler far more than the students. The undergraduates, he asserts, cheat a lot on exams and papers; they obtain pocket money by stealing books from the college bookstore; they keep library books out as long as they like and let fines go unpaid; they deny their roommates "the slightest considerateness"; students of both sexes live "pig-style" in their dormitories; their conversations "usually cannot follow a logical pattern," and so on.

The first thing to be said about these accusations is that Barzun has seized upon the occasional practices of a few undergraduates in order to damn a whole generation. The second is that even if these qualities did characterize a whole generation, they hardly seem heinous when compared with the sins of the fathers—when compared, that is, with racism at home and imperialism abroad.

The distressing consequence of this obsession with the peccadillos of the young is an avoidance of those genuinely important problems to which the young are calling attention. Mandarins like Barzun, Kennan, and Hook are so preoccupied with manners that they forget matter. They are so certain of the rightness of their own patterns of thought and action and so eager to denounce all deviations by the young from those patterns that they blind themselves (and others) to the serious questions this new generation has raised—questions about the nature of education, the proper functions of a university, the very quality of American life.

What Activists Are Really Like

A dozen or so studies have been made of student activists at a variety of universities, and the findings have been conveniently summarized in a recent essay by Stanford's Nevitt Sanford. The group portrait that emerges (confirmed by Kenneth Keniston's new book, *Young Radicals*) is strikingly different from the slanderous one being peddled by Messrs. Barzun and Hook.

The activists, first of all, constitute only a small minority, though a growing one, of all college students; at Berkeley, for example, their number is put at about 15 percent. Second, there are important differences, in almost all measurable categories, between activists on the campus and other students. The activists score consistently higher on a wide variety of personality tests, including theoretical skills, aesthetic sensitivity, degree of psychological autonomy, and social maturity. They are also the better students, with significantly higher grade-point averages than the nonactivists. In trying to account for the recent emergence of student activism, Sanford points to various changes since the 1930s in family life and child training. But he feels that student activism is primarily a response to social conditions both within the university and in the world at large. Since the latter are the more widely known determinants of student rebelliousness, I will confine my remarks to conditions in the university.

One set of grievances on the campus centers on what does—or does not—go on in the classroom. As David Riesman has written, "Colleges on the whole have been very backward as compared with industry or the Army in their curiosity about their own inner processes." Until recently they have accepted lectures, grading, and examination as part of the Natural Order of Things and have seen no reason to question the long-standing assumptions that Teacher is the possessor and arbiter of Truth, that his function is to transmit knowledge (narrowly defined as accumulated information) to students, and that their function is to memorize it.

Any challenge to this conventional wisdom is still viewed with scorn by the vast majority of faculty and administrators—and of the student population as well. Barzun, for example, gives short shrift to any protest against grades and tests; "no person by way of being educated," he announces, "resents examinations; they are so instructive." Should a student activist or one of his allies among the younger faculty reply that exams and grades chiefly instruct students in how to please their professors, in how to compete with one another, in how to settle for orthodox questions and answers, and in how to suppress their own originality, Barzun's answer would be—hogwash. He sees the activists' demand for autonomy and for the freedom to pursue their own lines of inquiry as cant, as another example of their "mental confusion." By way of proof, Barzun triumphantly recounts a recent episode in a large Midwestern university: when students in a philosophy of education class of 300 complained that they had little say in their own education, the professor asked how many did in fact want to take responsibility for their work, and only ten hands went up. The moral, as Barzun draws it, is that students calling for self-regulation merely "ape the advertiser's soapy mind." But that is not the moral at all. Our educational system has been so successful in turning out automatons that the vast majority of its products are terrified at the thought of taking over responsibility for their own lives. The fact that only ten hands went up is itself a severe indictment of our educational practices. Instead of proving that "all is well," it proves that we are in desperate trouble—that maybe only 3.3 percent of our *citizens* are willing to make their own decisions.

Barzun similarly misses the point the undergraduate dissenters are making about the lecture system. That point has been well put in a recent issue of the *Yale Alumni Magazine* by Alan Weiner, a graduating senior. The present system, he wrote, encourages "debilitating dependence"; each student, taking dutiful notes at lecture, produces by the end of the semester (and for exams) a "paraphrased copy" of the lecturer's text, "one copy differing from the other less in content than in penmanship." Weiner recognizes that lectures, at their best, can be useful—a good lecture can provide a lucid introduction to some particularly difficult area of study so that the student "is spared the initial paralysis of venturing alone into *terra incognita*"; it can offer a fundamental reinterpretation not yet published or widely accepted; and it can "show a brilliant man in the process of putting ideas together." But such moments in the lecture room are rare, so rare that they do not justify the maintenance of a system which far more typically inculcates sloppiness, omniscience, plagiarism, and theatricality in the lecturer, and passivity, boredom, resentment, and cynicism in the student.

And what is the answer of men like Barzun to the growing resentment of the lecture system? That the protesters do not understand the true nature of their dissatisfaction. The real trouble, Barzun declares, is that the university has "let lapse the *formality* of lecturing—its form—which was its principal merit." What is wanted by way of change, in other words, is not to dismantle the lecture system but to return it to its pristine shape, to reintroduce formal presentation" and even "staginess and rhetorical effects," since these impart something Barzun labels "didactic energy." Given this gross misreading of student discontent, it might be well to remember in speaking hereafter of the "generation gap" that incomprehension is not confined to one side.

Where the System Fails

Discontent with teaching practices in our universities embraces more than the lecture system. Even where small seminars or discussion groups prevail (an expensive device few universities can afford), the needs of the students are not given anything like equal consideration with the needs of teachers. As two students in the *Yale Daily News* recently put it, the present system fails to help undergraduates appropriate facts and skills "in the interest of making lives, not just living." In assuming that the university's main, almost exclusive, function is to produce and transmit information, we have given top priority to promoting those faculty members most likely to assist in the manufacture of knowledge. This means, of course, that the university has come to be staffed chiefly by those concerned with research and writing rather than those concerned with educating the young—that is, with helping them to change. As Alfred North Whitehead said long ago, "So far as the imparting of information is concerned, no university has had any justification for existence since the popularisation of printing in the fifteenth century." Yet most professors do look on the imparting of information as the sum and substance of their responsibility. They make little or no effort to show, either in their subject or in their person, how knowledge can influence conduct and inform action (which, as William Arrowsmith has pointed out, is not really surprising, since they are themselves products of the same noneducation).

Most professors are interested only in students who are themselves potential scholars; they are concerned with training future colleagues, not with helping the individual young person grow in his own directions. The lack of interest taken by most professors in most students, their refusal to reveal or engage more than a small share of their own selves, have made many of the best students cynical about knowledge and about those who purvey it. They hoped to find in their professors models on whom they might pattern their lives; instead they find narrow specialists busy with careers, with government contracts, with the augmentation of status and income. They hoped to find a curriculum which would help them to uncover and pursue their interests; instead they find one primarily tailored to the needs of the faculty specialists. They hoped to discover a mode of living which would help them to integrate their intellectual curiosity with the demands of their sense and emotions; instead they find, in Erich Fromm's words, an education "more and more cerebral . . . [where] people are taught concepts, but are not taught or confronted with the experience which corresponds to these concepts." They hoped to find some acknowledgment of their worth and some encouragement toward its further development; instead they find disinterest, patronization, overt dislike. They find, in short, what Nietzsche called "the advancement of learning at the expense of man."

With considerable justice, therefore, the students, particularly the more talented and sensitive ones, reject the university and its faculty as self-serving, self-justifying, self-enclosed. They learn to seek their education—the expanding of insight and option—outside the formal academic curriculum, to seek it in talk and games with friends, in films, clothes, and cars, in Sergeant Pepper's Lonely Hearts Club Band, in the lyrics of Bob Dylan, in the Doors, in pot and acid. And if some of these sources prove as phony or as dangerous as the mechanical exercises of the campus, surely much of the responsibility lies with an academic community that has encouraged, almost forced, its students to look for life-enhancement where it can.

Is the University a Democracy?

Most of the powers within the academic community will not even acknowledge the right of students to complain, let alone the cogency of those complaints. To the request that they be allowed a voice in planning the curriculum, a Jacques Barzun replies that they have done nothing to "earn" a voice. To the lament that their studies seem out-moded or irrelevant, Barzun retorts that "relevance is a relationship in the mind and not a property of things"—which apparently means that although students might want to study urban affairs, if they will instead study cockle shells *in the right way*, they will discover all there is to know about life in the ghettos. And to the students' suggestion that they have some formal power in such matters as choosing faculty, passing on applications for admission, or helping to decide on the expansion of the physical plant, Barzun responds with hoots of derision and George Kennan with cold anger.

Both gentlemen remind the undergraduates that the university is not, and was never meant to be, a democracy. Barzun does believe that students should have the right of self-government in their own dormi-tories, for he acknowledges that they are "socially mature enough not to need domestic proctoring" (a curious and seemingly arbitrary depar-ture from his usual premise that undergraduates are children). But Kennan will not go even this far in extending power to undergraduates. The university, by virtue of its position as owner of the dormitories, has no choice in Kennan's view but "to lay down certain minimal norms for the manner in which that use can proceed. This would be true," he insists, "even if the inhabitants were older people." But it is not true, for Kennan's (and my own) university. Princeton owns a great deal of faculty housing, and in none of it are the tenants sub-jected to the demeaning regulations in regard to visitors, and so on, which are imposed upon the students.

With the exception of this disagreement over parietal rules, Barzun and Kennan are firmly united in their contention that the university cannot and should not be a democracy. Kennan, in his instance, is the more peremptory of the two. "Even if university trustees and administrators had a right to shift a portion of their responsibilities for university affairs to the student, which they do not," he writes, the student would in any case "be unqualified to receive it." The very suggestion, he warns, is part of the current tendency of American society "to press upon the child a premature external adulthood."

Barzun rests most of his case on the grounds of impracticality. The university cannot function as a democracy, he argues, because it is "extremely difficult to get from student bodies either a significant vote, or a council or committee that is representative. . . . Add that student newspapers have long ceased to purvey anything approaching a public opinion, and it is clear that democracy is that last name a political scientist would apply to the government by outcry which has lately gained favor as an extracurricular activity." The absurdity of this argument (and its loaded terminology) is best seen when placed in another context. Is it *easy* to get a "significant" or "representative" vote from the United States Congress? Do our commercial newspapers "purvey anything approaching a public opinion"? Shall we, on those accounts, abandon both the Congress and the public press as unworkable institutions? In trying to make a case against democracy in the university, in other words, Barzan has forced himself—I assume, inadvertently—into making a case against democracy in general. The "insurmountable obstacles" which he finds to democratic institutions on the campus are likewise in the path of democracy within the larger society. Indeed, they loom less large on campus; given the limited size of a university, the opinions of its constituency could be canvassed and tabulated far more easily than in the society as a whole—that is, if the will to do so existed.

The other argument most often heard for denying students any say in university affairs is that they are "mere transients." True, but so are many professors, and so (to change the context) are members of the House of Representatives, who are elected for only two years. Besides, the *interests* of the student population do not shift as often as the population itself; Clark Kerr, in fact, detects signs that students are beginning to look upon themselves as a "class." But even if the interests of the undergraduates did continually change (and they probably should), life does, after all, belong to the living, or, in the case of the universities, a campus to its *present* constituents.

The University as Landlord

In addition to student grievances over what happens in the classroom and on the campus, there is another major source of disaffection: the university's relationship to the world around it—its role as landlord of neighboring property, and, on the broader canvas, its role as the recipient of government largesse and provider of government expertise.

The upheavals of last spring at Columbia brought to focus the problem of the university's relationship to the society at large. One of two key issues during that upheaval was Columbia's pending construction of a gym in a public park used by Harlem residents. This issue by itself might be thought of minor importance (if, that is, one is not a resident of Harlem), but in fact it was the latest of a long series of encroachments by Columbia into the surrounding ghetto, an encroachment which usually involved evicting tenants with little concern for their wishes and welfare. (Even now Columbia continues its encroachment; as James Ridgeway reports in his new book, *The Closed Corporation: American Universities in Crisis*, Columbia is still secretly extending its real estate holdings in Harlem, and its "relocation office" is still forcing families out of buildings it wants to tear down.)

Various groups, including students, faculty, Harlem residents, and the city, had appealed to the Columbia administration to review its policies on the gym construction—all to no avail. It is simply false to say, as Sidney Hook has, that "instead of seeking peacefully to resolve them [grievances] through existing channels of consultation and deliberation, the SDS seeks to inflame them." Not only did student groups, including SDS, attempt to get a peaceful hearing, but they had to make those attempts against formidable obstacles, for as Amitai Etzioni, professor of sociology at Columbia, has written, "due process, even in the loose sense of established channels for expression and participation, is not institutionalized at Columbia or at most other universities."

Even after the unheavals of last spring, the suggestion that precise channels be established for student participation continues to infuriate men like Barzun. One would think that anyone who deplores student "immaturity" would at least recognize the standard argument of psychologists that immaturity is prolonged, even heightened, by an exclusion from responsibility. But apparently, despite his rhetoric in defense of "orderly process," Barzun prefers occasional barricades to regularized communication.

He even goes so far as to deny the reality of issues like the gym construction. Universities must expand, he argues, and expansion inevitably brings conflict with the university's immediate neighbors. But shall the needs of several hundred citizens, he rhetorically asks, "prevail over the needs of . . . a national university?" Besides, the area around a university is usually a "deteriorating" one (as regards Columbia, Barzun has elsewhere referred to its surrounding neighborhood as "uninviting, abnormal, sinister, dangerous"), so it is a matter of simple "self-protection" for the university to take "steps." The "steps," as Barzun defines them, include bringing in the police against crime and vice, hiring special patrols, and buying real estate as fast as funds and the market permit." This might look, Barzum concedes, like "waging war on the inhabitants," but what they forget is that with the university's expansion goes "increased employment and trade." The residents of Harlem apparently do not see it that way, and they and their student allies have decided that all else failing, it becomes necessary to invoke the doctrine of "self-protection" for themselves as well. (In his long book, Barzun has almost no discussion of Columbia's relations with Harlem; when I came to a chapter entitled "Poverty in the Midst of Plenty," I thought I had finally come to a detailed review of those relations, but the chapter turned out instead to be about the financial problems of the university.)

Why Innovation Is Crucial

The second major issue in the Columbia dispute last spring concerned the university's affiliation with the Institute for Defense Analyses (IDA), an affiliation which in turn symbolized the university's dependence on government grants and involvement with government research. Barzun and others like to defend the university as a "center of research," and they contrast that "proper" function with the "misguided" one of the university becoming a center of "experience." But it is one thing to defend the university theoretically as a research center, and quite another to ask specifically "research in what and for what?"

The multiple and tangled relationships that have developed between our leading universities and the large corporations and the federal government raise doubts about the proper boundaries of "research." This is especially true of what James Ridgeway calls the university's "war machinery"—its complicity in everything from antisubmarine-warfare research at Columbia to counterinsurgency planning at the University of Michigan. Today more than two thirds of university research funds come from agencies closely connected with defense matters, and about one quarter of the 200 largest industrial corporations in the country have university officials on their board of directors. It is certainly an open question these days whether the university is engaged in research in order to pursue "truth" or to acquire status, power, and profit. Columbia's own farcical involvement with the Strickman cigarette filter is but one of many examples of the university's placing greed ahead of integrity.

There are, I should stress, no simple formulas for establishing the "right" relationship universities should form with public corporations and governments. It is *because* there are no easy answers that the matter should be subjected to open debate, with all interested parties bringing to bear their insights and perspectives. And by "all," I include students. They are rightly disturbed over the university's entanglement with war and private profit, and they ask that their concern be registered and their views considered. They are entitled to nothing less, for until students began to protest such matters as IDA affiliation, the universities were doing business as usual, blind to the implications of their own actions. The same is true of the university's record regarding innovation in education and the procedures of campus government— I mean real innovation, not the substitution of blue tape for red. Before student activists began forcing a variety of campus and classroom issues into the open, the university's concern was minimal.

What we are witnessing, then, is not a sporadic and superficial, but a sustained and far-reaching, attack on the university's smug and antique bearing. The student activists are not rebelling against their parents' values, but applying those values to the institutions with which they find themselves involved. They are not confused children, uncertain of their motives or aims, but determined adults who have found their education and their society seriously wanting.

I doubt if we have ever had a generation—or at least a minority one—that has engaged itself so earnestly on the side of principled action, that valued people so dearly and possessions so little, that cared enough about our country to jeopardize their own careers within it, that wanted to have institutions and a society which would make such lives possible. It is a generation for which we should be immensely grateful and of which we should be immensely proud. Instead, we tell them that they are frenzied children; that we will try to be patient with them but that they should not push us too far; that they too in time will grow to understand the *real* ways of the world. To say that this condescension or blindness on the part of the older generation is a "pity" does not fit the dimensions of the case. It is a crime.

The Free Universities

"An Investigation into Sex" is now offered at Dartmouth. "Analogues to the LSD Experience" can be studied at Penn. "Guerrilla Warfare" is being examined by DePauw students. Stanford undergraduates are studying "American Youth in Revolt," and "The Origins and Meaning of Black Power" is a course at Brooklyn College.

Has higher education finally caught up with the times? The colleges and universities themselves have not, but some of their members are trying to fill the gap with side shows. The above courses and hundreds like them are currently offered at student-organized "free universities" and "experimental colleges" on campuses across the country.

Bob Reich is one of the organizers. A short, ivy-leaguish senior, he is concerned about the quality and content of education at Dartmouth. Ten years ago Reich would have done little more than grumble discreetly about large lecture courses or grade-motivated learning. Five years ago he might have mustered up a minor demonstration. But in the winter of 1966, Reich, a top history student and former class president simply gathered some colleagues around him and seceded.

"I had heard about student-organized experimental colleges at San Francisco State and Princeton," he recalls, "so I talked to a couple of guys, put a notice in the paper and held a meeting." Fifty people attended and out of it emerged the Dartmouth Experimental College (DEC). Fraternities, social clubs and dormitories agreed to organize courses.

The result was first presented to the community in the form of an elegantly printed catalogue. "When you're trying to explain a sex course to some townspeople, it sure helps to have a fancy catalogue," explains one DEC organizer. Listed were seventeen courses on such topics as "Man Faces Death," The Development of Conservative Thought" and "Contemporary Marriage." Each course had an undergraduate coordinator who was responsible for writing a syllabus, constructing a reading list, and inviting speakers. "The emphasis of these courses will be on the participants, rather than on the structures and requirements of an institution," reads the catalogue. "Innovation will be the rule; free give and take will be the method; a provocative educational experience will be the goal."

A massive publicity campaign then began. DEC organizers made radio and TV appearances, newspaper articles described the venture,

Ralph Keyes, "The Free Universities." Copyright © 1967 by *The Nation* (October 2, 1967). Reprinted by permission of *The Nation*.

and mailings were sent out—not only to Dartmouth students but to faculty, townspeople and girls at nearby Colby Junior College. Doubling the most optimistic prediction, 1,057 people applied for the first quarter's offerings. These included 585 Dartmouth students (about one-fifth of the student body); 230 townspeople; seventy faculty members; and 173 Colby girls. For a while, the Dartmouth Experimental College was the fourth largest college in New Hampshire. The dean of Dartmouth applied for a course, as did his two secretaries. (He missed the first class, but wrote the student coordinator asking for a "Dean's Excuse.") Since the seminars were to be kept small, only half the applicants could be accepted. Thirty-eight of seventy faculty members applying were admitted, and the Director of Admissions just missed being turned away.

"Great!" wrote in one student, "this has made Dartmouth meaningful." "It's wonderful to pursue a subject out of sheer interest and sans pressures of any kind," commented another. An older lady from town bubbled: "For so many years I've tried to get students into my home to talk. . . . This is the first time anything like this has happened and I'm so thrilled. . . . I'd do anything to keep it going." Even the Dean of Faculty endorsed the venture, saying soberly: "A healthy institution will work very hard to promote this kind of insurgence."

Dartmouth's experience is not unique. Banding together with faculty and townspeople, young academic seditionists have formed more than forty free universities and experimental colleges in the past two years.

Growing out of the civil rights "Freedom Schools" and Vietnam "Teach-ins," free universities began cropping up during 1965 in New York, Berkeley, Chicago, Detroit and Los Angeles. These early efforts were generally more militant than free and too often suffered from what Harvey Wheeler, a staff member of the Center for the Study of Democratic Institutions, called "a suffocating Marxist commitment." New Left groups, particularly Students for a Democratic Society (SDS), quickly picked up the idea and began to organize free universities. Michigan, Texas, Colorado, Ohio State, Florida, Wisconsin and Minnesota became nervous hosts to "counter-university" squatters.

But an interesting evolution soon began to occur in these academic fifth columns. If free university founders were often left-wing ideologues, many of the teachers and most of the students wanted simply to teach and learn in a free atmosphere. The anti-establishmentarians were soon faced with the choice of trying to whip their creations into line, allowing them to go their own way, or simply letting them die.

The Free University of Pennsylvania (FUP), an early venture, founded in the winter of 1966 by the local SDS chapter, ran into this problem: "When we first started discussing having a free university we expected 100 to 150 to get involved at most," recalls Bob Brand, a stocky, garrulous SDS senior in economics. "We had thirty to forty courses planned and were really worried about how to explain a poor sign-up to the teachers of the courses." "But," marvels a girl who was involved in registration, "all these 'straight' people came out of the woodwork to get involved, people you never would have expected to sign up for something like this." In the end, about 750 people enrolled, and ten new seminars had to be organized on the spot to handle the overflow. It soon became obvious that the Free University of Pennsylvania had gone beyond its SDS roots, and the parent weaned its child because, as an SDS spokesman admitted, "it had outgrown us."

One of the most successful efforts of its kind, FUP has enrolled more than 700 students for forty to fifty courses in each of its three semesters, many participants coming from the surrounding community. Free University officials estimate that students or teachers from twenty-eight Philadelphia institutions other than Penn are involved.

Enthusiasm for Penn's Free University is generally high. Sophomore Rich Feigenberg took an FUP course because "in the regular university there are too many requirements, few electives allowed, and even these you have to fit into your schedule." Freshman Mary Knutch attended the FUP seminar on Contemporary Issues because "after two semesters at Penn I found that I had forgotten how to talk." Tom Knox, a junior, found that in the "New Left Ideologies" class, "you get a good discussion inasmuch as nobody feels like the professor is trying to make a point."

Penn's administration is less sanguine about this pearl in its shell. A point of friction has been the question of whether outsiders should be allowed to use the university facilities "for free." Though the students have won grudging consent on this issue, the dean's office points out that the Free University has yet to supply the reports and statistics that were promised in return. "There doesn't seem to be much planning," concludes Dean of Women Alice Emerson. Her complaint is well grounded. In its quest for freedom the Free University of Pennsylvania has created a bureaucratic structure so ill defined that work tends to fall upon whoever will do it—usually the hard-working coordinator Steve Kuromiya, a senior in architecture.

This type of problem caused three FUP Coordinating Committee members to write a public letter last year contending: "The Free University is in trouble. . . . The majority of courses are ill attended, the creative thought has been at a minimum in many courses, the minimal office work required has not been done, and that which has was done by a few people." The letter caused a flurry of controversy. A large public meeting was held to discuss the issues and many volunteers came forward.

But from beneath this crisis a more interesting and subtle kind of disagreement came to light. The worriers came from the original SDS crew who had started the Free University. Their conception of what it should be was expressed by Bob Brand who says: "The way I wanted it to go was to have people asking the basic questions about their disciplines." This, he admits, is "basically a very conservative academic position." But Brand's constituency is small. The new hero of today's Free University at Penn is Ira Einhorn, a thirtyish, long-haired, bearded, "Be-in" organizer. Einhorn, who wears a daffodil behind one ear, graduated from Penn ten years ago, and has been moving in beat and hip subcultures ever since. Last term he taught two courses in the Free University: "Analogues to the LSD Experience" and "The World of Marshall McLuhan."

"Kids are learning more wandering around cities and on TV than in the universities," says Einhorn in explaining his approach to education. "I like to move around and you need more mobile classrooms. My classroom is just an extension of myself. It's the same kind of thing that happened in the Be-in. After living in the insane asylum you've got to get sane yourself."

Einhorn rambles, darting wildly from subject to subject. He is obviously intelligent and well read. His McLuhan course syllabus ("subject to change as I grow into the course or it grows into me") recommends thirty-six books, from Nietzche to Goodman, and Roethke to Ginsberg. His teaching tools ranged from candles and incense to rock 'n' roll and free-word association. Einhorn's courses are easily the most popular in the Free University. "LSD" had an enrollment of more than 100, and "McLuhan" actually *rose* in participation from sixty to seventy-five, more people attending the last class than the room would hold.

"Old New Leftists" like Bob Brand are basically concerned with the limitations of course *content* in existing institutions, and want to create a setting where people can study society in a rigorous way. Leftism and pedagogy are hardly inconsistent. The new breed of insurgent looks to a hipper, freer, "celebration" form of learning. To them method and content cannot be separated because freedom, opening up, living and loving are themselves the goals. Randomness can only help that process, as surely as a junior bureaucracy will hinder it. As the hippies ascend, the "Be-in" and the free university become more and more indistinguishable.

Similar disputes have occurred at San Francisco State's Experimental College. Senior English major Cynthia Carlson brought some freshmen together there in the fall of 1965 to discuss and critically examine their education. By spring, twenty-one seminars had grown up, organized by students and loosely grouped under the heading of "The Experimental College" (EC). More than 350 students were involved as participants, as well as twenty-five student seminar organizers and thirty faculty members who donated time as advisers.

Although influenced by the free university movement, the students at State aimed at special goals from the start. They deliberately avoided getting stuck in a posture of self-conscious militancy, preferring instead to "build a model," a positive alternative that would parallel the existing college. "Creative tension" was to exist between the two, said Jim Nixon, 25-year-old graduate student in philosophy who coordinated the original effort. "If you can get the sense of what you want to build," he explained, "then you can go to the college, take what is useful in it and avoid hostilities."

State's venture quickly mushroomed. Seventy courses were set up in the fall of 1966 for some 1,200 registrants. The national news media began to take notice of this "quiet revolution" just across the bay from Berkeley. Nixon, a persuasive and extremely bright leader, ran for president of State's Associated Students on a pro-EC platform and won overwhelmingly. The future sparkled and the EC's fall catalogue declared:

> The idea is that students ought to take responsibility for their own education. The assertion is that you can start learning anywhere, as long as you really care about the problem you tackle and how well you tackle it. The method is one which asks you to learn how you learn, so you can set the highest conceptual standards of accomplishment for yourself. The assumption is that you are capable of making an open-minded contract with yourself to do some learning, and capable of playing a major role in evaluating your own performance. The claim is that if people, students, faculty and administrators work with each other in these ways, the finest quality education will occur.

In its first year and a half, the Experimental College has had a tempestuous history. At best it has provided an open creative learning situation, spiced by a heavy dose of West Coast *avant-gardism*. A course in "Competition and Violence" had participants study conflict by learning and practicing judo, speaking to one another about their reactions while they fought. The "Involvement Theatre Workshop" was "an attempt to create a genre of theatre in which the audience is involved to the greatest extent possible—perplexed, threatened and ultimately seduced into intellectual, emotional and physical participation in the action." Last year, EC sponsored a thirty-six hour, 6,000-person light show, rock and soul, "sensory awakening happening" called "Whatever It Is."

Problems soon confronted the EC. State's newspaper, *The Daily Gater*, sniped regularly at the "Other College." Wrote city editor Phil Garlington: "The Other College, in truth, is quite harmless, for the most part a playschool for the S.F. State hippie element." Former chairman of the faculty, Dr. Richard Axen, commented that "Any professor who teaches in the Experimental College loses respectability within his department." When a *Newsweek* article lauding the Experimental College hit the stands, several faculty members reportedly called on the vice president for academic affairs to ask who was running the college—the president or Jim Nixon.

Harder to combat than external debunking has been perpetual strife within the "parallel college." EC's key debate centered around the question of planning versus spontaneity. As at Penn, the question of what *type* of learning is best receives constant attention. Former coordinator Cynthia Carlson Nixon, Jim's wife, has consistently pushed for greater structure and rigorous learning. She worries that students who cut their teeth on the Experimental College may reject "the beautiful, great thoughts of the ages," and confuse real learning with simple fun. Before resigning as coordinator, she reported hopefully: "Kids might have tried a course for a couple of semesters and found they were screwing up, not attaining what they wanted, and had to figure out how to do it. Now, they're having to make an investment of time and energy. They can't just bop in saying, 'teach me, and make it fun.' " Graduate student Floyd Turner, who has been studying the Experimental College, compared what he finds there to "the traditional problem that students faced when they got to Oxford. It often takes them a year to adjust to the shock of being responsible for their own learning."

But harder times now face EC. Their gadfly critic, Phil Garlington, was recently elected president of the associate students against an EC-backed slate. Internal dissension has left its toll in disunity. The original leadership has left the campus, and a hipper breed of students is in charge. Academic credit problems have created ill will, and after a year and a half the faculty is increasingly resistant to Experimental College demands and encroachment.

Staters who have been involved in the Experimental College for any length of time feel generally discouraged. But one wonders how they could possibly see the venture as in any way a failure. San Francisco State itself, in large part because of prodding from the Experimental College, now offers experimental courses which a faculty member can create for a trial semester, with only departmental approval. It has a much loosened general education program, with a student-faculty committee working to revise it still more. It is considering a Work-Study degree program, growing in part out of the Urban Communities and Change Area of the Experimental College. And when one considers the thousands of State students who were stimulated by direct or indirect contact with the EC to question the roots of their education, failure seems hardly the term.

It is risky to generalize about the scores of free universities and experimental colleges, since their diversity is at least as great as their similarity. Stanford's aggressively anti-establishment "Experiment" bears little resemblance to Dartmouth's low-key Experimental College. "Valley Centre" students (from Smith, Mount Holyoke, the University of Massachusetts and Amherst) happily rented a house for their venture, but FUPers wouldn't hear of such a thing. ("Too many ties, less freedom," contends coordinator Kuromiya. "The way we do it all you need is a few leaflets.") On the other hand, while Penn students gladly use university facilities, DEC organizers refuse to jeopardize their autonomy, preferring to meet in clubrooms and fraternities. The EC at San Francisco State relies on student teachers. At Penn and San Francisco State new teaching methods are eagerly being sought, but Dartmouth organizers have been content to rely on a standard seminar format. Students at Stanford and State can seek degree credit for their extracurricular learning, but the FUP and DEC want no such entanglement.

Despite this diversity some common aspects can be found and evaluated. These include:

Creating a new learning environment. Particularly in the multiversities where huge lecture classes are the rule, there is no doubt that the free universities and experimental colleges have responded to massive frustration with the existing learning environment. "The Free University did seem to fill a need students feel for small group discussion of intellectual matters," concedes Penn Dean Emerson. "It was the only chance I got to talk," says a Penn freshman of her FUP class.

Of course this informal atmosphere is not without its price. Extensive reading for a free university course is rare and discussions of the "bull-session" variety are all too frequent. Dartmouth English Prof. Alan Gaylord, who took the DEC course on J. R. R. Tolkien, laments: "If learning involves more than just an exchange of opinion, includes real digging, then I think there's a real question about the value of our course. Superficial discussion has value up to a point, but there are so many decisions about what to do with one's time that this rapidly loses value."

Focusing learning on more relevant, interesting and integrated subjects. If nothing else, the subjects studied in student-run colleges are more contemporary and lively than those taught in normal institutions. They must be to attract and hold an audience.

One of the DEC courses last term was on the Cuban Revolution. Freshman Camilo Garzón, the son of a Colombian military officer, eagerly enrolled. Asked if he had learned anything in the short time the class had been meeting, he replied, "Oh, yes, I learned for example that Castro had changed his mind about Marxism during the revolution. I hadn't known that and got a better view of Castro." He found that the most exciting thing was the debate between two anti-Fidel Cuban refugees and the Castro supporters in the class.

One enterprising 18-year-old junior science student at Dartmouth wanted to organize a course on Immanuel Velikovsky, a scientific heretic who has constructed an elaborate historical hypothesis of cataclysmic world development. Realizing that his subject was esoteric, the student, Ron Silverman, posted signs around campus reading, "WHO IS IMMANUEL VELIKOVSKY?" These were followed a few days later by posters asking "WHERE IS IMMANUEL VELIKOVSKY?" and later still "WHAT DOES IMMANUEL VELIKOVSKY SAY?" and "WHAT DOES IMMANUEL VELIKOVSKY DO?" "Who *is* Immanuel Velikovsky?" soon became a form of friendly greeting around Dartmouth, and when the first Experimental College catalogue appeared, sure enough, there was a course entitled, "The Works of Immanuel Velikovsky." Its description began, "In response to the current wave of interest in the theories of Dr. Immanuel Velikovsky. . . ."

About fifteen students and seven professors from different fields involved themselves in this course, the climax of which was a visit by Velikovsky himself. Word that he was coming spread as far as Ambassador College in Pasadena, where the dean sent money to tape the sessions and came across country himself for the two days. By most reports this was one of the most diverse and intensive grillings Velikovsky had ever received (he was eager to come for that reason), and he defended himself so limply that the few students who had started out in any way "believers" ended up as skeptics. "But," reports Silverman, "in order to understand Velikovsky we had to study so many side issues —Egyptian history, Bibical studies, geology, physics, astronomy, etc.— that this in itself was of great value." The class shared his enthusiasm, and the professors were delighted at the opportunity to get together with colleagues in other fields. Recently, letters have come from the *Saturday Review* and from as far away as Holland, asking for transcripts of the taped class sessions.

Although the sparkle and relevance of student-organized courses can be impressive, one wonders about their lasting value. Is the diligent student teacher at Dartmouth's course on "Gambling in the United States" really serving a useful function? "People will gamble," he explains, "and I might as well make them better at it."

Improved student-faculty relations. At best these ventures can fulfill a City College student's dream that a professor will "sit down, take off his tie, you'll call him Harry and he'll call you Mickey and you'll discuss physics together." Some have come close.

At Pennsylvania they tell of a psychology professor who had a reputation as a sort of "bad guy"—a tough, sour teacher. He had generally taught huge lecture courses which he hated. Lots of cheating went on, and there was little opportunity for personal contact. When the Free University first started he wrote a letter to the *Daily Pennsylvanian* offering to teach a course on "Pride." "We thought it was a put-on," recalls an FUP organizer, "but we called him and found out he was serious." Twenty people signed up for the course and most finished it. The Free University later got a letter from the professor saying how much he loved teaching it, having been able to relate to his students on a good intellectual and personal level. "I really dug that, since I had heard for so long that he was a bastard," marvels the FUP functionary.

But too often the traditional inhibitions of student-faculty relationships are not so easily broken down. History of Science instructor, David Kubrin, who took the Dartmouth Velikovsky course, expressed disappointment that the DEC had not achieved a "community of scholars." "I'm still referred to as 'sir,'" he notes sardonically. A Penn student tells of attending an FUP seminar held at a friend's apartment. Even there, he reported, the professor sat apart from the students, who directed all discussion at him. "They just couldn't break down old barriers," laments the visitor, "so I went for the punch to break down my own barriers."

Broadening the pool of teachers. Student-run educational experiments commonly involve as teachers people hardly acceptable to existing institutions. The most successful course at DePauw's Free University, on guerrilla warfare, was taught by an Air Force major. He enrolled several girls, a few professors, and had to divide his class in two sections to accommodate the overflow. In another vein, the Pre-University at the University of Wisconsin (Milwaukee) brought in the past state Communist Party chairman to teach Marxism, causing acute pain to some state legislators.

Lawyers, businessmen, housewives, writers, political activists—even a gardener (at SF State) and a Goldwater adviser (at Penn) have been considered qualified to teach free university-experimental college courses.

At San Francisco State the students hired social critic Paul Goodman to be "their professor" for a semester last year. The experience was less productive than it should have been because neither Goodman nor his students could figure out exactly what he was there to do. "Goodman's used to attacking his employers," observed one Stater more drolly, "but when students were in that role he kept maneuvering around but could never figure out a good posture from which to do that."

Broadening the pool of students. At the larger ventures such as Seattle, Penn and Dartmouth a number of the students consist of townspeople. Ira Einhorn was pleased to find that more than half the sixty-odd students in his McLuhan course were past 35. "All colleges must attract over-35s and bring them back to school," he argues with conviction. "The young hippies are so alienated from older people that they can't even talk to them. The over-35s can't understand how you can operate without a program like we do today. I'd tell them that my only program is what I'm doing at any given time. I don't think I got them to agreeing on much, but at least I got them in touch with one another."

FUP's open-door policy had one curious result for Einhorn when twelve right wingers showed up for three consecutive classes of his LSD course, the last time armed with cameras. One of them, a fundamentalist girl, became enraged when they started discussing the religious aspects of LSD. Asked if this didn't cramp his style, Einhorn replied off-handedly: "No. My policy is maximum jeopardy at all times."

At Dartmouth, junior Bob DuPuy had several townspeople in his course on "The Adolescent Subculture." "They enjoyed it and had as much to say as anyone," he reports, adding: "On the whole, in fact, they were more serious than the students. One older guy, a newspaper editor, used to drive 60 miles for every class, and do a lot of extra reading. I once asked him why he was taking the class and he replied, 'I've got several teenagers working for me, and I'm trying to learn how to get blood out of a stone.'"

A recent session of the DEC seminar on "Poverty in America" met in the easy chairs of the Union Lounge to listen to a community worker from rural Vermont. After the class, a young student nurse said she had read Michael Harrington's *The Other America* and was enjoying the course very much because it was teaching her how much poverty actually existed in this country. A soldier stationed nearby said he was there because "I'm against the poverty program, so I came to see what all the do-gooders are up to." Two high school girls reported they liked the seminar but didn't find the level of discussion any higher than in their high school. An older architect, a Dartmouth graduate, was taking the course with his wife and found it a welcome change from what he had known, because, "it puts the burden upon the individual."

Developing new subjects and teaching methods. If nothing else, free universities and experimental colleges have developed some strikingly creative courses and approaches to teaching. Almost every venture offers a few courses like "Bob Dylan and Other Folk as Contemporary Theologians" (Seattle), "The Philosophical Ramifications of Modern Drama: Or What in the Hell are We Doing in South Vietnam?" (Ohio State), or "The Biblical Roots of American Democracy" (Penn). The Free University of DeKalb (Illinois) offers not only "Eclectic Ecstasy" but an "Eclectic Ecstasy Laboratory."

Some ventures have made vigorous efforts to develop new teaching methods. Lawrence Lipton, teaching a course on "West Coast Avant-Garde Literature" at the Free University of California (Los Angeles), attempted a "reintegration of the arts in a workshop manner." In this "Teach-out" he employed tapes of poetry, films, a jazz combo and a "phono montage" of radio and TV commercials, football games and evangelical speeches.

At Penn, Ira Einhorn has been eager to come up with new approaches. "The first LSD class was in a huge lecture hall with lots of people, so I tried to break this down by turning out the lights and passing out candles and incense. This brought people closer together, made it more like a gathering, made people more conscious of one another's voices because they couldn't see faces. Then another time I spent a whole class period on four words—just put them on the board and let people free associate. I did a body eruption session using (Wilhelm) Reich, then a two and a half hour rock 'n' roll session and the next class gave a lecture on schizophrenia."

Though most free universities or experimental colleges have one or a few wild courses like this, the more striking fact is how conventional most of them are, in teaching approach if not course subject. "We need more daring people," complains instructor Paul Dorpat of Seattle's Free University. But too many participants feel like the Penn student who endorsed the lecture system used in his FUP course saying: "If somebody knows more about a subject than I, I expect him to lecture."

In Mike Vozick's experimental Biology I course at San Francisco State, the students quickly became dissatisfied with the random reports they were giving one another and decided that all future presentations should deal with cells. His students ended up taking the regular Biology Department exams as well as attending some of the laboratory sessions and lectures. "We're developing into a regular Biology I course," explains Vozick cheerfully. "The only difference is kids are learning because they want to, not because they have to."

If nothing else, these students' creations, by their very existence, constitute a critique of existing colleges and universities. That some faculty, administrators and townspeople are willing to involve themselves in the ventures indicates that the sentiment goes beyond mere youthful exuberance.

Political scientist Andrew Hacker, in a recent article on college presidents, noted that they often "prefer to work with the foundation-sponsored and government-underwritten programs that are rising parallel to the conventional curriculum. . . . For it is at this margin that a president has his freest hand, in new territory where he does not face the barricades of departmental baronies." Cannot something of the same motivation be ascribed to free university and experimental college founders?

What better way is there to reform outmoded structures than to create a better model at the side? Of course this involves much more than most initial enthusiasts realize. It calls on them to debate issues of education. How do you learn? What should you learn? Who is qualified to teach? Even if the practical pressures of running their own learning communities serve only to give these seditionists greater sympathy for the centuries-old dilemmas of education, the experiments might justify their existence.

But more than recognition of difficulties is occurring. The free universities and experimental college may be serving all higher education by having the gall to deal with the old problems in daring ways. They are discovering what it is that people really want to learn about, and are trying to create an environment in which this can be done. For every course that dies another will attract and hold an audience. Since the free curriculum must renew itself each semester, it can constantly question the validity of any course or field of learning. Their faculty failures are matched by the discovery of "born teachers." If too many classes rely on conventional methods, a few create and test exciting new approaches.

More than a century ago, American higher education was bogged down in the pious and anti-intellectual irrelevancy of its religious origins. Students then, as today, grew quickly frustrated and created their own literary and debating societies to examine more relevant issues. They discussed the topics of the day, invited stimulating speakers and developed libraries (in many cases overshadowing those of the regular institution). For decades, most college students belonged to these societies which were their major source of intellectual stimulation. Finally, after the Civil War, the colleges and universities reformed themselves to the extent that the student societies were no longer essential, and they slowly died out. Historian of education, Frederick Rudolph, attributes this wave of change to the pressure of example exerted by the lively undergraduates. "What is remarkably instructive about what they did is how much more effective they were than the would-be reformers in the ranks of the presidents and professors."

Is a similar process beginning today? Some slight evidence can be detected. Many of the recent reforms in San Francisco State's system can be directly traced to the ferment of the Experimental College. A faculty committee at Dartmouth is trying to develop more experimental opportunities in the curriculum, and Dean Thaddeus Seymour says: "There's no doubt this is directly related to the success of the Experimental College." In a clear response to the challenge of the Free University, Penn this year offered for the first time eight wildly successful noncredit seminars conducted by top faculty members.

Perhaps the highest function of the student educators will be to work themselves out of a job.

American Education as an Addictive Process and Its Cure*

The topic is the individual in the college, his commitments and his work. A broad subject indeed! Let us define the task more specifically. Let's aim the dialogue to each of you, who are, after all, individuals in the college. Let's talk directly and prophetically to your situation.

Let's set an ambitious goal to present the most important message you have ever listened to, to present a challenge which will change some of your lives. This may sound immodest but it's not, really, because what we shall consider has nothing to do with me personally. Like the other speakers, I, too, have been sent over by Central Casting to read my lines in the scenario we are working on today. I am simply a temporary mouthpiece for the message you are about to hear. Another reason for setting a bold goal is that this is my last performance in this particular drama. This is my last lecture as a college teacher to a college audience, and after the performance I'm going to take off the greasepaint and change uniform and move on to another show.

The third reason for claiming that my ambition today is not immodest is that I am saying nothing new. I didn't write the script. The lines were written by the oldest playwright in the business. I am simply repeating the oldest message in human history. We know, of course, that the wise men don't talk. The Book of Tao tells us that he who knows, speaks not and he who speaks, knows not. When the wise men in the past did talk, they have always written the same book. They have always told us the same message, repeated in a different dialect, using the metaphor of their time, using the vocabulary of their tribe, but it is always the same message. "Turn off your mind. Step for a moment or two out of your own ego. Stop your robot activity for a while. Stop the game you are in. Look within."

O, words! More good advice! The words that I have just given you are pretty trite and cliché today in the twentieth century, aren't they? But 3,000 years ago, when they were first enunciated, they were tre-

Timothy Leary, "American Education as an Addictive Process and Its Cure." Reprinted by permission of G. P. Putnam's Sons from *The Politics of Ecstasy* by Timothy Leary. Copyright © 1968 by The League for Spiritual Discovery, Inc.
* This chapter is a revision of a lecture given by Dr. Timothy Leary at the Second Annual Symposium on American Values, Central Washington State College, Ellensburg, Washington, April 1963. One week following the lecture, the speaker was fired from Harvard University for being absent from class, a paradoxical charge since his regularly scheduled courses had been assigned to other professors the preceding September.

mendously exciting. They probably brought about biochemical changes in the neurosystems of the people that heard these chants for the first time. Of course, now in the twentieth century, we are bombarded by words, thousands of words an hour, so that what I've just said is only another tattoo of syllables bouncing off your ears. Today we don't know what to look for if we try to get out of our game, and we don't know how to do it.

Now if you look at some of the metaphors that were used by these men in the past who changed the course of human history, the great visionaries, the great religious leaders, the great poets, you find an interesting correlation, a similarity. They all found the same thing when they looked within. They talked about the inner light, about the soul, the divine flame, the spark, or the seed of life, or the white light of the void. You will recognize that I have just ranged in these metaphors through several great philosophers, both Eastern and Western. All of these metaphors rang true and were right at the time. We can recognize now that they were clumsy within our nervous system. Listen! Each of those poetic images within the next 2 to 5 years is going to be validated by modern biochemistry and modern pharmacology.

Let me define the problem as I see it. I want to define it first of all ontologically, in the scientific sense, and then later I'll talk about the social aspects of the problem which we now face.

Ontologically there are an infinite number of realities, each one defined by the particular space-time dimension which you use. From the standpoint of one reality we may think that the other realities are hallucinatory, or psychotic, or far out, or mysterious, but that is just because we're caught at the level of one space-time perception.

For many people it's an infuriating thought that there are many, many realities. Last week, I was giving a lecture on consciousness expansion with Professor Alpert at the Aero-Space Institute in Los Angeles. A young engineer happened to be in the building that night, busy with some aerospace activity, and as he was leaving the building, he saw this crowd in a large room, and he came in to listen. After the lecture was over and we were on the way out, he stopped us and started to argue about reality. He could hardly talk, he was so mad. He said, "There is only one reality, the reality that is here, the reality of our physical laws, and for you to say that there is a range of realities, and particularly to say that this range might be brought about by drugs, is intellectual fraud, deceiving your fellow man!" It seemed to disturb him and make him angry to think that this solidity (which we are convinced exists around us) is perhaps just one level of an enormously complex continuum of realities. Now it's bad enough to say that there are other realities, but it's really intolerable if we suggest that some of the other realities are more conducive to ecstasy, happiness, wisdom, to more effective activity, than our familiar reality. So much for the general ontological situation. Let us try to spell this out in more exact terms.

The social reality in which we have been brought up and which we have been taught to perceive and deal with is a fairly gross and static affair. But it misses the real excitement. The real hum and drama, the beauty of the electronic, cellular, somatic, sensory energy process have no part in our usual picture of reality. We can't see the life process. We are surrounded by it all the time. It is exploding inside of us in a billion cells in our body, but most of the time we can't experience it. We are blind to it. For example, how do we know when another person is alive? We have to poke his robot body and listen to his heart, look for some movement. If he breathes, he is alive. But that is not the life process. That is just the external symptom. It's like seeing that the car moves, and from the fact that the body of the car moves, inferring that the motor is going inside. We can hear the car motor, we can brake, but we can't tune in on the machinery of life inside ourselves or around us. Now at this point you must be thinking, well, poor Leary, he has gone too far out. But really I don't think that it should be this difficult to accept logically the fact that there are many realities and that the most exciting things that happen, cellular and nuclear processes, the manufacture of protein from DNA blueprints, are not at the level of our routine perception. And for that matter, that the most complex communications, the most creative processes exist at levels of which we are not ordinarily aware.

Let's take an analogy. Suppose that you had never heard of the microscope, and I came before you and said, "Ladies and gentlemen, I have an instrument which brings into view an entirely different picture of reality, according to which this world around us which seems to have solidity and symmetry and certain form is actually made up of organisms, each of which is a universe; there is a world inside a drop of water. A drop of blood is like a galaxy. A leaf is a fantastic organization perhaps more complicated than our own social structure." You would think that I was pretty far out, until that moment when I could persuade you to put your eye down to the microscope, show you how to focus, and then you would share the wonder which I had tried to communicate to you. All right, we know that cellular activity is infinitely complex.

We tend to think of our external, leatherlike skin body as the basic ontological frame of reference. The center of our universe. This foolish egocentricity becomes apparent when we compare our body with a tractor. We usually think of a tractor or a harvesting machine as a clumsy, crude instrument which just organizes and brings food for us to feed our mouths. But from the standpoint of the cell, the animal's body, the human being's body, your body, is a clumsy instrument, the function of which is to transport the necessary supplies to keep the cellular life process going. And we realize, when we study biology textbooks, that our body is actually a complex set of soft-divine machines serving in myriad ways the needs of the cell. These concepts can be a little disturbing to our egocentric and our anthropocentric point of view.

But then we've just started, because the fellow with the electron microscope comes along. And he says, "Well, your microscope and your cell is nothing! Sure, the cell is complicated, but there's a whole universe inside the atom in which activities move with the speed of light, and talk about excitement, talk about fun, talk about communication, well, now here at the electron level we're just getting into it." And then the astronomer comes along with his instruments, and off we go again!

The interesting thing to me about this new vision of many realities that science confronts us with (however unwilling we are to look at it) is this: the closer and closer connection between the cosmology of modern science and the cosmology of some of the Eastern religions, in particular, Hinduism and Buddhism. I have a strong suspicion that within the next few years, we are going to see many of the hypotheses of our Christian mystics and many of the cosmological and ontological theories of Eastern philosophers spelled out objectively in biochemical terms. Now, all of these phenomena "out there" made visible by the electron microscope, the telescope, are wounding enough to our pride and our anthropomorphism (which Robert Ardry calls the "romantic fallacy"), but here, perhaps the most disturbing of all, comes modern pharmacology. Now we have evidence which suggests that by ingesting a tiny bit of substance which will change biochemical balances inside our nervous system, it's possible to experience directly some of the things which we externally view through the lenses of the microscope.

I will have more to say about the applications and implications of educational chemistry shortly. I'd like to stop and consider briefly the social-political and educational problems which are the subject of our symposium. We have told each other over and over again during the last two days of the conference that we're in pretty bad shape. Well, I'm not quite that pessimistic. What's in bad shape? The cellular process isn't in bad shape. The supreme intelligence, if you want to use that corny twentieth-century phrase for the DNA molecule, isn't in bad shape. For that matter, the human species is going to survive, probably in some mutated form. What's in bad shape? Our social games. Our secular traditions, our favorite concepts, our cultural systems. These transitory phenomena are collapsing and will have to give way to more advanced evolutionary products.

I'm very optimistic about the cellular process and the human species because they are part, we are part of the fantastic rushing flow which has been pounding along from one incredible climax to another for some 2 billion years. And you can't stay back there, hanging on to a rock in the stream. You've got to go along with the flow; you've got to trust the process, and you've got to adapt to it, and you might as well try to understand it and enjoy it. I have some suggestions in a moment as to how to do exactly that.

We are all caught in a social situation which is getting increasingly set and inflexible and frozen. A social process which is hanging on to a rock back there somewhere and keeping us from flowing along with the process. All the classic symptoms are there: professionalism, bureaucracy, reliance and overreliance on the old clichés, too much attention to the external and material, the uniformity and conformity caused by mass communication. The old drama is repeating itself. It happened in Rome and it happened to the Persian Empire and the Turkish Empire and it happened in Athens. The same symptoms. We're caught in what seems like an air-conditioned anthill, and we see that we're drifting helplessly toward war, overpopulation, plastic stereotyping. We're diverted by our circuses—the space race and television—but we're getting scared, and what's worse, we're getting bored and we're ready for a new page in the story. The next evolutionary step.

And what is the next step? Where is the new direction to be found? The wise men have been telling us for 3,000 years: it's going to come from *within*, from within your head.

The human being, we know, is a very recent addition to the animal kingdom. Sometime around 70,000 years ago (a mere fraction of a second in terms of the evolutionary time scale), the erect primate with the large cranium seems to have appeared. In a sudden mutational leap the size of the skull and the brain is swiftly doubled. A strange cerebral explosion. According to one paleo-neurological theory (Dr. Tilly Edinger), "Enlargement of the cerebral hemisphere by 50 percent seems to have taken place without having been accompanied by any major increase in body size."

Thus we come to the fascinating possibility that man, in the infancy of his existence, has never learned to use this new neurological machinery. That perhaps, like a child turned loose in the control room of a billion-tube computer, man is just beginning to catch on to the idea, just beginning to discover that there is an infinity of meaning and complex power in the equipment he carries around behind his own eyebrows.

The first intimation of this incredible situation was given by Alfred Russel Wallace, co-discoverer with Charles Darwin of what we call the theory of evolution. Wallace was the first to point out that the so-called savage—the Eskimo, the African tribesman—far from being an offshoot of a primitive and never-developed species, had the same neural equipment as the literate European. He just wasn't using it the same way. He hadn't developed it linguistically and in other symbolic game sequences. "We may safely infer," said Wallace, "that the savage possesses a brain capable, if cultivated and developed, of performing work of a kind and degree far beyond what he is ever required to do." We shall omit discussion of the ethnocentric assumptions (Protestant ethic, primitive-civilized) which are betrayed in this quote and follow the logic to its next step.

Here we face the embarrassing probability that the same is true of us. In spite of our mechanical sophistication we may well be savages, simple brutes quite unaware of the potential within. It is highly likely that coming generations will look back at us and wonder: how could they so childishly play with their simple toys and primitive words and remain ignorant of the speed, power, and relational potential within? How could they fail to use the equipment they possessed?

According to Loren Eiseley (whose argument I have been following in the last few paragraphs), "When these released potentialities for brain growth began, they carried man into a new world where the old laws no longer held. With every advance in language, in symbolic thought, the brain paths multiplied. Significantly enough, these which are most recently acquired and less specialized regions of the brain, the 'silent areas,' mature last. Some neurologists, not without reason, suspect that here may lie other potentialities which only the future of the race may reveal."

We are using, then, a very small percentage of the neural equipment, the brain capacity which we have available. We perceive and act at one level of reality when there are any number of places, any number of directions in which we can move.

Ladies and gentlemen, it is time to wake up! It's time to really use our heads. But how? Let's consider our topic: the individual in college. Can the college help us use our heads? To think about the function of the college, we have to think about the university as a place which spawns new ideas or breaks through to new visions. A place where we can learn how to use our neurological equipment.

The university, and for that matter, every aspect of the educational system, is paid for by an adult society to train young people to keep the same game going. To be sure that you do not use your heads. Students, this institution and all educational institutions are set up to anesthetize you, to put you to sleep. To make sure that you will leave here and walk out into the bigger game and take your place in the line. A robot like your parents, an obedient, efficient, well-adapted social game player. A replaceable part in the machine.

Now you *are* allowed to be a tiny bit rebellious. You can have fancy ways of dress, you can become a cute teen-ager, you can have panty raids, and that sort of thing. There is a little leeway to let lou think that you are doing things differently. But don't let that kid you.

I looked at television last night for a few minutes and watched a round table of high school students discussing problems. Very serious social problems. They were discussing teen-age drinking. Now the problem seems to be that young people want to do the grown-up things a little too fast. You want to start using the grown-ups' narcotics before you're old enough. Well, don't be in such a hurry! You'll be doing the adult drinking pretty soon. You'll be performing all the other standardized adult robot sequences because that is what they're training you to do. The last thing that an institution of education wants to allow you to do is to expand your consciousness, to use the untapped potential in your head, to experience directly. They don't want you to evolve, to grow, to really grow. They don't want you to move on to a different level of reality. They don't want you to take life seriously, they want you to take their game seriously. Education, dear students, is anesthetic, a narcotic procedure which is very likely to blunt your sensitivity and to immobilize your brain and your behavior for the rest of your lives.

I also would like to suggest that our educational process is an especially dangerous narcotic because it probably does direct physiological damage to your nervous system. Let me explain what I mean by that. Your brain, like any organ of your body, is a perfect instrument. When you were born, you brought into the world this organ which is almost perfectly adapted to sense what is going on around you and inside of you. Just as the heart knows its job, your brain is ready to do its job. But what education does to your head would be like taking your heart and wrapping rubber bands around it and putting springs on it to make sure it can pump. What education does is to put a series of filters over your awareness so that year by year, step by step, you experience less and less and less. A baby, we're convinced, sees much more than we do. A kid of ten or twelve is still playing and moving around with some flexibility. But an adult has filtered experience down to just the plastic reactions. This is a biochemical phenomenon. There's considerable evidence showing that a habit is a neural network of feedback loops. Like grooves in a record, like muscles, the more you use any one of the loops, the more likely you are to use it again. If there were time, I could spell out exactly how this conditioning process, this educational process works, how it is based on early, accidental, imprinted emotions.

So here we are once again. The monolithic, frozen empire is about to fall. We have been in this position many times in the last few thousand years. What can we do about educational narcosis? How can you "kick" the conformist habit? How can you learn to use your head?

We're all caught in this social addictive process. You young people know that it's not working out the way it could. You know you're hooked. You dread the robot sequence. But there is always the promise, isn't there? There's always the come-on. "Keep coming. It's going to get better. Something great is going to happen tomorrow if you're good today." It's not true! As a matter of fact, it gets worse, dear robots.

All right, where do we go? What can we do? I have two answers to those questions. The first is: *drop out!* Go out where you are closer to reality, to direct experience. Go out to where things are really happening. Go out to the frontier. Go out to those focal points where important issues are being played out. Why don't you pick out the most important problem in the world, as you see it, and go exactly to the center of the place where it's happening, where it is being studied and worked on? Why not? Someone has to be there, in the center. Why not you?

Now, there's a risk to this. The first risk is that you'll lose your foothold on the ladder that you've been climbing. You'll lose your social connection.

Undergraduates come to me very often and say, "I want to go on to graduate school in psychology. Where should I go?" And I always ask them the question, "Why do you want to study psychology?" And as I listen to them, usually one of two answers develops. Answer number one is: " I want to become a psychologist. I want to play the psychology game. I want to be able to play the role and use the terms you use, and I want to be an assistant professor and then an associate professor and then a full professor, and I want to get tenure, and maybe if I'm really ambitious, I might get to be president of the American Psychological Association." Well, that's fair enough, and for someone who has ambition I can give them advice about the strategic universities to go to, like go to Michigan or Yale but don't go to XYZ.

Some students, though, will say, "I want to study psychology because I want to study human nature" or "I want to find out what's what." To do some good. And then I can tell them, well, forget about graduate school. What kind of good do you want to do? Do you want to help the mentally ill? Then get yourself committed to a mental hospital. Stay there for a year or two; you'll learn more about mental illness in that two years than our profession has learned in a hundred years. If you want to learn about delinquency and reducing crime, go down to the tough section, learn the crime game, learn how to make a man-to-man contact with tough guys, learn from them why they are crooks and criminals. Spend a year in prison, not as a psychologist, but maybe as a guard, or cleaning up the garbage, and you'll learn more than you will ever learn in a criminology textbook. That is how it goes. There is no problem that can't be best solved and best worked out at this stage of ignorance by getting right into the reality.

Of course, another objection to this suggestion is: "After all, we do need some information and we do need facts and we have to learn them in university courses." And I say, "Sure, there are existential problems; there are certain times when in trying to solve an existential problem you will want to borrow the experience and the data of previous investigators." You can use the library, but again, beware, it's just like a narcotic. Library books are very dangerous addictive substances. Like heroin, books become an end in themselves. I made the suggestion two years ago at Harvard University that they lock up Widener Library, put chains on the doors, and have little holes in the wall like in bank tellers' windows, and if a student wanted to get a book, he would have to come with a little slip made out showing that he had some existential, practical question. He wouldn't say that he wanted to stuff a lot of facts in his mind so that he could impress a teacher or be one up on the other students in the intellectual game. No. But if he had an existential problem, then the library would help him get all the information that could be brought to bear on that problem. Needless to say, this plan didn't make much of a hit, and the doors of the Harvard Library are still open. You can still get dangerous narcotic volumes without a prescription at Harvard.

Where can we go?

Answer number one is to get out into the world, go to where the really important events, the events that you think are important, are happening and climb into them. That, by the way, is how all the great advances in science as well as politics have taken place.

Answer number two to the question, where can we go, is: Go inside. Go to your own brain; start using the untapped region of your head. Here, my friends, is the real frontier, the real challenge, the real opportunity.

Well, how do we do that? For centuries, for thousands of years, men have been studying this problem of how to expand their own consciousness, how to get into their own brains. One of the classic methods of doing it is the simple process of meditation. But today in 1963 this method seems far out. You'd be called eccentric if you said to an American that it would be useful for him to spend one hour a day alone—not thinking but just turning off all of the outside stimulation and the internal mental machinery and seeing where that will take him. We have to remind ourselves that meditation has been the classic psychological technique for thousands of years for most of the human race. Every one of our great visionaries, every one of the men who changed the course of human history, worked it out during a meditative experience.

Modern psychology calls this "turning on" by the fancy name "sensory deprivation." A few years ago psychologists discovered that if you took an American and put him in a dark room and you cut off all the sound and you cut off all the light and you cut off all tactile stimulation, in other words, if you turned off all the outside games, he couldn't keep his mind going and strange things would take place in his consciousness and he would begin to have hallucinations, revelations, visions, or he'd get in a panic and leap out of the room and shout "Help!" The reason for this is (and now we are getting back into neuro-psychology) that your mind, your game-playing verbal mind, like a drug habit, requires continual stimulation. You have to keep feeding it. In order to keep up the pretense that you are you and that your level of reality is really reality, you have to have feedback all the time. You have to have people around you reminding you that you are you; you have to have people around you participating in the same immediate realities, sharing the same social delusion, to keep this social reality going.

Now whenever you get out there, away from the social and sensory stimulation (as with men who are shipwrecked, men who are lost in a desert, men who are lost in the snow, men who go into monasteries, men who go into cells), there are withdrawal symptoms. The people panic because they are moving on to a different level of reality. How many of our great visionaries, our great history-making decisions, have come from men who have gone off in the desert? Jesus Christ went off in a cave in the mountain; Mohammed sat alone in a cave; Buddha lived in solitude for many years, so did St. John of the Cross. So have most of our other great visionaries. The problem now is that it is getting harder to let these physiological events happen. To be alone in order to look within.

Recently our technology, which has done so much to narrow our consciousness and to produce this robotlike conformity, has turned up two very disturbing processes which are going to cause all of us to do a lot of serious thinking in the next few years. These processes are electrical stimulation of the brain, and the new drugs, which also allow for increased control of consciousness, either by you or by someone else. The next evolutionary step is going to come through these two means, both of which involve greater knowledge, greater control, greater use and application of that major portion of our brain which we now do not use and of which we are only dimly aware.

These potentialities and these promises aren't going to go away. Your head, with its unused neurons, is there. Electrical stimulation and biochemical expansion of the neural processes are here, too. They aren't going to go away just because they upset our theories of psychology or our new words of education.

In 1943, a most dramatic event took place in a laboratory in Switzerland when Dr. Albert Hoffman accidentally ingested a tiny amount of semisynthetic ergot fungus known as LSD 25 and found himself thrown onto a level of reality which he had never experienced before. This had probably happened to many chemists in the past and to many other people in the past. Hoffman was the man on the spot who was able to understand what was going on. And because of Albert Hoffman of Sandoz Laboratory, we face today the challenge and dilemma of consciousness-expanding drugs. They are not addictive in the sense that there is no physiological attachment to them. I must point out that the very question of addiction is humorous to those of us who feel that we are all hopelessly addicted to words and to our tribal games. These drugs are physiologically safe. Over two thousand studies have been published, and as of 1968 despite the rumors there is no evidence of somatic or physical side effects. But they are *dangerous*; the socio-political dangers are there. We have incontrovertible evidence that these drugs cause panic, poor judgment, and irrational behavior on the part of some college deans, psychiatrists and government administrators *who have not taken them*.

What we think is going to happen is that a system of licensing and training will be developed, very similar to the way we train and license people to use motorcars and airplanes. People have to demonstrate that they can use their expanded neural machinery without hurting themselves and without danger to their fellow men. They will have to demonstrate proficiency, experience, training, and then we feel it is their right to be licensed. As in the case of airplane and auto, the license can be taken away from those who injure themselves or injure their fellow men.

There are many new by-products of this research in consciousness expansion and these studies. First of all, it is inevitable that a new language will develop to communicate the new aspect of experience. The language of words we now use is extremely clumsy, static, and heavy. We are now going to have to develop, as chemistry has developed, a language that will pay respect to the fact that our experience, our behavior, our social forms are flowing all the time. And if your language isn't equipped to change and flow with them, then you are in trouble, you're hooked. You're drugged by the educational system. There are going to be new values, rest assured, based on a broader range of reality. Our present values, based on certain ethnocentric tribal goals, are going to recede in importance after we see where man really belongs in the biological evolutionary process. There are going to be new social forms; there are going to be new methods of education.

I'll give you one example here. In the last few months, we have been studying accelerated learning by the use of the expanded consciousness. It's your trained mind, you remember, which prevents you from learning. If a professor of linguistics who doesn't know any French goes to France with his five-year-old son and they both spend equal time with the French people, who is going to learn French faster? The five-year-old son will quickly outstrip his dad even with that Ph.D. in linguistics. Why? Because Dad has stuffed his mind with all sorts of censoring and filtering concepts that prevent him from grooving with the French process. The psychedelic experience can release these learning blocks. We took, for example, a brilliant woman who had an emotional block against learning language. She wanted to learn Spanish. We gave her a very heavy dose of LSD, put her in a quiet room and put earphones on her, and for eight hours she was flooded with spoken Spanish from records. Every hour or so, we would go in and take the earphones off and say, "How are you?" She answered ecstatically in Spanish! She had been wallowing in Spanish for a thousand years. By the sixth or seventh hour, she was repeating back the Spanish words with the right enunciation, the dialectic tempo and so forth. The problem now is that when she hears Spanish spoken, she is likely to go into another level of consciousness, to get suddenly very high, which leads to other interesting possibilities of auto-conditioning. All of us, adults and students, have been censored so much, the filters have been applied for so long, the neuro-physiological processes are so firmly set that if we want to expand our consciousness, we are probably going to have to use chemical means. We adults, if we are going to move on to different levels of reality, are going to have to rely on some direct means of this sort. We have high hopes for the next generation, and particularly the next generation after that. It is the goal of our research and of our educational experiments that in one or two generations, we will be witnessing the appearance of human beings who have much more access, without drugs, to a much greater percentage of their nervous systems.

So there you have it. I'm sure that a few or none of you will follow the advice and the prophetic warnings that I have been giving. I have had to tell you with words. But I'm also going to take my own advice. I'm dropping out of the university and educational setup. I'm breaking the habit. I hope in the coming years as you drift into somnambulance that some of you will remember our meeting this morning and will break your addiction to the system. I'll be waiting for you.

I want to leave one final warning. There will be many people who will see the utility of the electrical and chemical techniques I have been talking about and will want to use them, as the Western, scientific mind has always wanted to use them, for their own power and their own control. Whenever new frontiers open up, you have the new problem of exploitation and selfish use. There will be no lack of people who will be delighted to use the underdeveloped areas of *your* cortex. We have coined the term "internal freedom." It is a political, didactic device; we want to warn you not to give up the freedom which you may not even know you have. In the Seattle paper yesterday, in one of the columns, I read a very interesting item to the effect that the Russians were developing extrasensory-perception techniques and studying ways which can eventually control consciousness. We can do that, of course, with television now. If 60 million people all watch one program, they are being controlled. But still we have that choice of turning it on or off. The next step, and I warn you it is not far off, involves some fellow using electrical implants and drugs to control consciousness. Then, dear friends, it may be too late. We won't know where the buttons are to turn them off. The open access to these methods is the key to internal freedom. If we know what we are doing, do it openly and collaboratively, free from government control, then we will be free to explore the tremendous worlds which lie within.

NEW LIFE STYLES

The sense of urgency which characterizes contemporary youth is of course not restricted to their "new" political ideas. From the first, many young people—the media invariably called them "hippies"—were convinced that a meaningfully restructured society was not possible until its citizens were liberated from their traditional and burdensome mores and values—from the "hangups" characteristic of our country. Other young people despaired of any kind of social reform, and were concerned only in liberating themselves and other like-minded spirits. How was this liberation to be achieved? Through "mind-expanding" drugs for some; through "mystical" disciplines like Zen and Yoga; through a reassertion of the "body," as the word is used by Norman O. Brown. In short, young people had decided to do their own "thing"—and they followed through to such an extent as to cause some to question whether real communication between young and old was any longer possible. If this resulting "gap" is real, it is to be defined by the nature of these new interests.

Most of the selections in this section explore new ways of reawakening the adult self to the possibilities and joys of existence which most of us have never, or rarely, realized. R. E. L. Masters has recorded some remarkable examples of his subjects' reactions after taking LSD or peyote. Norman O. Brown's provocative address to Columbia University students and Leo Litwak's "Joy Is the Prize: A Trip to Esalen Institute" are about the rediscovery of the senses, the first advocating the need and the latter recording the experience. Paul Reps' suggestive and ineffable transcriptions of Zen koans point to the differences in sensibility between East and West. Both Warren Hinckle and Gary Snyder treat a phenomenon which the media have often distorted—communal living. While Hinckle presents its more glamorous aspects, Snyder describes the regenerative implications of this new life style. The commune, what Snyder calls the "Tribe," combines the most salutary elements of East and West. Marshall McLuhan deserves special mention because he alone has emphasized the positive—indeed redeeming—aspects of modern culture. Among other things, McLuhan believes that the Western stress on separateness and containment is already being replaced by an Eastern sense of fluidity and relationship.

Apocalypse: The Place of Mystery in the Life of the Mind

I didn't know whether I should appear before you—there is a time to show and a time to hide; there is a time to speak, and also a time to be silent. What time is it? It is fifteen years since H. G. Wells said Mind was at the End of its Tether—with a frightful queerness come into life: there is no way out or around or through, he said; it is the end. It is because I think mind is at the end of its tether that I would be silent. It is because I think there is a way out—a way down and out—the title of Mr. John Senior's new book on the occult tradition in literature—that I will speak.

Mind at the end of its tether: I can guess what some of you are thinking—*his* mind is at the end of its tether—and this could be; it scares me but it deters me not. The alternative to mind is certainly madness. Our greatest blessings, says Socrates in the *Phaedrus*, come to us by way of madness—provided, he adds, that the madness comes from the god. Our real choice is between holy and unholy madness: open your eyes and look around you—madness is in the saddle anyhow. Freud is the measure of our unholy madness, as Nietzsche is the prophet of the holy madness, of Dionysus, the mad truth. Dionysus has returned to his native Thebes; mind—at the end of its tether—is another Pentheus, up a tree. Resisting madness can be the maddest way of being mad.

And there is a way out—the blessed madness of the maenad and the bacchant: "Blessed is he who has the good fortune to know the mysteries of the gods, who sanctifies his life and initiates his soul, a bacchant on the mountains, in holy purifications." It is possible to get the illuminations without the derangement. Derangement is disorder: the Dionysian faith is that order as we have known it is crippling, and for cripples; that what is past is prologue; that we can throw away our crutches and discover the supernatural power of walking; that human history goes from man to superman.

No superman I; I come to you not as one who has supernatural powers, but as one who seeks for them, and who has some notions which way to go to find them.

Sometimes—most times—I think that the way down and out leads out of the university, out of the academy. But perhaps it is rather that we should recover the academy of earlier days—the Academy of Plato in Athens, the Academy of Ficino in Florence, Ficino who says, "The spirit of the god Dionysus was believed by the ancient theologians and Platonists to be the ecstasy and abandon of disencumbered minds, when partly by innate love, partly at the instigation of the god, they transgress the natural limits of intelligence and are miraculously transformed into the beloved god himself; where, inebriated by a certain new draft of nectar and by an immeasurable joy, they rage, as it were, in a bacchic frenzy. In the drunkenness of this Dionysian wine, our Dionysius (the Areopagite) expresses his exultation. He pours forth enigmas, he sings in dithyrambs. To penetrate the profundity of his meanings, to imitate his quasi-Orphic manner of speech, we too require the divine fury."

At any rate the point is first of all to find again the mysteries. By which I do not mean simply the sense of wonder—that sense of wonder which is indeed the source of all true philosophy—by mystery I mean secret and occult; therefore unpublishable; therefore outside the university as we know it; but not outside Plato's Academy, or Ficino's.

Why are mysteries unpublishable? First because they cannot be put into words, at least not the kind of words which earned you your Phi Beta Kappa keys. Mysteries display themselves in words only if they can remain concealed; this is poetry, isn't it? We must return to the old doctrine of the Platonists and Neo-Platonists, that poetry is veiled truth; as Dionysus is the god who is both manifest and hidden; and as John Donne declared, with the Pillar of Fire goes the Pillar of Cloud. This is also the new doctrine of Ezra Pound, who says: "Prose is not education but the outer courts of the same. Beyond its doors are the mysteries. Eleusis. Things not to be spoken of save in secret. The mysteries self-defended, the mysteries that cannot be revealed. Fools can only profane them. The dull can neither penetrate the secretum nor divulge it to others." The mystic academies, whether Plato's or Ficino's, knew the limitations of words and drove us on beyond them, to go over, to go under, to the learned ignorance, in which God is better honored and loved by silence than by words, and better seen by closing the eyes to images than by opening them.

And second, mysteries are unpublishable because only some can see them, not all. Mysteries are intrinsically esoteric, and as such an offense to democracy: is not publicity a democratic principle? Publication makes it republican—a thing of the people. The pristine academies were esoteric and aristocratic, self-consciously separate from the profane vulgar. Democratic resentment denies that there can be anything that can't be seen by everybody; in the democratic academy truth is subject to public verification; truth is what any fool can see. This is what is meant by the so-called scientific method: so-called science is the attempt to democratize knowledge—the attempt to substitute method for insight, mediocrity for genius, by getting a standard operating procedure. The great equalizers dispensed by the scientific method are the tools, those analytical tools. The miracle of genius is replaced by the standardized mechanism. But fools with tools are still fools, and don't let your Phi Beta Kappa key fool you. Tibetan prayer wheels are another way of arriving at the same result: the degeneration of mysticism into mechanism—so that any fool can do it. Perhaps the advantage is with Tibet: for there the mechanism is external while the mind is left vacant; and vacancy is not the worst condition of the mind. And the resultant prayers make no futile claim to originality or immortality; being nonexistent, they do not have to be catalogued or stored.

The sociologist Simmel sees showing and hiding, secrecy and publicity, as two poles, like Yin and Yang, between which societies oscillate in their historical development. I sometimes think I see that civilizations originate in the disclosure of some mystery, some secret; and expand with the progressive publication of their secret; and end in exhaustion when there is no longer any secret, when the mystery has been divulged, that is to say profaned. The whole story is illustrated in the difference between ideogram and alphabet. The alphabet is indeed a democratic triumph; and the enigmatic ideogram, as Ezra Pound has taught us, is a piece of mystery, a piece of poetry, not yet profaned. And so there comes a time—I believe we are in such a time—when civilization has to be renewed by the discovery of new mysteries, by the undemocratic but sovereign power of the imagination, by the undemocratic power which makes poets the unacknowledged legislators of mankind, the power which makes all things new.

The power which makes all things new is magic. What our time needs is mystery: what our time needs is magic. Who would not say that only a miracle can save us? In Tibet the degree-granting institution is, or used to be, the College of Magic Ritual. It offers courses in such fields as clairvoyance and telepathy; also (attention physics majors) internal heat: internal heat is a yoga bestowing supernatural control over body temperature. Let me succumb for a moment to the fascination of the mysterious East and tell you of the examination procedure for the course in internal heat. Candidates assemble naked, in midwinter, at night, on a frozen Himalayan lake. Beside each one is placed a pile of wet frozen undershirts; the assignment is to wear, until they are dry, as many as possible of these undershirts before dawn. Where the power is real, the test is real, and the grading system dumfoundingly objective. I say no more. I say no more; Eastern Yoga does indeed demonstrate the existence of supernatural powers, but it does not have the particular power our Western society needs; or rather I think that each society has access only to its own proper powers; or rather each society will only get the kind of power it knows how to ask for.

The Western consciousness has always asked for freedom: the human mind was born free, or at any rate born to be free, but everywhere it is in chains; and now at the end of its tether. It will take a miracle to free the human mind: because the chains are magical in the first place. We are in bondage to authority outside ourselves: most obviously— here in a great university it must be said—in bondage to the authority of books. There is a Transcendentalist anticipation of what I want to say in Emerson's Phi Beta Kappa address on the American Scholar:

"The books of an older period will not fit this. Yet hence arises a grave mischief. The sacredness which attaches to the act of creation, the act of thought, is transferred to the record. Instantly the book becomes noxious: the guide is a tyrant. The sluggish and perverted mind of the multitude having once received this book, stands upon it, and makes an outcry if it is destroyed. Colleges are built on it. Meek young men grow up in libraries. Hence, instead of Man Thinking, we have the bookworm. I had better never see a book than to be warped by its attraction clean out of my own orbit, and make a satellite instead of a system. The one thing in the world, of value, is the active soul."

How far this university is from that ideal is the measure of the defeat of our American dream.

This bondage to books compels us not to see with our own eyes; compels us to see with the eyes of the dead, with dead eyes. Whitman, likewise in a Transcendentalist sermon, says, "You shall no longer take things at second or third hand, nor look through the eyes of the dead, nor feed on the specters in books." There is a hex on us, the specters in books, the authority of the past; and to exorcise these ghosts is the great work of magical self-liberation. Then the eyes of the spirit would become one with the eyes of the body, and god would be in us, not outside. God in us: *entheos*: enthusiasm; this is the essence of the holy madness. In the fire of the holy madness even books lose their gravity, and let themselves go up into the flame: "Properly," says Ezra Pound, "we should read for power. Man reading should be man intensely alive. The book should be a ball of light in one's hand."

I began with the name of Dionysus; let me be permitted to end with the name of Christ: for the power I seek is also Christian. Nietzsche indeed said the whole question was Dionysus versus Christ; but only the fool will take these as mutually exclusive opposites. There is a Dionysian Christianity, an apocalyptic Christianity, a Christianity of miracles and revelations. And there always have been some Christians for whom the age of miracle and revelation is not over; Christians who claim the spirit; enthusiasts. The power I look for is the power of enthusiasm; as condemned by John Locke; as possessed by George Fox, the Quaker; through whom the houses were shaken; who saw the channel of blood running down the streets of the city of Litchfield; to whom, as a matter of fact, was even given the magic internal heat—"The fire of the Lord was so in my feet, and all around me, that I did not matter to put on my shoes any more."

Read again the controversies of the seventeenth century and discover our choice: we are either in an age of miracles, says Hobbes, miracles which authenticate fresh revelations; or else we are in an age of reasoning from already received Scripture. Either miracle or Scripture. George Fox, who came up in spirit through the flaming sword into the paradise of God, so that all things were new, he being renewed to the state of Adam which he was in before he fell, sees that none can read Moses aright without Moses' spirit; none can read John's words aright, and with a true understanding of them, but in and with the same divine spirit by which John spake them, and by his burning shining light which is sent from God. Thus the authority of the past is swallowed up in new creation; the word is made flesh. We see with our own eyes and to see with our own eyes is second sight. To see with our own eyes is second sight.

Twofold Always. May God us keep
From single vision and Newton's sleep.

Joy Is the Prize: A Trip to Esalen Institute

Big Sur is an 80-mile stretch of California coast below the Monterey Peninsula. It is approximately midway between Los Angeles and San Francisco and difficult of access from either direction. Before the coastal highway was completed in 1936, the shore was accessible only by foot. The Los Padres National Forest, one of the largest preserves in the country, extends 30 miles inland and is 200 miles long; it occupies most of the area. Not much land is available for private ownership. There are only 300 residents. The rugged terrain of Los Padres includes redwood canyons, barren mountain ranges, desert flora, thick forests. It is the province of mountain lions and wild boar.

Stone cliffs rise 2,000 feet above the ocean. Beyond a wedge of meadow, the steeply inclined hillside begins. For great distances there is no meadow at all and the serpentine coastal highway hangs on the cliffside. It is a two-lane road, sometimes impassable after heavy rains. The fog bank wavers off shore. When it sweeps in, the traveler faces an uncanny trip, guided entirely by the few white dashes of the center line that are visible. With hairpin turns, sharp rises and declines, the road can be dangerous in bad weather. On clear days when the setting sun ignites dust particles on your windshield you are forced to drive blind for dangerous seconds.

Nonetheless, 4,000 people traveled this road last year, in disregard of weather, aimed toward the Esalen Institute, famous until a few years ago under a different name, Big Sur Hot Springs. These are unlikely adventurers. They are doctors, social workers, clinical psychologists, teachers, students, business executives, engineers, housewives—or just fun lovers who have come to take the baths.

Big Sur Hot Springs was originally renowned as the Eden discovered by Henry Miller and Jack Kerouac. Joan Baez once lived there. The springs were purchased in 1910 from a man named Slade by Dr. Henry C. Murphy of Salinas. It was Dr. Murphy's intention to establish a health spa. In order to use the mineral waters he brought in two bathtubs by fishing sloop. They were hauled up the cliff and placed on a ledge at the source of the springs. But because of their inaccessibility, the springs did not flourish as a spa. Not until Dr. Murphy's grandson,

Leo Litwak, "Joy Is the Prize: A Trip to Esalen Institute," from *The New York Times Magazine*, December 31, 1967. © 1967 by The New York Times Company. Copyright © 1967 by Leo Litwak. Reprinted by permission of the Author and his agent, James Brown Associates, Inc., and by permission of The New York Times Company.

Michael, assumed operation of the property in the mid-nineteen-fifties did the baths begin to receive attention—attention that has grown with the development of Esalen Institute.

Michael Murphy at 37 appears to be in his early 20's. He is slender and boyish and has a marvelous smile. I took part in a panel discussion at Hot Springs some years ago and I was not impressed either by the topic, my performance or the audience. I did enjoy the baths. I had misgivings about Murphy's program, yet none about him. He seemed to me generous, charming, innocent, credulous, enthusiastic and enormously sympathetic. A Stanford alumnus who had done some graduate work in psychology and philosophy, he had recently returned from an 18-month study of the art of meditation at the Aurobindo Ashram in Pondicherry, India, and he devoted a considerable part of each day to meditation. I believe he had—and still has—in mind some great mission, based on his Indian experience. I am not quite sure what the scope of his mission is. A friend of his told me: "Mike wants to turn on the world." Esalen Institute is his instrument for doing so. It has come a long way from the shoddy panels of a few years ago. Its spreading impact may seriously affect our methods of therapy and education.

In the course of a year, almost 1,000 professional persons—social workers, psychiatrists, clinical psychologists—enroll in Esalen workshops. Close to 700 psychotherapists have been trained to administer techniques devised by staff members—Frederick Perls, Virginia Satir, Bernard Gunther and William Schutz. These techniques have been demonstrated at hospitals, universities and medical schools. This year Esalen has opened a San Francisco extension which in the first two months of operation has attracted an attendance in excess of 10,000, offering the same workshops and seminars that are available at Big Sur. Esalen-type communities have begun to appear throughout the country, in Atlanta, Chicago, Los Angeles, Cleveland, La Jolla. One has even appeared in Vancouver, Canada. Murphy offers advice and help, and permits use of his mailing list.

Consider some offerings of the Esalen winter brochure. Seminars led by Alan Watts, the Zen interpreter, and Susan Sontag, the camp interpreter. Workshops for professional therapists conducted by Frederick Perls, an early associate of Freud and Wilhelm Reich and a founder of Gestalt therapy. A lecture panel including the psychologist Carl Rogers and Herman Kahn, the "thinking about the unthinkable" man. Some of the titles are: "Kinetic Theater," "Psychotechnics," "Do You Do It?

Or Does It Do You?" "Dante's Way to the Stars," "Creativity and the Daimonic," "On Deepening the Marriage Encounter," "Tibetan Book of the Dead," "Anxiety and Tension Control," "Racial Confrontation as a Transcendental Experience."

What principle guides a mélange that consists of dance workshops, therapy workshops, sensory-awareness experiments, the Tibetan Book of the Dead, Herman Kahn, Carl Rogers, Frederick Perls and Susan Sontag?

Esalen's vice president, George B. Leonard, has written a general statement of purpose. He says: "We believe that all men somehow possess a divine potentiality; that ways may be worked out—specific, systematic ways—to help, not the few, but the many toward a vastly expanding capacity to learn, to love, to feel deeply, to create. We reject the tired dualism that seeks God and human potentialities by denying the joys of the senses, the immediacy of unpostponed life." The programs, he says, are aimed toward "the joys of the senses."

I had signed up for a workshop led by Dr. William Schutz, a group therapist who has taught at Harvard and the Albert Einstein College of Medicine, among other institutions, and has served on the staff of the National Training Laboratories Interne Training Program at Bethel, Me. His latest book, "Joy," was published in 1967 by Grove Press.

In the brochure description of Dr. Schutz's workshop I read a warning that the experience would be more than verbal: "An encounter workshop with body movements, sensory awareness, fantasy experiments, psychodrama. "Developing the ability to experience joy is the workshop's guiding theme."

Joy as the prize of a five-day workshop?

"How can we speak of joy," Leonard has written, "on this dark and suffering planet? How can we speak of anything else? We have heard enough of despair."

It was easy enough to dismiss the language. It seemed naive to promise so great a reward for so small an investment. Joy for $175 seemed cheap at the price, especially since The New York Times was paying. I did have considerable anxieties that some of those "body movements" might be humiliating. And what precisely was meant by "sensory awareness"?

Esalen has changed considerably since my previous visit. Rows of new cabins are ranged along terraces on the hillside. The lodge is located at the bottom of a steep incline, in a meadow. The meadow is perhaps

200 yards deep and ends at the cliff edge. The Pacific Ocean is 150 feet below. A staff of 50 operates the kitchen, supervises the baths, cleans the cabins and garden and works on construction.

I passed hippy laborers, stripped to the waist, long hair flowing, operating with pick and shovel. Dreamy girls in long gowns played flutes near the pool.

I was somewhat put off by what I considered to be an excessive show of affection. Men hugged men. Men hugged women. Women hugged women. These were not hippies, but older folks, like myself, who had come for the workshop. People flew into one another's arms, and it wasn't my style at all.

After dinner, 30 of us met in the gallery for our first session. We began our excursion toward joy at 9 P.M. of a Sunday in a woodsy room on a balmy, starry night.

William Schutz, solidly built, with bald head and muzzle beard, began by telling us that in the course of the workshop we would come to dangerous ground. At such times we ought not to resist entering, for in this area lay our greatest prospect for self-transcendence. He told us to avoid verbal manipulations and to concentrate on our feelings.

We began with exercises. A fat lady in leotards directed us to be absurd. We touched our noses with our tongues. We jumped. We ran, We clutched one another, made faces at one another. Afterward, we gathered in groups of five and were given an ambiguous instruction to discover one another by touching in any way we found agreeable. I crouched in front of a strange-looking young man with an underslung jaw and powerful shoulders. I tried unlocking his legs and he glared at me.

When Schutz asked each group of five to select one couple that seemed least close, the young man with the underslung jaw selected me. The hostile pairs were than requested to stand at opposite diagonals of the room and approach each other. They were to do whatever they felt like doing when they met in the center of the room. A burly middle-aged man marched toward a petite lady. They met, they paused, stared, then suddenly embraced. The next couple, two husky men, both frozen rigid, confronted each other, stared, then also embraced. The young man and I came next. We started at opposite diagonals. We met in the center of the room. I found myself looking into the meanest, coldest eyes I had ever seen. He pressed his hands to his sides, and it was clear to me that we were not going to embrace. I reached for his hand to shake it. He jerked free. I put my hand on his shoulder; he shrugged me off. We continued staring and finally returned to our group.

There was a general discussion of this encounter. Some feared we might start fighting. Nothing, of course, was farther from my mind. I had gone out, intending to play their game and suddenly found myself staring at a lunatic. He had very mean, cold eyes, a crazy shape to his jaw, lips so grim that his ill-feeling was unmistakable. Back in our group he said to me, in a raspy, shrill voice: "You thought I was going to bat you in the face; that's why you turned away." There was a slurred quality to his speech, and it occurred to me that I might have triggered off a madman. I denied that I had turned away and I was challenged to stare him down. I was annoyed that I had been forced into something so silly.

We proceeded, on the basis of our first impressions, to give one another names, which we kept for the duration of the workshop. My nemesis accepted the name of Rebel. There was a plump, lovely girl we called Kate. A silent, powerful man with spectacles we named Clark. Our fat group leader received the name of Brigitte. A lumpy, solemn man with thick spectacles we named Gary. An elegant, trim, middle-aged woman we named Sheba. A buxom, mournful woman with long hair became Joan. A jovial middle-aged pipe smoker with a Jean Hersholt manner we named Hans. A fierce, mustached swaggerer in Bermuda shorts was Daniel. A quiet man with a little boy's face we named Victor. I was named Lionel. We were addressed by these names at all times.

I considered this renaming of ourselves a naive attempt to create an atmosphere free of any outside reference. Many of the techniques impressed me as naive. It seemed tactless and obvious to ask so blunt and vague a question as: "What are you feeling?" Yet what happened in the course of five days was that the obvious became clarified. Clichés became significant.

I found myself discovering what had always been under my nose. I had not known how my body felt under conditions of tension or fear or grief. I discovered that I was numb. I had all sorts of tricks for avoiding encounter. I didn't particularly like to be touched. I avoided looking strangers in the eye. I took pride in my coolness and trickery. I didn't believe one should give oneself away. It seemed to me a virtue to appear cool, to be relatively immune to feeling, so that I could receive shocks without appearing to. I considered it important to keep up appearances. I'm no longer proud of what I now believe to be an incapacity rather than a talent.

I thought my group rather dull. I saw no great beauty and a great deal of weakness. I felt somewhat superior, since I was there on assignment, not by choice. I hated and feared Reb.

But in the next few days, I became enormously fond of these apparently uninteresting strangers. We encountered one another in violent and intimate ways, and I could no longer dismiss them.

I was convinced that Rebel was insane. He opened our second meeting with gratuitous insults. He referred to me as "Charley Goodguy." When Brigitte, the leader of our group, told him not to think in stereotypes, he sneered at her: "Why don't you shut up, Fats?" It is difficult to convey the nastiness of his tone—an abrasive, jeering quality.

Daniel exploded. He called Rebel a shark and a rattlesnake. He said he wanted to quit the group because he despised this frightening, violent kid. "You scare me," he told Reb. "It's people like you who are responsible for Vietnam and Auschwitz. You're a monster and you're going to suck up all the energy of this group and it's not worth it. I want to get out."

I told Daniel his response seemed excessive. Vietnam and Auschwitz? "He's a little hostile," I said.

Reb didn't want any favors from me. "Hostile?" he sneered. "Say, I bet I know what you are. You sound to me like a professor. Or a pawnbroker. Which are you, a professor or a pawnbroker?"

Schutz intervened. He said to me and Rebel: "I feel you have something going. Why don't you have it out?" He suggested that we arm wrestle, an innocuous contest, but, under the circumstances, there seemed to be a great deal invested in winning or losing. My arm felt numb, and there was some trembling in my thighs. I feared I might not have all my strength, and Rebel appeared to be a powerful kid.

I pinned him so easily, however, that the group accused him of having quit. Daniel was jubilant: "You're a loser. You're trying to get clobbered."

Rebel was teased into trying again. On the second trial, he pressed my left arm down and demanded a re-match with the right hand. We remained locked together for close to 20 minutes. It was unbearable. I lost all sensation in my hand and arm. I willed my hand not to yield. Finally, I hoped he would press me down and get it over with. It ended when Rebel squirmed around and braced his foot against the wall and the contest was called.

Daniel was delighted by the outcome. He felt as though I had won something for him. Schutz asked: "Why don't *you* wrestle Reb?" Daniel despised violence. He probably would lose and he didn't want to give that monster the satisfaction of a victory. Violence was right up that shark's alley. He refused to play his games. Nonetheless, Daniel was on the ground with Rebel a moment later, beet red with strain, trembling down to his calves. Rebel raised his elbow, pressed Daniel down and the match was called off. Daniel leaped to his feet, circled the room. He suddenly charged Rebel, who was seated, and knocked him from his chair. He then rushed at Schutz, yelling: "It's you I hate, you bastard, for making me do this." Schutz did not flinch, and Daniel backed off. I could see that his impulse was histrionic. I felt sorry for Reb, who mumbled: "I copped out. I should have hit him."

Reb later presented a different guise. Far from being an idiot, he was an extremely precocious 20-year-old computer engineer, self-taught in the humanities. His father had abandoned the family when he was a child. His mother was a cold customer—never a sign of feeling. He didn't know where he stood with her. She taunted him in the same abrasive style which he tried with us.

Reb suffered sexual agonies that had brought him several hundred miles in search of a solution. He considered himself perverse and contemptible, the only impotent 20-year-old kid in the world. He admitted he found women repugnant as sexual objects, and it was hardly surprising that his crude advances were rebuffed. He admitted that his strategy had been to strike out in hope that someone would strike back so that he might *feel*. He was boyish and affectionate outside the group.

My feeling for him underwent a complete reversal. He began to impress me as an intelligent kid, trying with great courage to repair terrible injuries. The monster I had seen simply vanished.

I never anticipated the effect of these revelations, as one after another of these strangers expressed his grief and was eased. I woke up one night and felt as if everything were changed. I felt as if I were about to weep. The following morning the feeling was even more intense.

Brigitte and I walked down to the cliff edge. We lay beneath a tree. She could see that I was close to weeping. I told her that I'd been thinking about my numbness, which I had traced to the war. I tried to keep the tears down. I felt vulnerable and unguarded. I felt that I was about to lose all my secrets and I was ready to let them go. Not being guarded, I had no need to put anyone down, and I felt what it was to be unarmed. I could look anyone in the eyes and my eyes were open.

That night I said to Daniel: "Why do you keep diverting us with intellectual arguments? I see suffering in your eyes. You give me a

glimpse of it, then you turn it off. Your eyes go dead and the intel-
tual stuff bores me. I feel that's part of your strategy."

Schutz suggested that the two of us sit in the center of the room
and talk to each other. I told Daniel that I was close to surrender. I
wanted to let go. I felt near to my grief. I wanted to release it and be
purged. Daniel asked about my marriage and my work. Just when he
hit a nerve, bringing me near the release I wanted, he began to speculate on the tragedy of the human condition. I told him: "You're letting
me off and I don't want to be let off."

Schutz asked if I would be willing to take a fantasy trip.

It was late afternoon and the room was already dark. I lay down,
Schutz beside me, and the group gathered around. I closed my eyes.
Schutz asked me to imagine myself very tiny and to imagine that tiny
self entering my own body. He wanted me to describe the trip.

I saw an enormous statue of myself, lying in a desert, mouth open
as if I were dead. I entered my mouth. I climbed down my gullet,
entering it as if it were a manhole. I climbed into my chest cavity.
Schutz asked me what I saw. "It's empty," I said. "There's nothing
here." I was totally absorbed by the effort to visualize entering myself
and lost all sense of the group. I told Schutz there was no heart in
my body. Suddenly, I felt tremendous pressure in my chest, as if tears
were going to explode. He told me to go to the vicinity of the heart
and report what I saw. There, on a ledge of the chest wall, near where
the heart should have been, I saw a baby buggy. He asked me to look
into it. I didn't want to, because I feared I might weep, but I looked,
and I saw a doll. He asked me to touch it. I was relieved to discover
that it was only a doll. Schutz asked me if I could bring a heart into
my body. And suddenly there it was, a heart sheathed in slime, hung
with blood vessels. And that heart broke me up. I felt my chest con-
vulse. I exploded. I burst into tears.

I recognized the heart. The incident had occurred more than 20
years before and had left me cold. I had written about it in a story
published long ago in *Esquire*. The point of the story was that such
events should have affected me but never did. The war in Germany was
about over. We had just taken a German village without resistance. We
had fine billets in German houses. The cellars were loaded with jams
and sausages and wine. I was the aid man with the outfit, and was
usually summoned by the call of "Aid man!" When I heard that call
I became numb, and when I was numb I could go anywhere and do
anything I figured the battles were over. It came as a shock when I
heard the call this time. There were rifle shots, then: "Aid man!" I

ran to the guards and they pointed to bushes 10 yards from where they had been posted. They had spotted a German soldier and called to him to surrender. He didn't answer and they fired. I went to the bushes and turned him over. He was a kid about 16, blond, his hair strung out in the bushes, still alive. The .30-caliber bullets had scooped out his chest and I saw his heart. It was the same heart I put in my chest 23 years later. He was still alive, gray with shock, going fast. He stared up at me—a mournful, little boy's face. He asked: "Why did you shoot? I wanted to surrender." I told him we didn't know.

Now, 23 years later, I wailed for that German boy who had never mattered to me and I heaved up my numbness. The trip through my body lasted more than an hour. I found wounds everywhere. I remembered a wounded friend whimpering: "Help me, Leo," which I did—a close friend, yet after he was hit no friend at all, not missed a second after I heard of his death, numb to him as I was to everyone else, preparing for losses by anesthetizing myself. And in the course of that trip through my body I started to feel again, and discovered what I'd missed. I felt wide open, lightened, ready to meet others simply and directly. No need for lies, no need to fear humiliation. I was ready to be a fool. I experienced the joy Schutz had promised to deliver. I'm grateful to him. Not even the offer of love could threaten me.

This was the transformation I underwent in the course of that fantasy trip. The force of the experience began to fade quickly, and now, writing two weeks later, I find that little remains. But I still have a vision of a possibility I had not been aware of—a simple, easy connection with my own feeling and, consequently, with others'.

I had great difficulty emerging from my body. I was pinned against my intestines, pregnant with myself. When I finally began to move and restored all the missing organs and repaired those that were damaged, I feared that all this work was temporary, that if I were to leave the heart would vanish, the stomach dry up, the intestines be exposed. Schutz asked if there was anyone who could help me get out. I said: "My daughter." So I invited my daughter to enter my body. She stood near my heart and said: "Come on out, Daddy," and led me out. I ran to a meadow on my chest. I ran through long grass, toward a gate, directly toward the sun. There I lay down and rested.

Occasionally, during my trip, I heard others crying, but I had lost track of the group. I opened my eyes. I had an initial sense of others as darts of candlelight about me. The room seemed to have shifted. It was pitch black outside. Everyone was very close to me—Reb, Daniel, Brigitte, Bill, Joan, Victor, Kate, Clark, Gary, Sheba. Sheba still wept.

Brigitte directed us all to lie down and to reach out and touch one another. She turned out the lights and gave us various instructions designed to release us and finally we parted.

It was not easy leaving these people I had met only five days before. Time was distorted and we seemed to have lived years together. It was not easy leaving Big Sur. On the final morning, the entire workshop met to say good-by. Our group gathered in a tight circle, hugging and kissing, and I found myself hugging everyone, behaving like the idiots I had noticed on first arriving at Esalen. I hugged Rebel. I told him he was a great kid and that a few years from now he might not even recall his present trouble. I told him not to envy his peers. He was probably much better than they.

Schutz ended our last meeting by playing a record from "The Man of La Mancha," "The Impossible Dream." We were at that point of sentiment where corny lyrics announced truths and we could be illuminated by the wisdom of clichés.

The condition of vulnerability is precious and very fragile. Events and people and old routines and old habits conspire to bring you down. But not all the way down. There is still the recollection of that tingling sense of being wide awake, located in the here and now, feeling freely and entirely, all constraints discarded. It remains a condition to be realized. It could change the way we live.

From *The Varieties of Psychedelic Experience*

Turning to the forthcoming examples of psychedelic drug experiences, it is not possible to say that they are "typical." Every such experience is in many significant ways very *individual* and depends for its structure and content upon what the subject brings to the session in the way of personal history and frame of reference—"who he is" at that time. The other principal determinants of the experience will be the physical environment and the other person or persons present, most notably the *guide* conducting the session. The drug itself makes certain experiences possible; but rarely would it be accurate to say that the drug in any other sense determined a particular experience.

Finally, before passing on to the examples, something should be said about the remarkably high quality of the writing of those drug subjects who have given us first-person accounts of their psychedelic experiences. In many cases, the style is worthy of a professional author and the idea content is almost equally impressive. As others before us have noted, this surprising display of literary talent is not at all uncommon among former psychedelic subjects writing accounts of their experiences, and we think the reasons for it are clear. First of all, the subject has had what he regards as an enormously impressive and important experience and this valuation of the experience provides a very high degree of motivation to describe the session well and to try to convey to others the details, flavor, and impact of what occurred. Also, the psychedelic experience almost always is so unusual and richly various that all the materials are at hand for a vivid prose statement that requires no imagination to construct while, at the same time, the contents seem to the writer to rival the creative productions of even the most imaginative authors. In the case of our own subjects, it is relevant, too, that many were persons of superior intelligence and considerable education. Moreover, many were educators, clergymen, attorneys, and other such persons whose day-to-day work demands a fairly high degree of verbal facility.

Example No. 1: This contains no especially unusual elements but does describe a good many of the more common components of the psychedelic experience. Of particular interest is the summation by the subject (S), at the end of his account, of the reasons why he considers the term "consciousness-expanding" to be warranted.

S, a thirty-six-year-old assistant professor of English literature, had his peyote session in the company of the guide and S's wife, neither of whom took the drug. Several pre-session interviews and some correspondence and other reading had prepared S for his experience and eliminated misconceptions and most of the anxiety concerning it. S's own account follows:

"My peyote experience began in a house on a farm in the rugged hill country of Northwest Arkansas. A kind of tea had been brewed from the green 'buttons' or tops of the cactus plants and I had no trouble consuming an amount the guide told me was sufficient. The Dramamine I took ahead of time apparently was instrumental in keeping the hour or so of nausea within manageable proportions.

"Apart from this nausea and some feelings of being alternately too hot and too cold, no effects of the drug were noticeable for about one and one-half hours from the time of consumption. Then I suddenly became extremely aware of the croaking of frogs and then of the chirping of crickets. The former came from a stream about a block or so away from the house but sounded very close and I fancied that the frogs had come down to stand before the door and serenade me.

"Darkness had come on almost unnoticed and my attention was first called to the dimness of the light when my wife got up to turn on a small lamp that was standing on a table in one corner of the room. Very shortly after this I saw moving toward me across the room a ball of red fire about the size of a golf ball. It drifted, swaying a little from side to side, while moving toward me at about the level of my shoulders as I was seated in a chair. I felt no uneasiness, only interest, and when the ball of fire had come close enough I poked at its center with my finger. It then exploded, a lavish shower of multicolored sparks cascading and dropping on the rug at my feet. I smiled happily at the others and remarked: 'It has started. Now let's see what kind of traveler I am going to make.'

"Ever since I first had heard of the peyote I had wanted to observe the effects of such a drug on myself. I sought no particular experience but I expected to have a happy and interesting time and also possibly to learn a good bit about my own psychology. The beautiful images some writers have described were something I hoped would be a part of my experience. While outside the house were lovely natural surroundings that later I planned to explore.

"To see if the images would come I closed my eyes and perceived at first a succession of geometric forms, mostly circles and triangles. The colors were soft pastels and aroused in me a kind of emotional warmth that encompassed my wife, the guide and all of my surroundings and remained with me throughout most of the session. This warmth was accompanied by a sensation of relaxing muscles, although the mind kept very much alert and alive. Then began the images I had wanted to see, brilliantly colored and drenched in white and golden light. Also, objects in the images seemed to generate a light of their own and cast off glowing and pulsating or rippling waves of color. The first image I remember was of an Egyptian tomb made of granite, alabaster and marble. Behind it great golden sculptures of pharaohs rose to awesome heights and there was the fragrance of eucalyptus burning in brass bowls mounted upon tripods of iron that had the feet of falcons. Priests in ornate headdress ringed the tomb and raised their arms to greet a procession of many brightly robed figures bearing torches and with faces obscured by masks resembling the heads of various beasts. Funerary orations seemed to blend into marriage ceremonies where fruit and great platters of meat, even the forbidden pig, were served up by fierce glistening black slaves. The platters were placed upon massive stone steps leading to a dais upon which were seated royal figures in carved black chairs whose arms were the heads of solemn cats.

"From a distance, after that, I saw pyramids and knew that in one of these the ceremony just observed was unfolding. But the pyramids were transformed into haystacks, golden under a huge red sun, and then these became dunes in a great desert. Here, tents were clustered half-buried by swirling stinging sands. Inside one of these, in appropriate garb, my wife and I were seated on pillows of camel's hair. Girls in filmy garments were dancing, their dark eyes flashing above gleaming white teeth. There were tambourines, a drum, and strange stringed instruments, playing a music I could hear and that seemed intended to lay bare and set quivering the elemental passions of the listeners. Swarthy, scowling, bearded men were ranged near the tent's entrance. They had black, glaring eyes, wore daggers, and some held naked swords in lean weather-beaten hands.

"In many of the images that came to me I saw myself, sometimes with my wife, more often alone. I was a fur-capped Mongol huntsman, cold-eyed and cruel, bow in hand, striking down a running rabbit from the back of a racing, gaunt half-wild stallion. I was a stark black-robed figure, protected by an amulet suspended from a heavy gold chain that was worn about my neck, somberly wandering, lost in bitter ascetic reflection, among the crumbling walls of old temples overgrown by thick, twisted and gnarled vines. At other times there were legions of warriors, darkening deserts or in ranks that extended across immense bone-littered plains. There were brown-cowled monks, pacing cloisters in silent, shared but unadmitted desperation. Image after image after image, flowing in succession more rapid than I would have wished, but all exquisitely detailed and with colors richer and more brilliant than those either nature or the artist has yet managed to create.

"Again and again I returned to the images, so numerous I could not begin to recount them, but in between times many other curious phenomena came to my attention. So extended was time that once it seemed to me I lighted a cigarette, smoked it for hours, looked down and noticed that the cigarette still had its first ash. A few moments were hours, possibly longer, and any one event seemed to take almost no time at all. I remarked to my wife that 'We are out of time, but that is not to say that time has run out.' What I meant was that, in the moment when I spoke, time's fingers had ceased their nervous, incessant strumming upon the space that contained us. But that space was—how can one put it?—*irregular*. A space that expanded and contracted and imposed upon us (actually, of course, upon *me*) the arbitrary quickening rhythms of its pulsations. For, as I remarked, this timeless space was a bubble, and would burst. Then I experienced a dull sort of sadness, since I wanted to remain forever out of time. Or, if not that, then in a world of moments which, like those I was experiencing, were enormously extended. I wanted to know that those moments would not, in some instant to be dreaded, snap back like an elastic drawn out for a while but then released as if God were punishing some pleasure so great as to be an unforgivable transgression.

· "I believe it was simultaneous with this that I became aware of the body that encased me as being very heavy and amorphous. Inside it, everything was stirring and seemed to be drawing me inward. I felt that I could count the beats, the throbbing of my heart, feel the blood moving through my veins, feel the passage of the breath as it entered and left the body, the nerves as they hummed with their myriad messages. Above all, I was conscious of my brain as teemingly alive, cells incredibly active, and my mental processes as possessing the unity of perfect precision. Yet this last, I suspected, was not really true and instead my mind, 'drunk on its own ideas,' was boastfully over-estimating its prowess.

"Sensations were acute. I heard, saw, felt, smelled and tasted more fully than ever before (or since). A peanut butter sandwich was a delicacy not even a god could deserve. Yet, I took only a few bites and was too full to eat more. To touch a fabric with one's fingertip was to simultaneously know more about both one's fingertip and the fabric than one had ever known about either. It was also to experience intense touch-pleasure and this was accentuated even further when, at the guide's suggestion, I 'localized consciousness' in the fingertip with the consequence that all phenomena at that point were greatly enhanced.

"I took my wife's hand and it seemed to me a great force of love flowed through my hand into hers, and also from her hand into mine, and that then this love was diffused throughout our bodies. Her smile, her whole face was beautiful beyond description, and I wondered if I would be able to see her like this when the drug experience had ended.

"Together we walked to one end of the room, where a large reproduction of Rousseau's *Sleeping Gypsy* was hanging on the wall. Try as I might I could not at that time decide if the Gypsy was a man or a woman, but my wife said 'A man,' and I accepted her judgment. Studying the bulging-eyed beast in that painting, I saw that its mane is all dendrites and energy pulses through each branch and is transmitted to the brain of the sleeping Gypsy. The beast seemed to be sniffing, while the moon shimmered and winked and smiled, and the strings of the instrument that lay upon the ground were plucked by an invisible hand. I saw that in the painting gray-green waters never stir to wash upon brown sands. The sleep of the Gypsy was endless. The beast hovered, rooted forever in its place, and the life that I now breathed into that scene gave new life to me but not to those figures transfixed in captive immortality projected by a brain long since gone to its rest and returned to the dust. Better, I said, to be a live beholder than to be a great artist in his grave. Better life, than to be an immortal but immobile Gypsy or moon or sea or beast. My life suddenly seemed to me infinitely precious and I cried out with joy at the thought that I was now living so much in so short a span of time.

"Later, we walked in the woods and by the river and it seemed that my love was so great it evoked a response from animals, birds and plants, and even from inanimate things. On the river bank, as the sky began to brighten, I threw my arms around my wife and at once the birds broke into a song that bespoke a universal harmony always existing but requiring that one approach it in a certain way before it can reveal itself. The silver-surfaced river, bathed in fresh dawnlight, reflected trees reaching down as if yearning toward the heart of the earth. The leaves of the trees were as intricately patterned as great snowflakes and at other times resembled webs spun by God-inspired spiders of a thread of unraveled emeralds. The beauty of nature was such that I cannot describe it, although I have managed to retain some measure of the *feeling* it awakened in me.

"Along with all this there were torrents of ideas, some amplifications of my own past thinking, but others that were strange and entered my mind as if from without. At the house, when we returned and the effects were much less, it seemed to me that what I had experienced was essentially, and with few exceptions, the usual content of experience but that, of everything, there was MORE. This MORE is what I think must be meant by the 'expansion of consciousness' and I jotted down at that time something of this MORE I had experienced.

"The consciousness-expanding drugs, I wrote then, enable one to sense, think and feel MORE.

"Looking at a thing one sees MORE of its color, MORE of its detail, MORE of its form.

"Touching a thing, one touches MORE. Hearing a sound, one hears MORE. Tasting, one tastes MORE. Moving, one is MORE aware of movement. Smelling, one smells MORE.

"The mind is able to contain, at any given moment, MORE. Within consciousness, MORE simultaneous mental processes operate without any one of them interfering with the awareness of the others. Awareness has MORE levels, is many-dimensioned. Awareness is of MORE shades of meaning contained in words and ideas.

"One feels, or responds emotionally with MORE intensity, MORE depth, MORE comprehensiveness.

"There is MORE of time, or within any clock-measured unit of time, vastly MORE occurs than can under normal conditions.

"There is MORE empathy, MORE unity with people and things.

"There is MORE insight into oneself, MORE self-knowledge.

"There are MORE alternatives when a particular problem is considered, MORE choices available when a particular decision is to be made. There are MORE ways of 'looking at' a thing, an idea or a person . . ."

In an appraisal of the effects of his session, made about five months later, S said that his view of the psychedelic experience as "essentially a MORE" still seemed to him to be valid. What he had "carried away from" his session was "above all a feeling of very great enrichment." He retained "a more acute awareness of color, a much increased appreciation of the great beauty of my wife, and a wonderful awareness of the almost infinite detail that objects will yield up if only one will give them one's attention."

Most important of all, S thought, was "the knowledge and certainty I now have that it is truly possible to attain to a sense of harmony with all creatures and things." He felt that this sense of harmony as he had experienced it during his session provides the person with "a strength, serenity and capacity for loving not possible when the experience of harmony is wanting." S was having some success at "re-invoking" the harmonious state and making it a part of his everyday life. He felt that this must be done without the "invaluable help of peyote which shows one the way but then, quite properly, leaves one to follow that way through one's own efforts. This has to be so, since the way pointed out has its application in this world, not in the peyote wonder-world." S added that his experiencing of the "universal harmony and what it confers was the richest single event of my session and probably, also, of my life."

In evaluating the session just described, we regarded it as being a very positive and pleasant one for the subject. However, it was not one of those more profound experiences met with in the drug-state in which the subject confronts himself on the deepest levels of his being, receives some basic insight or understanding, and emerges transformed in some fundamental way.

Possibly these deeper levels were not reached because the subject had no *need* to reach them. His adjustment already was superior and this is reflected in the thoroughly wholesome or healthy-minded character of his session. Few psychedelic experiences are so free of "negative" elements as this one, although *all* of our subjects had to meet such basic requirements as: 1) successful present functioning; 2) absence of detectable signs of psychosis or serious neurosis; 3) absence of past history of major mental illness; and 4) adequate preparation for and positive expectations concerning the drug experience.

We would add that when these and a few other preconditions are met and when the session is adequately managed, the chances of any subject's "getting into trouble" are reduced to very slight proportions.

Example No. 2: The second example to be presented is of an unguided "session." The "subject" was, of course, not observed during his experience, but he was interviewed subsequently on several occasions and at length. He also submitted a written report of his experience.

We present an example of an unguided drug experience both so that it may be compared in certain respects with the examples of guided ones and because it illustrates some of the more common painful and delusive varieties of ideation and perception met with in the sessions.

Most of these negative aspects will not be found in the other examples given in this chapter, but will be further exemplified and discussed later on. In general, the negative aspects of the experience occur less often and in much milder form in the properly guided session than in the unguided or mismanaged one.

In this case, S, a male university student, age twenty-two, obtained a supply of LSD by "borrowing" it from his older brother, a physician. He took a very strong dose of the drug (estimated afterwards to have been 400 to 500 micrograms) and experienced what he believes was a "transient psychosis." The following is a condensed account by S of his experience:

"I had been thinking for some time about having some LSD. I finally made a decision and at about nine o'clock in the morning I went to the refrigerator where my brother kept a supply and took what I thought would be a sufficient amount. The amount, as I soon discovered, was more than sufficient! For the next ten hours I moved through a world that sometimes was beautiful and intensely interesting, but more often resembled a nightmare. For four of those hours I seem to have an almost complete amnesia. The experience as a whole I regard as a temporary psychotic distortion of consciousness.

"The experience did not begin badly. At first there was a very strange sense that all perception and abstract cognition had become kinesthetic —that these were no more than extensions of one's neuromuscular being. Then came a profound sense of the tragic and comical aspects of life, with a sense of walking around inside of my own brain.

"I closed my eyes and at once there appeared to me a great variety of Egyptian motifs, statues and *bas relief* forms with a rigorous symmetry. Everything was very precise and geometrical. When I opened my eyes and looked at the objects around me, it was as if they were made of tallow and were melting. There was a drippiness of colors, and it also seemed that these things might be made of waxen candy. It occurred to me that this was probably due not only to my heightened awareness of objects, but also to the liquid in my eyes that now imparted to everything a liquid coating. Along with these perceptions there was the sense of the intense sensuality of oneself, an extremely luxurious sensuality.

"I had several hallucinations that I recognized as such. At one point elves appeared and accepted me as a jolly fellow spirit. They spoke to me in verse and wanted to guide me to magical places—to castles and mythological realms. Many different personalities, all of them part of oneself, became autonomous and spoke of various things. There was a great concern with personal destiny and a sense that the total attention and concern of the universe was focused upon me. I thought that I was participating in a test, was being observed, and that the observing forces were benevolent. All people seemed to me to be no more than simply different forms of oneself, different masks of oneself. They were all of the different lives that one has, or that one is to live. And there was the sense that the world has no greater claim to substance than does a dream; that all authority, all validity rests with oneself and the world is entirely one's possession. Later, when I went out, this resulted in a total unconcern for social forms, such as not sitting down on the sidewalk or in the street; for now one knew that the sidewalk was a part of one's brain and one could do with it what one liked.

"My solipsism was accompanied by delusions of grandeur not logically consistent with it, yet reconcilable for the reason that they had a logic of their own. Although I was the All, I participated in the test of living that somehow was connected with the training of the future God. I was awed by the stereoscopic solidity of reality, the sheer substantiality of it all. Yet reality was my own thought and I was struck with wonder that one's thoughts could suddenly become so substantive and stereoscopic. I congratulated myself upon being able to create reality so well. I felt that others should be grateful to me for supporting their existence. I was holding them up, containing them, giving them air. I was benevolent, and did not kick them.

"I went out and walked through the streets where people were experienced as epiphenomena of oneself. They were also waxen mechanical toys, part of a mechanical toy process and were made out of candy. (This may have been because they were seen as having the bright colors of those little candies that are sometimes made in images of persons.) People were an utter absurdity as they went about their rituals, which I contained completely and knew to be absurd in their circularity, unconstructiveness and superstitiousness. But they went about their rituals with a sense of absolute self-righteousness, hilarious zombies who failed to recognize me as the one who beneficently supported their existence. I forgave them for failing to recognize me, knowing them to be as ignorant as children or animals. I took in the world as my private menagerie, a banquet I have provided for myself. It occurred to me to give them commands, but I knew it was better that I respect their ignorance; at the same time I was telling myself: 'You are under drugs and in a psychotic state and had better be as withdrawn and restrained as possible in a world that is liable to blow up if you make the wrong move.'

"The streets bounce, of course. The world is experienced as a physical extension of oneself, of one's own nervous system. Consequently I felt the blows of pick axes wielded by construction men tearing up the street. One possessed a kinesthetic identity with the street, and yet the blows did not hurt. For the street knows in its own being that it is being broken up and yet does not experience the judgment of pleasure or pain. Related to this was an acute awareness of energy in the world. One felt one's body to be supercharged with 'energy,' a word that was variously associated with 'nervous' and 'spirit.' Or it could be associated with tension of the spirit. The other, when it is person, is supercharged with energy like neonized electric generators, sizzling firecrackers as distinguished from the other when it is object and is perceived as static electricity. Only water fountains, among things, have energy. Other objects are frozen.

"The persona of people, I thought, are not to be respected. With this thought, they became the absence of materiality—smiling ghosts. However, they are similar to oneself and therefore are no more to be respected than oneself, or feared or approved of. All of my ideas about politics, religion, state and race were, at this point, embellished. I thought about all of the perversions of myself, by which I meant the rest of humanity. These perversions were not to be hated, just to be pitied and forgotten. They are the dead-end of evolution.

"I noticed that events in the world occurred or started just where one's own thought left off. One could think 'It's getting warm,' and then naturally someone just behind you would say 'It's getting warm.' One always anticipates—no, *knows*—the next stage, the next link in the process, or something in the world may take up at the point anticipated by one's thought. For example, I created a symphonic structure that reached a peak calling for a solo instrument, but there I broke off and at once was answered by an event in the world that was the objective resolution in the world of my subjective harmonies. This event was a man who came up to me and asked 'Are you all right, buddy?' This was the completion of the symphony, and I had anticipated his words and even his very tone of voice.

"A phenomenon of importance under the drug is the non-connective tactile awareness of things that consists of an extension of visual awareness to incorporate tactile awareness into its scope. The substance of a thing was both seen and felt through the visual perception. And along with this there was the sense that one must speak to beauty and commune with beauty in all of its forms, including persons. This included not just pretty girls, but also trees. A major revelation was that of the spiritual nature of trees: the obedient benevolence of trees. One was obliged to commune with them, and with statues. This imperative was part of a larger imperative that seemed to stand out absolutely from all other thought as the one overriding imperative statement: That one must seek God. The beautiful is a part of the imperative that one must approach the Godhead. This was the ultimate procedural prescription. All of the rest of thought was dispensable and this prescription alone could guide one. Related to this was the falling away of all the normal power and authority sanctions and seeming rightness of familiar social and prescriptive forms of behavior and purpose and attitude. These melted away with awareness of what was truly important, valid and authoritative. Since there was no reason not to, I sat down in the middle of a busy sidewalk and let people pass around me. I noticed that mannikins in windows were smiling and Elizabeth Taylor from an enormous poster advertising the film *Cleopatra* several times gestured for me to come to her.

"I got onto the subway thinking that I would ride it to the end of the line. At once these words, 'end of the line,' assumed awesome and multiple proportions. I felt drawn and impelled toward this 'end of the line' where Some Thing was waiting, and beckoning. I felt that I might find there fulfillment or destruction, or both. I recognized now that always at the core of the experience there had been this nightmarish rhythm of acceleration toward some impending unknown. Even so, there was some part of oneself that held to one's sense of mature sobriety.

"I remembered a patient described by my brother. He was schizophrenic, oblivious to circumstances and to his orientation in the world, and concerned himself only with considering what was going on in his head—a 'buzzing' in his head, as if it contained a nest of hornets. Now, with all of the stimuli from the environment swarming in upon me, I also felt my internal state to be one of a vast and buzzing colony of bees. Tingling, vibratory feelings overwhelmed my nervous system and I felt myself lifted upwards toward some unknown bliss or terror.

"I left the subway and lay down on a bench in a park and it was there that I lost my four hours. I had long nightmare dreams that came to me in a state that was different from sleeping but still somehow resembled it. These dreams, I think I have forgotten in self-defense against their horror. Yet I recall that they were just as vivid and real as conscious experience, but had gross although somehow symmetrical distortions as one would go through the same motions countless times. One would walk through the same door again and again, endlessly passing out through the door. There was a sense of the normal world having run riot and that it was now transformed into its antithesis. At other times, I 'awakened' into increasingly incredible and terrifying worlds. It seems to me that giant elevator shafts extended down into the infinite and insane-looking men kept passing into the elevators and coming out again—the same men, over and over. I sensed that I was moving toward some final undefined cataclysm of total damnation, but then awakened into what I supposed was another of the nightmare worlds and discovered that instead it was the 'real world.' The vividness and verisimilitude of the dream world is demonstrated by the length of time it took me to realize that now I was back in the 'real world.' From this point on, the drug intoxication diminished steadily and I made my way back home. Afterwards I felt that I had been in a feverish, drunken state that had left me with a head tied in knots and a feeling of shell-shock, or possibly a feeling like that of one who is undergoing withdrawal from a schizophrenic state.

"I felt also that things might have been much worse: That in the drug intoxication one might lose one's sense of balance and be in utter terror and helplessness before the nature of the universe—just as, for instance, should one lose one's sense of gravitational balance, of upness and downness, one would find oneself in terrified estrangement from the normally beneficent, supporting terrestrial environment."

Several things need to be said about S's account of an experience that contained psychosis-like elements if it was not, as he believes, an actual temporary psychosis. First of all, while the drug experience was definitely a very bad one, it also contained (as interviews brought out) a good many positive elements that S has played down in his account and which suggest that the "psychosis" may have been sporadic and intermittent, rather than continuous. It is characteristic of those persons who have painful experiences with psychedelic drugs that they attack the experience with great vehemence. Thus S, in his summation, insists that the "cosmic and mystical unions some drug subjects claim to experience in the drug-state are *always* [our italics] mere chemically imbalanced, epileptic-type states." And that all of the drug-state insights "are the insights of madness, which may or may not be valid but whose validity only can be determined by one in a normal state of consciousness."

The unfortunate experience of this subject almost certainly resulted in the main from several crucial factors. First of all, S would not have been accepted by a responsible researcher as a volunteer subject. Although a very brilliant young man, he has a history of *petit mal* seizures and this alone would have been a basis for disqualification. Secondly, he took the drug with the expectation of experiencing a "model psychosis"; and this expectation, as the scientific literature makes painfully evident, is frequently fulfilled. Third, not only did he have no supportive and directional guidance, but he exposed himself to a variety of stress situations that generated anxiety and accentuated his pathological ideation.

In the following example we offer a first-person account of an LSD experience that was thoroughly pleasurable to the subject, but comparatively innocuous. The drug was administered by a guide who was on hand for the session, but whose role was only to provide support and to deal with difficulties should any arise (as they did not). S, apart from the few tests she was given, was allowed complete free rein to experience what she would and her session, although she termed it rewarding, was relatively shallow and in that sense typical of sessions where the guide does no real guiding, only observes and, by his presence, enables the subject to feel more secure than she might feel otherwise.

Example No. 3: S, a twenty-four-year-old university instructor, was given 225 micrograms of LSD. (She had had one previous LSD experience with a 100-microgram dose.) Her account is as follows:

"The experience began in my fourth floor walk-up in Greenwich Village. After the initial physical sensations (a very mild nausea and stiffness of the neck) had passed, I began to notice that the wooden floor had started to ripple. I walked across the floor, climbing up its steep waves and sliding down its inclines. Occasionally, I would catch one of its oaken crests and ride it to the wall in much the same way that a surf rider travels on the waves.

"I looked first at the guide, whose appearance was unchanged, and then at my co-subject R, who was sitting in the lotus position. His well-fringed face was alternately shifting from Christ to satyr, then back to Christ again, and he opened his eyes and came out of his private Nirvana for a moment to say to me: 'Well, this it IT! What more is there to say?'

"I directed my attention towards the room and suddenly everything was holy. The stove, and the pottery and the chairs and the record player and the soup ladles and the old bottles—all were touched with sacrality, and I bowed to each of them in turn and worshiped. One pot in particular was so well endowed with divinity I dared not come closer to it than four or five feet lest I be burned to ashes for my unclean lips and impure heart. But a godly peach proved friendlier and accepted my adoration with kindly beneficence, radiating on me the preternatural light of its numinous fuzz. I bowed my gratitude and moved on, transfigured by the deity of things.

"I remember looking at a finely detailed photograph of the Swiss Alps. I had admired this photograph before, in my pre-LSD days an hour or an aeon ago, but now its precision became reality and the temperature plunged and fine crystals of snow whipped across my face and I circled like an eagle above the crags and snowy summits of the mountain top. An expedition of climbers waved up at me and I lifted one talon to wave back.

"I was called back to Greenwich Village by obscenity. A sound, a chant, lascivious and brutal, a whining pornography assaulted my ears and left me furious with moral indignation. "How dare you say things like that to me!" said I to the disembodied chant. It suddenly ended, as quickly as it had begun, and I saw R removing a record which he explained to me was a recording of fertility mantras directed to the goddess Kali. A Bach toccata then was put on the phonograph and the music of the spheres left their archetypal abode and took up residence in the walk-up on —— Street.

"It was at this time that I closed my eyes and experienced a vision of the future that unfolded in vivid colors before my closed eyes and was accompanied by voices that were audible, however, only inside my head. I found myself and the rest of mankind standing together on the foothills of the earth, being addressed by two splendid and luminous figures many hundreds of miles high. They could be seen plainly in spite of their height and they told us that they were the elders of this particular part of the cosmos and had lost their patience with the human creatures of this earth. The recalcitrance of greedy, warring, barbarous mankind had overexceeded itself and now that nuclear power had been discovered the outrageous breed evolved on our planet might yet attempt to subvert the whole cosmos. And so it had been decided in the Council of Elders that unless mankind could find something in its creations with which to justify itself, it would have to be destroyed.

"Having heard this message, we earthlings scattered and searched our libraries, museums, histories and parliaments for some achievement that might be seen as a justification for our being. We brought forth our greatest art objects, our Leonardos, Michelangelos, Praxiteles—But the elders only shook their heads and said solemnly: 'It is not sufficient.' We brought forth our great masterpieces of literature, the works of Shakespeare, Milton, Goethe, Dante. But these also were deemed insufficient. We searched in our religious literature and offered the figures of the religious geniuses—Jesus, Buddha, Moses, St. Francis, but the elders only laughed and said: 'Not sufficient.'

"It was then, when destruction seemed imminent and all had given themselves up to their fate, that I came forward and offered to the elders the music of Johann Sebastian Bach. They listened to the entire corpus and great silver tears of incredible brilliance shimmered and trickled down the length of their luminous bodies, after which they were silent. On and on this silence extended, until they broke it to say only: 'It is sufficient. You of the Earth are justified.' And then they went away.

"For a period of time I had neither capacity nor wish to measure, I pondered this vision. Then, when the music had ended, I lay on my back and looked up at the ceiling where a kaleidoscope of images from ancient civilizations flickered rapidly before my eyes. Egypt and Greece, Assyria and old China sped across the ceiling. Flickering pharaohs, fluttering parthenons and a palpitating Nebuchadnezzar—all contributed to this panoramic, historical agitation.

"And suddenly—destruction! The air was thick with the ammonia smell of death. Noxious vapors stung the eyes and choked the throat. The stench of the Apocalypse rose up with the opening of the graves of the new and old dead. It was the nostrils' view of the *Night on Bald Mountain*, an olfactory *Walpurgisnacht* rite. The world had become a reeking decay. Then I heard R rebuking someone with the words: 'Christ, Timmy, couldn't you have used your sandbox?' Timmy was the cat and the apocalyptic smell had issued from a single turd he had deposited in the middle of the floor.

"I turned my attention from Timmy's tangible residues to Timmy himself. He stretched himself with infinite grace and arched his back to begin—*The Ballet*. Leaping through time and space, he hung like Nijinsky—suspended in the air for a millennium, and then, drifting languidly down to the ground, he pirouetted to a paw-licking standstill. He then stretched out one paw in a tentative movement and propelled himself into a mighty spiral, whirling into cosmic dust, then up on his toes for a bow to his creation.

"He was a cat no longer—but Indra, the primeval God dancing the cosmic dance in that that time before time, setting up a rhythmic flux in nonbeing until it at last had attained to Life. The animating waves of the Dance of Creation pulsed all around me and I could no longer refuse to join in the dance. I arose to perform a *pas de deux* with the cat-Indra, but before I could allow myself more than a cursory leap into the cosmic fray a great flame erupted somewhere in the vicinity of my left elbow and I felt obliged to give it my attention. The guide had started a fire burning in the hearth and it commanded I concentrate upon it to the exclusion of all else.

"It was a lovely fire. Mandalas played in it and so did gods, and so did many hundreds of beings, known and unknown, rising in El Greco attenuations for one brilliant moment, only to lapse again into nothing. I fell into musing and after aeons had gone by and worlds within worlds within worlds had been explored, I looked up and said something to R. It was an attempt to define our relationship at that precise moment, and I said: 'You and I, we are ships that sometimes pass one another on the seas but never meet.' 'Bull——!' said R—and my vast, rippling reflections were shattered.

" 'Let's get out of here!' I said. 'Where to?' he asked, and seemed to find his question very funny. 'Where to?' he asked again, convulsed with laughter, and managed to add: 'as if there were any other "where" or "to." ' 'Where to, Bruté?' he howled, and along with our guide we headed for the second-floor apartment of a friend whose roomful of Buddhas I had planned to inspect.

"We began to descend the two flights of stairs and they never ended. Down, down, down, down, down, down, down—into the bowels of some ultimate cavern—into the center of the earth, no doubt—or perhaps into nowhere—to descend the stairs, forever and ever. 'Will they never end?' I asked, starting to panic. 'Only one more flight,' I was assured. And then, an infinity of stairsteps later, we arrived and entered the roomful of Buddhas and everything brightened.

"The room was a cacophony of Buddhas! Screaming gold Guatamas seared the eye from their sun-spot Satoris. Seething stone saviors revealed a Buddha-to-come in each of their granular particles. Wooden hermaphrodite Lords-of-the-East reconciled all opposites, all dualities, all dialectics. 'Yin, Yang, Jung!' I cried, and dragged R toward another room with a balcony just over the street. But the journey was long, and I felt like Alice when she had to go twice as fast in order just to stay in the same place.

"From the balcony the crowded street leaped up to greet us and it seemed we had only to reach out to touch the passersby. A painted elf skipped past us and I looked after him in astonishment. 'Just a fairy,' R explained. 'I thought it was an elf,' said I—for all double meanings were lost on me. A decrepit old gargoyle tottered by. 'Poor old gargoyle,' said I. 'He can't find his chapel.' And suddenly I felt very sad, for the whole of life became explainable in terms of men losing their potentialities by default and decaying into gargoyles which could yet be happy if only they could find their proper niche—their own flying buttress, overlooking eternity.

"Continuing to observe the scene below from the balcony, it seemed that my consciousness was projected downward, and with it my perceptions, so that I saw the passersby as if I were standing on the sidewalk and confronting them. From this perspective, they became an animated waxworks, escapees from Madame Tussaud, who bit their wax nails, clutched their wax newspapers, and knit their wax brows as they thought waxen thoughts. I kept wondering how long they could keep up this charade before they melted down into puddles and oozed away along the pavement.

"One strange creature approached us slowly, then yawned to reveal little stalagmite clay teeth set in a grotto of red dust. Suddenly, as if just making his decision, he turned and climbed onto a bus. I then noticed that people got on and got off of this bus. On and off. On and off. On and off. The eternal return. Primitive yet Christian. Circular but linear. And the bus plunged ahead along the route of its manifest destiny, then stopped a short distance down the street, while people kept climbing aboard at intervals to catch its life force, but only to be deposited unceremoniously along the byways of their partial, all-too-partial life segments. But where was the bus going? Toward what ultimate destination? Heaven? Fort Tryon Park? Utopia? Perhaps it was a million years away.

"It seemed that a horde of people came bearing down upon us— tides of gray automata threatening to engulf us. 'Don't worry,' I counseled R. 'I shall be Moses.' And, raising my arm, the crowd parted and we were free to enter the Promised Land.

"People continued to stream towards us and past us. I focused on an old lady in her late seventies, a dowdy pathetic creature dressed in shabby black and carrying impossibly huge shopping bags. As she made her way heavily towards us I saw, no longer much to my astonishment, that she began to lose years. I saw her as an Italian matriarch in her sixties, then in her fifties. As she continued to bloom backwards in time, she entered her portly forties and, after that, her housewifely thirties. Her face softened, her body grew more shapely, and still the years kept on dropping away. In her twenties she was carrying a child, and then she was a bride and carried orange blossoms. A moment later and she was a child who, in turn, shrank into a newborn baby carried by a midwife. The baby's umbilical cord was still intact and it let out a howl of awakening life. But then the process was reversed and the baby grew back into childhood, became again a bride, passed through her thirties, forties, fifties, sixties, and was the old lady in her seventies I had seen at the beginning. The old woman blinked, her eyes closed for a fraction of a second, and in that instant I clearly saw her death mask. She passed us by and had moved a little down the street when I heard from the direction she had come a baby's howl of awakening life. I turned my head, expecting to perceive afresh Our Lady of the Eternal Return, but saw instead the vortex of a crowd.

"The vortex was streaming into the giant doorway of a giant building. It atomized into points of energy, radial lights and shimmering vortices converging into a single solar concentration that seethed in thermal fury to explode at last into a kaleidoscope burst of falling jewels. Some sound had evidently come to my attention and a golden shovel crunched into a mound of opals near which was a sign that bore the incomprehensible words: DIG WE MUST FOR A GROWING NEW YORK. An iron-clad tympany bruised the ears with a raucous counterpoint of digging. Construction, destruction or something was in process and two protean tractors loomed before us, large and living. In their cabs these vital creatures bore little robot mannikins—absurd toy trinkets which undoubtedly they wound up every morning to mimic the motions of life. How proper it all seemed—the Man-machine playing at *noblesse oblige* with the machine-man. But between themselves, the living tractors maintained an uneasy truce. A crystal shelf shattered under the collective impact of their heavy, separate blows. Its sonic vibration stung the nervous system and prepared one for war. The tractors made ready for mutual assault, swinging their shovel-antennae high in the air and bellowing metallic curses at one another. Dive and attack! Attack and dive! But then their clanging vituperations acquired a primeval resonance. Voices were screaming from out of an early swamp. And I saw that the warring tractors were warring dinosaurs, their long necks diving and attacking in sinuous combat. 'Too much!' I thought, and with what seemed a great effort of will I returned through the centuries to —— Street.

"We continued our vigil from the terrace, but now I looked down on the scene below as if from a very high place. I chanced to observe a particularly rough square of pavement and what I saw there caused me to cry out to R to come over and share in this latest wonder. For there below us in that square of pavement lay all of Manhattan—its canyons, and skyscrapers and parks and people—laid out beneath us in miniature. The proportions, the infinite detail were perfect. We could have been in an airplane flying low over the city. But here it was in a common block of pavement—the city within the city. We could have swooped down like gods and lifted up the Empire State Building if we had so wished. But our ethics precluded that, and we left the little microcosm as it was.

"And so it went—a ten thousand years'-long adventure condensed somehow into a few brief hours. It all ended very suddenly for me, when a parking meter I was watching abruptly flipped its red Time Expired flag. And I knew it was over."

The account just concluded describes quite a few of the usual phenomena of the psychedelic drug experience. The altered awareness of time is frequently mentioned and is well exemplified in the subject's description of the interminable descent down the stairs. Mood changes abruptly, often in response to awareness of some perceptual stimulus. A great many altered perceptions—visual, auditory, and olfactory—are mentioned. There are vivid eyes-closed images, the empathic experiencing of a picture and the "projection" of consciousness to a point some distance from the body with visual perception appearing to be from that point and not from the actual physical location of the organs of sight.

Making some order out of and deriving something of value from these curious experiences and others like them will be a main concern of this book.

Necessarily, the subject describing a psychedelic experience is able to mention only a very few items selected from the wealth of events that make up the total experience. Usually the subject writes down what seems most important, unusual, or entertaining to her, or what she thinks will be of most value to the guide. In practice, these accounts by the subject are supplemental to the extensive notes made by the guide in the course of the session—notes recording both what the subject has said, and what the guide is able to observe apart from what is said.

Drugs: A Seminar

Attending drug conferences these days is a heady experience. I was invited to speak at the USNSA's Midwestern Regional Conference on Student Drug Involvement, in Chicago, November 24th through 26th, '67. The NSA has been putting together the best such conferences, starting with the First National one this summer. Chuck Hollander, head of drug studies desk for NSA, works energetically to make sure these conferences bring together all sorts of viewpoints and information-sources. If your school is planning any kind of drug conference, be sure to contact him at USNSA national offices, 2115 "S" St., N.W., Washington, D.C. 20008.

The following is a compilation of remarks by various beautiful people, both during speeches and informally—I made lots of notes during the speeches and went out of my way to get private interviews with whomever I could. Biographical notes in parentheses are mine, otherwise everything is quoted verbatim.

JOEL FORT, M.D. (formerly consultant to World Health Organization on problems of drug abuse and public health official in San Francisco, now lecturer at Berkeley and San Francisco State and Co-director of the National Sex and Drug Forum, San Francisco.)

A *First Basic Principle:* We can only understand use of any mind-altering drug within the context of society, and within the context of drug use. The true context begins with the most widely used and abused drug, alcohol . . . and tobacco . . . and over-the-counter preparations. Take Compoz every day. This is the climate. It goes *on* to include marijuana, LSD, and narcotics

Several thousand children die every year from an overdose of aspirin. This helps to put the whole matter in perspective. We entertain a false dichotomy—seeing alcohol and tobacco as beverages, or pleasurable substances, not as drugs; while the "drugs" are the ones less socially acceptable, with corresponding images of the "drug addict" on the corner . . .

Only with narcotics, barbiturates, and alcohol does daily excessive use involve physical injury or addiction. Formerly, marijuana was said to produce physical addiction. This turned out to be a lie and the idea that it was a "soft narcotic" was the next line. "Soft narcotics!" That

Michael Aldrich, "Drugs: A Seminar." Reprinted from *Chelsea*, #24/25 (Fall, 1968), by permission of the Author and *Chelsea*.

makes as much sense as talking about soft pregnancy. Then they tried "psychological dependence." Which means that you're psychologically uncomfortable when deprived of the drug—like millions of Americans when there's no TV. A whole demonology has grown up around "drug effects." A mind-altering drug effect is NOT: that within minutes or hours of smoking marijuana you murder, rape, go berserk. NOR is the obverse true, that you become totally self-realized. Both, described as effects of a drug, are absurd. The best illustration of what a drug effect really is: a cocktail party. Various people behaving in various different ways, though they are all about the same age, same social background, same setting. What we call a "drug effect"—usually relative to *illegal* drugs—is actually a function of three distinct things:

A) The pharmacology of the drug, its action;

B) The character or personality of the drugtaker;

C) The setting in which the drug is taken.

The most important of these is (B): there is no drug that will turn a normally happy "conforming" person—if there is one—into a monster.

The *only* drug where we have established proof of a causal relation between use of the drug and criminal or socially dangerous behavior, is alcohol. . . . There are more alcoholics in the San Francisco Bay area alone—about 100,000—than there are narcotics addicts in the whole United States.

The most common pattern of drug *abuse*—besides alcoholism—is barbiturate and amphetamine abuse, among middle or upper class older people who get their drugs on prescription and abuse them.

There are at least a million present users of pot in the country. More important than the number is the fact that it pervades all social classes. Why? Because we are a drug-ridden society. The average adult consumes 3 to 5 drugs a day, starting with coffee and cigarettes in the morning, cokes, booze, aspirin, stimulants, tranquilizers, and a sleeping pill or medication at night. Television is a perfect reflection of this: every time there's a pain or problem, turn to a drug. This is the context.

What do we do?

First we must conceptualize drug usage as a health matter, take it entirely out of the realm of criminal law. Our present barbaric system is exactly that which sent mentally sick people to prisons, in earlier eras, instead of to hospitals and clinics.

We must avoid both extremes of overpolarization—the one whereby total legalization means we would have overavailability and undercontrol, and the present one, prohibition. First we must take it out of cop and criminal control; the implications of arresting someone for use of *some* drugs, social ruin . . .

We have a model control law in the Dangerous Drugs Act of 1965—because it excludes the *user* from criminal punishment.

And a final comment:

If we can make the American educational experience more mind-expanding, not as many people will be looking to drugs for mind-expansion.

(Compare Dr. Fort's statements with that of William Burroughs, who advocates the Apomorphine treatment for junkies and says: "The razor inside, sir. Jerk the handle. If we wish to annihilate the junk pyramid, we must start with the bottom of the pyramid: the *Addict in the street*, and stop tilting quixotically for the 'higher ups' so called, all of whom are immediately replaceable."—Deposition: Testimony Concerning a Sickness, 1960.)

DAVID ISRAELSTAM, M.D. (psychological research consultant at Napa State Hospital, California. Everywhere I've heard him speak, he is more and more beautiful. He has taken LSD, likes it, and admits it in public, though he is not a proselytizer. He recently published the results of the most careful series of experiments yet done on the question of LSD chromosome damage. Dig.)

ALDRICH *What's this latest report of yours?*

ISRAELSTAM "It's in *Science*, Oct 27th. We—Laughman, Sargent, and I, at U.C. Berkeley's Donner Lab of Biophysics and Medical Physics— did chromosome cultures of leukocytes (white blood cells) of LSD users and found no difference of chromosome breakage rates between those cultures and the control cultures, thus providing the first published study disagreeing with earlier findings that LSD causes abnormally high rates of chromosome breakage. We started with 12 subjects, but only 8 cultures provided test material, so that's our base. The current unofficial (unpublished) "box score" is: five studies in favor for LSD chromosome damage, and four against such a positive correlation. Additional corroborative studies by other groups will be published in the near future.

ALDRICH *What about bad trips?*

ISRAELSTAM "They're actually good trips in disguise, if one knows how to work with and through them. Bad trips, in a way I don't begin to understand, radiate their panic, terror, and anxiety (as the case may be) to those around them. This can include friends, family, emergency room personnel of the general physician or psychiatrist variety. Even the treatment personnel, as analogous emotional states are included in them by the bad tripper, begin to feel quite uncomfortable. But because of the inability of even well-trained psychiatrists to tolerate such intense emotional states themselves, they often prefer to turn off the source of the discomfort—the bad tripper—rather than work through the unique or threatening personal situation.

I believe bad trips are really good trips in disguise, and contain central symbolic statements of who we are; and as such are critical to work through, if significant life alteration is to proceed in a direction desired by the person involved, i.e., the bad tripper or a person in an analogous non-drug "bad trip" life situation. The magnitude of the ecstasy when bad trips are resolved is equal and opposite to the agony of the bad trip preceding the breakthrough.

It's difficult for the bad tripper to have faith that the above transformation will occur—namely that by "letting go" and accepting the threatening situation, the threat will disappear. When bad trips start to occur, if you fight them, they get worse.

ALDRICH *I know that your medical background has been, until fairly recently, doing metabolic studies in schizophrenia. And now you're doing psychology, student counselling. Yet during your speech you said something about doctors being more afraid of death, and psychiatrists being more afraid of insanity, than most people. Care to elaborate on that idea?*

ISRAELSTAM "Sure. It's a question of the people you want working with LSD, both with medical and sociological research. I agree with Grof, the research doctor in Prague who says that anyone—especially psychotherapists—who wants to do LSD research, should have taken at least five trips himself. It's for the doctors, not the patients. And as for "guides," I'd rather have almost any caring, experienced Haight-Ashbury hippie around as a guide for a trip, than any randomly selected doctor or psychiatrist.

ALDRICH *Why?*

ISRAELSTAM "Many psychosocial workers—psychiatrists, psychologists, social workers—are in general to me a very sick group. Frequently they straddle the uncomfortable border between sanity and insanity. Pathologically, however, as a way of controlling their own incipient insanity ("insanity," at best, to me, is a continuous transition period between sanity and greater sanity), they project their own problem to the external world and expand their efforts suppressing incipient insanity in those with whom they come in contact. If it *weren't* for the fact that insanity, called "enlightenment" in the Orient, I'm told, is to me an important life-learning stage, the above would seem desirable

—what they do would seem reasonable. R. D. Laing, in the *Politics of Experience*, says "The current treatment of psychotics by psychiatrists is like the blind leading the half-blind."

As a general statement, those in our society most threatened by various thoughts, behaviors and actions, for their own vested psychologic interests, wind up in the control positions—i.e., police are most "threatened" by violent behavior, physicians are most "threatened" by death situations (often leading them to do extraordinary things, including *polarizing* pain and suffering, and their battle to "fight off" death), and psychiatrists are the ones most "threatened" by bizarre thoughts.

ALFRED R. LINDESMITH, PH.D. (Dr. Lindesmith, the Grand Pioneer of drug sociology in America, began studying the drug situation in 1935. His *The Addict and the Law* is one of the earliest, and still one of the best, studies of our various drug policies. He has traveled all over the world in search of the truth; is now a Professor of Sociology at the University of Indiana. See his introduction and careful article in *The Marihuana Papers*, for his approach.)

"We should keep the established vices in mind as we consider the coming vices. It *was* alcohol, caffeine, nicotine . . . now it's pot, amphetamines, LSD, others. Some of them are fads and will decline in the future. With pot it's different—a poor man's drug, easily grown everywhere. It is the alcohol-consuming (upper) classes which have had the most voice in the making of the laws. Marijuana, formerly an emblem of conflict between classes, is now a symbol of conflict between generations.

The "bother" about pot laws is a phenomenon and furor of the last few years, a product of the biggest change in marijuana use—the middle class now smokes pot, and objects to the penalties and arrests, which have also increased.

In California alone, the authorities report that in the first half of 1967, there were 11,587 arrests of adults, and 4,526 arrests of juveniles on marijuana charges. These are, respectively, *five times*, and *fifteen times*, the 1960 figures.

Chinese Emperor Shen Nung noted the use of marijuana for gout, "female weakness," constipation, and absent-mindedness, about 2737 B.C. Practice of using the plant for psychic effect spread West, through India and into the Middle East, on both sides of the Mediterranean, up to the "hashshashin" cult of writers and artists in Paris. The hemp plant was brought to North America more than 300 years ago, cultivated in the colonies as early as 1632. The idea of smoking it didn't develop until this century, even though the last century had "cannabis indica" as a medicine. A company once produced a medicinal pot cigarette and it was a failure—it didn't catch on. *Smoking* pot was probably a combination of two other practices—smoking opium and smoking hashish in the East.

Marijuana, as the name suggests, probably entered this country from Mexico. Corroboration of this may be suggested in the word "roach"— probably from "La Cucaracha."

La cucaracha, la cucaracha	The cockroach, the cockroach
Ya no puede caminar	Is not able to walk
Porque no tiene,	Because he doesn't have
Porque le falta,	Because is lacking to him
Marihuana que fumar.	Marijuana to smoke.

200 million pounds of hemp seed were imported in this country during the 300 years when it wasn't used for smoking. Besides all that grows wild. A botanist has reported that 17% of the pollen in Nebraska's air during the pollen seasons is marijuana.

If one goes to an Indian wedding and there is no *bhang*, marijuana in cakes or candies or drinks, one goes home and criticizes the host the same way one would if there were no champagne at an American wedding. Yet now, in America, the penalties are atrocious, since they were increased in 1951 and 1956. During the years 1952–1958, Federal prosecutions on marijuana charges actually diminished, from 1288 to 179. Yet the *Wall Street Journal* recently reported that *last year* there were 667 Federal prosecutions, and, of these, only 8 involved students.

Yet even the Attorney General's office in California, their Justice Department, reports that there is virtually no evidence to substantiate the various narcotics-bureau arguments against marijuana. Quote from Drug Arrests and Dispositions in California, 1964, issued in 1965: "There have been a number of attempts recently in California, deliberately or otherwise, to remove the legal and social stigma attached to marijuana usage. It has been stated that marijuana is not addicting and that smoking it is no worse than smoking tobacco and might even be less harmful. Since no scientific studies have ever been made which would show otherwise, these statements cannot be entirely refuted . . . The alleged progression from marijuana or dangerous drug usage to heroin has never been fully documented."

(Some notes on Dr. Lindesmith's remarks by me. First, marijuana's *military use* has always interested militarists. "La Cucaracha" was Pancho Villa's marching song. The 12th-century Persian assassin (Hashshashin, hashish-users) cult is infamous, though there is little or no historic proof that the assassin sect ever used hashish; see Bernard Lewis's *The Assassins*. Recent reports from Vietnam indicate that up to 85% of U.S. soldiers smoke pot regularly there. But the military use is always as relaxation from the fighting, rather than during the fighting; though some Army studies, it is rumored, have been done on actual in-combat use. Secondly, the 1965 Lynch Report is wrong, but couldn't admit it. There have been *many* studies made which *do* show that marijuana is not addicting, not as harmful as tobacco, and in fact less harmful. The Attorney General's Report, of course, had to turn this fact inside out.)

SENATOR ROGER E. CRAIG (Michigan State Senator Craig, from the Dearborn district, has introduced a bill to the State legislature to re-classify marijuana. He is a brilliant speaker and, with a lawyer's back-ground, is father of the Michigan State medicaid bill and also of a workmen's compensation law.)

ALDRICH *What is the status of your bill now?*

CRAIG "It has been drafted and is going to come up in the Senate Judi-ciary Committee for a hearing sometime in mid-January 1968.

ALDRICH *What, exactly, does your bill do?*

CRAIG "It would eliminate *Cannabis sativa* from the Michigan General Narcotics Act. Practically, however, it's just to get the bill in front of the committee which is really all I want to do at this time. A hearing, with open testimony on the issue, is what I want. Even if the bill were passed into law, the practical impact would not be to legalize marijuana, because of the federal laws against the drug.

ALDRICH *What are the bill's chances of passing?*

CRAIG "Practically nil. I don't think the legislative route offers much hope. But the judicial process does. Brother Oteri and I hold the key, in some Burkean way to bring the law into some more appropriate relation to the facts.

ALDRICH *You mean the Courts will be the ones to do it?*

CRAIG "I think our real hope—because of the politics involved—is in a judicial striking down of the laws which—I agree—are unconstitu-tional. The judiciary is the branch best able *politically* to handle this issue. There is no bill going to be passed in Michigan to legalize pot, this year, or next year, or . . .

ALDRICH *Has voter reaction been that bad?*

CRAIG "My district is totally out of sympathy with any efforts to change the marijuana law, mainly, I think, because of the press, which some-how keeps wanting to convince people that pot is opium. My mail has been heavy with hate—if I was running for Dean at Michigan State, I'd be all right—but most of those over voting age seem to hate it. I repeat, I had to introduce the bill to get a *hearing*. It may never get out of committee.

ALDRICH *What about the distortions of the press?*

CRAIG "Well, take for instance that *Life* article. (July 7, '67) I spent a whole afternoon with their people, going over reports, showing them facts, talking reasonably. When the article came out, I was reduced to saying that pot is no more dangerous than alcohol.

ALDRICH *Why have you staked your political career on this issue?*

CRAIG Because it's an important issue. If I can't talk about these kinds of issues, then who needs it? I will go where the facts take me.

JOSEPH OTERI (Mr. Oteri is a big, beautiful, ebullient trial lawyer from Boston whose brilliant defense of two kids on pot charges has earned him nationwide publicity and adoration. His is the most important of the many "unconstitutionality" cases now being heard in courts across the land. Note 1969: Massachusetts Supreme Court has denied Oteri's appeal in the Weiss-Leis case and it will now be appealed to the U.S. Supreme Court.)

ALDRICH *What's happening with your case?*

OTERI "Judge Tauro's opinion should be in within the next week or ten days. But I don't expect it to be favorable. We're already got the appeal brief ready—took the 48-page original brief and boiled down the most relevant testimony from the hearings—over 1800 pages of transcript that will soon be published—we have over 100 pages of appellant's brief to take to the final court of Massachusetts, the Supreme Judiciary Court of Appeals.

ALDRICH *How'd the hearing go?*

OTERI "It was a lawyer's dream. The first thing we discovered was that most of the "experts" on marijuana really aren't. For our defense testimony we grilled each witness several times before we put him on the stand. The prosecution's witnesses, though usually only their first testimony made the papers, were destroyed in cross-examination. It was beautiful. Don Louria, for instance, was supposed to be one of their stars. His major point was that chronic use of hashish, according to a study made quite some time ago in Morocco, was a contributing factor in insanity. He made it sound so positive during his presentation. Luckily, we'd done some preliminary research on that study, the Benabud Report.

Benabud was supposed to have proved that more than 25% of the people in Moroccan insane asylums were there because of chronic hashish-smoking. When we got Louria for cross-examination we fired some questions at him, like this:

"How many certified psychiatrists were there in all of Morocco at the time of the survey?"

Louria didn't know, so we had the correct answer. None.

"And how many medical doctors in Morocco at the time?"

Again he didn't know. There were *three* licensed doctors in the whole country then, one was purely an administrator, the other two general practitioners.

"So who *did* the actual research reported in the Benabud study?"

It turns out that the report was arrived at by having two French clerks translate the hospital *admissions* cards from Moroccan. "Who filled out the original admission cards?" There were not even *interns* there to do preliminary entrance diagnoses on all these admissions to the mental hospital where the study was made. The cards weren't prepared by doctors, or even by clerks; the admitting diagnosis, on the cards, was the opinion of whatever *policeman* had brought the person in to the hospital.

And on the basis of that kind of evidence, the Benabud report has been plaguing responsible medical doctors trying to do actual research on any possible correlations between insanity and pot ever since. We utterly destroyed that kind of "proof."

ALDRICH *Allen Ginsberg told me last year that the Benabud Report, so dear to a local judge who argues that pot contributes to insanity, was probably as fishy as that, but I've simply been arguing that a country like Morocco where maybe 85% of the population smokes hash, it's not surprising that 30% or however many in the insane asylums also have smoked it.*

OTERI That wasn't the worst one. The prosecution brought in some witnesses that were easy enough to destroy—they had no actual experience with, or research on, marijuana, and were just offering opinions based on what they'd heard. And the ones they brought in who supposedly *had* done research—the beauty here was the younger Chopra, Ismir Chopra. He came in talking about all this research he'd done with his father, telling about the results he'd supposedly arrived at—when we started questioning during cross-examination more closely and it turned out that he'd been in London at medical school, while he was claiming to have been helping his father with his research project. That discredits his personal testimony . . .

ALDRICH *That was a fairly common practice in India—the old man who*

*does whatever scientific research, some project, puts his son's name on
the report, too—it provides the kid with a kind of formal or nominal
reputation when and if he goes into the field.*

OTERI And that's not all, with young Ismir Chopra. His father's report
is one of the strongest links—so the younger doctor claimed—in
showing that marijuana causes crime. During cross-examination we
discovered more facts about the actual study his father'd done. There
was a 27-question questionnaire they used. Many of the questions were
just personal-background stuff, about family and social status. Then
came the questions about drug use. And there was *one* question.
"Were you ever convicted of a crime?" No mention of whether the
crime or conviction was before, during, after, or in any way involved
with use of marijuana or hashish. Didn't make any connection with
pot. Yet on the basis of the answers to that question, Chopra and
Chopra stated that this "scientific" study indicated that marijuana
was a determining factor in the commission of crimes.

ALDRICH *How did you dig all this stuff out?*

OTERI It took us months of research and a lot of money. Some people
have a vested interest in keeping the real facts about these "scientific"
studies hidden. I believe it was Tod Mikuriya, a San Francisco psychiatrist, who did the stuff on the Benabud Report. I think the
Chopra stuff just came out during cross-examination.

ALDRICH *Why have you been doing this?*

OTERI Remember your history? We once fought a Revolution, because
we wanted a self-determining government to give people the right to
decide for themselves what's right, if their actions didn't hurt anybody. Individual freedom. The right to smoke. If you believe in the
right of human beings to act in certain ways they enjoy as long as
they don't hurt others, then you believe in the right to be let alone,
and you'll fight for it.

A *Question Period*

Q Dr. Lindesmith, you've been investigating drug dangers for a long time
now. What do you think about reports of heavy hashish use being
dangerous to health?

LINDESMITH With hashish, the so-called danger of overuse is strongly
mitigated by the fact that a user will usually fall asleep before he can
smoke too much. There may be some danger in hashish preparations
made to be eaten—you could eat a lot before passing out—but
usually it is not hashish but bhang, relatively mild, that's used in
food or candy or drinks.

Q What do you gentlemen recommend about criminal punishment of actual heroin addicts?

LINDESMITH In most countries of the world, sane people do not like to put people in jail for having bad personal habits, but rather for activities which are dangerous to other people.

OTERI I thought the Robinson case, in California in 1962, took care of that. California law allowed arresting users; but the result of the case was that people could not be arrested just for being addicts.

LINDESMITH Yes, but California and other states have gotten around that very easily. You still can be arrested and thrown in jail just for unlawfully *using* drugs.

Q Dr. Becker (Howard Becker, Professor of Sociology at Northwestern, who'd talked about drug incidents on campus and how today's students are not "cool" like the old marijuana users of the fifties), what can we do about narcotics cops and informers on campus?

BECKER Not much. Try to get your school not to cooperate with them. Be cool—don't exhibit your drug use.

OTERI Universities are publically owned, but you have the absolute right to put your own lock on a dorm room door and not let anybody in without a search warrant. Just make sure you don't have a fink for a roommate. And the best answer, of course, is to just not hold.

Q Does the university have the right to search rooms?

OTERI Board contracts. Did you sign it? Or your parents. It makes some difference what the board contract says. Though if public hotel situations are analogous, you pay for the room and they don't have the right to search without a proper warrant.

Q What rights does a student have if he's hauled before the Administration and charged with possession or something?

OTERI Well—free legal advice is worth exactly what you pay for it— nothing. But you probably could demand and get counsel. But they'd probably still throw you out, if they wanted to. Perhaps your best move would be to not answer questions.

Q How do you know all this?

OTERI I used to be a cop.

Q Why are so many students so open about drug use?

BECKER One component motive is ideological. One can make of marijuana use in some ways a satisfactory symbol of the war between generations. The prohibitionist, whether police or administrator, is challenged by the young who back up their case with the best scientific information available. University controllers are in a peculiar situation: they can't, in fact, answer many of the arguments favoring drug use. So the prohibitionist administration is wide open to attack.

Secondly, people get caught because they are stupid in a particular way. Fifteen or sixteen years ago drug-users were members of a tight, well-established cult. It was a private matter, under conditions in which it was safe to use drugs. They had a whole catalogue of precautions: don't sell to unknowns, beware of all strangers, etc. Many students today don't understand the necessity for all this caution. Because they don't have this kind of cultural background. In a way, they're "culturally deprived."

Q What do you think of the openness, Dr. Oteri?

OTERI Well, it's part of demonstration of new ethics. The week our trial stopped in Boston, there was a huge smoke-in, and about 3000 kids showed up to puff pot in the faces of the cops standing around. But then next week there were fewer and fewer, and the week after that they didn't even get one line of newspaper coverage. The demonstration only works if it's new.

Q Senator Craig, you mentioned press distortion. Do you think this will continue?

CRAIG Well, the articles have been getting slightly more accurate, in the nationwide home journals. Given another year, respectable journals will be coming out and saying it should at most be a misdemeanor, should be regulated like liquor.

Q How can we have fewer drug incidents on campus?

BECKER It's important to do that, because of university public relations. And strong measures against student drug use can promote strong student responses, making more bad relations. It's obvious that we're not going to be able to command a decrease in drug *use*. And we can't *stop* drug use except by extreme totalitarian measures—daily frisking of suspects, room searches, etc.

So we've got to educate administrators to a calmer, more rational view, in which they do not react so madly to outside pressure. And we've got to take some of the pressure from inside off, too. This means stop students from doing things that provoke publicity.

The best thing to do would be an educational program designed to show students how to use drugs without attracting attention or publicity. But universities might have trouble with a program called how to smoke pot and not get caught.

The media contribute to the incidents, too. They love anything that can be made to sound sensational, because it sells. After *Life* and *Newsweek* came out with their big pot articles, for instance, someone asked *Time*, well, they like it, what've you got against it?

But often, open use and attendant bad publicity is not an open attempt to confront the administration. A local TV station ran a film recently that was supposed to be a "pot party" on the Northwestern campus. It generated only heat. The response was, "Those damn fool kids." That sort of thing does no good.

RALPH METZNER (Dr. Metzner is one of the most beautiful people in the world. Gentlemanly, calm, scholarly, Ph.D. in psychology from Harvard, one of the original LSD triumvirate with Leary and Alpert, co-author with them of the bible—THE PSYCHEDELIC EXPERI- ENCE—, editor since its inception of "The Psychedelic Review." Here are my notes from his speech, which was the highlight of the conven- tion—delivered so unassumingly that one hardly noticed.)

Two associations with word "drug"—medical and "fiends." The question "why do kids take drugs" overlooks the *basic* thing—that all kinds of people use drugs, alcohol, tobacco, etc. . . . The practice of taking a chemical to alter one's consciousness is universal. One might even call it a natural instinct of man. To alter the way in which he perceives the world.

This also to some extent explains people who take anything. Society has prevented him from having any objective (way to judge) knowledge whatsoever. "All drugs" are bad—meaning the ones some people don't like.

Distinction between a person's initial motive in using a drug, why a person continues to use a drug.

Initial: 1. Curiosity. 2. Peer pressure to do so. 3. "Kicks." The word taps one strain in American puritanism. It means, give pleasure. 4. Desire to cure one's problems, or to improve oneself. 5. Genuine reli- gious or spiritual quest. "I used to believe myself, in the common stereotype—what about all these kids? They must be taking it for kicks. Now I believe that among the teenagers there is more *genuine* search- ing for spiritual values from drugs. They already know much more than we do. And they're so far . . . we will never catch up with them." 6. The media. Play an important role in encouraging drug use. June *Newsweek* cover. On the back of the mag was an ad for liquor—paid for. The front-cover ad was free. Medium is message. And pictures of people involved with drugs—woman lying back, beautiful, looking stoned. The *Life* picture of the Ph.D. and the pregnant mother in a penthouse, blowing a joint. Implications.

Speed? Methedrine is a very puzzling drug—nobody knows quite how many are using it, or whether use is continuing. It produces a feeling of power and confidence and ability. Without doing anything. Some users are very bright people who feel unable to do anything about the society around them. The alcoholic or junkie tries to blot himself out, the speeder boosts his own feelings of his own effectiveness. It back-fires later, because it burns up the body's own energy reserves. And—though at first he might have been more effective—he goes into a coma.

Speed vs. acid. Speed accelerates your mental functioning at the ordinary level, speeded up. Whereas psychedelics add dimensions. If the metaphor for non-drug condition or "normal" activity is *walking*, speed is *running*, but acid is *flying*. The important change of percep-tion with acid is, "You become aware that your ordinary perception of the world is only one level, and that there are others."

LSD is not a hallucinogen, if, by hallucinations, you mean seeing something not there. It is a vision, multilevel perception. You become aware of how your mind selects out only those things it wants to, or has been conditioned to want to, out of the stream. 60–70% of the people who use acid never experience the high-dose effect. A very low dose of acid is like pot. But high doses get into another type of thing altogether, a death-birth or ego-transcendence thing, completely detached from the physical world including your body.

There may be a whole class of "psycho-synthesizers" that enhance *feelings*, especially positive feeling-states. Become identified with a group or core that includes positives and negatives, accepting all. May be better as a therapeutic tool.

Pot: partly a trank and partly a psychedelic, I suppose.

Mental health field. Working in that. Training the person who *treats*. With acid.

May be able to convert alcoholic from a socially liable person to a socially more harmonious one—with pot.

Our society is very phobic about TOUCH. People trying to get over that, crawling around under sheets, blindly groping each other to try to get rid of that phobia.

Influence of psychedelics on hand crafts. More than a fad involved here—an attempt to create clothing, utensils, etc., that have a natural rhythmic relation to one's life, rather than stuff turned out by computer factories. Personalization.

Religious effect. You will see increasing numbers of people engaged in spiritual quest of some kind. Often they stop using drugs (at least for a while) because LSD is *too* good. Too good for us to know how to use properly yet. Very tricky and very strange. We haven't even begun to know it yet—or what to do with it.

(Later I had dinner with Dr. Metzner, Charlie Scribner, Helen Nowlis, the Israelstams, Tom Ungerleider, and Chuck Hollander. Asked Ralph Metzner some more questions.)

ALDRICH *Has the Mafia moved into the Haight?*

METZNER Not that I really know of. It's possible, but I don't think it's happening. The really big pot and acid dealers are getting rougher, but I don't think it's organized crime moving in. How could the Mafia cut into the marijuana from Mexico? It's too easy for anyone to go get, and not lucrative enough for the Mafia.

ALDRICH Have you heard of China or Russia using LSD for brainwashing? Allen Ginsberg talks about a researcher in Prague who's discovered that acid can be used to remove conditional response.

METZNER Who's that? Stan Grof?

ALDRICH No, the name Allen gave in the latest *Humanist* was Elia Rubichek.

METZNER I haven't heard of that research. Grof, who's now at Johns Hopkins, worked in Prague and was famous for his requirement of all future psychotherapists who wanted to use LSD in treating patients—he requires that the therapist have 5 trips himself. Brainwashing? No, I haven't heard of experiments with brainwashing. It's funny what fright some people have about these drugs. Like the cop who's walking through the park and sees a hippie sitting in a flower patch. "Hey, kid!" he yells, "Are you doin' sumpthin' *psychedelic?*"

From *Zen Flesh, Zen Bones*

Muddy Road

Tanzan and Ekido were once traveling together down a muddy road. A heavy rain was still falling.

Coming around a bend, they met a lovely girl in a silk kimono and sash, unable to cross the intersection.

"Come on, girl," said Tanzan at once. Lifting her in his arms, he carried her over the mud.

Ekido did not speak again until that night when they reached a lodging temple. Then he no longer could restrain himself. "We monks don't go near females," he told Tanzan, "especially not young and lovely ones. It's dangerous. Why did you do that?"

"I left the girl there," said Tanzan. "Are you still carrying her?"

Trading Dialogue for Lodging

Provided he makes and wins an argument about Buddhism with those who live there, any wandering monk can remain in a Zen temple. If he is defeated, he has to move on.

In a temple in the northern part of Japan two brother monks were dwelling together. The elder one was learned, but the younger one was stupid and had but one eye.

A wandering monk came and asked for lodging, properly challenging them to a debate about the sublime teaching. The elder brother, tired that day from much studying, told the younger one to take his place. "Go and request the dialogue in silence," he cautioned.

So the young monk and the stranger went to the shrine and sat down.

Shortly afterwards the traveler rose and went in to the elder brother and said: "Your young brother is a wonderful fellow. He defeated me."

"Relate the dialogue to me," said the elder one.

"Well," explained the traveler, "first I held up one finger, representing Buddha, the enlightened one. So he held up two fingers, signifying Buddha and his teaching. I held up three fingers, representing Buddha, his teaching, and his followers, living the harmonious life. Then he shook his clenched fist in my face, indicating that all three

Paul Reps, Koans 14, 26, 76, and 82 from *Zen Flesh, Zen Bones*. Reprinted by permission of the Charles E. Tuttle Publishing Co., Inc.

come from one realization. Thus he won and so I have no right to remain here." With this, the traveler left.

"Where is that fellow?" asked the younger one, running in to his elder brother.

"I understand you won the debate."

"Won nothing. I'm going to beat him up."

"Tell me the subject of the debate," asked the elder one.

"Why, the minute he saw me he held up one finger, insulting me by insinuating that I have only one eye. Since he was a stranger I thought I would be polite to him, so I held up two fingers, congratulating him that he has two eyes. Then the impolite wretch held up three fingers, suggesting that between us we only have three eyes. So I got mad and started to punch him, but he ran out and that ended it!"

The Stone Mind

Hogen, a Chinese Zen teacher, lived alone in a small temple in the country. One day four traveling monks appeared and asked if they might make a fire in his yard to warm themselves.

While they were building the fire, Hogen heard them arguing about subjectivity and objectivity. He joined them and said: "There is a big stone. Do you consider it to be inside or outside your mind?"

One of the monks replied: "From the Buddhist viewpoint everything is an objectification of mind, so I would say that the stone is inside my mind."

"Your head must feel very heavy," observed Hogen, "if you are carrying around a stone like that in your mind."

Nothing Exists

Yamaoka Tesshu, as a young student of Zen, visited one master after another. He called upon Dokuon of Shokoku.

Desiring to show his attainment, he said: "The mind, Buddha, and sentient beings, after all, do not exist. The true nature of phenomena is emptiness. There is no realization, no delusion, no sage, no mediocrity. There is no giving and nothing to be received."

Dokuon, who was smoking quietly, said nothing. Suddenly he whacked Yamaoka with his bamboo pipe. This made the youth quite angry.

"If nothing exists," inquired Dokuon, "where did this anger come from?"

Why Tribe

We use the term Tribe because it suggests the type of new society now emerging within the industrial nations. In America of course the word has associations with the American Indians, which we like. This new subculture is in fact more familiar to that ancient and successful tribe, the European Gypsies—a group without nation or territory which maintains its own values, its language and religion, no matter what country it may be in.

The Tribe proposes a totally different style: based on community houses, villages and ashrams; tribe-run farms or workshops or companies; large open families; pilgrimages and wanderings from center to center. a synthesis of Gandhian "village anarchist" and I.W.W. syndicalism. Interesting visionary pamphlets along these lines were written several years ago by Gandhians Richard Gregg and Appa Patwardhan. The Tribe proposes personal responsibilities rather than abstract centralized government, taxes and advertising-agency-plus-Mafia type international brainwashing corporations.

In the United States and Europe the Tribe has evolved gradually over the last fifty years—since the end of World War I—in response to the increasing insanity of the modern nations. As the number of alienated intellectuals, creative types and general social misfits grew, they came to recognize each other by various minute signals. Much of this energy was channeled into Communism in the thirties and early forties. All the anarchists and left-deviationists—and many Trotskyites—were tribesmen at heart. After World War II, another generation looked at Communist rhetoric with a fresh eye and saw that within the Communist governments (and states of mind) there are too many of the same things as are wrong with "capitalism"—too much anger and murder. The suspicion grew that perhaps the whole Western Tradition, of which Marxism is but a (Millennial Protestant) part, is off the track. This led many people to study other major civilizations—India and China— to see what they could learn.

It's an easy step from the dialectic of Marx and Hegel to an interest in the dialectic of early Taoism, the *I Ching*, and the yin-yang theories. From Taoism it is another easy step to the philosophies and mythologies of India—vast, touching the deepest areas of the mind, and with a view of the ultimate nature of the universe which is almost identical with the most sophisticated thought in modern physics—that truth, whatever it is, which is called "The Dharma."

Next comes a concern with deepening one's understanding in an experiential way: abstract philosophical understanding is simply not enough. At this point many, myself included, found in the Buddha-Dharma a practical method for clearing one's mind of the trivia, prejudices and false values that our conditioning had laid on us—and more important, an approach to the basic problem of how to penetrate to the deepest non-self Self. Today we have many who are exploring the Ways of Zen, Varjrayana, Yoga, Shamanism, Psychedelics. The Buddha-Dharma is a long, gentle, human dialog—2,500 years of quiet conversation—on the nature of human nature and the eternal Dharma—and practical methods of realization.

In the course of these studies it became evident that the "truth" in Buddhism and Hinduism is not dependent in any sense on Indian or Chinese culture; and that "India" and "China"—as societies—are as burdensome to human beings as any others; perhaps more so. It became clear that "Hinduism" and "Buddhism" as social institutions had long been accomplices of the State in burdening and binding people, rather than serving to liberate them. Just like the other Great Religions.

At this point, looking once more quite closely at history both East and West, some of us noticed the similarities in certain small but influential heretical and esoteric movements. These schools of thought and practice were usually suppressed, or diluted and made harmless, in whatever society they appeared. Peasant witchcraft in Europe, Tantrism in Bengal, Quakers in England, Tachikawa-ryū in Japan, Ch'an in China. These are all outcroppings of the Great Subculture which runs underground all through history. This is the tradition that runs without break from Paleo-Siberian Shamanism and Magdalenian cave-painting; through megaliths and Mysteries, astronomers, ritualists, alchemists and Albigensians; gnostics and vagantes, right down to Golden Gate Park.

The Great Subculture has been attached in part to the official religions but is different in that it transmits a community style of life, with an ecstatically positive vision of spiritual and physical love; and is opposed for very fundamental reasons to the Civilization Establishment.

It has taught that man's natural being is to be trusted and followed; that we need not look to a model or rule imposed from outside in searching for the center; and that in following the grain, one is being truly "moral." It has recognized that for one to "follow the grain" it is necessary to look exhaustively into the negative and demonic potentials of the Unconscious, and by recognizing these powers—symbolically acting them out—one releases himself from these forces. By this profound exorcism and ritual drama, the Great Subculture destroys the one credible claim of Church and State to a necessary function.

All this is subversive to civilization: for civilization is built on hierarchy and specialization. A ruling class, to survive, must propose a Law: a law to work must have a hook into the social psyche—and the most effective way to achieve this is to make people doubt their natural worth and instincts, especially sexual. To make "human nature" suspect is also to make Nature—the wilderness—the adversary. Hence the ecological crisis of today.

We came, therefore (and with many Western thinkers before us), to suspect that civilizations may be overvalued. Before anyone says "This is ridiculous, we all know civilization is a necessary thing," let him read some cultural anthropology. Take a look at the lives of South African Bushmen, Micronesian navigators, the Indians of California; the researches of Claude Lévi-Strauss. Everything we have thought about man's welfare needs to be rethought. The tribe, it seems, is the newest development in the Great Subculture. We have almost unintentionally linked ourselves to a transmission of gnosis, a potential social order, and techniques of enlightenment, surviving from prehistoric times.

The most advanced developments of modern science and technology have come to support some of these views. Consequently the modern Tribesman, rather than being old-fashioned in his criticism of civilization, is the most relevant type in contemporary society. Nationalism, warfare, heavy industry and consumership, are already outdated and useless. The next great step of mankind is to step into the nature of his own mind—the real question is "just what is consciousness?"—and we must make the most intelligent and creative use of science in exploring these questions. The man of wide international experience, much learning and leisure—luxurious product of our long and sophisticated history—may with good reason wish to live simply, with few tools and minimal clothes, close to nature.

The Revolution has ceased to be an ideological concern. Instead, people are trying it out right now—communism in small communities, new family organization. A million people in America and another million in England and Europe. A vast underground in Russia, which will come out in the open four or five years hence, is now biding. How do they recognize each other? Not always by beards, long hair, bare feet or beads. The signal is a bright and tender look; calmness and gentleness, freshness and ease of manner. Men, women and children—all of whom together hope to follow the timeless path of love and wisdom, in affectionate company with the sky, winds, clouds, trees, waters, animals and grasses—this is the tribe.

A Social History of the Hippies

An elderly school bus, painted like a fluorescent Easter egg in orange, chartreuse, cerise, white, green, blue and, yes, black, was parked outside the solitary mountain cabin, which made it an easy guess that Ken Kesey, the novelist turned psychedelic Hotspur, was inside. So, of course, was Neal Cassady, the Tristram Shandy of the Beat Generation, proto-type hero of Jack Kerouac's *On The Road*, who had sworn off allegiance to Kerouac when the beat scene became menopausal and signed up as the driver of Kesey's fun and games bus, which is rumored to run on LSD. Except for these notorious luminaries, the Summit Meeting of the leaders of the new hippie subculture, convened in the lowlands of California's High Sierras during an early spring weekend last month, seemed a little like an Apalachin Mafia gathering without Joe Bananas.

Where was Allen Ginsberg, father goddam to two generations of the underground? In New York, reading his poetry to freshmen. And where was Timothy Leary, self-styled guru to tens or is it hundreds of thousands of turned-on people? Off some nowhere place like Stockton, to preach the gospel of Lysergic Acid Diethylamide to nice ladies in drip-dry dresses.

The absence of the elder statesmen of America's synthetic gypsy movement meant something. It meant that the leaders of the booming psychedelic bohemia in the seminal city of San Francisco were their own men—and strangely serious men, indeed, for hippies. Ginsberg and Leary may be Pied Pipers, but they are largely playing old tunes. The young men who make the new scene accept Ginsberg as a revered observer from the elder generation; Leary they abide as Elmer Gantry on their side, to be used for proselytizing squares only.

The mountain symposium had been called for the extraordinary purpose of discussing the political future of the hippies. Hippies are many things, but most prominently the bearded and beaded inhabitants of the Haight-Ashbury, a little psychedelic city-state edging Golden Gate Park. There, in a daily street-fair atmosphere, upwards of 15,000 unbonded girls and boys interact in a tribal, love-seeking, free-swinging, acid-based type of society where, if you are a hippie and you have a dime, you can put it in a parking meter and lie down in the street for an hour's suntan (30 minutes for a nickel) and most drivers will be careful not to run you over.

Warren Hinckle, "A Social History of the Hippies," from *Ramparts* Magazine, March, 1967. Reprinted by permission of *Ramparts*.

Speaking, sometimes all at once, inside the Sierra cabin were many voices of conscience and vision of the Haight-Ashbury—belonging to men who, except for their Raggedy Andy hair, paisley shirts and pre-mod western levi jackets, sounded for all the world like Young Republicans.

They talked about reducing governmental controls, the sanctity of the individual, the need for equality among men. They talked, very seriously, about the kind of society they wanted to live in, and the fact that if they wanted an ideal world they would have to go out and make it for themselves, because nobody, least of all the government, was going to do it for them.

The utopian sentiments of these hippies were not to be put down lightly. Hippies have a clear vision of the ideal community—a psychedelic community, to be sure—where everyone is turned on and beautiful and loving and happy and floating free. But it is a vision that, despite the Alice in Wonderland phraseology hippies usually breathlessly employ to describe it, necessarily embodies a radical political philosophy: communal life, drastic restriction of private property, rejection of violence, creativity before consumption, freedom before authority, de-emphasis of government and traditional forms of leadership.

Despite a disturbing tendency to quietism, all hippies *ipso facto* have a political posture—one of unremitting opposition to the Establishment which insists on branding them criminals because they take LSD and marijuana, and hating them, anyway, because they enjoy sleeping nine in a room and three to a bed, seem to have free sex and guiltless minds, and can raise healthy children in dirty clothes.

The hippie choice of weapons is to love the Establishment to death rather than protest it or blow it up (hippies possess a confounding disconcern about traditional political methods or issues). But they are decidedly and forever outside the Consensus on which this society places such a premium, and since the hippie scene is so much the scene of those people under 25 that Time magazine warns will soon constitute half our population, this is a significant political fact.

This is all very solemn talk about people who like to skip rope and wear bright colors, but after spending some time with these fun and fey individuals you realize that, in a very unexpected way, they are as serious about what they're doing as the John Birch Society or the Junior League. It is not improbable, after a few more mountain seminars by those purposeful young men wearing beads, that the Haight-Ashbury may spawn the first utopian collectivist community since Brook Farm.

That this society finds it so difficult to take such rascally looking types seriously is no doubt the indication of a deep-rooted hang-up. But to comprehend the psychosis of America in the computer age, you have to know what's with the hippies.

Ken Kesey—I

GAMES PEOPLE PLAY, MERRY PRANKSTER DIVISION

Let us go, then, on a trip.

You can't miss the Tripmaster: the thick-necked lad in the blue and white striped pants with the red belt and the golden eagle buckle, a watershed of wasted promise in his pale blue eyes, one front tooth capped in patriotic red, white and blue, his hair downy, flaxen, straddling the incredibly wide divide of his high forehead like two small toupees pasted on sideways. Ken Kesey, Heir Apparent Number One to the grand American tradition of blowing one's artistic talent to do some other thing, was sitting in a surprisingly comfortable chair inside the bus with the psychedelic crust, puffing absentmindedly on a harmonica.

The bus itself was ambulatory at about 50 miles an hour, jogging along a back road in sylvan Marin County, four loudspeakers turned all the way up, broadcasting both inside and outside Carl Orff's Carmina Burana and filled with two dozen people simultaneously smoking marijuana and looking for an open ice cream store. It was the Thursday before the Summit Meeting weekend and Kesey, along with some 15 members of the turned-on yes men and women who call him "Chief" and whom he calls the "Merry Pranksters" in return, was demonstrating a "game" to a delegation of visiting hippie firemen.

Crossing north over the Golden Gate Bridge from San Francisco to Marin County to pay Kesey a state visit were seven members of The Diggers, a radical organization even by Haight-Ashbury standards, which exists to give things away, free. The Diggers started out giving out free food, free clothes, free lodging and free legal advice, and hope eventually to create a totally free cooperative community. They had come to ask Kesey to get serious and attend the weekend meeting on the state of the nation of the hippies.

The dialogue had hardly begun, however, before Kesey loaded all comers into the bus and pushed off into the dark to search for a nocturnal ice cream store. The bus, which may be the closest modern man has yet come to aping the self-sufficiency of Captain Nemo's submarine, has its own power supply and is equipped with instruments for a full rock band, microphones, loudspeakers, spotlights and comfortable seats all around. The Pranksters are presently installing microphones every three feet on the bus walls so everybody can broadcast to everybody else all at once.

At the helm was the Intrepid Traveler, Ken Babbs, who is auxiliary chief of the Merry Pranksters when Kesey is out of town or incommunicado or in jail, all three of which he has recently been. Babbs, who is said to be the model for the heroes of both Kesey novels, *One Flew Over the Cuckoo's Nest* and *Sometimes A Great Notion*, picked up a microphone to address the guests in the rear of the bus, like the driver of a Grayline tour: "We are being followed by a police car. Will someone watch and tell me when he turns on his red light."

The law was not unexpected, of course, because any cop who sees Kesey's bus just about *has* to follow it, would probably end up with some form of professional D.T.'s if he didn't. It is part of the game: the cop was now playing on their terms, and Kesey and his Pranksters were delighted. In fact, a discernible wave of disappointment swept across the bus when the cop finally gave up chasing this particular U.F.O. and turned onto another road.

The games he plays are very important to Kesey. In many ways his intellectual rebellion has come full circle; he has long ago rejected the structured nature of society—the foolscap rings of success, conformity and acceptance "normal" people must regularly jump through. To the liberated intellect, no doubt, these requirements constitute the most sordid type of game. But, once rejecting all the norms of society, the artist is free to create his own structures—and along with any new set of rules, however personal, there is necessarily, the shell of the tortoise, a new set of games. In Kesey's case, at least, the games are usually fun. Running around the outside of an insane society, the healthiest thing you can do is laugh.

It helps to look at this sort of complicated if not confused intellectual proposition in bas relief, as if you were looking at the simple pictures on Wedgewood china. Stand Successful Author Ken Kesey off against, say, Successful Author Truman Capote. Capote, as long as his game is accepted by the system, is free to be as mad as he can. So he tosses the biggest, most vulgar ball in a long history of vulgar balls, and achieves the perfect idiot synthesis of the upper middle and lower royal classes. Kesey, who cares as much about the system as he does about the Eddie Cantor Memorial Forest, invents his own game. He purchases a pre-40's International Harvester school bus, paints it psychedelic, fills it with undistinguished though lovable individuals in varying stages of eccentricity, and drives brazenly down the nation's highways, high on LSD, watching and waiting for the cops to blow their minds.

At the least, Kesey's posture has the advantage of being intellectually consistent with the point of view of his novels. In *One Flew Over the Cuckoo's Nest*, he uses the setting of an insane asylum as a metaphor for what he considers to be the basic insanity, or at least the fundamentally bizarre illogic, of American society. Since the world forces you into a game that is both mad and unfair, you are better off inventing your own game. Then, at least, you have a chance of winning. At least that's what Kesey thinks.

Ken Kesey—II

THE CURRY IS VERY HOT; MERRY PRANKSTERS ARE HAVING POT

There wasn't much doing on late afternoon television, and the Merry Pranksters were a little restless. A few were turning on; one Prankster amused himself squirting his friends with a yellow plastic watergun; another staggered into the living room, exhausted from peddling a bicycle in ever-diminishing circles in the middle of the street. They were all waiting, quite patiently, for dinner, which the Chief was whipping up himself. It was a curry, the recipe of no doubt cabalistic origin. Kesey evidently took his cooking seriously, because he stood guard by the pot for an hour and a half, stirring, concentrating on the little clock on the stove that didn't work.

There you have a slice of domestic life, February 1967, from the swish Marin County home of Attorney Brian Rohan. As might be surmised, Rohan is Kesey's attorney, and the novelist and his *aides de camp* had parked their bus outside for the duration. The duration might last a long time, because Kesey has dropped out of the hippie scene. Some say that he was pushed, because he fell, very hard, from favor among the hippies last year when he announced that he, Kesey, personally, was going to help reform the psychedelic scene. This sudden social conscience may have had something to do with beating a jail sentence on a compounded marijuana charge, but when Kesey obtained his freedom with instructions from the judge "to preach an anti-LSD warning to teenagers" it was a little too much for the Haight-Ashbury set. Kesey, after all, was the man who had turned on the Hell's Angels.

That was when the novelist was living in La Honda, a small community in the Skyline moutain range overgrown with trees and, after Kesey invited the Hell's Angels to several house parties, overgrown with sheriff's deputies. It was in this Sherwood Forest setting, after he had finished his second novel with LSD as his co-pilot, that Kesey inaugurated his band of Merry Pranksters (they have an official seal from the State of California incorporating them as "Intrepid Trips, Inc."), painted the school bus in glow sock colors, announced he would write no more ("Rather than write, I will ride buses, study the insides of jails, and see what goes on"), and set up funtime housekeeping on a full-time basis with the Pranksters, his wife and their three small children (one confounding thing about Kesey is the amorphous quality of the personal relationships in his entourage—the several attractive women don't seem, from the outside, to belong to any particular man; children are loved enough, but seem to be held in common).

When the Hell's Angels rumbled by, Kesey welcomed them with LSD. "We're in the same business. You break people's bones, I break people's heads," he told them. The Angels seem to like the whole acid thing, because today they are a fairly constant act in the Haight-Ashbury show, while Kesey has abdicated his role as Scoutmaster to fledgling acid heads and exiled himself across the Bay. This self-imposed Elba came about when Kesey sensed that the hippie community had soured on him. He had committed the one mortal sin in the hippie ethic: *telling* people what to do. "Get into a responsibility bag," he urged some 400 friends attending a private Halloween party. Kesey hasn't been seen much in the Haight-Ashbury since that night, and though the Diggers did succeed in getting him to attend the weekend discussion, it is doubtful they will succeed in getting the novelist involved in any serious effort to shape the Haight-Ashbury future. At 31, Ken Kesey is a hippie has-been.

Ken Kesey—III

THE ACID TESTS—FROM UNITARIANS TO WATTS

Kesey is now a self-sufficient but lonely figure—if you can be lonely with dozens of Merry Pranksters running around your house all day. If he ever gets maudlin, which is doubtful, he can look back fondly on his hippie memories, which are definitely in the wow! category, because Ken Kesey did for acid roughly what Johnny Appleseed did for trees, and probably more.

He did it through a unique and short-lived American institution called the Acid Test. A lot of things happened at an Acid Test, but the main thing was that, in the Haight-Ashbury vernacular, everyone in the audience got zonked out of their minds on LSD. LSD in Pepsi. LSD in coffee. LSD in cake. LSD in the community punch. Most people were generally surprised, because they didn't know they were getting any LSD until it was too late. Later, when word got around that this sort of mad thing was happening at Acid Tests, Kesey sometimes didn't give out LSD on purpose, just so people wouldn't know whether they did or did not have LSD. Another game.

The Acid Test began calmly enough. In the early versions Kesey merely gave a heart-to-heart psychedelic talk and handed LSD around like the Eucharist, which first happened at a Unitarian conference in Big Sur in August of 1965. He repeated this ritual several times, at private gatherings in his home in La Honda, on college campuses, and once at a Vietnam Day Committee rally at Berkeley. Then Kesey added the Grateful Dead, a pioneer San Francisco rock group, to his Acid Tests and, the cherry on the matzos, the light show atmospheric technique of projecting slides and wild colors on the walls during rock dances. This combination he called "trips." Trip is the word for an LSD experience, but in Kesey's lexicon it also meant kicks, which were achieved by rapidly changing the audience's sensory environment what seemed like approximately ten million times during an evening by manipulating bright colored lights, tape recorders, slide projectors, weird sound machines, and whatever else may be found in the electronic sink, while the participants danced under stroboscopic lights to a wild rock band or just played around on the floor.

It was a fulgurous, electronically orgiastic thing (the most advanced Tests had closed circuit television sets on the dance floor so you could see what you were doing), which made psychedelics very "fun" indeed, and the hippies came in droves. Almost every hippie in the Bay area went to at least one Acid Test, and it is not exceeding the bounds of reasonable speculation to say that Kesey may have turned on at least 10,000 people to LSD during the 24 presentations of the Acid Test. (During these Tests the Merry Pranksters painted everything including themselves in fluorescent tones, and bright colors became the permanent in-thing in psychedelic dress.)

Turning so many unsuspecting people on to LSD at once could be dangerous, as the Pranksters discovered on a 1965 psychedelic road show when they staged the ill-fated Watts Acid Test. Many of the leading citizens of Watts came to the show, which was all very fine except that whoever put the LSD in the free punch that was passed around put in too much by a factor of about four. This served to make for a very wild Acid Test, and one or two participants "freaked out" and had a very hard time of it for the next few days.

After the California legislature played Prohibition and outlawed LSD on October 6, 1966, Kesey wound up the Acid Test with what was billed as a huge "Trips Festival" in San Francisco. People who regularly turn on say the Trips Festival was a bore: it embodied all the Acid Test elements except acid and, happily for the coffers of Intrepid Trips, Inc., attracted a huge crowd of newspapermen, narcotics agents and other squares, but very few hippies. The Merry Pranksters slyly passed out plain sugar cubes for the benefit of the undercover agents.

Suddenly San Francisco, which for a grown-up city gets excited very easily, was talking about almost nothing but "trips" and LSD. Hippies, like overnight, had become fashionable.

If you are inclined to give thanks for this sort of thing, they go to the bad boy wonder of Psychedelphia, disappearing there over the horizon in his wayward bus.

Historian Chester Anderson—I

THE GHOSTS OF SCENES PAST, OR HOW WE GOT HERE FROM THERE

Like Frederick J. Turner and Arnold Toynbee, Chester Anderson has a theory of history. His theory is psychedelic, but that is perfectly natural since he is a veteran acid head. Anderson, a 35-year-old professional bohemian who looks 45, considers himself the unofficial historian of the psychedelic movement and has amassed enough footnotes to argue somewhat convincingly that the past 15 years of social change in the United States—all the underground movements, and a significant part of the cultural changes—have been intimately connected with drugs.

If he is going to press his argument all the way, he may have to punch it out with Marshall McLuhan, who no doubt would assert that such phenomena as hippie colonies are nothing but a return to "tribal" culture, an inevitable reaction to our electronic age. And any social historian worth his salt will put it that every society has found some way to allow the sons and daughters of its middle class to drop out and cut up (most hippies by the way, are from middle class stock, so what's the difference from, say, the Teddy Boys?). Maybe lots, maybe none. But there is no disputing the cultural and artistic flipflops this country has gone through in the last decade. The jazz musicians' vogue meant something. So did the Beat Generation. So, we suppose, did Pop Art, and Rock and Roll, and so, of course, the hippies. If, in briefly tracing the derivation of the hippies from their seminal reasons in the intellectual uneasiness of the early 1950's, we chance to favor the testimony of Chester Anderson, it is only because he was there.

That was some bad year, 1953. There was a war on in Korea, a confusing, undefined war, the first big American war that wasn't the one to end all wars, because the aftermath of World War II had blown that phobia. And now the Bomb was with us, and with it the staccato series of disturbing headline events that stood for the Cold War; college was the only escape from the draft, but eggheads were becoming unpopular; Stevenson had lost the election and the Rosenbergs had been executed. It was all gloom, gloom, and dullsville, and if you were young and intellectual you were hard-pressed to find a hero or even a beautiful person. The only really alive, free thing, it seemed, was jazz—and the arrival of the long playing record had sparked a jazz renaissance, and with it the first drug heroes; most kids sympathized with Gene Krupa's marijuana busts, the agony of Lady Day's junk hangup was universal, and Charlie Parker had his own drugstore.

Lady Day's way wasn't the way of the new generation, Chester Anderson will be quick to tell you, because she was on "body" drugs. Whatever else body drugs—heroin, opium, barbiturates, alcohol, tranquilizers—may do, they eventually turn you off, and contemporary heads like to be turned on—i.e., senses intensified, stimulated rather than depressed. "Head" drugs, which do the latter, are both cheaper and easier to get than body drugs, and come in approximately 18 varieties in three different classifications—natural drugs like marijuana, hashish, peyote, morning glory seeds, Hawaiian wood rose seeds, and certain types of Mexican mushrooms; artificial psychedelics like mescaline, LSD, psilocybin and psilocin, and whatever the ingredient is that makes Romilar cough syrup so popular with young heads; and synthetic stimulants which, used in large doses by heads are known as "speed"—dexedrine, benzedrine and methedrine.

But in the early 1950's there wasn't such a complete psychedelic medicine shelf to choose from, and the culturally disenchanted pioneers who began to settle new colonies in New York's Village and San Francisco's North Beach had to make do with pot. In a climate dominated by Dwight Eisenhower in the newspapers and Ed Sullivan on television, they also began to turn on to the pacifist, humanist philosophies of Asia—particularly Buddhism, most especially Zen—while Christianity as a workable concept became more meaningless, despite the exemplary efforts of such men as Brother Antoninus and Thomas Merton. American churchmen seemed to have neither the patience nor the fortitude to deal with people who were, well, *unsettled*. Folk music, which had been slowly dying, perked up a little, and there was a new interest in fresh tuned-in poetry. As the '50s approached middle age and McCarthy went on the rampage, the few signs of life in a stagnant society centered around the disoriented peace movement, the fledgling civil rights movement, the young political left, jazz and folk music, poetry and Zen. Most of these followers were, of course, taking pot, while the rest of the country remained on booze and sleeping pills.

(If, in memory of the 85th anniversary of Anthony Trollope's death, we may be permitted an aside to the reader, it would be to say that one of the things that is considered original, but is in fact not, about the hippies is the concept of "dropping out" of society. Without adopting the histrionics of Hogarth crusading against the masses drinking gin, it is true that alcohol is an opiate which serves to help tens of millions of busy businessmen and lethargic housewives to "drop out" of any essential involvement in life and remain political and artistic boors. But alcohol is legal so nobody cares. If pot and LSD were ever legalized, it would be a mortal blow to this bohemia. Hippies have a political posture essentially because of the enforced criminality of their daily dose, and if taking LSD meant no more in society than the commuter slugging down his seventh martini, the conspiratorial magic would go out of the movement.)

Meanwhile, in San Francisco, Allen Ginsberg remembers an evening in 1955 which could stand as well as any for the starting point of what was to become the most thorough repudiation of America's middlebrow culture since the expatriates walked out on the country in the 1930's. The vanguard of what was to be the Beat Generation had gathered at the 6 Galley on Fillmore Street for a poetry reading moderated by Kenneth Rexroth, a respectable leftish intellectual who was later to become the Public Defender of the Beats. Lawrence Ferlinghetti was in the audience, and so were Kerouac and his then sidekick, Neal Cassady, listening to Michael McClure, Phil Lamantia, Gary Snyder and Philip Whalen read their poetry. Ginsberg was there too, and delighted everyone with a section of the still unfinished "Howl," better known to Beats as the Declaration of Independence.

Two distinct strains in the underground movement of the '50s were represented at this salient gathering. One was a distinctly fascist trend, embodied in Kerouac, which can be recognized by a totalitarian insistence on action and nihilism, and usually accompanied by a Superman concept. This strain runs, deeper and less silent, through the hippie scene today. It is into this fascist bag that you can put Kesey and his friends, the Hell's Angels, and, in a more subtle way, Dr. Timothy Leary.

The other, majority, side of the Beats was a cultural reaction to the existential brinkmanship forced on them by the Cold War, and a lively attack on the concurrent rhetoric of complacency and self-satisfaction that pervaded the literary establishment all the way from the Atlantic Monthly to Lionel Trilling. Led by men like Ginsberg and Ferlinghetti, the early Beats weighed America by its words and deeds, and found it pennyweight. They took upon themselves the role of conscience for the machine. They rejected all values and when, in attempting to carve a new creative force, they told America to "go fuck itself," America reacted, predictably, with an obscenity trial.

The early distant warnings of the drug-based culture that would dominate the Haight-Ashbury a decade later were there in the early days of North Beach. Marijuana was as popular as Coke at a Baptist wedding, and the available hallucinogens—peyote and mescaline—were part of the Beat rebellion. Gary Snyder, poet, mountain climber, formal Yamabushi Buddhist, and a highly respected leader of the hippie scene today, first experimented with peyote while living with the Indian tribe of the same name in 1948; Ginsberg first took it in New York in 1951; Lamantia, Kerouac and Cassady were turned on by Beat impresario Hymie D'Angolo at his Big Sur retreat in 1952. And Beat parties, whether they served peyote, marijuana or near beer, were rituals, community sacraments, setting the format for contemporary hippie rituals.

But the psychedelic community didn't really begin to flourish until late 1957 and 1958 in New York, and for that story we take you to Chester Anderson in the Village.

Historian Chester Anderson—II

WAS THE KINGSTON TRIO REALLY RED GUARDS?

On Thanksgiving Day, 1957, Chester Anderson was turned on to grass by a bongo-playing superhippie who went by the code name of Mr. Sulks. Grass, if you don't know and don't have an underground glossary handy, is translated marijuana, and from that day forward, Anderson, who once studied music at the University of Miami so he could write string quartets like Brahms, became a professional Turn-On and migrated with bohemia, east to west to east to west, from the Village to North Beach back to the Village to the Haight-Ashbury, where he can be found today—a prototype of the older psychedelic type who mixes with the drifting, turning on kids to form the central nervous system of any body of hippies.

The first psychedelic drug to reach the Village in any quantity was peyote, an obscure hallucinatory cactus bud used by Indians in religious ceremonies. Peyote was cheap and plentiful (it can still be ordered by mail from Laredo at $10 for 100 "buttons") and became highly touted —Havelock Ellis and Aldous Huxley recommended it. The only problem with peyote was that it tasted absolutely terrible, and, as peyote cults sprang up, peyote cookbooks came out with recipes for preparing the awful stuff in ways that would kill the taste. "Man," Chester recalls a head telling him at the time, "if I thought it'd get me high, I'd eat shit." As with most new head drugs, the taking of peyote was treated as a quasi-religious event. The first time Chester took it, he did so with great ritual before a statue of the Buddha.

Peyote was the thing in late 1957, and by the summer of 1958 mescaline, the first synthetic psychedelic, was widely distributed, The heads reacted like unwed mothers being handed birth control pills—they were no longer dependent on nature. Turn-ons could be *manufactured!*

According to Chester's files, LSD didn't arrive in any large, consumer-intended supply in the Village until the winter of 1961-62, and not in the Bay Area until the summer of 1964, but by that time something unusual had happened to America's psychedelic gypsies: they had become formal enemies of the State. Massive harassment by the cops in San Francisco, by the coffeehouse license inspectors in New York, had led the heads and the young middle class types who came in caravan proportions, to test the no-more-teachers, no-more-books way of bohemian life, to view the Establishment as the bad guy who would crush their individuality and spirituality in any way he could. This is the derivation of whatever political posture the hippies have today. It will be significant, of course, only if the Haight-Ashbury scene doesn't go the way of the Beat Generation—assimilated by a kick-hungry society. For the serious, literary Beats, it was all over but the shouting when the Co-existence Bagel Shop became a stop on sightseeing tours.

In 1962, the Village was pulsating with psychedelic evangelism. LSD was so cheap and so plentiful that it became a big thing among heads to turn on new people as fast as they could give LSD away.

Pot, also, was being used more widely than ever by middle class adults, and spread from the urban bohemias to the hinterlands by small folk music circles that were to be found everywhere from Jacksonville, Florida, to Wausau, Wisconsin. At the same time, almost the entire Village was treating LSD like it was a selection on a free lunch counter, and a scruffy folknik called Bobby Dylan was beginning to play charitable guest sets in the Washington Square coffeehouses. "Things," Chester said, "were happening more rapidly than we knew."

What was happening, Mr. Jones, was that folk music, under the influence of early acid culture, was giving way to rock and roll. Rock spread the hippie way of life like a psychedelic plague, and it metamorphosed in such rapid fashion from the popularity of folk music, that a very suspicious person might ask if seemingly safe groups like the Kingston Trio were not, in fact, the Red Guards of the hippie cultural revolution.

There was a rock and roll before, of course, but it was all bad seed. The likes of Frankie Avalon, Fabian and Elvis Presley sent good rock and roll musicians running to folk music. Then absolutely the world's greatest musical blitz fell and the Beatles landed, everywhere, all at once. The impact of their popular music was analogous to the Industrial Revolution on the 19th century. They brought music out of the juke box and into the street. The Beatles' ecstatic, alive, electric sound had a total sensory impact, and was inescapably participational. It was "psychedelic music." "The Beatles are a trip," Chester said. Whether the Beatles or Dylan or the Rolling Stones actually came to their style through psychedelic involvement (Kenneth Tynan says a recent Beatles song "Tomorrow Never Knows" is "the best musical evocation of LSD I've ever heard") is not as important as the fact that their songs reflect LSD values—love, life, getting along with other people, and that this type of involving, turn-on music galvanized the entire hippie underground into overt, brassy existence—particularly in San Francisco.

Drug song lyrics may, in fact, be the entire literary output of the hippie generation. The hippies' general disregard for anything as static as a book is a fact over which Chester Anderson and Marshall McLuhan can shake hands. For acid heads are, in McLuhan's phrase, "post-literate." Hippies do not share our written, linear society—they like textures better than surfaces, prefer the electronic to the mechanical, like group, tribal activities. Theirs is an ecstatic, do-it-now culture, and rock and roll is their art form.

The Merchant Princes—I

DR. LEARY—PRETENDER TO THE HIPPIE THRONE

The suit was Brooks Brothers '59, and the paisley tie J. Press contemporary, but the bonecarved Egyptian mandala hanging around his neck, unless it was made in occupied Japan, had to be at least 2000 years old. Dr. Timothy Leary, B.A. University of Alabama, Ph.D. University of California, LSD Cuernavaca and 86'd Harvard College, was dressed up for a night on the town, but as his devotees say of this tireless proselytizer of the psychedelic cause, it was work, work, work. Tonight Leary was scouting somebody else's act, a Swami's at that, who was turning on the hippies at the Avalon Ballroom by leading them in an hour-long Hindu chant without stopping much for breath. The Avalon is one of the two great, drafty ballrooms where San Francisco hippies, hippie-hangers-on and young hippies-to-be congregate each weekend to participate in the psychedelic rock and light shows that are now as much a part of San Francisco as cable cars and a lot noisier.

This dance was a benefit for the new Swami, recently installed in a Haight-Ashbury storefront, with a fair passage sign from Allen Ginsberg whom he had bumped into in India. The hippies were turning out to see just what the Swami's *schtick* was, but Dr. Leary had a different purpose. He has a vested, professional interest in turning people on, and here was this Swami, trying to do it with just chant, like it was natural childbirth or something.

The word professional is not used lightly. There is a large group of professionals making it by servicing and stimulating the hippie world—in the spirit of the Haight-Ashbury we should refer to these men as merchant princes—and Timothy Leary is the pretender to the throne.

Dr. Leary claims to have launched the first indigenous religion in America. That may very well be, though as a religious leader he is Aimee Semple McPherson in drag. Dr. Leary, who identifies himself as a "prophet," recently played the Bay Area in his LSD road show, where he sold $4 seats to lots of squares but few hippies (Dr. Leary's pitch is to the straight world), showed a technicolor movie billed as simulating an LSD experience (it was big on close-ups of enlarged blood vessels), burned incense, dressed like a holy man in white cotton pajamas, and told everybody to "turn on, tune in, and drop out."

In case you are inclined to make light of this philosophic advice you should not laugh out loud. Because Dr. Leary is serious about his work, he can not be dismissed as a cross between a white Father Divine and Nietzche, no matter how tempting the analogy. He has made a substantial historical contribution to the psychedelic scene, although his arrest records may figure more prominently than his philosophy in future hippie histories.

Since, something like Eve, he first bit into the sacred psychedelic mushroom while lounging beside a swimming pool in Cuernavaca, he has been hounded by the consequences of his act. Since Dr. Leary discovered LSD, he has been booted out of Harvard for experimenting a little too widely with it among the undergraduate population, asked to leave several foreign countries for roughly the same reasons, and is now comfortably if temporarily ensconced in a turned-on billionaire friend's estate near Poughkeepsie, New York, while awaiting judicial determination of a 30-year prison sentence for transporting a half-ounce of marijuana across the Rio Grande without paying the Texas marijuana tax, which has not been enforced since the time of the Lone Ranger.

If he were asked to contribute to the "L" volume of the World Book Encyclopedia, Dr. Leary would no doubt sum up his work as "having turned on American culture," though his actual accomplishments are somewhat more prosaic. Together with Richard Alpert, who was to Dr. Leary what Bill Moyers was to President Johnson, Leary wrote an article in May 1962 in, surprise, The Bulletin of the Atomic Scientists. The article warned that in event of war, the Russians were likely to douse all our reservoirs with LSD in order to make people so complacent that they wouldn't particularly care about being invaded, and as a civil defense precaution we ought to do it ourselves first—you know, douse our own reservoirs—so that when the reds got *their* chance the country would know just what was coming off. It was back to the old drawing board after that article, but Alpert and Dr. Leary made their main contribution to the incredibly swift spread of LSD through the nation in 1964 by the simple act of publishing a formula for LSD, all that was needed by any enterprising housewife with a B-plus in high school chemistry and an inclination for black market activity. Dr. Leary's religious crusade has been a bust, convert-wise, and not so salutary financially, either, so he announced recently that he was dropping out, himself, to contemplate his navel under the influence. It would be easier to take Dr. Leary seriously if he could overcome his penchant for treating LSD as a patent snake-bite medicine.

An enlightening example of this panacea philosophy is found back among the truss ads in the September 1966 issue of *Playboy*. In the midst of a lengthy interview when, as happens in *Playboy*, the subject got around to sex, Dr. Leary was all answers. "An LSD session that does not involve an ultimate merging with a person of the opposite sex isn't really complete," he said, a facet of the drug he neglected to mention to the Methodist ladies he was attempting to turn on in Stockton, California. But this time, Dr. Leary was out to turn on the *Playboy* audience.

The following selection from the interview is reprinted in its entirety. Italics are *Playboy*'s.

PLAYBOY We've heard that some women who ordinarily have difficulty achieving orgasm find themselves capable of multiple orgasms under LSD. Is that true?

LEARY In a carefully prepared, loving LSD session, a woman will inevitably have several hundred orgasms.

PLAYBOY Several *hundred?*

LEARY Yes. Several hundred.

After recovering from that intelligence, the *Playboy* interviewer, phrasing the question as diplomatically as possible, asked Dr. Leary if he got much, being such a handsome LSD turn-on figure. Dr. Leary allowed that women were always falling over him, but responded with the decorum of Pope Paul being translated from the Latin: "Any charismatic person who is conscious of his own mythic potency awakens this basic hunger in women and pays reverence to it at the level that is harmonious and appropriate at the time."

Dr. Leary also said that LSD is a "specific *cure* for homosexuality."

The final measurement of the tilt of Dr. Leary's windmill, his no doubt earnest claim to be the prophet of this generation, must be made by weighing such recorded conversations against his frequent and urgent pleas to young people to "drop out of politics, protest, petitions and pickets" and join his "new religion" where, as he said recently:

"You have to be out of your mind to pray."

Perhaps, and quite probably so.

The Merchant Princes—II

WHERE DUN & BRADSTREET FEARS TO TREAD

Allen Ginsberg asked 10,000 people to turn towards the sea and chant with him. They all did just that, and then picked up the papers and miscellaneous droppings on the turf of Golden Gate Park's Polo Field and went contentedly home. This was the end of the first Human Be-In, a gargantuan hippie happening held only for the joy of it in mid-January. The hippie tribes gathered under clear skies with rock bands, incense, chimes, flutes, feathers, candles, banners and drums. Even the Hell's Angels were on their good behavior—announcing that they would guard the sound truck against unspecified evil forces. It was all so successful that the organizers are talking about another be-in this summer to be held at the bottom of the Grand Canyon with maybe 200,000 hippies being-in.

The local papers didn't quite know how to treat this one, except for the *San Francisco Chronicle*'s ace society editor Frances Moffat, who ran through the crowd picking out local socialites and taking notes on the fashions.

Mrs. Moffat's intense interest reflects the very in, very marketable character of San Francisco Hippiedom. Relatively high-priced mod clothing and trinket stores are as common in the Haight-Ashbury as pissoirs used to be in Paris. They are run by hippie merchants mostly for square customers, but that doesn't mean that the hippies themselves aren't brand name conscious. Professing a distaste for competitive society, hippies are, contradictorily, frantic consumers. Unlike the Beats, they do not disdain money. Indeed, when they have it, which with many is often, they use it to buy something pretty or pleasureful. You will find only the best hi-fi sets in hippie flats.

In this commercial sense, the hippies have not only accepted assimilation (the Beats fought it, and lost), they have swallowed it whole. The hippie culture is in many ways a prototype of the most ephemeral aspects of the larger American society; if the people looking in from the suburbs want change, clothes, fun, and some lightheadedness from the new gypsies, the hippies are delivering—and some of them are becoming rich hippies because of it.

The biggest Robber Baron is dance promoter Bill Graham, a Jewish boy from New York who made it big in San Francisco by cornering the hippie bread and circuses concession. His weekend combination rock and roll dances and light shows at the cavernous, creaky old Fillmore Auditorium on the main street of San Francisco's Negro ghetto are jammed every night. Even Andy Warhol played the Fillmore. Althought Graham is happy providing these weekend spiritual experiences, he's not trying to be a leader. "I don't want to make cadres, just money," he said. Graham's cross-town competitor is Chet Helms, a rimless-glasses variety hippie from Texas who has turned the pioneer, non-profit San Francisco rock group called The Family Dog, into a very profit-making enterprise at the Avalon Ballroom.

A side-product of the light show dances, and probably the only other permanent manifestation of hippie culture to date, is the revival in a gangbusters way of Art Nouveau poster art. Wes Wilson, who letters his posters in 18, 24 and 36 point Illegible . . : , originated the basic style in posters for the Fillmore dances. Graham found he could make as much money selling posters as dance tickets, so he is now in the poster business, too.

Haight Street, the Fifth Avenue of Hippiedom, is geographically parallel to Golden Gate Park but several blocks uphill, where rows of half vacant store fronts once indicated the gradual decline of a middle class neighborhood. But all that changed, dramatically, during the past 18 months. Haight Street now looks like the Metropolitan Opera Company backstage on the opening night of Aida. The stores are all occupied, but with mercantile ventures that might give Dun & Bradstreet cause to wonder. Threaded among the older meat markets, discount furniture stores, laundromats and proletarian bars are a variety of leather goods shops, art galleries, mod clothing stores and boutiques specializing in psychedelic paraphernalia like beads, prisms and marijuana pipes, and of course there is the Psychedelic Shop itself.

The Psychedelic Shop is treated as a hippie landmark of sorts, but the Haight-Ashbury scene was percolating long before the Thelin brothers, Ron and Jay, stuffed a disconcertingly modern glass and steel store front full of amulets, psychedelic books, a large stock of the underground press and some effete gadgetry for acid heads. The hippie phenomena began to metamorphose from a personal to a social happening around the fall of 1965 after the kids at Berkeley turned on to LSD, Ken Kesey started holding Acid Tests, and The Family Dog staged its first dance.

Instrumental in spreading the word was the *Chronicle*'s highly regarded jazz critic, Ralph J. Gleason. Gleason is read religiously by hippies. Besides explaining to his square readers what is happening, he is also the unofficial arbitrator of good taste in the Haight-Ashbury community. Gleason was quick to tell Ken Kesey, in print, when he was out of line, and did the same for Dr. Leary. Gleason's writing tuned in other members of the *Chronicle* staff, and the extensive, often headline publicity the newspaper gave to the hippie scene (Kesey's return from a self-imposed Mexican exile was treated with the seriousness of a reasonably large earthquake) helped escalate the Haight-Ashbury population explosion.

So there is plenty of business for the hippie merchants, but some of them, like the Thelin brothers, are beginning to wonder where it will all lead. At the prodding of The Diggers, the Thelins are considering making the store a non-profit cooperative that will help "the kids get high and stay high" at low cost. They may also take the same steps with The Oracle, the Haight-Ashbury monthly tabloid. The majority of the hip merchants, however, are very comfortable with the ascending publicity and sales, and have as little vision of what they are helping create than did Alexander Bell when he spilled acid on himself.

If you have any doubts about the thoroughly successful commercialization of the entire hippie scene, you should look at the comic pages between Dick Tracy and L'il Abner, where a few weeks back there was this, well, episode, in the comic strip called Rex Morgan, M.D.:

Unless most parents sent their children to bed before they got to the comics that week, everybody now knows all about trips. This just goes to prove that somewhere in the wild, psychedelic world there's a buck to be made.

Emmett Grogan—I

WILL THE REAL FRODO BAGGINS PLEASE STAND UP?

Except for the obvious fact that he wasn't covered with fur, you would have said to yourself that for sure there was old Frodo Baggins, crossing Haight Street. Frodo Baggins is the hero of the English antiquarian J.R.R. Tolkien's classic trilogy, *Lord of the Rings,* absolutely the favorite book of every hippie, about a race of little people called Hobbits who live somewhere in pre-history in a place called Middle Earth. Hobbits are hedonistic, happy little fellows who love beauty and pretty colors. Hobbits have their own scene and resent intrusion, pass the time eating three or four meals a day and smoke burning leaves of herb in pipes of clay. You can see why hippies would like Hobbits.

The hustling, heroic-looking fellow with the mistaken identity was Emmett Grogan, kingpin of The Diggers and the closest thing the hippies in the Haight-Ashbury have to a real live hero. Grogan, 23, with blond, unruly hair and a fair, freckled Irish face, has the aquiline nose of a leader, but he would prefer to say that he "just presents alternatives."

He is in and out of jail 17 times a week, sometimes busted for smashing a cop in the nose (Grogan has a very intolerant attitude toward policemen), sometimes bailing out a friend, and sometimes, like Monopoly, just visiting. The alternatives he presents are rather disturbing to the hippie bourgeoisie, since he thinks they have no business charging hippies money for their daily needs and should have the decency to give things away free, like The Diggers do, or at least charge the squares and help out the hippies.

Grogan has a very clear view of what freedom means in society ("Why can't I stand on the corner and wait for nobody? Why can't everyone?") and an even clearer view of the social position of the hippie merchants ("They just want to expand their sales, they don't care what happens to people here; they're nothing but goddamn shopkeepers with beards.").

Everyone is a little afraid of Grogan in the Haight-Ashbury, including the cops. A one-man crusade for purity of purpose, he is the conscience of the hippie community. He is also a bit of a daredevil and a madman, and could easily pass for McMurphy, the roguish hero in Kesey's novel set in an insane asylum. There is a bit of J. P. Donleavy's *Ginger Man* in him, too.

A few weeks ago, out collecting supplies for The Diggers' daily free feed, Grogan went into a San Francisco wholesale butcher and asked for soup bones and meat scraps. "No free food here, we work for what we eat," said the head butcher, a tattooed Bulgar named Louie, who was in the icebox flanked by his seven assistant butchers. "You're a fascist pig and a coward," replied Grogan, whom Louie immediately smashed in the skull with the blunt side of a carving knife. That turned out to be a mistake, because the seven assistant butchers didn't like Louie much, and all jumped him. While all those white coats were grunting and rolling in the sawdust, a bleeding Grogan crawled out with four cardboard boxes full of meat.

This was a typical day in Dogpatch for Grogan, who has had his share of knocks. A Brooklyn boy, he ran away from home at 15 and spent the next six years in Europe, working as a busboy in the Alps, and, later, studying film making in Italy under Antonioni. Grogan had naturally forgotten to register for the draft, so when he returned to the United States he was in the Army four days later. That didn't last long, however, because the first thing Grogan had to do was clean the barracks. His idea of cleaning barracks was to throw all the guns out the window, plus a few of the rusty beds, and artistically displeasing foot lockers. Then he began painting the remaining bed frames yellow. "I threw out everything that was not esthetically pleasing," he told the sergeant.

Two days later Grogan was in the psychiatric ward of Letterman Hospital in San Francisco where he stayed for six months before the authorities decided they couldn't quite afford to keep him. That was shortly after an Army doctor, learning of his film training, ordered Grogan to the photo lab for "work therapy." It was a "beautiful, tremendously equipped lab," Grogan recalls, and since it wasn't used very much, he took a picture of his own big blond face and proceeded to make 5000 prints. When the doctors caught up with him, he had some 4700 nine by twelve glossies of Emmett Grogan neatly stacked on the floor, and all lab machines: driers, enlargers, developers were going like mad, and the water was running over on the floor. "What did you do *that* for?" a doctor screamed.

Grogan shrugged. "I'm crazy," he said.

He was released a little later, and acted for a while with the San Francisco Mime Troupe, the city's original and brilliant radical theatre ensemble. Then last fall, when the Negro riots broke out in San Francisco and the National Guard put a curfew on the Haight-Ashbury, the Diggers happened. "Everybody was trying to figure how to react to the curfew. The SDS came down and said ignore it, go to jail. The merchants put up chicken posters saying 'for your own safety, get off the street.' Somehow, none of those ideas seemed right. If you had something to do on the streets, you should do it and tell the cops to go screw off. If you didn't, you might as well be inside."

Something to do, to Grogan, was to eat if you were hungry, so at 8 p.m., at the curfew witching hour, he and an actor friend named Billy Landau set up a delicious free dinner in the park, right under the cops' noses, and the hippies came and ate and have been chowing down, free, every night since. The Haight-Ashbury has never been quite the same.

Emmett Grogan—II

A PSYCHEDELIC 'GRAPES OF WRATH'

Every Bohemian community has its inevitable coterie of visionaries who claim to know what it is all about. But The Diggers are, somehow, different. They are bent on creating a wholly cooperative subculture and, so far, they are not just hallucinating, they are doing it.

Free clothes (used) are there for whoever wants them. Free meals are served every day. Next, Grogan plans to open a smart mod clothing store on Haight Street and give the clothes away free, too (the hippie merchants accused him of "trying to undercut our prices"). He wants to start Digger farms where participants will raise their own produce. He wants to give away free acid, to eliminate junky stuff and end profiteering. He wants cooperative living to forestall inevitable rent exploitation when the Haight-Ashbury becomes chic.

Not since Brook Farm, not since the Catholic Workers, has any group in this dreadfully co-optive, consumer society been so serious about a utopian comunity.

If Grogan succeeds or fails in the Haight-Ashbury it will not be as important as the fact that he has tried. For he is, at least, providing the real possibility of what he calls "alternatives" in the down-the-rabbit-hole-culture of the hippies.

Grogan is very hung up on freedom. "Do your thing, be what you are, and nothing will ever bother you," he says. His heroes are the Mad Bomber of New York who blissfully blew up all kinds of things around Manhattan over 30 years because he just liked to blow things up, and poet Gary Snyder, whom he considers the "most important person in the Haight-Ashbury" because instead of sitting around sniffing incense and talking about it, he went off to Japan and became a Zen master. "He did it, man."

This is an interesting activist ethic, but it remains doubtful just what the hippies will do. Not that many, certainly, will join Grogan's utopia, because utopias, after all, have a size limit.

The New Left has been flirting with the hippies lately, even to the extent of singing "The Yellow Submarine" at a Berkeley protest rally, but it looks from here like a largely unrequited love.

The hip merchants will, of course, go on making money.

And the youngsters will continue to come to the Haight-Ashbury and do—what?

That was the question put to the hippie leaders at their Summit Meeting. They resolved their goals, but not the means, and the loud noise you heard from outside was probably Emmett Grogan pounding the table with his shoe.

The crisis of the happy hippie ethic is precisely this: it is all right to turn on, but it is not enough to drop out. Grogan sees the issue in the gap "between the radical political philosophy of Jerry Rubin and Mario Savio and psychedelic love philosophy." He, himself, is not interested in the war in Vietnam, but on the other hand he does not want to spend his days like Ferdinand sniffing pretty flowers.

This is why he is so furious at the hip merchants. "They created the myth of this utopia; now they aren't going to do anything about it."

Grogan takes the evils of society very personally, and he gets very angry, almost physically sick, when a pregnant 15-year-old hippie's baby starves in her stomach, a disaster which is not untypical in the Haight-Ashbury, and which Grogan sees being repeated ten-fold this summer when upwards of 200,000 migrant teenagers and college kids come, as a psychedelic "Grapes of Wrath," to utopia in search of the heralded turn-on.

The danger in the hippie movement is more than over-crowded streets and possible hunger riots this summer. If more and more youngsters begin to share the hippie political posture of unrelenting quietism, the future of activist, serious politics is bound to be affected. The hippies have shown that it can be pleasant to drop out of the arduous task of attempting to steer a difficult, unrewarding society. But when that is done, you leave the driving to the Hell's Angels.

Philosophy in a Pop Key: On Marshall McLuhan

Understanding Media has a dry, professional-sounding title, suggesting a handbook on magazines and television for advertising men, in particular those charged with buying space and time. It was written, however, by Professor Marshall McLuhan . . . whose conception of pop culture is no more conventional than an electronic opera. McLuhan is more likely to write a manual for the angel than for Madison Avenue. *Understanding Media* carries the subtitle "The Extensions of Man," which alerts readers at the start that more is at issue in this book than the relative merits of news and entertainment packages. We all know that radio, the movies, the press do things to us. For McLuhan they also *are* us: "They that make them," he quotes the Psalms, "shall be like unto them." So *Understanding Media* is nothing less than a book about humanity as it has been shaped by the means used in this and earlier ages to deliver information.

McLuhan's account of the effects of the media upon the human psyche lies between fact and metaphor. The instrumentalities through which words, images, and other human signals reach us transform our bodies as well as our minds. Our eyes are bulged out by vacuum tubes, our ears elongated by transistors, our skin ballooned by polyesters. ("Clothing and housing, as extensions of skin and heat-control mechanisms, are media of communication.") In his first book, *The Mechanical Bride,* published a dozen years ago and unmistakably inspired by Duchamp's erotic apparatuses, McLuhan dealt with the pop creations of advertising and other word-and-picture promotions as ingredients of a magic potion "composed of sex and technology," that was populating America with creatures half woman, half machine. "Noticed any very spare parts lately?" he inquired in a subhead of his title chapter. The legs, bust, hips of the modern girl have been dissociated from the human person as "power points," McLuhan claimed, reminding the reader that "the Hiroshima bomb was named 'Gilda' in honor of Rita Hayworth." Man, to McLuhan, often appears to be a device employed by the communications mechanisms in *their* self-development. "Any invention or technology," he writes in *Understanding Media,* "is an extension or self-amputation of our physical bodies, and such extension also demands new rations or new equilibriums among the other organs and extensions of the body. There is, for example, no way of refusing to comply with the new ratios or sense 'closure' evoked by the TV image."

In McLuhan's *The Gutenberg Galaxy*, the analysis of how the human organism has been remodeled by a single communications medium is turned into a full-scale interpretation of Western history. The outstanding characteristics of life in Europe and American from the Renaissance to the turn of the twentieth century are traced to the invention of moveable type and the diffusion of the printed word. The streaming of letters across a page brought into being an "eye culture" that found symbolic representation in *King Lear*, with its blindings and its wanderers stripped naked by the storm. (McLuhan got his Ph.D. in English at Cambridge.) With Gutenberg began the technological acceleration of history that has made constant change the norm of social life. The portability of books, McLuhan says, allowed "alphabetic man" to feed his intellect in isolation from others, thus introducing individualism and the Hamlet-like division between knowing and doing, as well as split personality ("Schizophrenia may be a necessary consequence of literacy") and the conflict between the ego and its environment. The separation of seeing from the other senses and the reduction of consciousness to sight-based concepts were compensated for by the emergence of the world of the unconscious. The fixed position of the reader vis-à-vis the page, says McLuhan, inspired perspective in painting, the visualization of three-dimensional objects in deep space, and the chronological narrative. The uniformity and repeatability of the phonetic bits that make up a line of type strengthened mechanistic philosophies, serial thinking in mathematics and the sciences, and ideals of social leveling, and they were the model for the assembly line. In replacing vernacular with mass media, print generated the centralizing forces of modern nationalism: "The citizen armies of Cromwell and Napoleon were the ideal manifestations of the new technology."

Understanding Media is McLuhan's good-bye to Gutenberg and to Renaissance, "typographic" man; that is, to the self-centered individual. As such, it takes its place in that wide channel of cultural criticism of the twentieth century that includes writers like T. S. Eliot, Oswald Spengler, D. H. Lawrence, F. R. Leavis, David Riesman, Hannah Arendt. *Understanding Media*, McLuhan's most neatly ordered and most comprehensive book, is an examination of how the eye-extended, print-reading individualist of the past five centuries is in our time undergoing metamorphosis under the bombardment of all his senses by new electronic media, the first of which was the telegraph. With the loss of the monopoly of the column of type has come the breakup of its peruser, and with this a landslide of all print-based social and art forms; e.g., the mechanical assembly line gives way to automation, and perspective in painting to two-dimensional, overall composition. Thus the changeover of media is synchronized with revolutionary phenomena in production and in cultural life and with an extreme crisis of values.

Of all crisis philosophers, McLuhan is by far the coolest. Though his notion of the "externalization" or "numbness" induced in the consumer of today's popular culture accords with Eliot's "hollow men," Riesman's "other-directedness," and Arendt's "banality," he is utterly unsympathetic to any concept of "decline." The collective trance of his contemporaries is to his mind a transitional phenomenon—one that recurs in all great historic shifts from one dominant medium to another. Current unfeeling and anxiety parallel states prevalent in the early Renaissance, when the printed document was replacing the handwritten script. Regarding us all in this light, McLuhan is immune to despair; in his terms, the theory that the modern world is a cultural wasteland is meaningless. What, he might ask, makes the inwardness of yesterday preferable to the shallowness of tomorrow, if both are by-products of more or less effective devices for conveying information? As the phonetic alphabet carried man from tribalism to individuality and freedom, the new electric media are taking him beyond "fragmented, literate, and visual individualism." If man today is part machine, this is not an effect of the Industrial Revolution. Technologies have been a component of human living for three thousand years, and our loftiest feelings have derived from that segment of us that is least ourselves: "By continuously embracing technologies, we relate ourselves to them as servo-mechanisms. That is why we must, to use them at all, serve these objects, these extensions of ourselves, as gods or minor religions. An Indian is the servo-mechanism of his canoe, as the cowboy of his horse or the executive of his clock." In line with Toynbee (the idea of the Eskimo as a merman, the cowboy as a centaur, is his), McLuhan has superseded Marx's "fetishism of commodities" with a fetishism of the medium to explain the forms of belief by which men have been governed in various epochs. Societies in which the sacred played a greater role than it does in ours were simply those ruled by media of communication more primitive than the visual. "To call the oral man 'religious,'" McLuhan observed in *The Gutenberg Galaxy*, "is, of course, as fanciful and arbitrary as calling blondes bestial."

McLuhan, then, is a modernist to the hilt; his own "sacred" touchstones are Cézanne and abstract art, the new physics, *Finnegan's Wake*. His is the kind of mind that fills with horror the would-be conservator of values (a Leavis, a Yeats, a Lukács). He is not tempted in the slightest to dig in at some bygone historical moment. Accepting novelty as inevitable, he is not only a modernist but a futurist. In his latest mood, he regards most of what is going on today as highly desirable, all of it as meaningful. His position is to be inside change; he is given over to metamorphosis on principle. The present worldwide clash between the new and old arouses him to enthusiasm, since "the meeting of two media is a moment of truth and revelation from which new form is born." It is this appreciation of innovating forms that distinguishes McLuhan from other writers on popular culture. Instead of discovering menace in the chatter of the disc jockey and the inanities of the commercial, or relief in New Wave films or in Shakespeare and ballet on TV, McLuhan probes beyond the content of the media to the impact of each medium itself as an art form. What takes place at any moment in the rectangle of the comic strip or on the screen of the TV set may not be worth serious reflection. But as you look, or look and listen, in the particular way demanded by the comic strip or the television image, something is slowly happening to one or more of your senses, and through that to your whole pattern of perception—never mind what gets into your mind. Hence the first axiom of *Understanding Media* is "The medium is the message." Radio tells us about bargains in secondhand cars, the great books, the weather, but the ultimate effect of radio is that, day after day, it is displacing reading and reintroducing on a new, technological level the oral communication of preliterate societies—or, as McLuhan calls it, "the tribal drum." The effect of a tale differs depending on whether we read it, hear it, or see it on the stage. McLuhan therefore ridicules the reformist idea that changes in programming could alter the cultural mix now produced by the popular arts. "Our conventional response to all media, namely that it is how they are used that counts, is the numb stance of the technological idiot. For the 'content' of a medium is like the juicy piece of meat carried by the burglar to distract the watchdog of the mind. . . . The effect of the movie form is not related to its program content." In fact, McLuhan suggests that one medium always uses another medium as its subject matter: "The content of the press is literary statement, as the content of the book is speech, and the content of the movie is the novel." Whether or not this is so in every case, it provides a suggestive description of much cotemporary art—for example, that of Rauschenberg, who through photographs and silk-screen reproductions makes news the content of painting

A remarkable wealth of observation issues from the play of McLuhan's sensibility upon each of today's vehicles of human intercourse, from roads and money to games and the computer. After *Understanding Media*, it should no longer be acceptable to speak of "mass culture" as a single lump. Each pop form, this work demonstrates, has its peculiar aesthetic features: the comics, a crude woodcut style; TV, a blurred "iconic" image shaped by the eye of the viewer out of millions of dots (in contrast to the shiny completed image of movie film). A further aesthetic complexity of the popular media pointed out by McLuhan lies in their division into "hot" and "cool." The hot medium, like radio and newspapers, is aggressive and communicates much information, while the cool, like TV and the Twist (also open-mesh stockings and dark glasses), is reticent and tends to draw its audience into participation. The varieties of aesthetic influences by which modern man is showered ought to dissolve the belief, prevalent among intellectuals, that today's man in the street, in contrast to the peasant or the bushman, has been cut down to a bundle of simple reflexes.

Responding to the man-made forms that flow continually through our senses, McLuhan arrives at happy conclusions for the future. No, man is not being impoverished by packaged cultural commodities. On the contrary, it was the split personality created by the book who was deprived of sensual self-realization: "Literacy is itself an abstract asceticism that prepares the way for endless patterns of privation in the human community." Though the shock of the sudden passage from mechanical to electrical technology has momentarily narcotized our nerves, integral man is in the process of formation. For the first time in history, the media are providing us with extensions not of one or more sense organs but of our sense structure as a whole, "since our new electric technology is not an extension of our bodies but of our central nervous systems." The mechanical age is departing, and with it the division of man within himself and his separation from his fellows. "Synaesthesia, or unified sense and imaginative life, had long seemed an unattainable dream to Western poets, painters, and artists in general. They had looked with sorrow and dismay on the fragmented and impoverished imaginative life of Western literate man in the eighteenth century and later. . . . They were not prepared to have their dreams realized in everyday life by the aesthetic action of radio and television. Yet these massive extensions of our central nervous systems have enveloped Western man in a daily session of synaesthesia." Instant communication through the electric media, McLuhan goes on to argue, is ending the age-old conflict between city and country; by "dunking entire populations in new imagery" and bringing them together in the "global village," it is eliminating, too, the conditions that make for war.

In sum, McLuhan has built a philosophy of history on art criticism, which he has directed not at styles in literature, painting, or architecture but at the lowly stuff of everyday life. In doing this, he has also sought to recast the meaning of art and literature since the Renaissance by finding in Shakespeare, Pope, or Blake "galaxies" of meaning related to the aesthetics and metaphysics of print. He has experimented with form in his own writings; that is, he has tried to function as an artist. *The Mechanical Bride* was a kind of early pop art, with a layout like a museum catalogue and with headlines, clips of advertising art, comic-strip boxes. *The Gutenberg Galaxy* and *Understanding Media* regard the human habitation as an enormous art pile, a throbbing assemblage of things that communicate, and they try to make it comprehensible by means of a mosaic of exhibits and comments that the author's "circulating point of view" has assembled from widely separated fields; McLuhan is attempting to imitate in his writing the form of the TV image, which he describes as "mosaic." The effort to develop an open, expressive social-science investigation in place of the customary learned research report may in time produce important results; McLuhan's version of this new form has the virtue of allowing the author to pick up bits of observation (e.g., that girls in dark glasses are engaged in "cool" communication) that are usually excluded, and it also enables him to bring into focus a remarkable spread of information (e.g., the measurement of time by smell mong the ancient Chinese and among modern brain-surgery patients). McLuhan's concern for style tempts him into discharges of epigrams, wisecracks, and puns. These have abated in *Understanding Media*, but the chapter titles are still haunted by gags ("Money: The Poor Man's Credit Card," "The Photograph: The Brothel-Without-Walls"). Some of this wit is low-grade ("Movies: The Reel World") even if we consider bad puns to be in keeping with the pop spirit. However, formulas like "If it works it's obsolete," to suggest the rate of change in media, and "Today, even natural resources have an informational aspect" more than balance the account.

McLuhan, then, is a kind of artist, and his quick leaps from datum to axiom ("Take off the dateline, and one day's paper is the same as the next") are often aesthetically pleasurable. In his communications-constructed world, the artist is the master figure—in fact, the only personage whom he differentiates from the media-absorbing mass. The artist, McLuhan believes, anticipates the changes in man that will be wrought by a new medium and through his work adjusts the collective psyche to it. Thus the artist provides an antidote to the numbness induced by change-over. Painting has long since gone beyond a merely visual medium; praising someone for having a "good eye," as if a modern painting were an object to be taken in by a single sense, is tantamount to praising him for being out of date. A Kandinsky or a Mondrian is actually apprehended through a "resonating interplay" of the whole keyboard of sense and consciousness; no wonder that eye-trained people continue to ask, "What does it mean?" One of McLuhan's most valuable contributions is to help dissolve the craft-oriented concept that modern art works still belong in the realm of things contemplated instead of being forces active in "the unified field of electric all-at-onceness" of tomorrow's world community.

Unfortunately, despite his insights into form, McLuhan's organization of his own ideas is far from first-rate. As a composition, *Understanding Media* is often out of control; "circular" perspective becomes synonymous with going round in circles. Endlessly repetitious, the book, for all its rain of bright intuitions, creates a total effect of monotony. This repetitiousness probably reflects McLuhan's uneasiness about his ability to make himself clear. For there are in his thesis inherent ambiguities. Given the advanced nature of the electric media, the implication is that older forms, like the book and the stage, are obsolete and that film and comic strip are the art forms of the future. In clinging to a sense extension (the eye) that has been surpassed, the novelist is a reactionary—except for the beatnik who gives readings in coffeehouses. Even being an individual is retrogressive, so turn the dial and slip into the new global kraal. Much as McLuhan lauds the artist, he has pitted the pop media against him, in disregard of the fact that the masterpieces of this century have been paintings, poems, plays, not movies or TV shows. The point is that while McLuhan is an aesthete, he is also an ideologue—one ready to spin out his metaphor of the "extensions" until its web covers the universe; if clothes are media, and trees and policemen are, too—if, in short, all of creation "speaks" to us—McLuhan is discussing as media what used to be called "Nature," and his notion of the "sensuously orchestrated" man of the future is a version of the pantheistic hero. He is a belated Whitman singing the body electric with Thomas Edison as accompanist. Yet to expect Adam to step out of the TV screen is utopianism of the wildest sort. For McLuhan, beliefs, moral qualities, social action, even material progress play a secondary role (if that) in determining the human condition. The drama of history is a crude pageant whose inner meaning is man's metamorphosis through the media. As a philosophy of cultural development, *Understanding Media* is on a par with theories that trace the invention of the submarine to conflicts in the libido or the decline of the handicrafts to the legalization of interest on loans.

"Usury," Ezra Pound wrote in the *Cantos,*

. . . rusts the man and his chisel
It destroys the craftsman, destroying craft;
Azure is caught with cancer.

McLuhan has taken with deadly literalness his metaphors of the media as extensions of the body and of a nervous system outside ourselves. "Man becomes, as it were, the sex organs of the machine world, as the bee of the plant world, enabling it to fecundate and to evolve ever new forms." His susceptibility to figures of speech leads him to describe possibilities of technological innovation as if they were already achieved facts. In his world, money and work are things of the past; we live on credit cards and "learn a living" as managers of computers, and the struggle, backwash, surprise of real events are somnambulistically brushed away. The chilly silence of science fiction reigns over a broad band of McLuhan's temperament.

These deficiencies might be decisive were there to arise a McLuhan "school" of cultural interpretation through media analysis. If one judges McLuhan as an individual writer, however, what remain paramount are his global standpoint and his zest for the new. As an artist working in a mixed medium of direct experience and historical analogy, he has given a needed twist to the great debate on what is happening to man in this age of technological speed-up. Other observers have been content to repeat criticisms of industrial society that were formulated a century ago, as if civilization had been steadily emptied out since the advent of the power loom. As against the image of our time as a faded photograph of a richly pigmented past, McLuhan, for all his abstractness, has found positive, humanistic meaning and the color of life in supermarkets, stratospheric flight, the lights blinking on broadcasting towers. In respect to the maladies of de-individuation, he has dared to seek the cure in the disease, and his vision of going forward into primitive wholeness is a good enough reply to those who would go back to it. *Understanding Media* is a concrete testimonial (illuminating, as modern art illuminates, through dissociation and regrouping) to the belief that man is certain to find his footing in the new world he is in the process of creating.

Classroom Without Walls

today we're beginning to realize that the new media aren't just
mechanical gimmicks for creating worlds of illusion, but new languages
with new and unique powers of expression.

—MARSHALL MC LUHAN

It's natural today to speak
of "audio and visual aids" to teaching
for we still think of the book as norm,
of other media as incidental.
We also think of the new media
—press, radio, movies, TV—
as MASS MEDIA
& think of the book
as an individualistic form.

Individualistic because it
isolated the reader in silence &
helped create the Western "I."
Yet it was the first product of
mass production.

With it everybody could have
the same books.
It was impossible
in medieval times for
different students, different institutions,
to have copies of the same book.
Manuscripts, commentaries, were dictated.
Students memorized.

Instruction was almost entirely oral,
done in groups.
Solitary study was reserved for
the advanced scholar.
The first printed books were
"visual aids" to oral instruction.

Marshall McLuhan, "Classroom Without Walls." Reprinted from *McLuhan:*
Hot and Cool, edited by Gerald Emanuel Stearn. Copyright © 1967 by
Gerald E. Stearn. Copyright © 1967 by Marshall McLuhan. A Brahmin Book.
Reprinted by permission of the publisher, The Dial Press, Inc.

Before the printing press,
the young learned by
listening, watching, doing.
So, until recently, our own
rural children learned the
language & skills of their elders.
Learning took place
outside the classroom.
Only those aiming at professional careers
went to school at all.

Today in our cities,
most learning occurs outside the classroom.
The sheer quantity of information conveyed by
press-mags-films-TV-radio
far exceeds
the quantity of information conveyed by
school instruction & texts.
This challenge has destroyed
the monopoly of the book as a teaching aid
& cracked the very walls of the classroom,
so suddenly,
we're confused, baffled.

In this violently upsetting social situation,
many teachers naturally view
the offerings of the new media
as entertainment,
rather than education.
**But this view carries
no conviction to the student.**

Find a classic
which wasn't first regarded
as light entertainment.
Nearly all vernacular works
were so regarded until the 19th century.

Many movies are obviously handled
with a degree of insight & maturity
at least equal to the level permitted
in today's textbooks.
Olivier's Henry V & Richard III
assemble a wealth of
scholarly & artistic skill

which reveal Shakespeare at a very high level,
yet in a way easy
for the young to enjoy.

The movie is to dramatic representation
what the book was to the manuscript.
It makes available
to many & at many times & places
what otherwise would be restricted
to a few at few times & places.
The movie, like the book,
is a ditto device.
TV shows to 50,000,000 simultaneously.
Some feel that the value
of experiencing a book
is diminished by being extended
to many minds.
This notion is always implicit
in the phrases "mass media," "mass entertainment"—
useless phrases obscuring the fact THAT
English itself
is a mass medium.
Today we're beginning to realize
that the new media aren't just
mechanical gimmicks
for creating worlds of illusion,
but new languages
with new & unique powers of expression.
Historically, the resources of English
have been shaped & expressed in
constantly new & changing ways.
The printing press changed,
not only the quantity of writing,
but the character of language
& the relations between author & public.
Radio, film, TV pushed
written English towards
the spontaneous shifts & freedom of
the spoken idiom.
They aided us in the recovery
of intense awareness of
facial language & bodily gesture.
If these "mass media"
should serve only
to weaken or corrupt

previously achieved levels of
verbal & pictorial culture,
it won't be because
there's anything inherently wrong with them.
It will be because we've failed
to master them as new languages in time
to assimilate them to
our total cultural heritage.

These new developments,
under quiet analytic survey,
point to a basic strategy of culture
for the classroom.
When the printed book first appeared,
it threatened
the oral procedures of teaching, and
created
the classroom as we now know it.
Instead of making
his own text, his own dictionary, his own grammar,
the student started out with these tools.
He could study, not one,
but several languages.
Today these new media
threaten, instead of merely reinforce,
the procedures of this traditional classroom.
It's customary to answer this threat
with denunciations of
the unfortunate character & effect
of movies & TV,
just as the comicbook
was feared & scorned & rejected
from the classroom.
Its good & bad features
in form & content,
when carefully set beside
other kinds of art & narrative,
could have become a major
asset to the teacher.

Where student interest is already
intensely focused
is the natural point
at which to be
in the elucidation of

other problems & interests.
The educational task
is not only
to provide
basic tools
of perception,
but to develop
judgement & discrimination
with ordinary social experience.

Few students ever acquire skill
in analysis of newspapers.
Fewer have any ability to discuss
a movie intelligently.
To be articulate & discriminating
about ordinary affairs & information
is the mark of an educated man.
It's misleading to suppose
        there's any basic difference between
        education & entertainment.
This distinction merely relieves people
        of the responsibility of
        looking into the matter.
It's like setting up a distinction between
        didactic & lyric poetry
        on the ground that one
        teaches, the other pleases.
However, it's always been true
        that whatever pleases
        teaches more effectively.

Marshall McLuhan's prediction that the shift from the "linear" to the "electronic" would inspire certain substantive changes in the culture has been reflected in the arts with their recent concentration on mixed-media entertainments such as happenings, kinetic sculpture, and electronic music—to name just a few. In the film, which has become our most resourceful medium, the hugely financed spectacles of Hollywood have been losing popularity to the moderately budgeted cinema of gifted European directors, and to the still more experimental works of young American filmmakers. Jonas Mekas and Leon Lewis both discuss aspects of this phenomenon. In theater, while "Broadway" still exists as a tourist attraction, "underground" theaters throughout the country have been presenting bold new attempts at environmental drama. One of the most influential advocates of this "new" theater was Antonin Artaud, who died in 1948. Artaud was especially fascinated by Oriental drama, as his insistence on the necessity for the trans-verbal and the ritualistic suggests. His ingenious attempts at breaking down the barriers between actor and audience anticipate the happening. The esthetic of this spontaneous participation is forcefully presented by Allan Kaprow, and the examples by Kaprow and Jerome Rothenberg illustrate the unique possibilities of the form.

The familiar distinction between "classical" and "popular" music has apparently all but eroded, as the pieces by John Cage and Ralph Gleason indicate. Cage has brilliantly fused elements of Zen, pop culture, electronics, and traditional music into the fabric of his own compositions, as many rock groups have attempted to do. The rock concert, which actually resembles a happening, often inspires in the participants (performers as well as audience) a feeling almost mystical in its intensity. Dancers wildly improvising, with no specific partners, seem transported. They have realized a desperate harmony not elsewhere available to them in this culture. Indeed, rock has created a kind of social gospel among the young which cannot be underestimated.

One of the most charming—or exasperating, depending on your perspective—developments in the graphic arts has been the Pop Movement. The interviews with Andy Warhol, Roy Lichtenstein, and James Rosenquist reveal the social significance of Pop art, and its attempt to depict, with often clinical candor, many of our unhealthy cultural attitudes. The serious intent of these artists warns us that Pop is more than just an ironic celebration of the most vulgar aspects of our culture. A resurrection of the vulgar—nothing less—is what Susan Sontag accomplishes in her well-known essay, "Notes on Camp." What were once regarded as embarrassing specimens of the modern sensibility have now become—art!

No More Masterpieces

One of the reasons for the asphyxiating atmosphere in which we live without possible escape or remedy—and in which we all share, even the most revolutionary among us—is our respect for what has been written, formulated, or painted, what has been given form, as if all expression were not at least exhausted, were not at a point where things must break apart if they are to start anew and begin fresh.

We must have done with this idea of masterpieces reserved for a self-styled elite and not understood by the general public; the mind has no such restricted districts as those so often used for clandestine sexual encounters.

Masterpieces of the past are good for the past: they are not good for us. We have the right to say what has been said and even what has not been said in a way that belongs to us, a way that is immediate and direct, corresponding to present modes of feeling, and understandable to everyone.

It is idiotic to reproach the masses for having no sense of the sublime, when the sublime is confused with one or another of its formal manifestations, which are moreover always defunct manifestations. And if for example a contemporary public does not understand *Oedipus Rex*, I shall make bold to say that it is the fault of *Oedipus Rex* and not of the public.

In *Oedipus Rex* there is the theme of incest and the idea that nature mocks at morality and that there are certain unspecified powers at large which we would do well to beware of, call them *destiny* or anything you choose.

There is in addition the presence of a plague epidemic which is a physical incarnation of these powers. But the whole in a manner and language that have lost all touch with the rude and epileptic rhythm of our time. Sophocles speaks grandly perhaps, but in a style that is no longer timely. His language is too refined for this age, it is as if he were speaking beside the point.

However, a public that shudders at train wrecks, that is familiar with earthquakes, plagues, revolutions, wars; that is sensitive to the disordered anguish of love, can be affected by all these grand notions and asks only to become aware of them, but on condition that it is addressed in its

Antonin Artaud, "No More Masterpieces," from *The Theater and Its Double* by Antonin Artaud. Translated from the French by Mary Caroline Richards. Reprinted by permission of Grove Press, Inc. Copyright © 1958 by Grove Press, Inc.

own language, and that its knowledge of these things does not come to it through adulterated trappings and speech that belong to extinct eras which will never live again.

Today as yesterday, the public is greedy for mystery: it asks only to become aware of the laws according to which destiny manifests itself, and to divine perhaps the secret of its apparitions.

Let us leave textual criticism to graduate students, formal criticism to esthetes, and recognize that what has been said is not still to be said; that an expression does not have the same value twice, does not live two lives; that all words, once spoken, are dead and function only at the moment when they are uttered, that a form, once it has served, cannot be used again and asks only to be replaced by another, and that the theater is the only place in the world where a gesture, once made, can never be made the same way twice.

If the public does not frequent our literary masterpieces, it is because those masterpieces are literary, that is to say, fixed; and fixed in forms that no longer respond to the needs of the time.

Far from blaming the public, we ought to blame the formal screen we interpose between ourselves and the public, and this new form of idolatry, the idolatry of fixed masterpieces which is one of the aspects of bourgeois conformism.

This conformism makes us confuse sublimity, ideas, and things with the forms they have taken in time and in our minds—in our snobbish, precious, aesthetic mentalities which the public does not understand.

How pointless in such matters to accuse the public of bad taste because it relishes insanities, so long as the public is not shown a valid spectacle; and I defy anyone to show me *here* a spectacle valid—valid in the supreme sense of the theater—since the last great romantic melodramas, i.e., since a hundred years ago.

The public, which takes the false for the true, has the sense of the true and always responds to it when it is manifested. However it is not upon the stage that the true is to be sought nowadays, but in the street; and if the crowd in the street is offered an occasion to show its human dignity, it will always do so.

If people are out of the habit of going to the theater, if we have all finally come to think of theater as an inferior art, a means of popular distraction, and to use it as an outlet for our worst instincts, it is because we have learned too well what the theater has been, namely, falsehood and illusion. It is because we have been accustomed for four hundred years, that is since the Renaissance, to a purely descriptive and narrative theater—storytelling psychology; it is because every possible ingenuity has been exerted in bringing to life on the stage plausible but detached beings, with the spectacle on one side, the public on the other—and because the public is no longer shown anything but the mirror of itself.

Shakespeare himself is responsible for this aberration and decline, this disinterested idea of the theater which wishes a theatrical performance to leave the public intact, without setting off one image that will shake the organism to its foundations and leave an ineffaceable scar.

If, in Shakespeare, a man is sometimes preoccupied with what transcends him, it is always in order to determine the ultimate consequences of this preoccupation within him, i.e., psychology.

Psychology, which works relentlessly to reduce the unknown to the known, to the quotidian and the ordinary, is the cause of the theater's abasement and its fearful loss of energy, which seems to me to have reached its lowest point. And I think both the theater and we ourselves have had enough of psychology.

I believe furthermore that we can all agree on this matter sufficiently so that there is no need to descend to the repugnant level of the modern and French theater to condemn the theater of psychology.

Stories about money, worry over money, social careerism, the pangs of love unspoiled by altruism, sexuality sugar-coated with an eroticism that has lost its mystery have nothing to do with the theater, even if they do belong to psychology. These torments, seductions, and lusts before which we are nothing but Peeping Toms gratifying our cravings, tend to go bad, and their rot turns to revolution: we must take this into account.

But this is not our most serious concern.

If Shakespeare and his imitators have gradually insinuated the idea of art for art's sake, with art on one side and life on the other, we can rest on this feeble and lazy idea only as long as the life outside endures. But there are too many signs that everything that used to sustain our lives no longer does so, that we are all mad, desperate, and sick. And I call for *us* to react.

This idea of a detached art, of poetry as a charm which exists only to distract our leisure, is a decadent idea and an unmistakable symptom of our power to castrate.

Our literary admiration for Rimbaud, Jarry, Lautréamont, and a few others, which has driven two men to suicide, but turned into café gossip for the rest, belongs to this idea of literary poetry, of detached art, of neutral spiritual activity which creates nothing and produces nothing; and I can bear witness that at the very moment when that kind of personal poetry which involves only the man who creates it and only at the moment he creates it broke out in its most abusive fashion, the theater was scorned more than ever before by poets who have never had the sense of direct and concerted action, nor of efficacity, nor of danger.

We must get rid of our superstitious valuation of texts and *written* poetry. Written poetry is worth reading once, and then should be destroyed. Let the dead poets make way for others. Then we might even come to see that it is our veneration for what has already been created, however beautiful and valid it may be, that petrifies us, deadens our responses, and prevents us from making contact with that underlying power, call it thought-energy, the life force, the determinism of change, lunar menses, or anything you like. Beneath the poetry of the texts, there is the actual poetry, without form and without text. And just as the efficacity of masks in the magic practices of certain tribes is exhausted—and these masks are no longer good for anything except museums—so the poetic efficacity of a text is exhausted; yet the poetry and the efficacity of the theater are exhausted least quickly of all, since they permit the *action* of what is gesticulated and pronounced, and which is never made the same way twice.

It is a question of knowing what we want. If we are prepared for war, plague, famine, and slaughter we do not even need to say so, we have only to continue as we are; continue behaving like snobs, rushing en masse to hear such and such a singer, to see such and such an admirable performance which never transcends the realm of art (and even the Russian ballet at the height of its splendor never transcended the realm of art), to marvel at such and such an exhibition of painting in which exciting shapes explode here and there but at random and without any genuine consciousness of the forces they could rouse.

This empiricism, randomness, individualism, and anarchy must cease.

Enough of personal poems, benefitting those who create them much more than those who read them.

Once and for all, enough of this closed, egoistic, and personal art.

Our spiritual anarchy and intellectual disorder is a function of the anarchy of everything else—or rather, everything else is a function of this anarchy.

I am not one of those who believe that civilization has to change in order for the theater to change; but I do believe that the theater, utilized in the highest and most difficult sense possible, has the power to influence the aspect and formation of things: and the encounter upon the stage of two passionate manifestations, two living centers, two nervous magnetisms is something as entire, true, even decisive, as, in life, the encounter of one epidermis with another in a timeless debauchery.

That is why I propose a theater of cruelty.—With this mania we all have for depreciating everything, as soon as I have said "cruelty," everybody will at once take it to mean "blood." But *"theater of cruelty"* means a theater difficult and cruel for myself first of all. And, on the level of performance, it is not the cruelty we can exercise upon each other by hacking at each other's bodies, carving up our personal anatomies, or, like Assyrian emperors, sending parcels of human ears, noses, or neatly detached nostrils through the mail, but the much more terrible and necessary cruelty which things can exercise against us. We are not free. And the sky can still fall on our heads. And the theater has been created to teach us that first of all.

Either we will be capable of returning by present-day means to this superior idea of poetry and poetry-through-theater which underlies the Myths told by the great ancient tragedians, capable once more of entertaining a religious idea of the theater (without meditation, useless contemplation, and vague dreams), capable of attaining awareness and a possession of certain dominant forces, of certain notions that control all others, and (since ideas, when they are effective, carry their energy with them) capable of recovering within ourselves those energies which ultimately create order and increase the value of life, or else we might as well abandon ourselves now, without protest, and recognize that we are no longer good for anything but disorder, famine, blood, war, and epidemics.

Either we restore all the arts to a central attitude and necessity, finding an analogy between a gesture made in painting or the theater, and a gesture made by lava in a volcanic explosion, or we must stop painting, babbling, writing, or doing whatever it is we do.

I propose to bring back into the theater this elementary magical idea, taken up by modern psychoanalysis, which consists in effecting a patient's cure by making him assume the apparent and exterior attitudes of the desired condition.

I propose to renounce our empiricism of imagery, in which the unconscious furnishes images at random, and which the poet arranges at random too, calling them poetic and hence hermetic images, as if the kind of trance that poetry provides did not have its reverberations throughout the whole sensibility, in every nerve, and as if poetry were some vague force whose movements were invariable.

I propose to return through the theater to an idea of the physical knowledge of images and the means of inducing trances, as in Chinese medicine which knows, over the entire extent of the human anatomy, at what points to puncture in order to regulate the subtlest functions.

Those who have forgotten the communicative power and magical mimesis of a gesture, the theater can reinstruct, because a gesture carries its energy with it, and there are still human beings in the theater to manifest the force of the gesture made.

To create art is to deprive a gesture of its reverberation in the organism, whereas this reverberation, if the gesture is made in the conditions and with the force required, incites the organism and, through it, the entire individuality, to take attitudes in harmony with the gesture.

The theater is the only place in the world, the last general means we still possess of directly affecting the organism and, in periods of neurosis and petty sensuality like the one in which we are immersed, of attacking this sensuality by physical means it cannot withstand.

If music affects snakes, it is not on account of the spiritual notions it offers them, but because snakes are long and coil their length upon the earth, because their bodies touch the earth at almost every point; and because the musical vibrations which are communicated to the earth affect them like a very subtle, very long massage; and I propose to treat the spectators like the snakecharmer's subjects and conduct them *by means of their organisms* to an apprehension of the subtlest notions.

At first by crude means, which will gradually be refined. These immediate crude means will hold their attention at the start.

That is why in the "theater of cruelty" the spectator is in the center and the spectacle surrounds him.

In this spectacle the sonorisation is constant: sounds, noises, cries are chosen first for their vibratory quality, then for what they represent.

Among these gradually refined means light is interposed in its turn. Light which is not created merely to add color or to brighten, and which brings its power, influence, suggestions with it. And the light of a green cavern does not sensually dispose the organism like the light of a windy day.

After sound and light there is action, and the dynamism of action: here the theater, far from copying life, puts itself whenever possible in communication with pure forces. And whether you accept or deny them, there is nevertheless a way of speaking which gives the name of "forces" to whatever brings to birth images of energy in the unconscious, and gratuitous crime on the surface.

A violent and concentrated action is a kind of lyricism: it summons up supernatural images, a bloodstream of images, a bleeding spurt of images in the poet's head and in the spectator's as well.

Whatever the conflicts that haunt the mind of a given period, I defy any spectator to whom such violent scenes will have transferred their blood, who will have felt in himself the transit of a superior action, who will have seen the extraordinary and essential movements of his thought illuminated in extraordinary deeds—the violence and blood having been placed at the service of the violence of the thought—I defy that spectator to give himself up, once outside the theater, to ideas of war, riot, and blatant murder.

So expressed, this idea seems dangerous and sophomoric. It will be claimed that example breeds example, that if the attitude of cure induces cure, the attitude of murder will induce murder. Everything depends upon the manner and the purity with which the thing is done. There is a risk. But let it not be forgotten that though a theatrical gesture is violent, it is disinterested; and that the theater teaches precisely the uselessness of the action which, once done, is not to be done, and the superior use of the state unused by the action and which, *restored*, produces a purification.

I propose then a theater in which violent physical images crush and hypnotize the sensibility of the spectator seized by the theater as by a whirlwind of higher forces.

A theater which, abandoning psychology, recounts the extraordinary, stages natural conflicts, natural and subtle forces, and presents itself first of all as an exceptional power of redirection. A theater that induces trance, as the dances of dervishes induce trance, and that addresses itself to the organism by precise instruments, by the same means as those of certain tribal music cures which we admire on records but are incapable of originating among ourselves.

There is a risk involved, but in the present circumstances I believe it is a risk worth running. I do not believe we have managed to revitalize the world we live in, and I do not believe it is worth the trouble of clinging to; but I do propose something to get us out of our marasmus, instead of continuing to complain about it, and about the boredom, inertia, and stupidity of everything.

A Manifesto on Happenings

Once, the task of the artist was to make good art; now it is to avoid making art of any kind. Once, the public and critics had to be shown; now the latter are full of authority and the artists are full of doubts.

The history of art and of esthetics are on all bookshelves. To this pluralism of values, add the current blurring of boundaries dividing the arts, and dividing art and life; and it is clear that the old questions of definition and standards of excellence are not only futile but naive. Even yesterday's distinction between art, anti-art and non-art are pseudo-distinctions which simply waste our time: the side of an old building recalls Clifford Still's canvases, the guts of a dishwashing machine doubles as Duchamp's "Bottle Rack," voices in a train station are Jackson Mac Low's poems, the sounds of eating in a luncheonette are by John Cage, and all may be part of a Happening. Moreover, as the "found-object" implies the found-word, -noise or -action, it also demands the found-environment. Art not only becomes life, but life refuses to be itself.

The decision to be an artist thus assumes both the existence of a unique activity and an endless series of deeds which deny it. The decision immediately establishes the context within which all of one's acts may be judged by others as art, and also conditions one's perception of all experience as probably (not possibly) artistic. Anything I say, do, notice, or think, is art—whether or not desired—because everyone else aware of what is occurring today will probably (not possibly) say, do, notice, and think of it, as art at some time or other.

This makes the identification of oneself as an artist an ironic one, attesting not to talent for a specialized skill, but to a philosophical stance before elusive alternatives of not-quite-art, or not-quite-life. "Artist" refers to a person willfully enmeshed in the dilemma of categories, who performs as if none of them existed. If there is no clear difference between an Assemblage with sound and a "noise" concert with sights, then there is no clear difference between an artist and a junkyard dealer.

Although it is a commonplace to do so, bringing such acts and thoughts to the gallery, museum, concert hall, stage or serious bookshop, blunts the power inherent in an arena of paradoxes. It restores that sense of esthetic certainty which these milieux once proclaimed in a

Allan Kaprow, "Manifesto," from *Manifestos* by Allan Kaprow, 1966, by Something Else Press, Inc.

philistine society, just as much as it evokes a history of cultural expectations that run counter to the poignant and absurd nature of art today. Conflict with the past automatically ensues.

But obviously this is not the issue. The contemporary artist is not out to supplant recent modern art with a better kind; *he wonders what art might be.* Art and life are not simply conmingled; *their identities are both uncertain.* To pose these questions in the form of acts that are neither art-like nor life-like, while at the same time locating them within the framed context of the conventional showplace, is to suggest that there are really no uncertainties at all: the name on the gallery or stage door assures us that whatever is contained within is art, and everything else is life.

Speculation. Professional philosophy of the twentieth century has generally removed itself from problems of human conduct and purpose, and plays instead art's late role as professionalistic activity; it could aptly be called philosophy for philosophy's sake. Existentialism for this reason is assigned a place closer to social psychology than to philosophy per se, by a majority of academicians for whom ethics and metaphysics are a definitional and logical inquiry at best. Paul Valéry, acknowledging philosophy's self-analytic tendency, and wishing to salvage from it something of value, suggests that even if Plato and Spinoza can be refuted, their thoughts remain astonishing works of art. Now, as art becomes less art, it takes on philosophy's early role as critique of life. Even if its beauty can be refuted, it remains astonishingly thoughtful. Precisely because art can be confused with life, it forces attention upon the aim of its ambiguities to "reveal" experience.

Philosophy will become steadily more important in its search for verbal knowledge, so long as it fails to recognize its own findings: that only a small fraction of the words we use are precise in meaning; and only a smaller proportion of these contain meanings in which we are vitally interested. When words alone are no true index of thought, and when sense and nonsense today rapidly become allusive and layered with implication rather than description, the use of words as tools to precisely delimit sense and nonsense may be a worthless endeavor. LSD and LBJ invoke different meaning clusters, but both partake of a need for code; and code performs the same condensing function as symbol in poetry. TV "snow" and Muzak in restaurants are accompaniments to conscious activity which, if suddenly withdrawn, produce a feeling of void in the human situation. Contemporary art, which tends to "think" in multi-media, intermedia, overlays, fusions and hybridizations, is a closer parallel to modern mental life than we have realized. Its judgments, therefore, may be acute. "Art" may soon become a meaningless word. In its place, "communications programming" would be a more imaginative label, attesting to our new jargon, our technological and managerial fantasies, and to our pervasive electronic contact with one another.

Soap: A Happening

(Commissioned by Florida State University. Performed in Sarasota on February 3rd and 4th, 1965. This work was first discussed in conference and then performed only once, without rehearsal and without spectators. Appropriate sites were chosen by the participants shortly before performance. Actions in parentheses are alternatives given to participants: either or both may be enacted.)

1st morning:	clothes dirtied by urination
1st evening:	clothes washed
	(in the sea)
	(in the laundromat)
2nd morning:	cars dirtied with jam on a busy street
	cars cleaned
	(in a parking lot)
	(in a car-wash)
2nd evening:	bodies dirtied with jam
	bodies buried in mounds at the sea edge
	bodies cleaned by the tide

Notes to "SOAP"

1st morning:
and
1st evening:

Each person privately soils some article of his own clothing. This is essential, for it refers to one's real experiences as an infant. In this act the person mingles his own water with the water of the sea or laundromat and consequently makes the cleansing of his clothing inescapably personal.

2nd morning:

Cars should be methodically and thoroughly smeared with jam, within sight of passers-by. The washing should be done as diligently. If a commercial car-wash is used, one should have this done as though nothing were out of the ordinary. Any questions asked should be answered in as noncommittal a way as possible.

2nd evening:

A vacant stretch of beach is best. Either couples or individuals may perform this. There should be long distances between each individual or couple. In the case of couples, one person covers the partner (who is preferably naked) with jam, digs a hole for him (or her) with sand to the neck, and sits quietly watching until the tide washes the partner. Then they depart.

Peacemaking Event: A Happening

Preparations: An open area of ground is set aside, and across it is erected what is called a *koro-cop*. Posts are put up in line, to the tops of these is attached a length of strong cane, and from the cane are suspended bundles of shredded palm leaf (*koro*). The "visitors" are the forgiving party, while the home party consists of those who have committed the last act of hostility.

Movements: The visitors enter dancing, the step being that of the ordinary dance. The women of the home party mark the time by clapping their hands on their thighs. The visitors dance forward in front of the men standing at the *koro-cop*, and then, still dancing all the time, pass backwards and forwards between the standing men, bending their heads as they pass beneath the suspended cane. The visitors may make threatening gestures at the men standing at the *koro-cop*, and every now and then break into a shrill shout. The men at the *koro* stand silent and motionless.

After dancing thus for a little time, the leader of the visitors approaches the man at one end of the *koro* and, taking him by the shoulders from the front, leaps vigorously up and down to the time of the dance, thus giving the man he holds a good shaking. The leader then passes on to the next man in the row while another of the visitors goes through the same performance with the first man. This is continued until each of the dancers has "shaken" each of the standing men. The dancers then pass under the *koro* and shake their enemies in the same manner from the back. After a little more shaking the dancers retire, and the women of the visiting group come forward and dance in much the same way, each woman giving each man of the other group a good shaking.

When the women have been through their dance the two parties of men and women sit down and weep together.

Jerome Rothenberg, "Peacemaking Event," from *Ritual: A Book of Primitive Rites and Events,* by Jerome Rothenberg, 1966, by Something Else Press, Inc.

Where Are We—The Underground?

When I was asked to accept the highest award of the Philadelphia College of Art, I hesitated for a moment. I said to myself: Who am I? Really, I haven't done much in my life. Everything I want to do, all my dreams, are still in the future. Then I thought again. What the College is really doing by awarding this honor to me, is directing people's attention to the avant-garde arts. This award doesn't, really, go to me; it goes to the new cinema—to all those avant-garde artists who are trying to bring some beauty into a world full of sadness and horror.

What are we really doing? Where are we—the Underground? What's the meaning of it all? I will try to answer, or to indicate, some of the meanings connected with our work—meanings that are closely connected with all of us.

There was a time, when I was sixteen or seventeen, when I was idealistic and believed that the world would change in my own lifetime. I read about all the suffering of man, wars, and misery that took place in the past centuries. And I somehow believed that in my own lifetime all this would change. I had faith in the progress of man, in the goodness of man. And then came the war, and I went through horrors more unbelievable than anything I had read in the books, and it all happened right before my eyes—before my eyes the heads of children were smashed with bayonets. And this was done by my generation. And it's still being done today, in Vietnam, by my generation. It's done all over the world, by my generation. Everything that I believed in shook to the foundations—all my idealism, and my faith in the goodness of man; all was shattered. Somehow, I managed to keep myself together. But, really, I wasn't one piece any longer; I was one thousand painful pieces.

It's really from this, and because of this, that I did what I did. I felt I had to start from the very beginning. I had no faith, no hope left. I had to collect myself again, bit by bit. And I wasn't surprised when, upon my arrival in New York, I found others who felt as I felt. There were poets, and filmmakers, and painters—people who were also walking like one thousand painful pieces. And we felt that there was nothing to lose any more. There was almost nothing worth keeping from our civilized inheritance. Let's clean ourselves out, we felt. Let's clean out everything that is dragging us down—the whole bag of horrors and

Jonas Mekas, "Where Are We—The Underground?" Reprinted by permission of the author and the Philadelphia College of Art.

lies and egos. The Beat Generation was the outgrowth, the result of this desperation; the mystical researches came out of this desperation. No price was too high, we felt, to pay for this cleaning job, no embarrassment too big to take. Let them laugh at us and our shabby appearances; let them spit into our beards. Even if we had nothing—some of us still have nothing to put in the cleared place—we couldn't remain as we were. We had to clean out not only the present but, through the drug experience or through meditation, to go back by several generations, to eliminate our egos, our bad faith, our mistrust, our sense of competition, of personal profit—so that if there was anything beautiful and pure, it would find a clear place and would settle in us and would begin to grow. It was a painful search, and it still is. We are still in the beginning of this search and growth, and many minds get broken to pieces. We are going through a dramatic end of the Christian Era and the birth of what we begin to call the Aquarian Age, and there are violent happenings taking place in man's spirit and they aren't always in our control. But it's a little bit easier because there are today many of us in various places of the country, of the world; we keep meeting each other, and we recognize each other; we know we are the traveling pioneers of the new age. We are the transitional generations. My generation, your generation, we have been marked by the sign of travel. We kept going and searching (we still do) in constant movement, from one side of the continent to another, between San Francisco and New York, between India and Mexico, and through all the inner journeys of the psychedelics and yoga systems, and macrobiotics. No generation since Columbus has traveled more than the current two generations of America. Yes, other generations have also traveled, but they always traveled as conquerors, to conquer the others, to teach them their own way of life. Our parents are still traveling through Vietnam as conquerors; they travel, yes—but how useless and unreal all their journeys and their conquerings seem to us today! For we are traveling, collecting the broken bits and pieces of knowledge, of love, of hope, of old ages; not the wisdom of our parents, nor our mothers' wisdom, but that wisdom which is as old as the earth, as the planets, as man himself—the mystical, the eternal—collecting, gathering ourselves bit by bit, having nothing to offer to others but taking gladly whatever is invested with love and warmth and wisdom, no matter how little that may be.

In cinema, this search is manifested through abandoning of all the existing professional, commercial values, rules, subjects, techniques, pretensions. We said: We don't know what man is; we don't know what cinema is. Let us, therefore, be completely open. Let us go in any direction. Let us be completely open and listening, ready to move to any direction upon the slightest call, almost like one who is too tired and too weary, whose senses are like a musical string, almost with no power of their own, blown and played by the mystical winds of the incoming Age, waiting for a slightest motion or call or sign—let's go in any direction to break out of the net that is dragging us down. Our mothers' wisdom! Don't get tied down to any of the establishments; they will go down and they will drag us down. The sun, that is our direction. The beauty, that is our direction—not money, not success, not comfort, not security, not even our own happiness, but the happiness of all of us together.

We used to march with posters protesting this and protesting that. Today, we realize that to improve the world, the others, first we have to improve ourselves; that only through the beauty of our own selves can we beautify the others. Our work, therefore, our most important work at this stage is ourselves. Our protest and our critique of the existing order of life can be only through the expansion of our own being. We are the measure of all things. And the beauty of our creation, of our art, is proportional to the beauty of ourselves, of our souls.

You may be wondering, sometimes, why we keep making little movies, underground movies, why we are talking about Home Movies, and you hope, sometimes, that all this will change soon. Wait, you say, until they begin making big movies. But we say, No, there is a misunderstanding here. We *are* making real movies. What we are doing comes from the deeper needs of man's soul. Man has wasted himself outside himself; man has disappeared in his projections. We want to bring him down, into his small room, to bring him home. We want to remind him that there is such a thing as home, where he can be, once in a while, alone and with himself and with a few that he loves close to him, and be with himself and his soul—that's the meaning of the home movie, the private visions of our movies. We want to surround this earth with our home movies. Our movies come from our hearts— our little movies, not the Hollywood movies. Our movies are like extensions of our own pulse, of our heartbeat, of our eyes, our fingertips; they are so personal, so unambitious in their movement, in their use of light, their imagery. We want to surround this earth with our film frames and warm it up—until it begins to move. We could continue expressing our own surroundings, being mirrors of the dirty cities, the black dailiness. But we have done that job already. There is pain in the arts of the last few decades. The whole period of so-called modern art is nothing but the pain of our ending civilization, the last decades of the Christian Era. Now we are looking, we are being pulled by a desire for something joyful deep within us, deep in the stars, and we want to bring it down to earth so that it will change our cities, our faces, our movements, our voices, our souls—we want an art of light. You'll see more and more of luminous colors and heavenly sounds coming through our art. The brush strokes will be charged with a different energy, not to express our egos, not to promote ourselves "as artists" (that is gone, all that is gone and gone), but to bring down the whispers of heaven to serve as strings, as instruments of ethereal winds, with our own personalities almost disappearing. I see it all over the country, and humble, unknown artists keep coming from various and distant countries, passing the town like monks stopping on their way somewhere, showing glimpses brought down from heaven. There is a renaissance, a spiritual renaissance coming upon us, and it's through artists that this new age is bringing to us its first voices and visions; it's through their intuition that the eternity communicates with us, bringing a new knowledge, new feelings. Let us then be very open to our art, to this new art, and to our work as artists. This isn't time for lowering ourselves, but for being ready to sing the most beautiful note.

I was talking in the beginning about my own disillusionment after the war. Today, for the first time in a long time, I suddenly again begin to see the broken pieces of myself coming together. I am listening, very openly, with all my senses, with my eyes and ears open, and I begin to hear and see a new man emerging. After fifteen years of disillusionment, slowly, during the last few months, I have gained again the belief and trust in man, and the knowledge that this is the generation that is building the bridge from horror to light. You, me—we are the one thousand painful pieces that are beginning to come together in one beautiful note. As if a completely new race of man were emerging on earth. Do you know what the rock 'n' roll group called *The Byrds* do with their money? They are making huge signs and putting them all along the roadsides of California, and the signs say one word: Love. But our parents would say: This is crazy, you should put your money into the bank. That's the difference. That's what I mean. That's where we stand in 1966 and midsummer.

The New Cinema

The present is filled with the past and great with the future. —LEIBNIZ

At a recent European Film Festival, Orson Welles began an address on "The Aesthetics of the Cinema" with a series of anecdotes describing the financial difficulties he had encountered as a producer and director. The audience was startled, then enraged, as Welles continued to talk about Money for over two hours. Finally, almost unable to contain himself, someone interrupted Welles and demanded to know what "money" had to do with Film Art.

"Without money," Welles replied, "there isn't any"—a rueful summary of his own uneven career as a filmmaker and a revealing commentary on an industry that has always found time to pay lip-service to Art while furiously pursuing a profit.

The technology of this science-struck century has substantially reduced the cost and complexity of the equipment that a film artist needs to render his personal visions on a celluloid strip, but the subsidiary costs involved in the production of anything other than a very short film escalate logarhythmically. Because of the elaborate, archaic working rules of the large studios, feature-length films are rarely made for less than one million dollars. And then, in order to interest an intricate distributional network in a particular film, a producer must usually make certain guarantees, promising that a film will have at least one "star," an understandable (even inspirational) story, a minimum of controversial material and the suggestion of some mildly erotic behavior. With a trained eye on the box office and sensitive finger on the fluctuating pulse of public morality, the studios constantly recalculate the permissible limits. Twentieth-Century-Fox makes a picture about Che Guevara, but they choose Omar Sharif to portray Che. Robert Aldrich directs a smouldering erotic confrontation in *The Killing of Sister George*, but today it is considered valid for the responsible adult to be interested in the once-taboo subject of lesbianism. The basic limitations remain, and the impetus of such a calculating, timid, economic-ordered system is inevitably toward the bland and the familiar. The culmination of its forces and pressures seems to be the Spectacular which runs for many hours and is devoid of interest throughout. The leaden, bloated *Cleopatra* was such an artistic failure and a financial fiasco that one might have expected it to permanently kill the maxi-budget Epic. But the large studios learn very slowly. There will surely be more.

Leon Lewis, "The New Cinema." Used by permission of the author.

Hollywood was once justifiably called "The Film Capital of the World," but the technical excellence and creative virtuosity of the commercial American cinema, so admired by contemporary European film critics, vanished before the end of World War II. The decline and demise of the big-studio production system occurred for many reasons, but it is not really an oversimplification to say that the insatiable greed and arrogant stupidity of the now-legendary tycoons who administered the system eventually destroyed the initiative and imagination of the talented men who had been working within its confines. When Hollywood no longer offered the filmmaker an adequate opportunity to make films that were artistic *and* entertaining, a vacuum of sorts appeared. It has been filled by two apparently separate groupings (in a casual sense) of filmmakers, each attempting to generate a completely free cinema with infinite artistic possibilities.

One might be called "the advanced European cinema" represented by Jean-Luc Godard, Federico Fellini, Michaelangelo Antonioni, by Ingmar Bergman, Alain Resnais, François Truffaut, and perhaps a few others. The other is the New American Cinema, the films of the so-called "underground" filmmakers of the United States. When these two groups have acknowledged each other's existence, it is usually with enmity and contempt. Louis Marcorelles of the French film magazine *Cahiers du Cinéma* claims that independent American films are unprofessional, unconcerned with the problems of mass communication and therefore negligible. Ken Kelman, in an informative review in *The Nation* (May 11, 1964) ripostes:

> In the old Europe, itself, a reaction is evident, which both the Continentals and many of us tend to take seriously as the new cinema. This centers around Resnais, Antonioni and Godard (surely not Bergman or Fellini). . . . If Schonberg had gone to a spare sonata form in 1910, that would have been the musical equivalent of such procedure; of Antonioni's dilution, of Godard's ellipsis of plot, anyhow. Resnais's reaction has been more that of late Mahler or very early Schonberg—to stretch the traditional form as far as it will go, to cast the old plot-film in as dense and complicated a guise as possible. Another element in the work of these three which seem to me reactionary in a bad sense is, as Jonas Mekas has remarked, a tired determinism, a rationality that is restrictive on more levels than just the formal.

Each group seems to be convinced that the other is pursuing a futile and sterile philosophy of filmmaking. Actually, what is most crucial to the future of the cinema in each has begun to coalesce into a single tradition. The young filmmakers of the United States are fascinated by

Godard's latest work (*La Chinoise, Weekend*) and Godard, his anger with "bourgeoisie politics" forcing him into increasingly unfashionable positions, moves closer to their methods of production.

Godard's career began in the middle 1950s when he worked for *Cahiers du Cinéma* as a film critic. His transition from film critic to filmmaker would be extremely unusual in the United States, but in France, almost all of the young film directors were once critics. As an aside, one might note that many filmmakers in the American underground have also written extensively about their craft and about each other's work. In 1959, Godard made his first feature film, *Breathless*, an artistic and critical triumph and a modest commercial success. Godard's reputation among an avant-garde audience in Europe and the United States was established almost immediately, but his next film, *Le Petit Soldat* (1960) was banned in France and all of his early films were relatively unsuccessful in finding a large audience. Then, with both men taking a gamble, Godard accepted an offer from Joseph Levine to make a film with Jack Palance and Brigitte Bardot. Godard used Levine's million to make a film which Levine considered appalling, and Levine cut and re-edited it until he had something which he felt "would sell." Since then, Godard has insisted on absolute control over every aspect of his films. When *One Plus One was* released in Toronto in the last part of 1968, the manager of the theater in which the film was playing added the Rolling Stones' song "Sympathy for the Devil" to the soundtrack, contending that it made the film "comprehensible" since it summarized what Godard had said with the Stones in the film. In addition to instituting legal action immediately, Godard, who was present at the premier as the guest of honor, demonstrated his wrath by throwing several punches at the manager's head.

After the debacle with Levine, Godard knew that he could not afford to trade his integrity as an artist for lavish backing. By working with a minimal crew that was totally devoted to him and by capitalizing on his awesome technical competence, Godard has been able to finish his latest films (*La Chinoise, Weekend*) for about two hundred thousand dollars. By Hollywood standards, this is an impossible feat of cost-cutting, but $200,000 is still an imposing and inaccessible figure. However, Godard hasn't been trapped on this level either. His brief, surreal, documentary footage of the uprising in Paris in June, 1968, was made with minimal, amateurish equipment and no prospect of any audience beyond a small coterie of friends and admirers. For his next project, Godard talks of working with an 8mm camera and of circulating the prints among the members of a committed "revolutionary" underground hidden within an oppressive social structure. Godard's conviction that there must be no gap between the private life style and the public act explains his adoption of an ethical stance that is strikingly similar to the guiding tenets of the New American Cinema.

Actually, there is nothing particularly "new" about the New American Cinema. The term is an invention designed to suggest the distance between the "Old" Hollywood movies and the work of the independent, underground filmmaker. The New American Cinema began in the years immediately following the end of World War II, partly as a reaction to the situation in Hollywood and partly as a consequence of the social milieu in the post-war United States. The psychological dislocation engendered by the war, the beginning of the Cold War and the threat of the A-Bomb impressed a pattern of retreat on the national psyche. Eventually, a repressive atmosphere which discouraged and limited artistic expression developed, and very few memorable films were made in Hollywood in the decade after the war. Some of the people whom we regard as the "first generation" of the New Cinema—Maya Deren, Harry Smith, Vern Zimmerman, Kenneth Anger—felt that the future of the film resided in the work of independent filmmakers who were, ultimately, independent men: free hearts and minds not committed to or controlled by the stifling and coercive forces of a pain-ridden, frightened society. Jones Mekas, the "evangelist" of the New American Cinema, emphasized this concern in asking:

> What's the use of a cinema if a man's soul goes rotten? It's not a question of films being good or bad artistically. It is a question of . . . a new understanding of life.

The implications of Mekas's statement are that *anything* made in the "new" way must be good and that everything made in the "old" (Hollywood) way has to be bad. The effect of this attitude, unfortunately, was to close or limit in certain ways a cinema that was dedicating itself to an expansion and exploration of *all* the possibilities of cinematic expression. Since the Old cinema boasted of its technical proficiency, some underground filmmakers purposely flaunted their amateurism. Crude and careless work was prized as a sign of sincerity. Expensive technical equipment (generally unavailable anyway) was shunned on the principle that it would corrupt an artist's soul. The dogmatic attitude toward everything that had ever been done in Hollywood is expressed in Kelman's review:

> Old American Cinema is doped, hooked and preconditioned by all the oughts and noughts of our society. It is a docile pet which apes the way things are not; it is the tame creature of an invalid culture.

By comparison, one should note Godard's comment that the filmmaker "must not exclude one aspect of the cinema in the name of another aspect of the cinema." What is at stake here is the maintenance of a sensibility which will not inhibit a fascination with the entire spectrum of cinematic possibilty. Or, as Godard has said, "A true historical formation" is vital.

Two decades have passed since Maya Deren's *Ritual in Transfigured Time* prefigured the emergence of the New Cinema in America. The freedom of inquiry which characterizes the New Cinema today is actually a realization of the ethical and aesthetic aspirations of the early days. Without attempting a definitive historical survey, it is possible to make certain judgments about what has been accomplished and what the future (the *near* future) holds.

In spite of Mekas's impressive manifestos, the underground filmmakers haven't been particularly successful in their efforts to encourage radical social change. Mekas's *Film Cinematheque*—the only real showcase for the New American Cinema—has been closed by the New York City police department for presenting "obscene" material. The social psychosis which Mekas railed against obviously still exists. The cinema itself seems to be a reflective medium designed to record action, rather than an active medium designed to induce it in the direct and immediate sense of Guerrilla or Street Theater. In spite of spacious claims like those by Resnais that the audience represented the "political reality" of *Last Year at Marienbad*, the film is sealed in the can by the director before the audience ever gets to see it. Still, film can be the critical factor in a chain reaction leading towards social reform or even revolution. Although the audience is unlikely to burst out of a cinematheque and begin burning buses and erecting barricades, a film may prepare a person for eventual participation in radical political activity. Mekas, or Godard, would argue that film fulfills a crucial function in a society by educating a person in terms of new possibilities; new, liberating modes of thought and action that make it possible for him to respond to the direct appeal of Street Theater or some similar dynamic stimulus. Once, literature provided the primary source for the construction of a sensibility, but that role seems to have been usurped by film and music today. It is no coincidence that Godard makes a film using The Rolling Stones (*One Plus One*) at the same time that Mick Jagger sings "Street Fighting Man."

The role that the cinema has played in the reconstruction of society cannot be described with accuracy. The theoretical speculation which centers about its potential for political evolution reveals more about the wishes of the theoretician than it does about the cinema. Whatever else the New American Cinema may have accomplished, the measure of its significance must be within the area of film itself—the cinema aesthetics that is has explored and invented. There seem to be four basic aspects to this aesthetic, which I would delineate—as concisely as possible—as follows:

1. *A conviction that the filmmaker must be totally involved in every part of the process of filmmaking.* Stan Brakhage vehemently insists that the director (creator) not only plan every shot, but actually hold and manipulate the camera at all times. Brakhage does all the cutting and editing himself, completely arranges the settings, and, in terms of his own belief that the filmmaker must somehow get under the *surface* of the film, has worked directly on the celluloid by painting it, burning it and exposing it to an ingenious variety of optical devices. Brakhage feels that his commitment to the total process of filmmaking has enabled him to render his own vision of the Universe in mythopoetic terms, and his finest work, *Dog Star Man, Blue Moses* and *Anticipation of the Night* support this. On the other hand, one of the greatest strengths of Godard's work is the magnificent camera work of Raoul Coutard.

2. *A constant attention to the process itself.* One of the most serious defects of the "old" cinema was that it dealt with the establishment of illusion. Consequently, the proponents of the New Cinema felt that illusion would be avoided by directing attention to a particular cinematic device while that device was being used. In this way, the filmmaker would involve the audience in the use of a particular effect and in an investigation of its visual potential. The filmmaker could alter or control perception as a part of a threefold system of response. First, the audience would respond to the material. Then, it would be made aware of the technique which induced that response. Finally, it would be encouraged to consider the reflexive action of its sudden, new awareness on its original response. This is similar to Godard's demand that his audience be aware at all times that it is watching a film and to Godard's determination to make clear the fact that the nature of film motion itself is illusory—single frames moving past a lens. A film concerned with the process of filmmaking becomes a comment upon the art of the cinema.

3. *A concern with the necessity to create a visual language.* Like the filmmakers of the silent era who feared the loss of "cinematic purity" with the introduction of sound-synch equipment, the New Cinema has been characterized by an attempt to order all experience in terms of visual images. This is undoubtedly due to a distrust for a language

system that has been debased and exhausted. It is paralleled by the search for a more satisfactory mode of discourse initiated by the so-called "Beat" poets and by the poets who attend to Charles Olson's request for a return to a language based on the logic of myth rather than the logic of science. But while the poets must still use "words"—their root/source materials—the film poet would use as little verbal material as possible. For Brakhage, or Ed Emschwiller (the director of *Relativity*), the camera is not merely an extension of the eye, but ultimately, an extension of the mind. Their films are an attempt to explore and expand the art of vision, to order the universe in terms of a complex, evolving visual logic—finally, to *create perception*.

4. *A commitment to the reevaluation of the narrative form*. The film-makers of the New Cinema question the necessity to "tell a story" or offer an ordered plot in the Aristotelian sense. The manipulation of Time has been the crux of cinematic "reality" since the days of Méliès, the nineteenth century conjuror who virtually invented the cinema, but the "old" cinema has been bound by the conventions of the traditional dramatic structure. When asked whether a film must have a beginning, middle and end, Godard replied, "Yes, but not necessarily in that order." A film like Emschwiller's *Relativity* carries this further so that the revelation of experience is ordered by a continuing response to a total sensory projection. *Relativity* appears to be an investigation of the shapes and textures of nature. It is also clearly a consideration of the way in which the mind and the skin react to these forms. Similarly, Brakhage's *Window Water Baby Moving* might be called the "story" of his wife giving birth to his son, but the literary terms which one uses to describe or discuss a story are not suitable or useful in understanding what is happening on the screen. There really is no satisfactory critical vocabulary yet for these films and this accounts for the anger and confusion which has surrounded their release so far. The films are developing a complex visual logic that must be understood on its own terms.

One of the most important things about the New American Cinema is its willingness to explore any subject, emotion or attitude and to carry through the implications of its vision. Many of the films that are offered to the public as "artistic revelations" or the work of "great" talents are undeniably rubbish. The claims that one makes for the cinema are sustained by only a handful of films. But these films are extraordinary. A work like William David Sherman's *Maximus, To Himself*, an example of the New American Cinema at its most creative, is a synthesis of the aesthetic concerns of the underground filmmaker and the inventive power of Godard. Sherman has succeeded in fusing the vocal and visual elements of his film into a unified projection that opens away from its subject (the poem by Charles Olson) to reveal an impressive *cinematic* mode of apprehension. At this moment in time, Sherman's audience is probably still rather limited, but films like this one will be instrumental in the education of an audience that is prepared to respond to a film on the filmmaker's terms. It may be difficult to articulate the precise nature of this response, but that isn't crucial now. What counts is to be alive to the experience of the film.

Concluding Note

The films of the New Cinema are available from the *Film-Maker's Cooperative* in New York City, and from The *British Film Institute* in London.

Experimental Music

Formerly, whenever anyone said the music I presented was experimental, I objected. It seemed to me that composers knew what they were doing, and that the experiments that had been made had taken place prior to the finished works, just as sketches are made before paintings and rehearsals precede performances. But, giving the matter further thought, I realized that there is ordinarily an essential difference between making a piece of music and hearing one. A composer knows his work as a woodsman knows a path he has traced and retraced, while a listener is confronted by the same work as one is in the woods by a plant he has never seen before.

Now, on the other hand, times have changed; music has changed; and I no longer object to the word "experimental." I use it in fact to describe all the music that especially interests me and to which I am devoted, whether someone else wrote it or I myself did. What has happened is that I have become a listener and the music has become something to hear. Many people, of course, have given up saying "experimental" about this new music. Instead, they either move to a halfway point and say "controversial" or depart to a greater distance and question whether this "music" is music at all.

For in this new music nothing takes place but sounds: those that are notated and those that are not. Those that are not notated appear in the written music as silences, opening the doors of the music to the sounds that happen to be in the environment. This openness exists in the fields of modern sculpture and architecture. The glass houses of Mies van der Rohe reflect their environment, presenting to the eye images of clouds, trees, or grass, according to the situation. And while looking at the constructions in wire of the sculptor Richard Lippold, it is inevitable that one will see other things, and people too, if they happen to be there at the same time, through the network of wires. There is no such thing as an empty space or an empty time. There is always something to see, something to hear. In fact, try as we may to make a silence, we cannot. For certain engineering purposes, it is desirable to have as silent a situation as possible. Such a room is called an anechoic chamber, its six walls made of special material, a room without echoes. I entered one at Harvard University several years ago and heard two sounds, one high and one low. When I described them to the engineer in charge, he informed me that the high one was my nervous system in operation, the low one my blood circulation. Until I die there will be sounds. And they will continue following my death. One need not fear about the future of music.

But this fearlessness only follows if, at the parting of the ways, where it is realized that sounds occur whether intended or not, one turns in the direction of those he does not intend. This turning is psychological and seems at first to be a giving up of everything that belongs to humanity—for a musician, the giving up of music. This psychological turning leads to the world of nature, where, gradually or suddenly, one sees that humanity and nature, not separate, are in this world together; that nothing was lost when everything was given away. In fact, everything is gained. In musical terms, any sounds may occur in any combination and in any continuity.

And it is a striking coincidence that just now the technical means to produce such a free-ranging music are available. When the Allies entered Germany towards the end of World War II, it was discovered that improvements had been made in recording sounds magnetically such that tape had become suitable for the high-fidelity recording of music. First in France with the work of Pierre Schaeffer, later here, in Germany, in Italy, in Japan, and perhaps, without my knowing it, in other places, magnetic tape was used not simply to record performances of music but to make a new music that was possible only because of it. Given a minimum of two tape recorders and a disk recorder, the following processes are possible: 1) a single recording of any sound can be made; 2) a rerecording may be made, in the course of which, by means of filters and circuits, any or all of the physical characteristics of a given recorded sound may be altered; 3) electronic mixing (combining on a third machine sounds issuing from two others) permits the presentation of any number of sounds in combination; 4) ordinary splicing permits the juxtaposition of any sounds, and when it includes unconventional cuts, it, like rerecording, brings about alternatives of any or all of the original physical characteristics. The situation made available by these means is essentially a total sound-space, the limits of which are ear-determined only, the position of a particular sound in this space being the result of five determinants: frequency of pitch, amplitude or loudness, overtone structure or timbre, duration, and morphology (how the sound begins, goes on, and dies away). By the alteration of any one of these determinants, the position of the sound in sound-space changes. Any sound at any point in this total sound-space can move to become a sound at any other point. But advantages can be taken of these possibilities only if one is willing to change one's musical habits radically. That is, one may take advantage of the appearance of images without visible transition in distant places, which is a way of saying "television," if one is willing to stay at home instead of gong to a theatre. Or one may fly if one is willing to give up walking.

Musical habits include scales, modes, theories of counterpoint and harmony, and the study of the timbres, singly and in combination of a limited number of sound-producing mechanisms. In mathematical terms these all concern discrete steps. They resemble walking—in the case of pitches, on steppingstones twelve in number. This cautious stepping is not characteristic of the possibilities of magnetic tape, which is revealing to us that musical action or existence can occur at any point or along any line or curve or what have you in total sound-space; that we are, in fact, technically equipped to transform our contemporary awareness of nature's manner of operation into art.

Again there is a parting of the ways. One has a choice. If he does not wish to give up his attempts to control sound, he may complicate his musical technique towards an approximation of the new possibilities and awareness. (I used the word "approximation" because a measuring mind can never finally measure nature.) Or, as before, one may give up the desire to control sound, clear his mind of music, and set about discovering means to let sounds be themselves rather than vehicles for man-made theories or expressions of human sentiments.

This project will seem fearsome to many, but on examination it gives no cause for alarm. Hearing sounds which are just sounds immediately sets the theorizing mind to theorizing, and the emotions of human beings are continually aroused by encounters with nature. Does not a mountain unintentionally evoke in us a sense of wonder? otters along a stream a sense of mirth? night in the woods a sense of fear? Do not rain falling and mists rising up suggest the love binding heaven and earth? Is not decaying flesh loathsome? Does not the death of someone we love bring sorrow? And is there a greater hero than the least plant that grows? What is more angry than the flash of lightning and the sound of thunder? These responses to nature are mine and will not necessarily correspond with another's. Emotion takes place in the person who has it. And sounds, when allowed to be themselves, do not require that those who hear them do so unfeelingly. The opposite is what is meant by response ability.

New music: new listening. Not an attempt to understand something that is being said, for, if something were being said, the sounds would be given the shapes of words. Just an attention to the activity of sounds.

Those involved with the composition of experimental music find ways and means to remove themselves from the activities of the sounds they make. Some employ chance operations, derived from sources as ancient as the Chinese *Book of Changes*, or as modern as the tables of random numbers used also by physicists in research. Or, analogous to the Rorschach tests of psychology, the interpretation of imperfections in the paper upon which one is writing may provide a music free from one's memory and imagination. Geometrical means employing spatial superimpositions at variance with the ultimate performance in time may be used. The total field of possibilities may be roughly divided and the actual sounds within these divisions may be indicated as to number but left to the performer or to the splicer to choose. In this latter case, the composer resembles the maker of a camera who allows someone else to take the picture.

Whether one uses tape or writes for conventional instruments, the present musical situation has changed from what it was before tape came into being. This also need not arouse alarm, for the coming into being of something new does not by that fact deprive what was of its proper place. Each thing has its own place, never takes the place of something else; and the more things there are, as is said, the merrier.

But several effects of tape on experimental music may be mentioned. Since so many inches of tape equal so many seconds of time, it has become more and more usual that notation is in space rather than in symbols of quarter, half, and sixteenth notes and so on. Thus where on a page a note appears will correspond to when in a time it is to occur. A stop watch is used to facilitate a performance; and a rhythm results which is a far cry from horse's hoofs and other regular beats.

Also it has been impossible with the playing of several separate tapes at once to achieve perfect synchronization. This fact has led some toward the manufacture of multiple-tracked tapes and machines with a corresponding number of heads; while others—those who have accepted the sounds they do not intend—now realize that the score, the requiring that many parts be played in a particular togetherness, is not an accurate representation of how things are. These now compose parts but not scores, and the parts may be combined in any unthought ways. This means that each performance of such a piece of music is unique, as interesting to its composer as to others listening. It is easy to see again the parallel with nature, for even with leaves of the same tree, no two are exactly alike. The parallel in art is the sculpture with moving parts, the mobile.

It goes without saying that dissonances and noises are welcome in this new music. But so is the dominant seventh chord if it happens to put in an appearance.

Rehearsals have shown that this new music, whether for tape or for instruments, is more clearly heard when the several loud-speakers or performers are separated in space rather than grouped closely together. For this music is not concerned with harmoniousness as generally understood, where the quality of harmony results from a blending of several elements. Here we are concerned with the coexistence of dissimilars, and the central points where fusion occurs are many: the ears of the listeners wherever they are. This disharmony, to paraphrase Bergson's statement about disorder, is simply a harmony to which many are unaccustomed.

Where do we go from here? Towards theatre. That art more than music resembles nature. We have eyes as well as ears, and it is our business while we are alive to use them.

And what is the purpose of writing music? One is, of course, not dealing with purposes but dealing with sounds. Or the answer must take the form of paradox: a purposeful purposelessness or a purposeless play. This play, however, is an affirmation of life—not an attempt to bring order out of chaos nor to suggest improvements in creation, but simply a way of waking up to the very life we're living, which is so excellent once one gets one's mind and one's desires out of its way and lets it act of its own accord.

When Xenia and I came to New York from Chicago, we arrived in the bus station with about twenty-five cents. We were expecting to stay for a while with Peggy Guggenheim and Max Ernst. Max Ernst had met us in Chicago and had said, "Whenever you come to New York, come and stay with us. We have a big house on the East River." I went to the phone booth in the bus station, put in a nickel, and dialed. Max Ernst answered. He didn't recognize my voice. Finally he said, "Are you thirsty?" I said, "Yes," He said, "Well, come over tomorrow for cocktails." I went back to Xenia and told her what had happened. She said, "Call him back. We have everything to gain and nothing to lose." I did. He said, "Oh! It's you. We've been waiting for you for weeks. Your room's ready. Come right over."

Dad is an inventor. In 1912 his submarine had the world's record for staying under water. Running as it did by means of a gasoline engine, it left bubbles on the surface, so it was not employed during World War I. Dad says he does his best work when he is sound asleep. I was explaining at the New School that the way to get ideas is to do something boring. For instance, composing in such a way that the process of composing is boring induces ideas. They fly into one's head like birds. Is that what Dad meant?

Like A Rolling Stone

*Forms and rhythms in music are never changed without producing
changes in the most important political forms and ways.*

Plato said that.

*There's something happenin' here. What it is ain't exactly clear. There's
a man with a gun over there tellin' me I've got to beware. I think it's
time we STOP, children, what's that sound? Everybody look what's
goin' down.*

The Buffalo Springfield said that.

For the reality of politics, we must go to the poets, not the politicians.

Norman O. Brown said that.

*For the reality of what's happening today in America, we must go to
rock 'n roll, to popular music.*

I said that.

For almost forty years in this country, which has prided itself on individualism, freedom and nonconformity, all popular songs were written
alike. They had an eight-bar opening statement, an eight-bar repeat, an
eight-bar middle section or bridge, and an eight-bar reprise. Anything
that did not fit into that framework was, appropriately enough, called
a novelty.

Clothes were basically the same whether a suit was double-breasted
or single-breasted, and the only people who wore beards were absent-
minded professors and Bolshevik bomb throwers. Long hair, which was
equated with lack of masculinity—in some sort of subconscious reference
to Samson, I suspect—was restricted to painters and poets and classical
musicians, hence the term "longhair music" to mean classical.

Four years ago a specter was haunting Europe, one whose fundamental
influence, my intuition tells me, may be just as important, if in another
way, as the original of that line. The Beatles, four long-haired Liverpool

teen-agers, were busy changing the image of popular music. In less than a year, they invaded the United States and almost totally wiped out the standard Broadway show—Ed Sullivan TV program popular song. No more were we "flying to the moon on gossamer wings," we were now articulating such interesting and, in this mechanistic society, unusual concepts as "Money can't buy me love" and "I want to hold your hand."

"Societies, like individuals, have their moral crises and their spiritual revolutions," R. H. Tawney says in *Religion and the Rise of Capitalism*. And the Beatles appeared ("a great figure rose up from the sea and pointed at me and said 'you're a Beatle with an "a" ' "—Genesis, according to John Lennon). They came at the proper moment of a spiritual cusp—as the martian in Robert Heinlein's *Stranger in a Strange Land* calls a crisis.

Instantly, on those small and sometimes doll-like figures was focused all the rebellion against hypocrisy, all the impudence and irreverence that the youth of that moment was feeling vis-à-vis his elders.

Automation, affluence, the totality of instant communication, the technology of the phonograph record, the transistor radio, had revolutionized life for youth in this society. The population age was lowering. Popular music, the jukebox and the radio were becoming the means of communication. Huntley and Brinkley were for mom and dad. People now sang songs they wrote themselves, not songs written *for* them by hacks in grimy Tin Pan Alley offices.

The folk music boom paved the way. Bob Dylan's poetic polemics, "Blowin' in the Wind" and "The Times They Are A-Changin'," had helped the breakthrough. "Top-40" radio made Negro music available everywhere to a greater degree than ever before in our history.

This was, truly, a new generation—the first in America raised with music constantly in its ear, weaned on a transistor radio, involved with songs from its earliest moment of memory.

Music means more to this generation than it did even to its dancing parents in the big band swing era of Benny Goodman. It's natural, then, that self-expression should find popular music so attractive.

The dance of the swing era, of the big bands, was the fox-trot. It was really a formal dance extended in variation only by experts. The swing era's parents had danced the waltz. The fox-trot was a ritual with only a little more room for self-expression. Rock 'n roll brought with it not only the voices of youth singing their protests, their hopes and their expectations (along with their pathos and their sentimentality and their personal affairs from drag racing to romance), it brought their dances.

"Every period which abounded in folk songs has, by the same token, been deeply stirred by Dionysiac currents," Nietzsche points out in *The Birth of Tragedy*. And Dionysiac is the word to describe the dances of the past ten years, call them by whatever name from bop to the Twist to the Frug, from the Hully Gully to the Philly Dog.

In general, adult society left the youth alone, prey to the corruption the adults suspected was forthcoming from the song lyrics ("All of me, why not take all of me," from that hit of the thirties, of course, didn't mean *all* of me, it meant, well . . . . er. . . . .) or from the payola-influenced disc jockeys. (Who ever remembers about the General Electric scandals of the fifties, in which over a dozen officials went to jail for industrial illegalities?)

The TV shows were in the afternoon anyway and nobody could stand to watch those rock 'n roll singers; they were worse than Elvis Presley.

But all of a sudden the *New Yorker* joke about the married couple dreamily remarking, when a disc jockey played "Houn' Dog" by Elvis, "they're playing our song," wasn't a joke any longer. It was real. That generation had suddenly grown up and married and Elvis was real memories of real romance and not just kid stuff.

All of a sudden, the world of music, which is big business in a very real way, took another look at the music of the pony-tail and chewing gum set, as Mitch Miller once called the teen-age market, and realized that there was one helluva lot of bread to be made there.

In a short few years, Columbia and R.C.A. Victor and the other companies that dominated the recording market, the huge publishing houses that copyrighted the music and collected the royalties, discovered that they no longer were "kings of the hill." Instead, a lot of small companies, like Atlantic and Chess and Imperial and others, had hits by people the major record companies didn't even know, singing songs written in Nashville and Detroit and Los Angeles and Chicago and sometimes, but no longer almost always, New York.

It's taken the big ones a few years to recoup from that. First they called the music trash and the lyrics dirty. When that didn't work, as the attempt more recently to inhibit songs with supposed psychedelic or marijuana references has failed, they capitulated. They joined up. R.C.A. Victor bought Elvis from the original company he recorded for—Sun Records ("Yaller Sun records from Nashville" as John Sebastian sings it in "Nashville Cats")—and then bought Sam Cooke, and A.B.C. Paramount bought Ray Charles and then Fats Domino. And Columbia, thinking it had a baby folk singer capable of some more sales of "San Francisco Bay," turned out to have a tiny demon of a poet named Bob Dylan.

So the stage was set for the Beatles to take over—"with this ring I can—dare I say it?—rule the world!" And they did take over so thoroughly that they have become the biggest success in the history of show business, the first attraction ever to have a coast-to-coast tour in this country sold out before the first show even opened.

With the Beatles and Dylan running tandem, two things seem to me to have been happening. The early Beatles were at one and the same time a declaration in favor of love and of life, an exuberant paean to the sheer joy of living, and a validation of the importance of American Negro music.

Dylan, by his political, issue-oriented broadsides first and then by his Rimbaudish nightmare visions of the real state of the nation, his bittersweet love songs and his pure imagery, did what the jazz and poetry people of the fifties had wanted to do—he took poetry out of the classroom and out of the hands of the professors and put it right out there in the streets for everyone.

I dare say that with the inspiration of the Beatles and Dylan we have more poetry being produced and more poets being made than ever before in the history of the world. Dr. Malvina Reynolds—the composer of "Little Boxes"—thinks nothing like this has happened since Elizabethan times. I suspect even that is too timid an assessment.

Let's go back to Plato, again. Speaking of the importance of new styles of music, he said, "The new style quietly insinuates itself into manners and customs and from there it issues a greater force . . . goes on to attack laws and constitutions, displaying the utmost impudence, until it ends by overthrowing everything, both in public and in private."

That seems to me to be a pretty good summation of the answer to the British rock singer Donovan's question, "What goes on? I really want to know."

The most immediate apparent change instituted by the new music is a new way of looking at things. We see it evidenced all around us. The old ways are going and a new set of assumptions is beginning to be worked out. I cannot even begin to codify them. Perhaps it's much too soon to do so. But I think there are some clues—the sacred importance of love and truth and beauty and interpersonal relationships.

When Bob Dylan sang recently at the Masonic Memorial Auditorium in San Francisco, at intermission there were a few very young people in the corridor backstage. One of them was a long-haired, poncho-wearing girl of about thirteen. Dylan's road manager, a slender, long-haired, "Bonnie Prince Charlie" youth, wearing black jeans and Beatle boots, came out of the dressing room and said, "You kids have to leave! You can't be backstage here!"

"Who are you?" the long-haired girl asked.

"I'm a cop," Dylan's road manager said aggressively.

The girl looked at him for a long moment and then drawled, "Whaaaat? With those boots?"

Clothes really do *not* make the man. But sometimes . . .

I submit that was an important incident, something that could never have happened a year before, something that implies a very great deal about the effect of the new style, which has quietly (or not so quietly, depending on your view of electric guitars) insinuated itself into manners and customs.

Among the effects of "what's goin' on" is the relinquishing of belief in the sacredness of logic. "I was a prisoner of logic and I still am," Malvina Reynolds admits, but then goes on to praise the new music. And the prisoners of logic are the ones who are really suffering most—unless they have Mrs. Reynolds' glorious gift of youthful vision.

The first manifestation of the importance of this outside the music— I think—came in the works of Ken Kesey and Joseph Heller. *One Flew Over the Cuckoo's Nest*, with its dramatic view of the interchangeability of reality and illusion, and *Catch-22*, with its delightful utilization of crackpot realism (to use C. Wright Mill's phrase) as an explanation of how things are, were works of seminal importance.

No one any longer really believes that the processes of international relations and world economics are rationally explicable. Absolutely the very best and clearest discussion of the entire thing is wrapped up in Milo Minderbinder's explanation, in *Catch-22*, of how you can buy eggs for seven cents apiece in Malta and sell them for five cents in Pianosa and make a profit. Youth understands the truth of this immediately, and no economics textbook is going to change it.

Just as—implying the importance of interpersonal relations and the beauty of being true to oneself—the under-thirty youth immediately understands the creed patiently explained by Yossarian in *Catch-22* that everybody's your enemy who's trying to get you killed, even if he's your own commanding officer.

This is an irrational world, despite the brilliant efforts of Walter Lippmann to make it rational, and we are living in a continuation of the formalized lunacy (Nelson Algren's phrase) of war, any war.

At this point in history, most of the organs of opinion, from the *New York Review of Books* through the *New Republic* to *Encounter* (whether or not they are subsidized by the C.I.A.), are in the control of the prisoners of logic. They take a flick like *Morgan* and grapple with it. They take *Help* and *A Hard Day's Night* and grapple with those two beautiful creations, and they fail utterly to understand what is going on because they try to deal with them logically. They complain because art doesn't make sense! Life on this planet in this time of history doesn't make sense either—as an end result of immutable laws of economics and logic and philosophy.

Dylan sang, "You raise up your head and you ask 'is this where it is?' And somebody points to you and says 'it's his' and you say 'what's mine' and somebody else says 'well, what is' and you say 'oh my god am i here all alone?' "

Dylan wasn't the first. Orwell saw some of it, Heller saw more, and in a different way so did I. F. Stone, that remarkable journalist, who is really a poet, when he described a *Herald Tribune* reporter extracting from the Pentagon the admission that, once the first steps for the Santo Domingo episode were mounted, it was impossible to stop the machine.

Catch-22 said that in order to be sent home from flying missions you had to be crazy, and obviously anybody who wanted to be sent home was sane.

Kesey and Heller and Terry Southern, to a lesser degree in his novels but certainly in *Dr. Strangelove*, have hold of it. I suspect that they are not really a *New Wave* of writers but only a *last* wave of the past, just as is Norman Mailer, who said in his Berkeley Vietnam Day speech that "rational discussion of the United States' involvement in Viet Nam is illogical in the way surrealism is illogical and national political discussion of Adolf Hitler's motives was illogical and then obscene." This is the end of the formal literature we have known and the beginning, possibly, of something else.

In almost every aspect of what is happening today, this turning away from the old patterns is making itself manifest. As the formal structure of the show business world of popular music and television has brought out into the open the Negro performer—whose incredibly beautiful folk poetry and music for decades has been the prime mover in American song—we find a curious thing happening.

The Negro performers, from James Brown to Aaron Neville to the Supremes and the Four Tops, are on an Ed Sullivan trip, striving as hard as they can to get on that stage and become part of the American success story, while the white rock performers are motivated to escape from that stereotype. Whereas in years past the Negro performer offered style in performance and content in song—the messages from Leadbelly to Percy Mayfield to Ray Charles were important messages—today he is almost totally style with very little content. And when James Brown sings, "It's a Man's World," or Aaron Neville sings, "Tell It Like It Is," he takes a phrase and only a phrase with which to work, and the Supremes and the Tops are choreographed more and more like the Four Lads and the Ames Brothers and the McGuire Sisters.

I suggest that this bears a strong relationship to the condition of the civil rights movement today in which the only truly black position is that of Stokely Carmichael, and in which the N.A.A.C.P. and most of the other formal groups are, like the Four Tops and the Supremes, on an Ed Sullivan-TV-trip to middle-class America. And the only true American Negro music is that which abandons the concepts of European musical thought, abandons the systems of scales and keys and notes, for a music whose roots are in the culture of the colored peoples of the world.

The drive behind all American popular music performers, to a greater or lesser extent, from Sophie Tucker and Al Jolson, on down through Pat Boone and as recently as Roy Head and Charlie Rich, has been to sound like a Negro. The white jazz musician was the epitome of this.

Yet an outstanding characteristic of the new music of rock, certainly in its best artists, is something else altogether. This new generation of musicians is not interested in being Negro, since that is an absurdity.

The clarinetist Milton Mezzrow, who grew up with the Negro Chicago jazzmen in the twenties and thirties, even put "Negro" on his prison record and claimed to be more at home with his Negro friends than with his Jewish family and neighbors.

Today's new youth, beginning with the rock band musician but spreading out into the entire movement, into the Haight-Ashbury hippies, is not ashamed of being white.

He is remarkably free from prejudice, but he is not attempting to join the Negro culture or to become part of it, like his musical predecessor, the jazzman, or like his social predecessor, the beatnik. I find this of considerable significance. For the very first time in decades, as far as I know, something important and new is happening artistically and musically in this society that is distinct from the Negro and to which the Negro will have to come, if he is interested in it at all, as in the past the white youth went uptown to Harlem or downtown or crosstown or to wherever the Negro community was centered because there was the locus of artistic creativity.

Today the new electronic music by the Beatles and others (and the Beatles' "Strawberry Fields" is, I suggest, a three-minute masterpiece, an electronic miniature symphony) exists somewhere else from and independent of the Negro. This is only one of the more easily observed manifestations of this movement.

The professional craft union, the American Federation of Musicians, is now faced with something absolutely unforeseen—the cooperative band. Briefly—in the thirties—there were co-op bands. The original Casa Loma band was one and the original Woody Herman band was another.

But the whole attitude of the union and the attitude of the musicians themselves worked against the idea, and co-op bands were discouraged. They were almost unknown until recently.

Today almost all the rock groups are cooperative. Many live together, in tribal style, in houses or camps or sometimes in traveling tepees, but always *together* as a *group*; and the young girls who follow them are called "groupies," just as the girls who in the thirties and forties followed the bands (music does more than soothe the savage breast!) were called "band chicks."

The basic creed of the American Federation of Musicians is that musicians must not play unless paid. The new generation wants money, of course, but its basic motivation is to play anytime, anywhere, anyhow. Art is first, then finance, most of the time. And at least one rock band, the Loading Zone in Berkeley, has stepped outside the American Federation of Musicians entirely and does not play for money. You may give them money, but they won't set a price or solicit it.

This seems to me to extend the attitude that gave Pete Seeger, Joan Baez and Bob Dylan such status. They are not and never have been for sale in the sense that you can hire Sammy Davis to appear, as you can hire Dean Martin to appear, any time he's free, as long as you pay his price. You have not been able to do this with Seeger, Baez and Dylan any more than Allen Ginsberg has been for sale either to *Ramparts* or the C.I.A.

Naturally, this revolt against the assumptions of the adult world runs smack dab into the sanctimonious puritan morality of America, the schizophrenia that insists that money is serious business and the acquisition of wealth is a blessing in the eyes of the Lord, that what we do in private we must preach against in public. Don't do what I do, do what I say.

Implicit in the very names of the business organizations that these youths form is an attack on the traditional, serious attitude toward money. It is not only that the groups themselves are named with beautiful imagery: the Grateful Dead, the Loading Zone, Blue Cheer or the Jefferson Airplane—all dating back to the Beatles with an A—it is the names of the nonmusical organizations: Frontage Road Productions (the music company of the Grateful Dead), Faithful Virtue Music (the Lovin' Spoonful's publishing company), Ashes and Sand (Bob Dylan's production firm—his music publishing company is Dwarf Music). A group who give light shows is known as the Love Conspiracy Commune, and there was a dance recently in Marin County, California, sponsored by the Northern California Psychedelic Cattlemen's Association, Ltd.

And, of course, there is the Family Dog, which, despite *Ramparts*, was never a rock group, only a name under which four people who wanted to present rock 'n roll dances worked.

Attacking the conventional attitude toward money is considered immoral in the society of our fathers, because money is sacred. The reality of what Bob Dylan says—"money doesn't talk, it swears"—has yet to seep through.

A corollary of the money attack is the whole thing about long hair, bare feet and beards. "Nothing makes me sadder," a woman wrote me objecting to the Haight-Ashbury scene, "than to see beautiful young girls walking along the street in bare feet." My own daughter pointed out that your feet couldn't get any dirtier than your shoes.

Recently I spent an evening with a lawyer, a brilliant man who is engaged in a lifelong crusade to educate and reform lawyers. He is interested in the civil liberties issue of police harassment of hippies. But, he said, they wear those uniforms of buckskin and fringe and beads. Why don't they dress naturally? So I asked him if he was born in his three-button dacron suit. It's like the newspaper descriptions of Joan Baez's "long stringy hair." It may be long, but *stringy?* Come on!

To the eyes of many of the elder generation, all visible aspects of the new generation, its music, its lights, its clothes, are immoral. The City of San Francisco Commission on Juvenile Delinquency reported adversely on the sound level and the lights at the Fillmore Auditorium, as if those things of and by themselves were threats (they may be, but not in the way the Commission saw them). A young girl might have trouble maintaining her judgment in that environment, the Commission chairman said.

Now this all implies that dancing is the road to moral ruin, that young girls on the dance floor are mesmerized by talent scouts for South American brothels and enticed away from their happy (not hippie) homes to live a life of slavery and moral degradation. It ought to be noted, parenthetically, that a British writer, discussing the Beatles, claims that "the Cycladic fertility goddess from Amorgos dates the guitar as a sex symbol to 4800 years B.C."

During the twenties and the thirties and the forties—in other words, during the prime years of the Old Ones of today—dancing, in the immortal words of Bob Scobey, the Dixieland trumpet player, "was an excuse to get next to a broad." The very least effect of the pill on American youth is that this is no longer true.

The assault on hypocrisy works on many levels. The adult society attempted to chastise Bob Dylan by economic sanction, calling the line in "Rainy Day Woman," "everybody must get stoned" (although there is a purely religious, even biblical, meaning to it, if you wish), an enticement to teen-agers to smoke marijuana. But no one has objected to Ray Charles's "Let's Go Get Stoned," which is about gin, or to any number of other songs, from the Kingston Trio's "Scotch and Soda" on through "One for My Baby and One More [ONE MORE!] for the Road." Those are about alcohol and alcohol is socially acceptable, as well as big business, even though I believe that everyone under thirty now knows that alcohol is worse for you than marijuana, that, in fact, the only thing wrong about marijuana is that it is illegal.

Cut to the California State Narcotics Bureau's chief enforcement officer, Matt O'Connor, in a TV interview recently insisting, à la Parkinson's Law, that he must have more agents to control the drug abuse problem. He appeared with a representative of the state attorney general's office, who predicted that the problem would continue "as long as these people believe they are not doing anything wrong."

And that's exactly it. They do not think they are doing anything wrong, any more than their grandparents were when they broke the prohibition laws. They do not want to go to jail, but a jail sentence or a bust no longer carries the social stigma it once did. The civil rights movement has made a jailing a badge of honor, if you go there for principle, and to a great many people today, the right to smoke marijuana is a principle worth risking jail for.

"Make Love, Not War" is one of the most important slogans of modern times, a statement of life against death, as the Beatles have said over and over—"say the word and be like me, say the word and you'll be free."

I don't think that wearing that slogan on a bumper or on the back of a windbreaker is going to end the bombing tomorrow at noon, but it implies something. It is not conceivable that it could have existed in such proliferation thirty years ago, and in 1937 *we* were pacifists, too. It simply could not have happened.

There's another side to it, of course, or at least another aspect of it. The Rolling Stones, who came into existence really to fight jazz in the clubs of London, were against the jazz of the integrated world, the integrated world arrived at by rational processes. Their songs, from "Satisfaction" and "19th Nervous Breakdown" to "Get Off of My Cloud" and "Mother's Little Helper," were antiestablishment songs in a nonpolitical sort of way, just as Dylan's first period was antiestablishment in a political way. The Stones are now moving, with "Ruby Tuesday" and "Let's Spend the Night Together," into a social radicalism of sorts;

but in the beginning, and for their basic first-thrust appeal, they hit out in rage, almost in blind anger and certainly with overtones of destructiveness, against the adult world. It's no wonder the novel they were attracted to was David Wallis' *Only Lovers Left Alive*, that Hell's Angels story of a teen-age, future jungle. And it is further interesting that their manager, Andrew Loog Oldham, writes the essays on their albums in the style of Anthony Burgess' violent *A Clockwork Orange*.

Nor is it any wonder that this attitude appealed to that section of the youth whose basic position was still in politics and economics (remember that the Rolling Stone Mick Jagger was a London School of Economics student, whereas Lennon and McCartney were artists and writers). When the Stones first came to the West Coast, a group of young radicals issued the following proclamation of welcome:

> Greetings and welcome Rolling Stones, our comrades in the desperate battle against the maniacs who hold power. The revolutionary youth of the world hears your music and is inspired to even more deadly acts. We fight in guerrilla bands against the invading imperialists in Asia and South America, we riot at rock 'n roll concerts everywhere. We burned and pillaged in Los Angeles and the cops know our snipers will return.
>
> They call us dropouts and delinquents and draftdodgers and punks and hopheads and heap tons of shit on our heads. In Viet Nam they drop bombs on us and in America they try to make us make war on our own comrades but the bastards hear us playing you on our little transistor radios and know that they will not escape the blood and fire of the anarchist revolution.
>
> We will play your music in rock 'n roll marching bands as we tear down the jails and free the prisoners, as we tear down the state schools and free the students, as we tear down the military bases and arm the poor, as we tattoo BURN BABY BURN! on the bellies of the wardens and generals and create a new society from the ashes of our fires.
>
> Comrades, you will return to this country when it is free from the tyranny of the State and you will play your splendid music in factories run by the workers, in the domes of emptied city halls, on the rubble of police stations, under the hanging corpses of priests, under a million red flags waving over a million anarchist communities. In the words of Breton, THE ROLLING STONES ARE THAT WHICH SHALL BE! LYNDON JOHNSON— THE YOUTH OF CALIFORNIA DEDICATES ITSELF TO YOUR DESTRUCTION! ROLLING STONES—THE YOUTH OF CALIFORNIA HEARS YOUR MESSAGE! LONG LIVE THE REVOLUTION!!!

But rhetoric like that did not bring out last January to a Human Be-In on the polo grounds of San Francisco's Golden Gate Park twenty thousand people who were there, fundamentally, just to see the other members of the tribe, not to hear speeches—the speeches were all a drag from Leary to Rubin to Buddah*—but just to *BE*.

In the Haight-Ashbury district the Love Generation organizes itself into Job Co-ops and committees to clean the streets, and the monks of the neighborhood, the Diggers, talk about free dances in the park to put the Avalon Ballroom and the Fillmore out of business and about communizing the incomes of Bob Dylan and the Beatles.

The Diggers trace back spiritually to those British millenarians who took over land in 1649, just before Cromwell, and after the Civil War freed it, under the assumption that the land was for the people. They tilled it and gave the food away.

The Diggers give food away. Everything is Free. So is it with the Berkeley Provos and the new group in Cleveland—the Prunes—and the Provos in Los Angeles. More, if an extreme, assault against the money culture. Are they driving the money changers out of the temple? Perhaps. The Diggers say they believe it is just as futile to fight the system as to join it and they are dropping out in a way that differs from Leary's.

The Square Left wrestles with the problem. They want a Yellow Submarine community because that is where the strength so obviously is. But even *Ramparts*, which is the white hope of the Square Left, if you follow me, misunderstands. They think that the Family Dog is a rock group and that political activity is the only hope, and Bob Dylan says, "There's no left wing and no right wing, only upwing and down wing," and also, "I tell you there are no politics."

But the banding together to form Job Co-ops, to publish newspapers, to talk to the police (even to bring them flowers), aren't these political acts? I suppose so, but I think they are political acts of a different kind, a kind that results in the Hell's Angels being the guardians of the lost children at the Be-In and the guarantors of peace at dances.

The New Youth is finding its prophets in strange places—in dance halls and on the jukebox. It is on, perhaps, a frontier buckskin trip after a decade of Matt Dillon and Bonanza and the other TV folk myths, in which the values are clear (as opposed to those in the world around us) and right is right and wrong is wrong. The Negro singers have brought the style and the manner of the Negro gospel preacher to popular music, just as they brought the rhythms and the feeling of the gospel music,

---

* The Be-In heard speeches by Timothy Leary, the psychedelic guru, Jerry Rubin, the leader of the Berkeley Vietnam Day movement, and Buddah, a bartender and minor figure in the San Francisco hippie movement who acted as master of ceremonies.

and now the radio is the church and Everyman carries his own walkie-talkie to God in his transistor.

Examine the outcry against the Beatles for John Lennon's remark about being more popular than Jesus. No radio station that depended on rock 'n roll music for its audience banned Beatles records, and in the only instance where we had a precise measuring rod for the contest—the Beatles concert in Memphis where a revival meeting ran day and date with them—the Beatles won overwhelmingly. Something like eight to five over Jesus in attendance, even though the Beatles charged a stiff price and the Gospel according to the revival preacher was free. Was my friend so wrong who said that if Hitler were alive today, the German girls wouldn't allow him to bomb London if the Beatles were there?

"Nobody ever taught you how to live out in the streets," Bob Dylan sings in "Like a Rolling Stone." You may consider that directed at a specific person, or you may, as I do, consider it poetically aimed at plastic uptight America, to use a phrase from one of the Family Dog founders.

"Nowhere to run, nowhere to hide," Martha and the Vandellas sing, and Simon and Garfunkel say, "The words of the prophets are written on the subway walls, in tenement halls." And the Byrds sing, "A time for peace, I swear it's not too late," just as the Beatles sing, "Say the word." What has formal religion done in this century to get the youth of the world so well acquainted with a verse from the Bible?

Even in those artists of the second echelon who are not, like Dylan and the Beatles and the Stones, worldwide in their influence, we find it. "Don't You Want Somebody To Love," the Jefferson Airplane sings, and Bob Lind speaks of "the bright elusive butterfly of love."

These songs speak to us in our condition, just as Dylan did with "lookout kid, it's somethin' you did, god knows what, but you're doin' it again." And Dylan sings again a concept that finds immediate response in the tolerance and the antijudgment stance of the new generation, when he says, "There are no trials inside the Gates of Eden."

Youth is wise today. Lenny Bruce claimed that TV made even eight-year-old girls sophisticated. When Bob Dylan in "Desolation Row" sings, "At midnight all the agents and the superhuman crew come out and round up everyone that knows more than they do," he speaks true, as he did with "don't follow leaders." But sometimes it is, as John Sebastian of the Lovin' Spoonful says, "like trying to tell a stranger 'bout a rock 'n roll."

Let's go back again to Nietzsche.

> Orgiastic movements of a society leave their traces in music [he wrote]. Dionysiac stirrings arise either through the influence of those narcotic

potions of which all primitive races speak in their hymns [—dig that!—] or through the powerful approach of spring, which penetrates with joy the whole frame of nature. So stirred, the individual forgets himself completely. It is the same Dionysiac power which in medieval Germany drove ever increasing crowds of people singing and dancing from place to place; we recognize in these St. John's and St. Vitus' dancers the bacchic choruses of the Greeks, who had their precursors in Asia Minor and as far back as Babylon and the orgiastic Sacea. There are people who, either from lack of experience or out of sheer stupidity, turn away from such phenomena, and strong, in the sense of their own sanity, label them either mockingly or pityingly "endemic diseases." These benighted souls have no idea how cadaverous and ghostly their "sanity" appears as the tense throng of Dionysiac revelers sweeps past them.

And Nietzsche never heard of the San Francisco Commission on Juvenile Delinquency or the Fillmore and the Avalon ballrooms.

"Believe in the magic, it will set you free," the Lovin' Spoonful sing. "This is an invitation across the nation," sing Martha and the Vandellas, and the Mamas and the Papas, "a chance for folks to meet, there'll be laughin', singin' and music swingin', and dancin' in the street!"

Do I project too much? Again, to Nietzsche. "Man now expresses himself through song and dance as the member of a higher community; he has forgotten how to walk, how to speak and is on the brink of taking wing as he dances . . . no longer the *artist*, he has himself become *a work of art.*"

"Hail hail rock 'n roll," as Chuck Berry sings. "Deliver me from the days of old!"

I think he's about to be granted his wish.

Interviews with Pop Artists: Andy Warhol, Roy Lichtenstein, James Rosenquist

Andy Warhol

Someone said that Brecht wanted everybody to think alike. I want everybody to think alike. But Brecht wanted to do it through Communism, in a way. Russia is doing it under government. It's happening here all by itself without being under a strict government; so if it's working without trying, why can't it work without being Communist? Everybody looks alike and acts alike, and we're getting more and more that way.

I think everybody should be a machine.

I think everybody should like everybody.

Is that what Pop Art is all about?

Yes. It's liking things.

And liking things is like being a machine?

Yes, because you do the same thing every time. You do it over and over again.

And you approve of that?

Yes, because it's all fantasy. It's hard to be creative and it's also hard not to think what you do is creative or hard not to be called creative because everybody is always talking about that and individuality. Everybody's always being creative. And it's so funny when you say things aren't, like the shoe I would draw for an advertisement was called a "creation" but the drawing of it was not. But I guess I believe in both ways. All these people who aren't very good should be really good. Everybody is too good now, really. Like, how many actors are there? There are millions of actors. They're all pretty good. And how many painters are there? Millions of painters and all pretty good. How can you say one style is better than another? You ought to be able to be an Abstract-Expressionist next week, or a Pop artist, or a realist, without feeling you've given up something. I think the artists who aren't very good should become like everybody else so that people would like things that aren't very good. It's already happening. All you have to do is read the magazines and the catalogues. It's this style or that style, this or that

Gene Swenson, "Interviews with Pop Artists: Andy Warhol, Roy Lichtenstein, James Rosenquist." Reprinted from the article "What Is Pop Art?" from *Art News*, November, 1963, and February, 1964. Reprinted by permission of *Art News*.

image of man—but that really doesn't make any difference. Some artists get left out that way, and why should they?

Is Pop Art a fad?

Yes, it's a fad, but I don't see what difference it makes. I just heard a rumor that G. quit working, that she's given up art altogether. And everyone is saying how awful it is that A. gave up his style and is doing it in a different way. I don't think so at all. If an artist can't do any more, then he should just quit; and an artist ought to be able to change his style without feeling bad. I heard that Lichtenstein said he might not be painting comic strips a year or two from now—I think that would be so great, to be able to change styles. And I think that's what's going to happen, that's going to be the whole new scene. That's probably one reason I'm using silk screens now. I haven't been able to make every image clear and simple and the same as the first one. I think it would be so great if more people took up silk screens so that no one would know whether my picture was mine or somebody else's.

It would turn art history upside down?

Yes.

Is that your aim?

No. The reason I'm painting this way is that I want to be a machine, and I feel that whatever I do and do machine-like is what I want to do.

Was commercial art more machine-like?

No, it wasn't. I was getting paid for it, and did anything they told me to do. If they told me to draw a shoe, I'd do it, and if they told me to correct it, I would—I'd do anything they told me to do, correct it and do it right. I'd have to invent and now I don't; after all that "correction," those commercial drawings would have feelings, they would have a style. The attitude of those who hired me had feeling or something to it; they knew what they wanted, they insisted; sometimes they got very emotional. The process of doing work in commercial art was machine-like, but the attitude had feeling to it.

Why did you start painting soup cans?

Because I used to drink it. I used to have the same lunch every day, for twenty years, I guess, the same thing over and over again. Someone said my life has dominated me: I liked that idea. I used to want to live at the Waldorf Towers and have soup and a sandwich, like that scene in the restaurant in *Naked Lunch* . . .

We went to see *Dr. No* at Forty-second Street. It's a fantastic movie, so cool. We walked outside and somebody threw a cherry bomb right in front of us, in this big crowd. And there was blood. I saw blood on people and all over. I felt like I was bleeding all over. I saw in the paper last week that there are more people throwing them, it's just part of the scene—and hurting people. My show in Paris is going to be called "Death in America." I'll show the electric chair pictures and the dogs in Birmingham and car wrecks and some suicide pictures.

Why did you start these "Death" pictures?

I believe in it. Did you see the *Enquirer* this week? It had "The Wreck that Made Cops Cry"—a head cut in half, the arms and hands just lying there. It's sick, but I'm sure it happens all the time. I've met a lot of cops recently. They take pictures of everything, only it's almost impossible to get pictures from them.

When did you start with the "Death" series?

I guess it was the big plane crash picture, the front page of a newspaper: 129 DIE. I was also painting the *Marilyns*. I realized that everything I was doing must have been Death. It was Christmas or Labor Day—a holiday—and every time you turned on the radio they said something like "4 million are going to die." That started it. But when you see a gruesome picture over and over again, it doesn't really have any effect.

But you're still doing "Elizabeth Taylor" pictures.

I started those a long time ago, when she was so sick and everybody said she was going to die. Now I'm doing them all over, putting bright colors on her lips and eyes.

My next series will be pornographic pictures. They will look blank; when you turn on the black lights, then you see them—big breasts and . . . If a cop came in, you could just flick out the lights or turn on the regular lights—how could you say that was pornography? But I'm still just practicing with these yet. Segal did a sculpture of two people making love, but he cut it all up, I guess because he thought it was too pornographic to be art. Actually it was very beautiful, perhaps a little too good, or he may feel a little protective about art. When you read Genêt you get all hot, and that makes some people say this is not art. The thing I like about it is that it makes you forget about style and that sort of thing; style isn't really important.

Is "Pop" a bad name?

The name sounds so awful. Dada must have something to do with Pop—it's so funny, the names are really synonyms. Does anyone know what they're supposed to mean or have to do with, those names? Johns and Rauschenberg—Neo-Dada for all these years, and everyone calling them derivative and unable to transform the things they are—are now called progenitors of Pop. It's funny the way things change. I think John Cage has been very influential, and Merce Cunningham, too, maybe. Did you see that article in the *Hudson Review* [*The End of the Renaissance?*, Summer, 1963]? It was about Cage and that whole crowd, but with a lot of big words like radical empiricism and teleology. Who knows? Maybe Jap and Bob were Neo-Dada and aren't any more. History books are being rewritten all the time. It doesn't matter what you do. Everybody just goes on thinking the same thing, and every year it gets more and more alike. Those who talk about individuality the most are the ones who most object to deviation, and in a few years it may be the other way around. Some day everybody will think just what they want to think, and then everybody will probably be thinking alike; that seems to be what is happening.

Roy Lichtenstein

What is Pop Art?

I don't know—the use of commercial art as subject matter in painting, I suppose. It was hard to get a painting that was despicable enough so that no one would hang it—everybody was hanging everything. It was almost acceptable to hang a dripping paint rag, everybody was accustomed to this. The one thing everyone hated was commercial art; apparently they didn't hate that enough either.

Is Pop Art despicable?

That doesn't sound so good, does it? Well, it *is* an involvement with what I think to be the most brazen and threatening characteristics of our culture, things we hate, but which are also powerful in their impingement on us. I think art since Cézanne has become extremely romantic and unrealistic, feeding on art; it is utopian. It has had less and less to do with the world, it looks inward—neo-Zen and all that. This is not so much a criticism as an obvious observation. Outside is the world; it's there. Pop Art looks out into the world; it appears to accept its environment, which is not good or bad, but different— another state of mind.

'How can you like exploitation?' 'How can you like the complete mechanization of work? How can you like bad art?' I have to answer that I accept it as being there, in the world.

Are you anti-experimental?

I think so, and anti-contemplative, anti-nuance, anti-getting-away-from-the-tyranny-of-the-rectangle, anti-movement and-light, anti-mystery, anti-paint-quality, anti-Zen, and anti all of those brilliant ideas of preceding movements which everyone understands so thoroughly.

We like to think of industrialization as being despicable. I don't really know what to make of it. There's something terribly brittle about it. I suppose I would still prefer to sit under a tree with a picnic basket rather than under a gas pump, but signs and comic strips are interesting as subject matter. There are certain things that are usable, forceful and vital about commercial art. We're using those things—but we're not really advocating stupidity, international teenagerism and terrorism.

Where did your ideas about art begin?

The ideas of Prof. Hoyt Sherman [at Ohio State University] on perception were my earliest important influence and still affect my ideas of visual unity.

Perception?

Yes. Organized perception is what art is all about.

He taught you "how to look"?

Yes. He taught me how to go about learning how to look.

At what?

At what, doesn't have anything to do with it. It is a process. It has nothing to do with any external form the painting takes, it has to do with a way of building a unified pattern of seeing . . . In Abstract-Expressionism the paintings symbolize the idea of ground-directedness as opposed to object-directedness. You put something down, react to it, put something else down, and the painting itself becomes a symbol of this. The difference is that rather than symbolize this ground-directedness I do an object-directed appearing thing. There is humor here. The work is still ground-directed; the fact that it's an eyebrow or an almost direct copy of something is unimportant. The ground-directedness is in the painter's mind and not immediately apparent in the painting. Pop Art makes the statement that ground-directedness is not a quality that the painting has because of what it looks like . . . This tension between apparently object-directed products and actual ground-directed processes is an important strength of Pop Art.

Antagonistic critics say that Pop Art does not transform its models. Does it?

Transformation is a strange word to use. It implies that art transforms. It doesn't, it just plain forms. Artists have never worked with the model—just with the painting. What you're really saying is that an artist like Cézanne transforms what we think the painting ought to look like into something he thinks it ought to look like. He is working with paint, not nature; he's making a painting, he's forming. I think my work is different from comic strips—but I wouldn't call it transformation; I don't think that whatever is meant by it is important to art. What I do is form, whereas the comic strip is not formed in the sense

I'm using the word; the comics have shape but there has been no effort to make them intensely unified. The purpose is different, one intends to depict and I intend to unify.

Abstract-Expressionism has had an almost universal influence on the arts. Will Pop Art?

I don't know. I doubt it. It seems too particular—too much the expression of a few personalities. Pop might be a difficult starting point for a painter. He would have great difficulty in making these brittle images yield to compositional purposes . . . Interaction between painter and painting is not the total commitment of Pop, but it is still a major concern—though concealed and strained.

Do you think that an idea in painting—whether it be 'interaction' or the use of commercial art—gets progressively less with time?

It seems to work that way. Cubist and Action Painting ideas, although originally formidable and still an influence, are less crucial to us now. Some individual artists, though—Stuart Davis, for example—seem to get better and better.

A curator at the Modern Museum has called Pop Art fascistic and militaristic.

The heroes depicted in comic books are fascist types, but I don't take them seriously in these paintings—maybe there is a point in not taking them seriously, a political point. I use them for purely formal reasons, and that's not what those heroes were invented for . . . Pop Art has very immediate and of-the-moment meanings which will vanish—that kind of thing is ephemeral—and Pop takes advantage of this "meaning," which is not supposed to last, to divert you from its formal content. I think the formal statement in my work will become clearer in time. Superficially, Pop seems to be all subject matter, whereas Abstract-Expressionism, for example, seems to be all esthetic . . .

I paint directly—then it's said to be an exact copy, and not art, probably because there's no perspective or shading. It doesn't look like a painting *of* something, it looks like the thing itself. Instead of looking like a painting *of* a billboard—the way a Reginald Marsh would look— Pop Art seems to be the actual thing. It is an intensification, a stylistic intensification of the excitement which the subject matter has for me; but the style is, as you said, cool. One of the things a cartoon does is to express violent emotion and passion in a completely mechanical and removed style. To express this thing in a painterly style would dilute it; the techniques I use are not commercial, they only appear to be commercial—and the ways of seeing and composing and unifying are different and have different ends.

Is Pop Art American?
Everybody has called Pop Art "American" painting, but it's actually industrial painting. America was hit by industrialism and capitalism harder and sooner and its values seem more askew . . . I think the meaning of my work is that it's industrial, it's what all the world will soon become. Europe will be the same way, soon, so it won't be American; it will be universal.

James Rosenquist

I think critics are hot blooded. They don't take very much time to analyze what's in the painting . . .

O.K., the critics can say [that Pop artists accept the mechanization of the soul]. I think it's very enlightening that *if* we do, we realize it instead of protesting too much. It hasn't been my reason. I have some reasons for using commercial images that these people probably haven't thought about. If I use anonymous images—it's true my images have not been hot-blooded images—they've been anonymous images of recent history. In 1960 and 1961 I painted the front of a 1950 Ford. I felt it was an anonymous image. I wasn't angry about that, and it wasn't a nostalgic image either. Just an image from old magazines—when I say old, I mean 1945 to 1955—a time we haven't started to ferret out as history yet. If it was the front end of an new car there would be people who would be passionate about it, and the front end of an old car might make some people nostalgic. The images are like no-images. There is a freedom there. If it were abstract, people might make it into something. If you paint Franco-American spaghetti, they won't make a crucifixion out of it, and also who could be nostalgic about canned spaghetti? They'll bring their reactions but, probably, they won't have as many relevant ones . . .

The images are now, already, on the canvas and the time I painted it is on the canvas. That will always be seen. That time span, people will look at it and say, "why did he paint a '50 Ford in 1960, why didn't he paint a '60 Ford?" That relationship is one of the important things we have as painters. The immediacy may be lost in a hundred years, but don't forget that by that time it will be like collecting a stamp; this thing might have ivy growing around it. If it bothers to stand up—I don't know—it will belong to a stamp collector, it will have nostalgia then, But still that time reference will mean something . . .

I have a feeling, as soon as I do something, or as I do something, nature comes along and lays some dust on it. There's a relationship between nature—nature's nature—and time, the day and the hour and the minute. If you do an iron sculpture, in time it becomes rusty, it gains a patina and that patina can only get to be beautiful. A painter searches for a brutality that hasn't been assimilated by nature. I believe there is a heavy hand of nature on the artist. My studio floor could be, some people would say that is part of me and part of my paintings because that is the way I arranged it, the way things are. But it's not, because it's an accidental arrangement: it *is* nature, like flowers or other things . . .

[Paint and paint quality] are natural things before you touch them, before they're arranged. As time goes by the brutality of what art is, the idea of what art can be, changes; different feelings about things become at home, become accepted, natural . . . [Brutality is] a new vision or method to express something, its value geared right to the present time . . .

When I was a student, I explored paint quality. . . . I had paint running down my armpits. I kept looking at everything I was doing—a wall, a gasoline tank, I kept looking to see what happened, looking at a rusty surface, at the nature, at changing color. I've seen a lot of different ways paint takes form and what it does, and what excited me and what didn't. After some Abstract-Expressionist painting I did then, I felt I had to slice through all that, because I had a lot of residue, things I didn't want. I thought that I would be a stronger painter if I made most of my decisions before I approached the canvas; that way I hoped for a vision that would be more simple and direct. I don't know what the rules for Abstract-Expressionism are, but I think one is that you make a connection with the canvas and then you discover; that's what you paint and eliminate what you don't want. I felt my canvases were jammed with stuff I didn't want . . .

I'm amazed and excited and fascinated about the way things are thrust at us, the way this invisible screen that's a couple of feet in front of our mind and our senses is attacked by radio and television and visual communications, through things larger than life, the impact of things thrown at us, at such a speed and with such a force that painting and the attitudes toward painting and communication through doing a painting now seem very old-fashioned . . .

I think we have a free society, and the action that goes on in this free society allows encroachments, as a commercial society. So I geared myself, like an advertiser or a large company, to this visual inflation—in commercial advertising which is one of the foundations of our society. I'm living in it, and it has such impact and excitement in its means of imagery. Painting is probably more exciting than advertising—so why shouldn't it be done with that power and gusto, with that impact. I see very few paintings with the impact that I've felt, that I feel and try to do in my work . . . My metaphor, if that is what you can call it, is my relations to the power of commercial advertising which is in turn related to our free society, the visual inflation which accompanies the money that produces box tops and space cadets . . .

When I use a combination of fragments of things, the fragments or objects or real things are caustic to one another, and the title is also caustic to the fragments . . . The images are expendable, and the images are in the painting and therefore the painting is also expendable. I only hope for a colorful shoe-horn to get the person off, to turn him on to his own feelings . . .

The more we explore, the more we dig through, the more we learn the more mystery there is. For instance, how can I justify myself, how can I make my mark, my "X" on the wall in my studio, or in my experience, when somebody is jumping in a rocket ship and exploring outer space? Like, he begins to explore space, the deeper he goes in space the more there is of nature, the more mystery there is. You may make a discovery, but you get to a certain point and that point opens up a whole new area that's never even been touched . . .

I treat the billboard image as it is, so apart from nature. I paint it as a reproduction of other things; I try to get as far away from the nature as possible . . .

An empty canvas is full, as Bob [Rauschenberg] said. Things are always gorgeous and juicy—an empty canvas is—so I put something in to dry it up. Just the canvas and the paint—that would be nature. I see all this stuff [pointing to the texture of a canvas]—that's a whole other school of painting. All that very beautiful canvas can be wonderful, but it's another thing. The image—certainly it's juicy, too—but it throws your mind to something else, into art. From having an empty canvas, you have a painted canvas. It may have more action; but the action is like a confrontation, like a blow that cancels out a lot of other stuff, numbing your appreciation for a lot of juicy things. Then, too, somebody will ask, why do I want that image there? I don't want that image, but it's there. To put an image in, or a combination of images, is an attempt to make it at least not nature, cancel it from nature, wrest it away. Look at that fabric, there, the canvas, and the paint—those are like nature . . .

I learned a lot more about painting paint when I painted signs. I painted things from photos and I had quite a bit of freedom in the interpretation, but still, after I did it, it felt cold to me, it felt like I hadn't done it, that it had been done by a machine. The photograph was a machine-produced image. I threw myself at it. I reproduced it as photographically and stark as I could. They're still done the same way; I like to paint them as stark as I can . . .

I thought for a while I would like to use machine-made images, silk-screens, maybe. But by the time I could get them—I have specifics in my mind—it would take longer or as long, and it would be in a limited size, than if I did them as detached as I could by hand, in the detached method I learned as a commercial painter . . .

When I first started thinking like this, feeling like this, from my outdoor painting, painting commercial advertising, I would bring home colors that I like, associations that I liked using in my abstract painting, and I would remember specifics by saying this was a dirty bacon tan, this was a yellow T-shirt yellow, this was a Man-Tan suntan orange. I remember these like I was remembering an alphabet, a specific color. So then I started painting Man-Tan orange and—I always remember Franco-American spaghetti orange. I can't forget it—so I felt it as a remembrance of things, like a color chart, like learning an alphabet. Other people talk about painting nothing. You just can't do it. I paint something as detached as I can; then I have one image, that's it. But in a sense the image is expendable; I have to keep the image so that the thing doesn't become an attempt at a grand illusion, an elegance . . .

If I use a lamp or a chair, that isn't the subject, it isn't the subject matter. The relationships may be the subject matter, the relationships of the fragments I do. The content will be something more, gained from the relationships. If I have three things, their relationship will be the subject matter; but the content will, hopefully, be fatter, balloon to more than the subject matter. One thing, though, the subject matter isn't popular images, it isn't that at all.

Notes on "Camp"

Many things in the world have not been named; and many things, even if they have been named, have never been described. One of these is the sensibility—unmistakably modern, a variant of sophistication but hardly identical with it—that goes by the cult name of "Camp."

A sensibility (as distinct from an idea) is one of the hardest things to talk about; but there are special reasons why Camp, in particular, has never been discussed. It is not a natural mode of sensibility, if there be any such. Indeed the essence of Camp is its love of the unnatural: of artifice and exaggeration. And Camp is esoteric—something of a private code, a badge of identity even, among small urban cliques. Apart from a lazy two-page sketch in Christopher Isherwood's novel *The World in the Evening* (1954), it has hardly broken into print. To talk about Camp is therefore to betray it. If the betrayal can be defended, it will be for the edification it provides, or the dignity of the conflict it resolves. For myself, I plead the goal of self-edification, and the goad of a sharp conflict in my own sensibility. I am strongly drawn to Camp, and almost as strongly offended by it. That is why I want to talk about it, and why I can. For no one who wholeheartedly shares in a given sensibility can analyze it; he can only, whatever his intention, exhibit it. To name a sensibility, to draw its contours and to recount its history, requires a deep sympathy modified by revulsion.

Though I am speaking about sensibility only—and about a sensibility that, among other things, converts the serious into the frivolous—these are grave matters. Most people think of sensibility or taste as the realm of purely subjective preferences, those mysterious attractions, mainly sensual, that have not been brought under the sovereignty of reason. They *allow* that considerations of taste play a part in their reactions to people and to works of art. But this attitude is naïve. And even worse. To patronize the faculty of taste is to patronize oneself. For taste governs every free—as opposed to rote—human response. Nothing is more decisive. There is taste in people, visual taste, taste in emotion— and there is taste in acts, taste in morality. Intelligence, as well, is really a kind of taste: taste in ideas. (One of the facts to be reckoned with is that taste tends to develop very unevenly. It's rare that the same person has good visual taste *and* good taste in people *and* taste in ideas).

Taste has no system and no proofs. But there is something like a logic of taste: the consistent sensibility which underlies and gives rise to a certain taste. A sensibility is almost, but not quite, ineffable. Any sensibility which can be crammed into the mold of a system, or handled with the rough tools of proof, is no longer a sensibility at all. It has hardened into an idea. . . .

To snare a sensibility in words, especially one that is alive and powerful,* one must be tentative and nimble. The form of jottings, rather than an essay (with its claim to a linear, consecutive argument), seemed more appropriate for getting down something of this particular fugitive sensibility. It's embarrassing to be solemn and treatise-like about Camp. One runs the risk of having, oneself, produced a very inferior piece of Camp.

These notes are for Oscar Wilde.

"One should either be a work of art, or wear a work of art."
—*Phrases & Philosophies for the Use of the Young*

1. To start very generally: Camp is a certain mode of aestheticism. It is *one* way of seeing the world as an aesthetic phenomenon. That way, the way of Camp, is not in terms of beauty, but in terms of the degree of artifice, or stylization.

2. To emphasize style is to slight content, or to introduce an attitude which is neutral with respect to content. It goes without saying that the Camp sensibility is disengaged, depoliticized—or at least apolitical.

3. Not only is there a Camp vision, a Camp way of looking at things. Camp is as well a quality discoverable in objects and the behavior of persons. There are "campy" movies, clothes, furniture, popular songs, novels, people, buildings. . . . This distinction is important. True, the Camp eye has the power to transform experience. But not everything can be seen as Camp. It's not *all* in the eye of the beholder.

4. Random examples of items which are part of the canon of Camp:

Zuleika Dobson
Tiffany lamps

* The sensibility of an era is not only its most decisive, but also its most perishable, aspect. One may capture the ideas (intellectual history) and the behavior (social history) of an epoch without ever touching upon the sensibility or taste which informed those ideas, that behavior. Rare are those historical studies—like Huizinga on the late Middle Ages, Febvre on 16th century France—which do tell us something about the sensibility of the period.

Scopitone films
The Brown Derby restaurant on Sunset Boulevard in LA
The Enquirer, headlines and stories
Aubrey Beardsley drawings
Swan Lake
Bellini's operas
Visconti's direction of *Salome* and *'Tis Pity She's a Whore*
certain turn-of-the-century picture postcards
Schoedsack's *King Kong*
the Cuban pop singer La Lupe
Lynd Ward's novel in woodcuts, *God's Man*
the old Flash Gordon comics
women's clothes of the twenties (feather boas, fringed and beaded
    dresses, etc.)
the novels of Ronald Firbank and Ivy Compton-Burnett
stag movies seen without lust

5. Camp taste has an affinity for certain arts rather than others. Clothes, furniture, all the elements of visual décor, for instance, make up a large part of Camp. For Camp art is often decorative art, emphasizing texture, sensuous surface, and style at the expense of content. Concert music, though, because it is contentless, is rarely Camp. It offers no opportunity, say, for a contrast between silly or extravagant content and rich form. . . . Sometimes whole art forms became saturated with Camp. Classical ballet, opera, movies have seemed so for a long time. In the last two years, popular music (post rock-'n'-roll, what the French call *yé yé*) has been annexed. And movie criticism (like the list of "The 10 Best Bad Movies I Have Seen") is probably the greatest popularizer of Camp taste today, because most people still go to the movies in a high-spirited and unpretentious way.

6. There is a sense in which it is correct to say: "It's too good to be Camp." Or "too important," not marginal enough. (More on this later.) Thus, the personality and many of the works of Jean Cocteau are Camp, but not those of André Gide; the operas of Richard Strauss, but not those of Wagner; concoctions of Tin Pan Alley and Liverpool, but not jazz. Many examples of Camp are things which, from a "serious" point of view, are either bad art or kitsch. Not all, though. Not only is Camp not necessarily bad art, but some art which can be approached as Camp (example: the major films of Louis Feuillade) merits the most serious admiration and study.

"The more we study Art, the less we care for Nature."
                                    —*The Decay of Lying*

7. All Camp objects, and persons, contain a large element of artifice. Nothing in nature can be campy. . . . Rural Camp is still man-made, and most campy objects are urban. (Yet, they often have a serenity— or a naïveté—which is the equivalent of pastoral. A great deal of Camp suggests Empson's phrase, "urban pastoral.")

8. Camp is a vision of the world in terms of style—but a particular kind of style. It is the love of the exaggerated, the "off," of things-being-what-they-are-not. The best example is in Art Nouveau, the most typical and fully developed Camp style. Art Nouveau objects, typically, convert one thing into something else: the lighting fixtures in the form of flowering plants, the living room which is really a grotto. A remarkable example: the Paris Métro entrances designed by Hector Guimard in the late 1890s in the shape of cast-iron orchid stalks.

9. As a taste in persons, Camp responds particularly to the markedly attenuated and to the strongly exaggerated. The androgyne is certainly one of the great images of Camp sensibility. Examples: the swooning, slim, sinuous figures of pre-Raphaelite painting and poetry; the thin, flowing, sexless bodies in Art Nouveau prints and posters, presented in relief on lamps and ash-trays; the haunting androgynous vacancy behind the perfect beauty of Greta Garbo. Here, Camp taste draws on a mostly unacknowledged truth of taste: the most refined form of sexual attractiveness (as well as the most refined form of sexual pleasure) consists in going against the grain of one's sex. What is most beautiful in virile men is something feminine; what is most beautiful in feminine women is something masculine. . . . Allied to the Camp taste for the androgynous is something that seems quite different but isn't: a relish for the exaggeration of sexual characteristics and personality mannerisms. For obvious reasons, the best examples that can be cited are movie stars. The corny flamboyant femaleness of Jayne Mansfield, Gina Lollobrigida, Jane Russell, Virginia Mayo; the exaggerated he-man-ness of Steve Reeves, Victor Mature. The great stylists of temperament and mannerism, like Bette Davis, Barbara Stanwyck, Tallulah Bankhead, Edwige Feuillière.

10. Camp sees everything in quotation marks. It's not a lamp, but a "lamp"; not a woman, but a "woman." To perceive Camp in objects and persons is to understand Being-as-Playing-a-Role. It is the farthest extension, in sensibility, of the metaphor of life as theater.

11. Camp is the triumph of the epicene style. (The convertibility of "man" and "woman," "person" and "thing.") But all style, that is, artifice, is, ultimately, epicene. Life is not stylish. Neither is nature.

12. The questions isn't, "Why travesty, impersonation, theatricality?" The question is, rather, "When does travesty, impersonation, theatricality acquire the special flavor of Camp?" Why is the atmosphere of Shakespeare's comedies (As You Like It, etc.) not epicene, while that of Der Rosenkavalier is?

13. The dividing line seems to fall in the 18th century; there the origins of Camp taste are to be found (Gothic novels, Chinoiserie, caricature, artificial ruins, and so forth.) But the relation to nature was quite different then. In the 18th century, people of taste either patronized nature (Strawberry Hill) or attempted to remake it into something artificial (Versailles). They also indefatigably patronized the past. Today's Camp taste effaces nature, or else contradicts it outright. And the relation of Camp taste to the past is extremely sentimental.

14. A pocket history of Camp might, of course, begin farther back—with the mannerist artists like Pontormo, Rosso, and Caravaggio, or the extraordinarily theatrical painting of Georges de La Tour, or Euphuism (Lyly, etc.) in literature. Still, the soundest starting point seems to be the late 17th and early 18th century, because of that period's extraordinary feeling for artifice, for surface, for symmetry; its taste for the picturesque and the thrilling, its elegant conventions for representing instant feeling and the total presense of character—the epigram and the rhymed couplet (in words), the flourish (in gesture and in music). The late 17th and early 18th century is the great period of Camp: Pope, Congreve, Walpole, etc., but not Swift, les précieux in France; the rococo churches of Munich; Pergolesi. Somewhat later: much of Mozart. But in the 19th century, what had been distributed throughout all of high culture now becomes a special taste; it takes on overtones of the acute, the esoteric, the perverse. Confining the story to England alone, we see Camp continuing wanly through 19th century aestheticism (Burne-Jones, Pater, Ruskin, Tennyson), emerging full-blown with the Art Nouveau movement in the visual and decorative arts, and finding its conscious ideologists in such "wits" as Wilde and Firbank.

15. Of course, to say all these things are Camp is not to argue they are simply that. A full analysis of Art Nouveau, for instance, would scarcely equate it with Camp. But such an analysis cannot ignore what in Art Nouveau allows it to be experienced as Camp. Art Nouveau is full of "content," even of a political-moral sort; it was a revolutionary

movement in the arts, spurred on by a utopian vision (somewhere between William Morris and the Bauhaus group) of an organic politics and taste. Yet there is also a feature of the Art Nouveau objects which suggests a disengaged, unserious, "aesthete's" vision. This tells us something important about Art Nouveau—and about what the lens of Camp, which blocks out content, is.

16. Thus, the Camp sensibility is one that is alive to a double sense in which some things can be taken. But this is not the familiar split-level construction of a literal meaning, on the one hand, and a symbolic meaning, on the other. It is the difference, rather, between the thing as meaning something, anything, and the thing as pure artifice.

17. This comes out clearly in the vulgar use of the word Camp as a verb, "to camp," something that people do. To camp is a mode of seduction—one which employs flamboyant mannerisms susceptible of a double interpretation; gestures full of duplicity, with a witty meaning for cognoscenti and another, more impersonal, for outsiders. Equally and by extension, when the word becomes a noun, when a person or a thing is "a camp," a duplicity is involved. Behind the "straight" public sense in which something can be taken, one has found a private zany experience of the thing.

"To be natural is such a very difficult pose to keep up."
—*An Ideal Husband*

18. One must distinguish between naïve and deliberate Camp. Pure Camp is always naïve. Camp which knows itself to be Camp ("camping") is usually less satisfying.

19. The pure examples of Camp are unintentional; they are dead serious. The Art Nouveau craftsman who makes a lamp with a snake coiled around it is not kidding, nor is he trying to be charming. He is saying, in all earnestness: Voilà! the Orient! Genuine Camp—for instance, the numbers devised for the Warner Brothers musicals of the early thirties (*42nd Street*; *The Golddiggers of 1933*; . . . *of 1935*; . . . *of 1937*; etc.) by Busby Berkeley—do not *mean* to be funny. Camping—say, the plays of Noël Coward—does. It seems unlikely that much of the traditional opera repertoire could be such satisfying Camp if the melodramatic absurdities of most opera plots had not been taken seriously by their composers. One doesn't need to know the artist's private intentions. The work tells all. (Compare a typical 19th century opera with Samuel Barber's *Vanessa*, a piece of manufactured, calculated Camp, and the difference is clear.)

20. Probably, intending to be campy is always harmful. The perfection of *Trouble in Paradise* and *The Maltese Falcon*, among the greatest Camp movies ever made, comes from the effortless smooth way in which tone is maintained. This is not so with such famous would-be Camp films of the fifties as *All About Eve* and *Beat the Devil*. These more recent movies have their fine moments, but the first is so slick and the second so hysterical; they want so badly to be campy that they're continually losing the beat. . . . Perhaps, though, it is not so much a question of the unintended effect versus the conscious intention, as of the delicate relation between parody and self-parody in Camp. The films of Hitchcock are a showcase for this problem. When self-parody lacks ebullience but instead reveals (even sporadically) a contempt for one's themes and one's materials —as in *To Catch a Thief*, *Rear Window*, *North by Northwest*—the results are forced and heavy-handed, rarely Camp. Successful Camp—a movie like Carné's *Drôle de Drame*; the film performances of Mae West and Edward Everett Horton; portions of the Goon Show—even when it reveals self-parody, reeks of self-love.

21. So, again, Camp rests on innocence. That means Camp discloses innocence, but also, when it can, corrupts it. Objects, being objects, don't change when they are singled out by the Camp vision. Persons, however, respond to their audiences. Persons begin "camping": Mae West, Bea Lillie, La Lupe, Tallulah Bankhead in *Lifeboat*, Bette Davis in *All About Eve*. (Persons can even be induced to camp without their knowing it. Consider the way Fellini got Anita Ekberg to parody herself in *La Dolce Vita*.)

22. Considered a little less strictly, Camp is either completely naïve or else wholly conscious (when one plays at being campy). An example of the latter: Wilde's epigrams themselves.

"It's absurd to divide people into good and bad. People are either charming or tedious."

—*Lady Windemere's Fan*

23. In naïve, or pure, Camp, the essential element is seriousness, a seriousness that fails. Of course, not all seriousness that fails can be redeemed as Camp. Only that which has the proper mixture of the exaggerated, the fantastic, the passionate, and the naïve.

24. When something is just bad (rather than Camp), it's often because it is too mediocre in its ambition. The artist hasn't attempted

to do anything really outlandish. ("It's too much," "It's too fantastic," "It's not to be believed," are standard phrases of Camp enthusiasm.)

25. The hallmark of Camp is the spirit of extravagance. Camp is a woman walking around in a dress made of three million feathers. Camp is the paintings of Carlo Crivelli, with their real jewels and *trompe-l'-oeil* insects and cracks in the masonry. Camp is the outrageous aestheticism of Sternberg's six American movies with Dietrich, all six, but especially the last, *The Devil Is a Woman*. . . . In Camp there is often something *démesuré* in the quality of the ambition, not only in the style of the work itself. Gaudí's lurid and beautiful buildings in Barcelona are Camp not only because of their style but because they reveal— most notably in the Cathedral of the Sagrada Familia—the ambition on the part of one man to do what it takes a generation, a whole culture to accomplish.

26. Camp is art that proposes itself seriously, but cannot be taken altogether seriously because it is "too much." *Titus Andronicus* and *Strange Interlude* are almost Camp, or could be played as Camp. The public manner and rhetoric of de Gaulle, often, are pure Camp.

27. A work can come close to Camp, but not make it, because it succeeds. Eisenstein's films are seldom Camp because, despite all exaggeration, they do succeed (dramatically) without surplus. If they were a little more "off," they could be great Camp—particularly *Ivan the Terrible I & II*. The same for Blake's drawings and paintings, weird and mannered as they are. They aren't Camp; though Art Nouveau, influenced by Blake, is.

What is extravagant in an inconsistent or an unpassionate way is not Camp. Neither can anything be Camp that does not seem to spring from an irrepressible, a virtually uncontrolled sensibility. Without passion, one gets pseudo-Camp—what is merely decorative, safe, in a word, chic. On the barren edge of Camp lie a number of attractive things: the sleek fantasies of Dali, the haute couture preciosity of Albicocco's *The Girl with the Golden Eyes*. But the two things—Camp and preciosity—must not be confused.

28. Again, Camp is the attempt to do something extraordinary. But extraordinary in the sense, often, of being special, glamorous. (The curved line, the extravagant gesture.) Not extraordinary merely in the sense of effort. Ripley's Believe-It-Or-Not items are rarely campy. These items, either natural oddities (the two-headed rooster, the eggplant in the shape of a cross) or else the products of immense labor (the man who walked from here to China on his hands, the woman who engraved

the New Testament on the head of a pin), lack the visual reward—the glamour, the theatricality—that marks off certain extravagances as Camp.

29. The reason a movie like *On the Beach*, books like *Winesburg, Ohio* and *For Whom the Bell Tolls* are bad to the point of being laughable, but not bad to the point of being enjoyable, is that they are too dogged and pretentious. They lack fantasy. There is Camp in such bad movies as *The Prodigal* and *Samson and Delilah*, the series of Italian color spectacles featuring the super-hero Maciste, numerous Japanese science fiction films (*Rodan, The Mysterians, The H-Man*) because, in their relative unpretentiousness and vulgarity, they are more extreme and irresponsible in their fantasy—and therefore touching and quite enjoyable.

30. Of course, the canon of Camp can change. Time has a great deal to do with it. Time may enhance what seems simply dogged or lacking in fantasy now because we are too close to it, because it resembles too closely our own everyday fantasies, the fantastic nature of which we don't perceive. We are better able to enjoy a fantasy when it is not our own.

31. This is why so many of the objects prized by Camp taste are old-fashioned, out-of-date, *démodé*. It's not a love of the old as such. It's simply that the process of aging or deterioration provides the necessary detachment—or arouses a necessary sympathy. When the theme is important, and contemporary, the failure of a work of art may make us indignant. Time can change that. Time liberates the work of art from moral relevance, delivering it over to the Camp sensibility. . . . Another effect: time contracts the sphere of banality. (Banality is, strictly speaking, always a category of the contemporary.) What was banal can, with the passage of time, become fantastic. Many people who listen with delight to the style of Rudy Vallee revived by the English pop group, The Temperence Seven, would have been driven up the wall by Rudy Vallee in his heyday.

Thus, things are campy, not when they become old—but when we become less involved in them, and can enjoy, instead of being frustrated by, the failure of the attempt. But the effect of time is unpredictable. Maybe "Method" Acting (James Dean, Rod Steiger, Warren Beatty) will seem as Camp some day as Ruby Keeler's does now—or as Sarah Bernhardt's does, in the films she made at the end of her career. And maybe not.

32. Camp is the glorification of "character." The statement is of no importance—except, of course, to the person (Loie Fuller, Gaudí, Cecil B. De Mille, Crivelli, de Gaulle, etc.) who makes it. What the

Camp eye appreciates is the unity, the force of the person. In every move the aging Martha Graham makes she's being Martha Graham, etc., etc. . . . This is clear in the case of the great serious idol of Camp taste, Greta Garbo. Garbo's incompetence (at the least, lack of depth) as an *actress* enhances her beauty. She's always herself.

33. What Camp taste responds to is "instant character" (this is, of course, very 18th century); and, conversely, what it is not stirred by is the sense of the development of character. Character is understood as a state of continual incandescence—a person being one, very intense thing. This attitude toward character is a key element of the theatricalization of experience embodied in the Camp sensibility. And it helps account for the fact that opera and ballet are experienced as such rich treasures of Camp, for neither of these forms can easily do justice to the complexity of human nature. Wherever there is development of character, Camp is reduced. Among operas, for example, *La Traviata* (which has some small development of character) is less campy than *Il Trovatore (which has none)*.

"Life is too important a thing ever to talk seriously about it."
—Vera, or The Nihilists

34. Camp taste turns its back on the good-bad axis of ordinary aesthetic judgment. Camp doesn't reverse things. It doesn't argue that the good is bad, or the bad is good. What it does is to offer for art (and life) a different—a supplementary—set of standards.

35. Ordinarily we value a work of art because of the seriousness and dignity of what it achieves. We value it because it succeeds—in being what it is and, presumably, in fulfilling the intention that lies behind it. We assume a proper, that is to say, straightforward relation between intention and performance. By such standards, we appraise *The Iliad*, Aristophanes' plays, The Art of the Fugue, *Middlemarch*, the paintings of Rembrandt, Chartres, the poetry of Donne, *The Divine Comedy*, Beethoven's quartets, and—among people—Socrates, Jesus, St. Francis, Napoleon, Savonarola. In short, the pantheon of high culture: truth, beauty, and seriousness.

36. But there are other creative sensibilities besides seriousness (both tragic and comic) of high culture and of the high style of evaluating people. And one cheats oneself, as a human being, if one has *respect* only for the style of high culture, whatever else one may do or feel on the sly.

For instance, there is the kind of seriousness whose trademark is anguish, cruelty, derangement. Here we do accept a disparity between intention and result. I am speaking, obviously, of a style of personal existence as well as of a style in art; but the examples had best come from art. Think of Bosch, Sade, Rimbaud, Jarry, Kafka, Artaud, think of most of the important works of art of the 20th century, that is, art whose goal is not that of creating harmonies but of overstraining the medium and introducing more and more violent, and unresolvable, subject-matter. This sensibility also insists on the principle that an *oeuvre* in the old sense (again, in art, but also in life) is not possible. Only "fragments" are possible. . . . Clearly, different standards apply here than to traditional high culture. Something is good not because it is achieved, but because another kind of truth about the human situation, another experience of what it is to be human—in short, another valid sensibility—is being revealed.

And third among the great creative sensibilities is Camp: the sensibility of failed seriousness, of the theatricalization of experience. Camp refuses both the harmonies of traditional seriousness, and the risks of fully identifying with extreme states of feeling.

37. The first sensibility, that of high culture, is basically moralistic. The second sensibility, that of extreme states of feeling, represented in much contemporary "avant-garde" art, gains power by a tension between moral and aesthetic passion. The third, Camp, is wholly aesthetic.

38. Camp is the consistently aesthetic experience of the world. It incarnates a victory of "style" over "content," "aesthetics" over "morality," of irony over tragedy.

39. Camp and tragedy are antitheses. There is seriousness in Camp (seriousness in the degree of the artist's involvement) and, often, pathos. The excruciating is also one of the tonalities of Camp; it is the quality of excruciation in much of Henry James (for instance, *The Europeans, The Awkward Age, The Wings of the Dove*) that is responsible for the large element of Camp in his writings. But there is never, never tragedy.

40. Style is everything. Genet's ideas, for instance, are very Camp. Genet's statement that "the only criterion of an act it is elegance"* is virtually interchangeable, as a statement, with Wilde's "in matters of great importance, the vital element is not sincerity, but style." But what counts, finally, is the style in which ideas are held. The ideas

---

* Sartre's gloss on this in *Saint Genet* is: "Elegance is the quality of conduct which transforms the greatest amount of being into appearing."

about morality and politics in, say, *Lady Windemere's Fan* and in *Major Barbara* are Camp, but not just because of the nature of the ideas themselves. It is those ideas, held in a special playful way. The Camp ideas in *Our Lady of the Flowers* are maintained too grimly, and the writing itself is too successfully elevated and serious, for Genet's books to be Camp.

41. The whole point of Camp is to dethrone the serious. Camp is playful, anti-serious. More precisely, Camp involves a new, more complex relation to "the serious." One can be serious about the frivolous, frivolous about the serious.

42. One is drawn to Camp when one realizes that "sincerity" is not enough. Sincerity can be simple philistinism, intellectual narrowness.

43. The traditional means for going beyond straight seriousness— irony, satire—seem feeble today, inadequate to the culturally oversaturated medium in which contemporary sensibility is schooled. Camp introduces a new standard; artifice as an ideal, theatricality.

44. Camp proposes a comic vision of the world. But not a bitter or polemical comedy. If tragedy is an experience of hyperinvolvement, comedy is an experience of underinvolvement, of detachment.

"I adore simple pleasures, they are the last refuge of the complex."
—*A Woman of No Importance*

45. Detachment is the prerogative of an elite; and as the dandy is the 19th century's surrogate for the aristocrat in matters of culture, so Camp is the modern dandyism. Camp is the answer to the problem: how to be a dandy in the age of mass culture.

46. The dandy was overbred. His posture was disdain, or else *ennui*. He sought rare sensations, undefiled by mass appreciation. (Models: Des Esseintes in Huysmans' *À Rebours, Marius the Epicurean*, Valéry's *Monsieur Teste*.) He was dedicated to "good taste."

The connoisseur of Camp has found more ingenious pleasures. Not in Latin poetry and rare wines and velvet jackets, but in the coarsest, commonest pleasures, in the arts of the masses. Mere use does not defile the objects of his pleasure, since he learns to possess them in a rare way. Camp—Dandyism in the age of mass culture—makes no distinction between the unique object and the mass-produced object. Camp taste transcends the nausea of the replica.

47. Wilde himself is a transitional figure. The man who, when he first came to London, sported a velvet beret, lace shirts, velveteen knee-breeches and black silk stockings, could never depart too far in his life

from the pleasures of the old-style dandy; this conservatism is reflected in *The Picture of Dorian Gray*. But many of his attitudes suggest something more modern. It was Wilde who formulated an important element of the Camp sensibility—the equivalence of all objects—when he announced his intention of "living up" to his blue-and-white china, or declared that a door-knob could be as admirable as a painting. When he proclaimed the importance of the necktie, the boutonniere, the chair, Wilde was anticipating the democratic *esprit* of Camp.

48. The old-style dandy hated vulgarity. The new-style dandy, the lover of Camp, appreciates vulgarity. Where the dandy would be continually offended or bored, the connoisseur of Camp is continually amused, delighted. The dandy held a perfumed handkerchief to his nostrils and was liable to swoon; the connoisseur of Camp sniffs the stink and prides himself on his strong nerves.

49. It is a feat, of course. A feat goaded on, in the last analysis, by the threat of boredom. The relation between boredom and Camp taste cannot be overestimated. Camp taste is by its nature possible only in affluent societies, in societies or circles capable of experiencing the psychopathology of affluence.

> "What is abnormal in Life stands in normal relations to Art. It is the only thing in Life that stands in normal relations to Art."
> —*A Few Maxims for the Instruction of the Over-Educated*

50. Aristocracy is a position vis-à-vis culture (as well as vis-à-vis power), and the history of Camp taste is part of the history of snob taste. But since no authentic aristocrats in the old sense exist today to sponsor special tastes, who is the bearer of this taste? Answer: an improvised self-elected class, mainly homosexuals, who constitute themselves as aristocrats of taste.

51. The peculiar relation between Camp taste and homosexuality has to be explained. While it's not true that Camp taste is homosexual taste, there is no doubt a peculiar affinity and overlap. Not all liberals are Jews, but Jews have shown a peculiar affinity for liberal and reformist causes. So, not all homosexuals have Camp taste. But homosexuals, by and large, constitute the vanguard—and the most articulate audience—of Camp. (The analogy is not frivolously chosen. Jews and homosexuals are the outstanding creative minorities in contemporary urban culture. Creative, that is, in the truest sense: they are creators of sensibilities. The two pioneering forces of modern sensibility are Jewish moral seriousness and homosexual aestheticism and irony.)

52. The reason for the flourishing of the aristocratic posture among homosexuals also seems to parallel the Jewish case. For every sensibility is self-serving to the group that promotes it. Jewish liberalism is a gesture of self-legitimization. So is Camp taste, which definitely has something propagandistic about it. Needless to say, the propaganda operates in exactly the opposite direction. The Jews pinned their hopes for integrating into modern society on promoting the moral sense. Homosexuals have pinned their integration into society on promoting the aesthetic sense. Camp is a solvent of morality. It neutralizes moral indignation, sponsors playfulness.

53. Nevertheless, even though homosexuals have been its vanguard, Camp taste is much more than homosexual taste. Obviously, its metaphor of life as theater is peculiarly suited as a justification and projection of a certain aspect of the situation of homosexuals. (The Camp insistence on not being "serious," on playing, also connects with the homosexual's desire to remain youthful.) Yet one feels that if homosexuals hadn't more or less invented Camp, someone else would. For the aristocratic posture with relation to culture cannot die, though it may persist only in increasingly arbitrary and ingenious ways. Camp is (to repeat) the relation to style in a time in which the adoption of style—as such—has become altogether questionable. (In the modern era, each new style, unless frankly anachronistic, has come on the scene as an antistyle.)

"One must have a heart of stone to read the death of Little Nell without laughing."

—In conversation

54. The experiences of Camp are based on the great discovery that the sensibility of high culture has no monopoly upon refinement. Camp asserts that good taste is not simply good taste; that there exists, indeed, a good taste of bad taste. (Genet talks about this in *Our Lady of the Flowers*.) The discovery of the good taste of bad taste can be very liberating. The man who insists on high and serious pleasures is depriving himself of pleasure; he continually restricts what he can enjoy; in the constant exercise of his good taste he will eventually price himself out of the market, so to speak. Here Camp taste supervenes upon good taste as a daring and witty hedonism. It makes the man of good taste cheerful, where before he ran the risk of being chronically frustrated. It is good for the digestion.

55. Camp taste is, above all, a mode of enjoyment, of appreciation— not judgment. Camp is generous. It wants to enjoy. It only seems like

malice, cynicism. (Or, if it is cynicism, it's not a ruthless but a sweet cynicism.) Camp taste doesn't propose that it is in bad taste to be serious; it doesn't sneer at someone who succeeds in being seriously dramatic. What it does is to find the success in certain passionate failures.

56. Camp taste is a kind of love, love for human nature. It relishes, rather than judges, the little triumphs and awkward intensities of "character.". . . Camp taste identifies with what it is enjoying. People who share this sensibility are not laughing at the thing they label as "a camp," they're enjoying it. Camp is a *tender* feeling.

(Here, one may compare Camp with much of Pop Art, which—when it is not just Camp—embodies an attitude that is related, but still very different. Pop Art is more flat and more dry, more serious, more detached, ultimately nihilistic.)

57. Camp taste nourishes itself on the love that has gone into certain objects and personal styles. The absence of this love is the reason why such kitsch items as *Peyton Place* (the book) and the Tishman Building aren't Camp.

58. The ultimate Camp statement: it's good *because* it's awful. . . . Of course, one can't always say that. Only under certain conditions, those which I've tried to sketch in these notes.

THE
LITERATURE

What can escape the artist's eye? Virtually every aspect of the American experience considered in this book is dealt with, squarely or peripherally, in the selections which follow.

Since his premature death, Lenny Bruce has emerged as a spokesman for the young because he relentlessly and brilliantly satirized deeply rooted prejudices of our culture. In his obsessively hilarious monologue, "The Dirty-Word Concept," Bruce vilifies a society that has stigmatized words describing natural functions, and, by extension, the natural functions themselves. According to Bruce, this repression has resulted in a distorted view of obscenity, which condones violence and murder while refusing to concede that a "Men's Room" is really a "Toilet." Lawrence Ferlinghetti's powerful litany "I Am Waiting" pleads for a rebirth of wonder in a time of apathy. The paralysis and self-alienation caused by the emphasis on the machine is the theme of John Tytell's "Meditation in a Machine." LeRoi Jones writes about the Negro in "Black Bourgeoisie," as do Alan and David Arkin in their lyric "The Klan" (we must recommend Richie Havens' rendition to appreciate its power).

George Economou and Jackson Mac Low have poems on the Vietnam War and oppression at home, respectively, the latter a "chance" poem, which depends as much on the environment in which it is read, and the nature of the performance, as on the words themselves. Barry Wallenstein's "John Lied" might also be called a chance or "concrete" poem, and could thus be related to McLuhan's notions of the simultaneous and nonlinear. Tom Paxton, in "Talking Vietnam Pot Luck Blues," humorously urges introducing marijuana as the bargaining agent to "end all hostilities" in Vietnam—while elevating spirits on both sides. Chet Powers' lyric "Get Together" (particularly as recorded by the Youngbloods) plaintively calls for an alliance of love to replace our separateness—an aspect of the "hippie" protest conveniently overlooked by many in the "establishment." Edward Field's disarming "Graffiti," also about love, recalls Norman Brown's words about reclaiming our body from its mental bondage. Susan Sontag's "Notes on 'Camp'" comes to mind as Toby Olson "recaps" the career of Gorgeous George. The selections from Denise Levertov, Gary Snyder, Mark Strand, and Robert Vas Dias, though quite different from each other in several ways, might all be seen to contain aspects of Zen in in that they encourage the act of living in contrast to the stasis of reading—even poetry! Harold Jaffe's Assassination, a one-act play which concludes the section, contains characters and situations which suggest the comic-strip recreations of Pop artists like Roy Lichtenstein.

The Dirty-Word Concept

If you've ever seen this bit before, I want you to tell me, stop me.
I'm going to piss on you.
Now, I tell you this because some of the ringsiders have objected to it,
and it's just fair to warn you, that's all. I don't make any great show
of it—I just do it, and that's all. You can't photograph it—it's like rain.

The point of view there is to help you with bad early toilet training. That
fact is that you and I have had such bad early toilet training, that the
worst sound in the world to all of us is when that toilet-flush noise
finishes before you do. I never could go over to your house and say:
"Excuse me, where's the toilet?"
I have to get hung up with that corrupt facade of
"Where's the little boy's room?"
"Oh, you mean the tinkle-dinkle ha-ha room? Where they have just
sashays and cough drops and pastels?"
"Yeah. I wanna shit in the cough-drop box."
"Oh, awright."
The *tsi gurnischt* is what puts you into the toilet every time, Jim. And
unfortunately, intellectual awareness does you no good.

And you know why we got this—this is really weird—the censorship?
It's motivated by bad early toilet training. Every time—
OLD WOMAN "He made a *sissy*! Call the police."
Yeah.
OLD WOMAN "Get the policeman up here, he made a *sissy*. He's not
gonna make it no more? Get the probation officer. That's all."
So if you're thirty-six years old, you drive down the street, you see the
red light in the rear vision mirror—you just crap out:
COP You know what you did?
"Yeah. I made a sissy."
COP What?
"I dunno, I . . . What'd I do?"
COP You made an illegal left turn!
"Oh, damn, I'm pissed with me. I'm no goddam good, man."
That's it. That's the dues.

Words, boy, they're too much. Forget it. Let's see. I started in show

Lenny Bruce, "The Dirty-Word Concept." Reprinted by permission of the
Douglas International Corporation and The Lenny Bruce Estate.

business in '50. I won the Arthur Godfrey Show, then I went to the Strand in New York, then, about ten years ago, I went right into the toilet, *Bong!*

But at this time I did, let's see, the Robert Q. Lewis Show, Broadway Open House, Arthur Godfrey and His Friends Show, and the comment of the day was:

"Lenny, you're gonna go a long way, because you're—you're not like those other comics, you don't have to resort to filthy toilet jokes. Anybody can get a laugh on toilet jokes, but you're clever . . ."

And I started thinking about that. I was proud, but then I started thinking, "How dirty is my toilet?" Yeah. That's sort of strange, that I have to resort to it, or even protest against it, or my bedroom—toilet jokes, bedroom jokes.

Then I would just lay in bed, and I wouldn't even say that word at that time, you know, I'd just think it, you know, then I'd thunder out of the bedroom and dash open the door and

"*Look* at you, you *dirty, dopey, Commie toilet,* you! And the tub and the hamper—you should know better."

Alright. I'm going to do something you never thought I'd do on stage. I'm going to a bit now that I was arrested for. I'm going to tell you the dirtiest word you've ever heard on stage. It is just *disgusting!*

I'm not going to look at you when I say it, cause this way we won't know who said it. I may blame that cat over there. It's a four-letter word, starts with an 's' and ends with a 't' . . . and . . . just don't take me off the stage, just . . . don't embarrass my Mom. I'll go quietly.

The word is—Oh, I'm going to *say* it and just get it *done* with. I'm tired of walking the streets.

[*Whispers*] "Snot!"

I can't look at you. But that's the word: snot. I know a lot of my friends are thinking now,

"He's so clever, and then, for a cheap laugh, he says 'snot.' He don't need that, that disgusting character."

But do you know anything about snot? Except that every time you heard it you go *Phah!* Or *Ich!* or *Keeriste!?* Do you think I would just take snot out of left field and use it for the shock value? *Nada.*

Suppose I tell you something about snot, something that was so unique about snot that you'd go:

"Is that the *truth* about snot?"

"Look, I'm gonna lie to ya? That's *right.* That's about snot."

"How do ya like that! I never knew that."
Cause you never listen, that's why. If you'd listen all the time, then
you'd learn about snot. I'll tell you something about snot—no. I know,
you're smug:

"We know all we wanna know about snot. We smoked that stuff
when we were kids."

Well, I've done some research about snot. How about this about snot:
you can't get snot off a suede jacket! Take any suede jacket straight from
Davega's and throw it in the cleaners and try to run out of the store:

"*Wait! Stop them!* Alright, block the door. *Get them!* Tell the wife
to stand over there. . . . Son, is this your jacket?"

"Well, . . . yeah."

"Son, do you know what this is on the sleeve of the jacket?"

"No."

"*You wanna go downtown?!*"

"No."

"Well, what's on the sleeve?"

"Well . . . ah . . . *snot.*"

"Son, you know you can't get snot off suede. It's a killer. Kills
velvet too."

"No, I didn't know that. I didn't know that it was snot."

"*You knew that was snot,* son. You can't get snot off suede. It's
ruined. You can flake it off, but the black mark will always be there."

"What'll I do?"

"Just snot all over the whole jacket! That's the only thing you
can do."

"Do you do that work?"

"No. There's no money in it. Can't get help."

Now, you've seen a lot of snot. You've seen it in back of radiators in
Milner hotels. Looks like bas-relief woodglue.

Now, I'm going to show you some snot. Just cause I like you—if I
really like you, boy! Then it's a show. Would Jack Benny or Bob Hope
show you any snot? Fake snot, from the magic store, maybe.

O.K. Snot. Snot that fools old Jewish mothers:

[*Jewish accent*] "You blew your nose in the *Playboy Magazine*
again?"

Here we go [*blows his nose*]. I did it! And I did it for one reason: to
show you how well adjusted I am. Why do I say I'm well adjusted?
Why?

Cause I didn't look later.

Now we see the same man, not well adjusted. See? Slow motion.
A lot of people say to me,
"Lenny, how come you don't look later?"
A lot of people ask me that:
"You never look *once?*"
"Nope! Nope. If you've seen one, you've seen 'em all."
Now I got a handful of snot! That's what I got.
"Which hand has the M&M? Agh! *Snot!*"
I'm going to take it and put it on the piano. Now, when the pianist
comes back for the intermission, she'll think it's a note:
"Oh, a request! They haven't forgotten the old tunes. Strange
envelope. . . . *Foo!* That's *snot!*"

The hangup is that the word repression—I'll tell you better this way.
You know—what is it, on Forty-Eighth Street here, next to the Latin
Quarter?—Fun Shops, they call them, those whoopee-cushion stores,
the stores that sell unjoyous buzzers, vomit, dog-crap. It's really bizarre.
It's fool-your-friend, hurt-your-friend, put a fly in his ice-cube.
"We have a cute little article here, it's, it's fake dog crap."
"*What?*"
"Yeah—fake dog shit—very humorous. Ya see, we take this fake
dog crap and we put it on the stairs, see"—
"Now who would buy that?"
"Oh, there's a market for it."
"Well, it doesn't seem very humorous to—"
"Oh, yeah—cause you can take it two ways, see? It's *double
entendre*. It could be real dog shit or fake dog crap. And then we
have this fake vomit—"
"*Now get the hell outta here!* There's no market—"
"I'm tellin' ya there's a market for it. You just donno how it works,
see?"
"Well, just don't bring the samples up here, that's all."
"Look. I mean, just picture this. See, here's what happens. The guy
comes home, see? The wife puts the fake dog shit on the stairs.
The real vomit or the fake vomit or the real dog shit and the fake
vomit, see. And he comes home and goes
'Yippee! Dog shit!'
And he grabs it and goes
'Ahhh, it's *fake!* Oh, here's some vomit!'
That's fake too, and then he cries his eyes out—and that's the fun.
That's after he drinks the fly in the sugar cube."

"Well, I dunno. That's certainly, a weird kind of humor."

If I could just rob fifty words out of your head I could stop the war. Just like that, Jim! It would end. *Pow!* Fifty words. Semantics. *Pchew! PowPowPow!* Take 'em away.

Hotel—three in the morning—filthy word. Motel—every "well" comedian, as opposed to the "sick" comedian, has given motels such a *schmutz* connotation that I couldn't ask my *grandmother* to go to a motel if I wanted to give her a Gutenburg Bible.

So hotel is dirty and motel is dirty—where's there a clean place to take some lady? A clean word that won't offend anyone.

Trailer!

GUY Hey, do you wanna come to my trailer?

GIRL All right. There's nothing dirty about trailers. Trailers are hunting and fishing and Salem cigarettes. Yes. Yes, of course I'll come to your trailer. Where is it?

GUY Inside my hotel room.

Then it's dirty again, man.

Here's a tip how the word suppression, the dirty words that you swallow, are a deterrent to this community. There is a disease called leukemia. Leukemia, there's no specific cure for. Talking about leukemia certainly would not help it. Here's a disease that's above that. How come? Cause no one talks about it. In fact, when the Community Chest hits on you, do you say,

"Excuse me, how much of my buck is going to the clap?"

Did you? No, I don't think you did. Why didn't you?

[*Aggressive male voice*] "Well son, I don't ask about the clap because only bums get it."

"Oh, I see."

"And communists!"

And seven million war heroes that must be bums and communists.

"Awright, whaddya wannus to do? Just get some people that's had it not to cop out?—

ELEANOR ROOSEVELT GAVE LOU GEHRIG THE CLAP!"

"O.K., that's good."

"Gave it to Chiang Kai-shek, too. That's why he couldn't get the puttees on."

You see, if you or I ever had it, the doctor would never cop out to us. Lose the account?

"Mrs. Schekner, you got the clap."
Forget it!
"Little discharge, dear, we're gonna give you a little, ah, tell you
      what, ah, I got a little, ah, vitamin-booster, a little penicillin."
No. She's not hip. No.

I wonder: if I were to work to a Bert Parks kind of audience—he smiles
when he defecates—and I were to ask,
      "Hey, I wonder how many of the family people out here, how many
      of the daughters—fifteen-year-olds and older—might have the
      clap?"
I'm sure there would be a portion of the audience that would want to
punch me out.
      Wouldn't you assume that the guy who would feel some hostility
toward me for verbalizing, just asking that question, if his daughter
had the clap—what if his daughter *had* the clap? Is she going to go to
her daddy? I doubt it.
      And V.D., right up on top—although with Aureomycins you could
whack it out in one day. But it stays there.
      "Well, you see, leukemia you get in a respectable way, that's all.
      You know how you get the clap, and, ah . . ."
Because, *doing it*, well, that's about the dirtiest thing we can do. But
dig how we have screwed the country. Dig what the good-good culture's
done to you.
      You only know this if you're about thirty-five or so, and you made at
least some of the war, the good war, the war that I was in, from '42 to
'45. And you know that if that four-letter word is dirty and doing it is
dirty—the good people don't do it, nuns and priests don't do it, and
someday we're going to rise above the physical and the carnal, the lustful
—well, you agree that it's not the nicest act. In fact, you don't want me
to do it to your mother or your sister. You get arrested for doing it in
the street. It's a filthy, rotten act.
      That's why they don't like Americans anywhere. That's why we have
lost the world completely—because we fucked all of their mothers for
chocolate bars. And don't you forget it, Jim. Don't ever forget that.
      And if you don't think those kids have heard that since 1942—that
bumper crop—those kids that now are twenty-three years old, that's now
in control—
      "Do you know what happened? Do you know what those Americans
      did to your poor mother while your poor father threw up his guts
      in the next room while those soldiers lined up your mother for their

stinking eggs and the chocolate bars and their friggin cigarettes?
Those bastards! What they did with their money over here!"
And that goes from Marseilles, St. Tropez, all the way, Jim, to Con-
stantinople. That's all they've heard, Jim. Those cats over there were
duking with their bread.

Now, intellectual awareness does them no good. They know, like, if
I'm hungry, I'll sell my sister's ass for an egg. It doesn't do any good
knowing it: it happened, Jim.

If this society was the least little bit correct, if religion helped it out
a little bit, and that act was the least bit the antithesis of what is
perverse, and you felt that it was a true Christian act of procreation, if it
was sweet hugging and kissing—watch. The fellow comes off the plane:

> BRITISH VOICE Is that the fellow who fucked Mother? Oh, yes! How
> *are* you? *Damn,* I haven't seen you in *so* long, and you're such a
> *wonderful* person. You certainly made Mother feel *good.* I certainly
> would like to *thank* you—that certainly was a nice thing to do. And
> I understand you gave her some candy besides.

But we don't agree that it's a nice act. It's a filthy, dirty act. In fact,
that's what any eighteen-year-old chick or thirty-year-old chick will tell
you when you take her out:

"You don't *love* me, you just want to *ball* me."

Boy! Listen to that:

> GIRL He was a *nice guy*—he didn't try to fool around with me.
> But *you* don't love me, you just want to ball me.
> GUY *What?* Of course I love you—I wouldn't want to sleep with
> you if I didn't love you.
> GIRL No, no. If you loved me you'd drive me to Wisconsin; punch
> me in the mouth; read the Bible to me all night; you'd borrow
> money from me. You wouldn't want to ball me. You don't do that
> to someone you love—you do that to somebody you hate. Really
> *hate.*

In fact, when you *really* hate them, what's the vernacular we use?

"*Screw you,* mister!"

If you were taught it was a sweet Christian act of procreation, it was the
nicest thing we can do for each other, you'd use the term correctly,
and say

"*Unscrew* you, mister."

But the best people in the tribe don't do it.

But you won't admit that—that they think doing it is dirty, filthy.
They'll never admit that the clap is here—they'll never admit that their

son *has it*. Their son has the clap—where can the son go? Can that boy go to his father? *Bullshit* he can go to his old man. He could never relate to his father. He can't even go to the doctor; he's lucky if he can go to some *schmuck* who sweeps up a drugstore:

"Hey Manny, mop later, can I talk to ya?"

"What is it?"

"I got the clap."

"You? Where'd ya get that?"

"Painting a car, *schmuck!* What's the difference? I got it."

"So whaddaya want from me? Why don't you go to your father? Why don't ya go to a doctor?"

"I can't. Gimme some pills—you work in a drug store."

"Awright. Here."

"Dexedrine spansules . . . Is this good?"

"Yeah, it's all the same horseshit. This is good—keeps you awake, so you know you got it."

"Awright. The reason I want these pills, I got a good job, and I donwanna lay off."

"Oh yeah? Where ya working?"

"The meat-packing plant. Want a couple of steaks?"

"No! Just burn the doorknobs on the way out. Do me a favor—stop kissing my mother goodbye, O.K."

Maybe Jerry Lewis would go on television, and instead of getting hung up with muscular dystrophy, he'd have a Clap-a-thon.

Dear Anne Landers:

This summer I met a boy on vacation, and I fell madly in love with him, even though he admitted he had a boy back home. As a result of our affection I became in a motherly way. I'm all mixed up—I'm only three years old. What'll I do?

Dear Knocked Up:

Call Doctor Mendoza, Tijuana 1-7300.

It's very tough. It's very tough to stop the information. That's where it's all at. Because the word itself is of no consequence. What the constitution forbids is any bar to the communication system. It doesn't want nobody to abridge the right to say it one time, and one time to hear it.

Because the information makes the country strong. Because a knowledge of syphilis is not an instruction to get it. Because if you don't have the knowledge of it, and you just know about the good, and they just let the good come through, seeping through, what they think is good, you end up like Hitler. Cause he really got screwed around like that. He kept saying,

HITLER Am I doing all right?
FIRST AIDE You're doing *great!* They *love* you.
HITLER Don't bullshit, Marty. Someday they don't like me—
FIRST AIDE They *love* you!
SECOND AIDE Don't listen to those liars!
HITLER *Kill him!* Who said that?

Now, the daughter that you love, yeah, the daughter that you love, the daughter that you kill in the back of a taxicab because of a bad curettage—that's how you love that daughter, because she's a tramp, because she's got life in her belly and she ain't got a hoop on her finger that some witch doctor blessed—that's how you love that daughter. That's that *roch munas* you've got for that daughter, that she can just talk to her old man just like that. Snap! When I hear that cat saying,
    "Ah, that tramp! My wife's a tramp, and I got custody of my kids."
    "Your wife's a tramp? Whaddaya mean—sterno, and the woods and all?"
    "No, you know what kinda tramp I mean."
    "No I don't, man, I dunno what kinda tramp you mean at all."
    "She goes to bed with guys."
    "Well that's certainly a very Christian act. I can't think of anything nicer to do for any guy."
    "Yeah, but she does it in front of the kids."
Well, I am not that well adjusted yet, but you know, man, I would rather your kids see that than you yelling at your old lady or whacking her out. In fact, I guess it really is no deterrent to his growth to see that, no. Isn't that the nicest time? Or is balling just balling? Or is it just that—you just carry around a little aspirin box and make it with that:
    "Gimme a little bufferin."
    "There it is—a buck and a half."
Chungchungchung! That's it.

The dirty-word concept is beautiful. Postmaster Summerfield is concerned with reporting any pornography and any Tilly and Mack books you have lying around. Right? Now, for your child, who is perhaps in the formative years, for his viewing in the schoolyard are the dirty books, the smut peddlers which Postmaster Summerfield is concerned with—and justly so: these are formative years. But how about some other films that he's not concerned with?

Psycho, for example. If your kid's going to see a dirty movie, and be affected by it, then you must assume he'll be affected by *Psycho*. We have Anthony Perkins, a psychotic misogynist who kills a beautiful chick, Janet Leigh. No reason at all, man. Method: stabbing in the shower, blood down the drain. Method of disposal of body: wrapping it in the shower curtain, *schlepping* it to the swamp, doing her in. For no purpose, man—death, destruction.

Now, the stag movie, the dirty movie—the sixteen millimeter reduction print that you drag from lodge hall to lodge hall, the dirty movie that the Kefauver committee would destroy and then recreate for private parties. Let's inspect the subject matter. What are they doing, that couple?

I can't think of anybody getting killed in that picture. I can't see anyone getting slapped in the mouth, rapped around. Is there any hostility in that film? No. Just a lot of hugging and kissing. And the first time one instrument of death appeared—that pillow that might have smothered the chick—it went under her ass, and that was the end of the picture.

Please tell me what the hell the couple is doing that's that rank, vicious, rotten. The only thing I find offensive in that film is that from an art concept, cinematically, it's a bore. Yeah, those *schtup* pictures—forget it, man. No idea of the sensual, there's no music track, you know. But as far as hurting your child—what are they doing, that couple?

No. it's vicious and rotten and dirty—that you've bred a generation of faggots and misogynists, lady-haters and homosexuals.

Well, it's part of our culture that we teach our children: "These are your eyes, your nose, your mouth—and your *ga-ga*." Part of the guilt for the dirty I'm sure relates back to several hundred thousands of years ago —when everybody was giving up something for the Lord—and how guys would cap each other and wait around, and put it up on the bulletin board, and one guy said,

"I love the Lord better'n anybody in the tribe. I'm giving up nine rivers for the Lord. Write it down. How about you?"

"Seventeen rivers, ten farms. That's for the Lord. How about you?"

"Well, today I'm gonna be the best man in the tribe cause I'm giving up seventy-eight rivers, fifty-five farms, ten sheep, six oxen, and a mountain for the Lord."

And St. Paul just watched these people, and after everyone had chucked in, and the best man in the tribe had stated he was best man by giving almost all away, St. Paul said,

"Wait a minute! Before you give out the prize for the best man in the tribe, I'm going to give up something for the Lord you'll all remember: *F-U-C-K NO MORE PAUL!* That's it!"

"Hey, Paul, are you bullshittin or somtin? You're givin at up? Faw how long?"

"I'm giving it up for ever and ever!"

"Just to prove a point, huh?" Well, that's *ridiculous*. He's, ah . . ."

"*The best man in the tribe.*"

Why?

"Cause I don't do it, that's why. You who do it—second best. And you who *talk* about it—*we'll bust your ass*. Celibacy is the way."

It's the clean way, it's the best way. So all the *schtuppers* . . . turn into *fressers!* Ha ha! Didn't figure on that! That would really be weird.

Now. You'd assume that in a society that says, "Alright, this is clean; this is dirty"—that in the entertainment capital of that society, the entertainment capital of the world, Les Vegas, that the attraction would be the most austere. What's the attraction at Las Vegas?

"Well, at the Stardust we have the Passion Play."

"Correct; then they're consistent. What follows the Passion Play?"

"Well, I think they're having a Monet exhibit, then Eugene Ormandy and the New York City ballet. It's a very spiritual type of show."

Is that the attraction that all the purists support in Las Vegas? No. What's the attraction? Tits and ass.

"*I beg your pardon?*"

"Ah, tits and ass, that's what the attraction is."

"*Just* tits and ass?"

"Oh, no. An Apache team and tits and ass."

"Well, that's about all I actually go to see—the Apache team. And that's just one hotel. What's the second biggest attraction?"

"More tits and ass."

"*Get off it!* The third?"

"Tits and ass, and more ass, and tits, and ass and tits and ass and tits and ass."

"Do you mean to tell me that *Life* magazine would devote three full pages to tits and ass?"

"Yes. Right next to the article by Billy Graham and Norman

Vincent Peale. *Life* and *Look* and *Nugget* and *Rogue* and *Dude* and *Cavalier* and *Swank* and *Gent* and *Pageant* (the Legion of Decency's *Playboy*) and millions of other stroke books—the antecedent to *Playboy, National Geographic* with the African chicks—oh yes, they're stroke books."

It takes the seriousness out of everything if you can imagine Kennedy in back of the bathroom door whacking it to Miss July once in a while.

I stroke it once in a while; I assume he does.

"Ah, well, that may be the truth, but you just can't put TITS AND ASS NITELY up on the marquee outside on the strip."

"Why not?"

"*Why not!* Cause it's *dirty* and *vulgar*, that's why not!"

"Titties are dirty and vulgar? Well, they're not to me, I like to hug 'em and kiss 'em."

"No, you're not going to bait me. It's not the titties, it's the words, the way you relate."

"I don't believe you. I believe to you it's the titty that's dirty. Cause I'll change the words to TUCHUSES AND NAY-NAYS NITELY.

"Hmmmm. That's a little better."

"Well, you're not anti-semitic. That's point one for you. But how about making it very austere—Latin: GLUTIUS MAXIMUS AND PECTORALIS MAJORS NITELY."

"Now that's *clean!*"

"To you, *schmuck*, but it's dirty to the Latins. And the fact that you're an illiterate doesn't get you off the hook."

"Well, I don't care what you say, you just can't put TITS AND ASS up there. You have to have something a little, ah—LA NOVELLE VOGUE! LA PARISIENNE!"

"Ah, the Follies! Lou Walters! French tits and ass. Class with ass."

"I'll buy that. Unless I can have something patriotic—how about THE MOST AMERICAN GIRLS IN THE WORLD?"

"American tits and ass—Grandma Moses' tits and Norman Rockwell's ass: draw my ass and win a Buick. My ass you can draw; you can draw my ass! My ass you can draw."

That's why the *word* isn't dirty—the *titties* are dirty. Oh yeah. The titties are *filthy*. That's why you can't have a marquee reading

TITS AND ASS NITELY

Uh um. Cause the titties are dirty and vulgar. And if we deny that—then it's all a lie.

Here's how the titties work. If the titty is bloodied and maimed, it's clean. But if the titty is pretty, it's filthy.

There's a time and place for the titty. That's why you never see any obscenity photos that are atrocity photos. Um Um. Any titty that's cut off and distended, that's good.

Yeah, its really weird.

Eleanor Roosevelt had nice tits. She really did. A friend of mine saw them and said they were terrific. That's not disrespectful; in fact, she would have liked that, I think. Yeah. He walked into the bedroom and she was fixing—

GUY Excuse me.

ELE That's all right. You were looking at my tits, weren't you?

GUY Well, I wasn't looking *at* them, I was looking at everything— the wall, and everything—

ELE That's all right. You can look at them.

GUY Uh, they're O.K.

ELE People say they're the nicest tits ever. Ever ever ever.

GUY They really are nice tits. Could I touch them?

ELE No. no. Nope. Cause a lot of people want to touch them and then they'd touch them too much. That's all. Just look at them. Just look at them and say they're nice tits.

GUY Awright—they're nice tits. In fact, I'm gonna tell my friends how nice they are. Heh heh. And what a terrific person you are for showing them to me.

Touch it once, touch it once.

What's "it"? That's what I got busted for: "It." "It" is Clara Bow. But I cannot be superstitious with that, the *double entendre*. Because to me your titties are no joke. They're pretty and they're not humorous to me. It's not a hahaha. That elbow-nudging sly-innuendo hahaha you-know-what-it-means, that Jack Paar with his cool, Alexander King the junkie Mark Twain—your Uncle Willie, who I would never let baby-sit for me. *He's* a nice moralist—when you're eleven years old he's grabbing your sister:

"What a *nice* little tickle-ikle-ikle!"

"Yeah, I'm hip, you tickle-ikle-ikle."

I Am Waiting

I am waiting for my case to come up
and I am waiting
for a rebirth of wonder
and I am waiting for someone
to really discover America
and wail
and I am waiting
for the discovery
of a new symbolic western frontier
and I am waiting
for the American Eagle
to really spread its wings
and straighten up and fly right
and I am waiting
for the Age of Anxiety
to drop dead
and I am waiting
for the war to be fought
which will make the world safe
for anarchy
and I am waiting
for the final withering away
of all governments
and I am perpetually awaiting
a rebirth of wonder

I am waiting for the Second Coming
and I am waiting
for a religious revival
to sweep thru the state of Arizona
and I am waiting
for the Grapes of Wrath to be stored
and I am waiting
for them to prove
that God is really American
and I am seriously waiting
for Billy Graham and Elvis Presley
to exchange roles seriously

and I am waiting
to see God on television
piped onto church altars
if only they can find
the right channel
to tune in on
and I am waiting
for the Last Supper to be served again
with a strange new appetizer
and I am perpetually awaiting
a rebirth of wonder

I am waiting for my number to be called
and I am waiting
for the living end
and I am waiting
for dad to come home
his pockets full
of irradiated silver dollars
and I am waiting
for the atomic tests to end
and I am waiting happily
for things to get much worse
before they improve
and I am waiting
for the Salvation Army to take over
and I am waiting
for the human crowd
to wander off a cliff somewhere
clutching its atomic umbrella
and I am waiting
for Ike to act
and I am waiting
for the meek to be blessed
and inherit the earth
without taxes
and I am waiting
for forests and animals
to reclaim the earth as theirs
and I am waiting
for a way to be devised
to destroy all nationalisms
without killing anybody
and I am waiting

for linnets and planets to fall like rain
and I am waiting for lovers and weepers
to lie down together again
in a new rebirth of wonder

I am waiting for the Great Divide to be crossed
and I am anxiously waiting
for the secret of eternal life to be discovered
by an obscure general practitioner
and save me forever from certain death
and I am waiting
for life to begin
and I am waiting
for the storms of life
to be over
and I am waiting
to set sail for happiness
and I am waiting
for a reconstructed Mayflower
to reach America
with its picture story and tv rights
sold in advance to the natives
and I am waiting
for the lost music to sound again
in the Lost Continent
in a new rebirth of wonder

I am waiting for the day
that maketh all things clear
and I am waiting
for Ole Man River
to just stop rolling along
and I am waiting
for the deepest South
to just stop Reconstructing itself
in its own image
and I am waiting
for a sweet desegregated chariot
to swing low
and carry me back to Ole Virginie
and I am waiting
for Ole Virginie to discover
just why Darkies are born
and I am waiting

for God to lookout
from Lookout Mountain
and see the *Ode to the Confederate Dead*
as a real farce
and I am awaiting retribution
for what America did
to Tom Sawyer
and I am perpetually awaiting
a rebirth of wonder

I am waiting for Tom Swift to grow up
and I am waiting
for the American Boy
to take off Beauty's clothes
and get on top of her
and I am waiting
for Alice in Wonderland
to retransmit to me
her total dream of innocence
and I am waiting
for Childe Roland to come
to the final darkest tower
and I am waiting
for Aphrodite
to grow live arms
at a final disarmament conference
in a new rebirth of wonder

I am waiting
to get some intimations
of immortality
by recollecting my early childhood
and I am waiting
for the green mornings to come again
youth's dumb green fields come back again
and I am waiting
for some strains of unpremeditated art
to shake my typewriter
and I am waiting to write
the great indelible poem
and I am waiting
for the last long careless rapture
and I am perpetually waiting
for the fleeing lovers on the Grecian Urn

to catch each other up at last
and embrace
and I am awaiting
perpetually and forever
a renaissance of wonder

Patriotic Poem

George Washington, your name is on my lips.
You had a lot of slaves.
I don't like the idea of slaves. I know I am
a slave to
too many masters, already
a red cardinal flies out of the pine tree in my eye swooping
down to crack a nut and the bird feeds on a tray draped with
a thirteen-starred flag. Underneath my heart where the fat clings
like bits of wool
I want to feel a man slipping his hand inside my body
massaging the heart, bathing
it in stripes, streams of new blood with stars floating in it
must pass through my arteries, each star pricking
the walls of veins with the prickly sensation of life.
The blood is old,
perhaps was shipped from Mt. Vernon
which was once a blood factory.
Mr. Washington, the pseudo aristocrat with two large fish instead of
feet, slapping around the plantation,
managing the country with surveyor's tools,
writing documents with sweet potatoes, yams, ham hocks, and black-eyed
peas,
oh I hate southern gentlemen, too bad he was one;
somehow I've always hated the men who ran my country
but I was a loyal citizen. "Take me to your leader,"
and I'll give him a transfusion of my AB negative blood with stars
floating in it. I often said this
in a spirit of devotion, chauvinistic passion,
pining secretly for the beautiful Alexander Hamilton but making do with
George who, after all, was the first president
and I need those firsts. On my wall, yes the wall of my stomach;
on my money, yes play money and real money, money I spend and
money I save, in and out of pocket; on documents, and deeds, statuary,
monuments, books, pictures, trains, old houses, whiskey bottles, and
even sewing machine shuttles there is his name
and my commitment, after all, is to names, how else, to what else
do we commit ourselves but names
and George I have committed myself to you. No Western sheriffs for me;
they only really like men and horses and sometimes gun play.
I guess I'm stuck with you, George, despite your absolute inability

to feel anything personal, or communicate it,
or at least share it with me.
Thank you at least for being first in your white linen and black coat.
My body, the old story, is my country, the only territory I control
and it certainly has been torn by wars. I'd like to think the
Revolution is over and that at last I am going to have my first president, at last I can have an inaugural ball;
the white house of my corpuscles
asks for new blood; I have given so many transfusions to others
When will you make me your first lady, George?
When will I finally become the first president's wife?

Meditation in a Machine

Precise mechanisms
Love us —JOHN ASHBERY: *"Europe"*

I

inside the whirring
assemblage
spinning wheels
hammering shafts
time an oiled
movement of steel

everything in this
room of tight screws
regulated and perfect

no flower stems
break
in your wind

here a man
could meditate
without soul

all this circumstance
of steel and springs
substitutes

II

some minds
riot
with precision

just fling one
hand
into the whirring wheel

watch the pistons
smash
each other

John Tytell, "Meditation in a Machine." Used by permission of the author.

breaking
through their
containment

the oil runs
smoother than blood
more colorfully

suggesting rust
and flowers springing
through the springs

Black Bourgeoisie

has a gold tooth, sits long hours
on a stool, thinking about money.
sees white skin in a secret room
rummages his sense for sense
dreams about Lincoln(s)
conks his daughter's hair
sends his coon to school
works very hard
grins politely in restaurants
has a good word to say
never says it
does not hate ofays
hates, instead, him self
him black self.

The Klan

The country-side was cold and still,
There was a cross upon the hill,
This cold cross wore a burning hood
To hide its rotten heart of wood.
Father, I hear the iron sound
of hoofbeats on the frozen ground.

Down from the hills the riders came,
Jesus, it was a crying shame
To see the blood upon their whips
And hear the snarling of their lips.
Mother, I feel a stabbing pain—
Blood flows down like summer rain.

Now each one wore a mask of white
To hide his cruel face from sight,
And each one sucked a little breath
Out of the empty lungs of death.
Sister, lift my bloody head,
It's so lonesome to be dead.

He who travels with the Klan
Is a monster and not a man,
Underneath that white disguise
I have looked into his eyes.
Brother, will you stand with me?
It's not easy to be free.

If Politicians Would Learn from Poets

Since they never overcome
their boyhood dreams to be
the biggest pricks
                in our body politic
let politicians learn from poets
                   if they will
the honest speech of an erection
                  unequivocal
and full
   of heart's blood's
desire
   to do something
unmistakably human.

Jail Break

(for Emmett Williams & John Cage) September 1963, April & August 1966

Tear now jails down all.
Tear all now down jails.
Tear now all jails down.
Tear jails now all down.
Tear jails now down all.
Tear now jails all down.
Tear now down all jails.
Tear all down jails now.
Tear jails down all now.
Tear jails all down now.
Tear all jails down now.
Tear jails all now down.
Tear jails down now all.
Tear down now all jails.
Tear now all down jails.
Tear down now jails all.
Tear now down jails all.
Tear down all jails now.
Tear down jails all now.
Tear all jails now down.
Tear all now jails down.
Tear down jails now all.
Tear down all now jails.
Tear down all now jails.

All jails now down tear.
All now tear down jails.
All jails down tear now.
All now jails down tear.
All now down tear jails.
All jails now tear down.
All tear now jails down.
All jails down now tear.
All down now tear jails.
All tear down jails now.
All tear jails down now.
All now down jails tear.
All down tear now jails.
All down tear jails now.
All down now jails tear.
All down jails now tear.
All down jails tear now.
All tear jails now down.
All now tear jails down.
All tear down now jails.
All jails tear now down.
All now jails tear down.
All jails tear down now.
All tear now down jails.

jails tear down all now.
jails tear down now all.
jails down now all tear.
jails now tear down all.
jails now tear all down.
jails tear now down all.
jails tear now all down.
jails all tear now down.
jails tear all now down.
jails all tear down now.
jails all down tear now.
jails now down all tear.
jails tear all down now.
jails down all tear now.
jails down now tear all.
jails now all tear down.
jails down tear all now.
jails now all down tear.
jails all down now tear.
jails down tear now all.
jails all now tear down.
jails down all now tear.
jails now down tear all.
jails all down now tear.

enviroing sounds, & let what they hear modify how they speak. In Way 1 they must be able to improvise together, let performance flow & their own impulses determine how they speak. Way 2 needs a precise conductor & 5 speakers who follow him accurately.

MATERIALS: 120 small cards, 5 equal squares of poster board (8 to 28 inches a side), paint/ink, pen/brush; for Way 1, 10 envelopes each large enough to hold 24 cards with room for easy removal & insertion of cards.

of sign easiest to handle; size, colors, letter shapes most visible in performance situation. Make 5 square signs, each with one of the 5 words on it. For Way 1 attach 2 envelopes to each sign back & put the 24 cards whose texts begin with the sign's word in one.

PERFORMANCE: Way 1: The speakers line up, holding signs parallel in the order TEAR DOWN ALL JAILS NOW. Each draws a card, listens closely to other speakers & environment until he & the situation are ready, then speaks the words as a connected sentence making good sense. Speed, loudness & voice coloration are free. He puts the card in the empty envelope & draws another, &c., until he's read each card once. It ends after last speaker finishes. Way 2: Lined up as above, speakers face conductor, who shuffles the 120 cards & draws one, pointing in turn, in the permutation's order, to each word's bearer, who says the word, connecting it with the others so the sentence makes sense tho said he said by 5. Way 2 needs long intense rehearsal; ends when all 120 permutations are read. Way 2 performed (2nd Jail Poets' Reading, Living Theatre, 9 Sept. 1963) by Judith Malina, Tom Cornell, Paul Prensky, & 2 others, conducted by JML. Way 1 1st performed in rain (reading against USSR jailing of writers, 30 April 1966: WIN, II, 9: 6-7) by JML, Paul Blackburn, Jerome Rothenberg, David Antin, & the Rt. Revd. Michael F. Itkin.

Jackson Mac Low, "Jail Break." Reprinted from Win magazine. © 1966 by Jackson Mac Low. Reprinted by permission of Win and the author, Jackson Mac Low, 1764 Popham Avenue, Bronx, New York 10453.

Down tear now jails all.
Down now tear jails all.
Down tear all jails now.
Down all now tear jails.
Down jails tear all now.
Down jails all tear now.
Down now all jails tear.
Down all jails now tear.
Down all tear now jails.
Down jails now tear all.
Down now jails all tear.
Down jails now all tear.
Down tear jails now all.
Down now all tear jails.
Down now tear all jails.
Down jails tear now all.
Down tear jails all now.
Down all jails tear now.
Down tear all now jails.
Down all now jails tear.
Down all tear jails now.
Down jails all now tear.
Down all now tear jails.
Down now all tear jails.

Now all down tear jails.
Now down all tear jails.
Now tear down jails all.
Now jails all down tear.
Now jails all tear down.
Now jails tear down all.
Now down jails all tear.
Now all tear jails down.
Now all tear down jails.
Now down all jails tear.
Now jails down all tear.
Now tear down all jails.
Now tear all down jails.
Now all down jails tear.
Now tear jails down all.
Now jails down tear all.
Now down tear all jails.
Now all jails tear down.
Now all jails down tear.
Now tear jails all down.
Now jails tear all down.
Now down tear jails all.
Now down jails tear all.
Now all jails tear down.

Poem Against the Rich

Each day I live, each day the sea of light
Rises, I seem to see
The tear inside the stone
As if my eyes were gazing beneath the earth.
The rich man in his red hat
Cannot hear
The weeping in the pueblos of the lily,
Or the dark tears in the shacks of the corn.
Each day the sea of light rises
I hear the sad rustle of the darkened armies,
Where each man weeps, and the plaintive
Orisons of the stones.
The stones bow as the saddened armies pass.

John Lied

There were rabbits in every fold
Watching, John saw
rabbits in every fold

After a decade of calm
rabbits in every fold

About all that
John lied   There were no rabbits
There were 30 men shot
There were thirty men shot

Who did did did it

(John is a liar
John lies for power)
    never tell never   never   never
    never tell STOP never   never
    never never never never   never
    never never never never   never
    never never never never   never
    I remember days of no falling
    never never never never   never
    never never never never   never
    FALLEN ROCK ZONE never never
    DANGER and DANGER and DANGER
    & never PROCEED WITH CAUTION
    & NO CROSSING   & dead DEER

Barry Wallenstein, "John Lied." Reprinted from *The Massachusetts Review*,
© 1969, The Massachusetts Review, Inc.

Talking Vietnam Pot Luck Blues

When I landed in Vietnam,
I hardly got to see Saigon
They shaped us up and called the roll,
And off we went on a long patrol,
Swattin' flies, swappin' lies
Firin' the odd shot here and there.

The captain called a halt that night
And we had chow by the pale moonlight.
A lovely dinner they planned for us—
With a taste like a seat on a crosstown bus.
Some of the veterans left theirs in the cans
    for the Viet Cong to find . . .
Deadlier than a land mine.

Well naturally somebody told a joke
And a couple of fellas began to smoke.
I took a whiff as a cloud rolled by
And my nose went up like an infield fly.
The captain, this blond fella from Yale, said,
"What's the matter with you, baby?"

Well, I may be crazy, but I think not.
I'd swear to God that I smell pot.
But who'd have pot in Vietnam?
He said, "What do you think you're sittin' on?"
These little plants, thousands of them.
Good God almighty . . . *Pastures of Plenty!*

We all lit up and by and by
The whole platoon was flying high.
With a beautiful smile on the captain's face
He smelled like midnight on St. Mark's Place.
Cleaning his weapon, chanting the Hare Krishna.

The moment came, as it comes to all,
When I had to answer Nature's call.
I was stumbling around in a beautiful haze
When I met a little cat in black P.J.'s,
Rifle, ammo-belt, B. F. Goodrich sandals.

He looked up at me and said,
"Whatsa' matta wit-choo, baby?"

He said, "We're campin' down the pass
And smelled you people blowin' grass,
And since by the smell you're smokin' trash
I brought you a taste of a special stash
straight from uncle Ho's victory garden.
We call it Hanoi Gold."

So his squad and my squad settled down
And passed some lovely stuff around.
All too soon it was time to go.
The captain got on the radio . . .
"Hello, Headquarters. We have met the enemy—
And they have been smashed!"

White Rabbit

One pill makes you larger
And one pill makes you small.
And the ones that mother gives you
Don't do anything at all.
Go ask Alice
When she's ten feet tall.

And if you go chasing rabbits
And you know you're going to fall.
Tell 'em a hookah smoking caterpillar
Has given you the call.
Call Alice
When she was just small.

When men on the chessboard
Get up and tell you where to go.
And you've just had some kind of mushroom
And your mind is moving low.
Go ask Alice
I think she'll know.

When logic and proportion
Have fallen sloppy dead,
And the White Knight is talking backwards
And the Red Queen's lost her head

Remember what the dormouse said:
"Feed your head.
Feed your head.
Feed your head."

Get Together

Love is but the song we sing
And fear's the way we die.
You can make the mountains ring
Or make the angels cry.
Know the dove is on the wing
And you need not know why.
C'mon people now—smile on your brother,
Let's get together
Try and love one another right now.

Some will come and some will go
And we shall surely pass
When the one who left us here
Returns for us at last,
We are but a moment's sunlight,
Fading on the grass
C'mon people now—smile on your brother
Hey let's get together
And love one another right now.

If you heard the song I sing
Then you must understand.
You hold the key to love and fear
All in your trembling hand.
One key unlocks them both you know
And it's at your command.
C'mon people now—smile on your brother,
Let's get together
Try and love one another right now.

Chet Powers, "Get Together." Copyright © 1963. IRVING MUSIC, INC.

Graffiti

An Excerpt from *Sex Stories*

When the Men's Room was being demolished
to make way for a newer model, all steel and cement,
he broke in, holding his breath against the ancient stink,
and cut out an old wooden partition between the booths,
with its writings and pictures, and its glory holes,
some sealed repeatedly by the authorities
and others barely begun
where defects in the wood allowed pencil points to dig in
and one well-used one hacked out with knives and fingernails
with dried come encrusted on the rim
decorated with lips of mouth and cunt,
and around that, the cheeks of an ass;

and telephone numbers saying "call me"
and dates and times when free and where,
and descriptions of partners wanted
and acts or roles desired:
  Sex slave, white, looking for black master
  Got a sister? Fix me up. Signed, Desperate
  Couple marié cherche troisième
  Have six hard inches meet me here tonight
and true sex stories written out at length,
and instructive drawings of the sex organs in all positions
some half-washed out by the char, or painted over
but dug so deep or traced lovingly so often
they were still visible through the paint;
and still faintly seen but nearly overwhelmed at last,
the political slogans of past generations.

He took that whole wall, the size of a school blackboard,
figured over as it was like an oriental temple,
the work of a people, a folk artifact,
the record of lifetimes of secret desires,
the forbidden and real history of man,
and leaving it just as it was, hung it up in his house.

Respecting tradition
he charged everyone a nickel to see it.

Gorgeous George

He wore
gold bobby-pins in his hair,
and raised turkeys

in California
years before the Olympic Stadium was air conditioned,
and old ladies swilled beer and yelled and sweated.

In the ring he would prance and strut
like a turkey, and say
"mess up my hair and I'll kill you"
But they always did it, escaping
barely with their lives.

His specialty
was the Flying-Mare.

He was a gentleman
in his golden briefs and curled locks,
and yet he was dainty.

Each Christmas
he gave away 500 turkeys
to orphan homes.

This was before
faggots were openly common
in California.

Toby Olson, "Gorgeous George," from *The Wrestlers*, The Pierrepont Press, Brooklyn, New York, 1969. Reprinted by permission of the author.

To the Reader

As you read, a white bear leisurely
pees, dyeing the snow
saffron,

and as you read, many gods
lie among lianas: eyes of obsidian
are watching the generations of leaves,

and as you read
the sea is turning its dark pages,
turning
its dark pages.

Things to Do Around San Francisco

Catch eels in the rocks below the Palace of the Legion of
    Honor.
Four in the morning—congee at Sam Wo.
Walk up and down Market, upstairs playing pool,
Turn on at Aquatic park—seagulls steal   bait-sardine
Going clear out to Oh's to buy bulghour.
Howard street goodwill—
Not paying traffic tickets; stopping the phone.
Merry-go-round at the beach, the walk up to the cliff-house,
    sea-lions and tourists—the old washed-out road
      that goes on—
Play chess at Mechanics'
Dress up and go looking for work.
Seek out the Wu-t'ung trees, park arboretum.
Suck in the sea air and hold it;
      miles of white walls
      sunset shoots back from somebody's window
      high in the Piedmont hills
Get drunk all the time. Go someplace and score.
Walk in and walk out of the Asp
Walk up Tam
Keep quitting and starting at Berkeley
Watch the Pike in the Steiner Aquarium:
                he doesn't move.
Sleeping with strangers
Keeping up on the news
Chanting sutras after sitting
Practising yr frailing on guitar;

Get dropped off   in the fog   in the night
Fall in love twenty times
Get divorced
Keep moving—move out to the Sunset—
Get lost   or
Get found

"Things to Do Around San Francisco" and "Things to Do Around a Ship at
Sea" first appeared in *Poetry*, December, 1966. Copyright © 1966 by The
Modern Poetry Association. Reprinted by permission of the Editor of *Poetry*,
and by permission of the author, Gary Snyder.

Things to Do Around a Ship at Sea

Go out with a small flashlight and a star chart, on a good night,
    and check out the full size of Eridanus.
Sunbathe on a cot on the boatdeck
Go forward and talk to the lookout, away from the engines,
    the silence and shudder
Watch running lights pass in the night.
Phosphorescing creatures alongside the shipside,
    burning spots in the wake.
Stag, Argosy, Playboy, and Time.
Do pushups.
Make Coffee in the galley, telling jokes.
Type letters to his girl friend in Naples for the
    twelve-to-four Oiler
Sew up jeans.
Practise tying knots and whipping
With the Chief Cook singing blues
Tell big story lies
Grow a beard
Learn to weld and run a lathe
Study for the Firemans Oilers and Watertenders exam
Tropic- and sea-bird watching
Types of ships
Listening to hours of words and lifetimes—fuck & shit—
Figuring out the revolution.
Hammer pipes and flanges
Paint a picture on a bulkhead with leftover paints
Jack off in the shower
Dream of girls, about yr girl friend, writing letters, wanting
    children,
Making plans.

Eating Poetry

Ink runs from the corners of my mouth.
There is no happiness like mine.
I have been eating poetry.

The librarian does not believe what she sees.
Her eyes are sad
and she walks with her hands in her dress.

The poems are gone.
The light is dim.
The dogs are on the basement stairs and coming up.

Their eyeballs roll,
their blond legs burn like brush.
The poor librarian begins to stamp her feet and weep.

She does not understand.
When I get on my knees and lick her hand,
she screams.

I am a new man.
I snarl at her and bark.
I romp with joy in the bookish dark.

Mark Strand, "Eating Poetry." Reprinted with permission from *The New York Review of Books*. Copyright © 1967 The New York Review.

Dump Poem

This is a genuine used poem
last-year's model poem
shirt off someone's back poem
chair minus a leg poem
scrap husk and rind poem
steakbone poem.
You can smell this poem when the wind is right
for miles, around it swoop
herring gulls and great-black-backed gulls,
leaves of a rainsoaked paperback now dry
flutter around it, and graffiti of stripped wallpaper.
This poem is to be thrown out
sprinkled with kerosene
set afire so you can hear its juices
sizzling and its light bulbs popping:
bulldozed, buried, used for fill.

Robert Vas Dias, "Dump Poem." Reprinted from *Sumac*. Copyright © 1968 by The Sumac Press.

Assassination: A Subway Ride in One Act

Characters

NARRATOR *wears various costumes, but retains same face, a luminescent skeleton's mask, which, however, does not cover his mouth*

FEMALE MODEL *curvy and young*

WOMAN FROM THE AUDIENCE *speaks her mind; wears a placard around her neck which reads "Plain Talk"; she should sit in the middle of the theater*

BALD RUSSIAN *salacious looking (though in his 60s); his placard reads "Smoked Meat"*

YOUNG MAN *of the wiseguy Wall Street clerk variety; his placard reads "Punk"*

BLACK MAN IN AFRICAN DRESS (BLACK 1) *in his late 20s; placard reads "Black"*

BLACK MAN IN BEGGAR'S GARB (BLACK 2) *in his late 20s or early 30s; obverse side of placard reads "White," reverse reads "Black"*

YOUNG WOMAN *late 20s; has taught herself to be "bohemian" and tolerant; her placard reads "Suck for Peace"; she carries a shopping bag*

NUN *no older than 40; placard reads "God."*

HASSIDIC RABBINICAL STUDENT *early 20s, unworldly, preoccupied; placard reads "God"*

JUNIOR EXECUTIVE *late 20s or early 30s; sonorous midwestern voice, attache case; placard reads "Money"*

HIPPY *late teens or early 20s; bearded, barefoot, contemplative; placard reads "Love"*

BEAR *someone in a bear outfit; a bear's head will do*

MANNEQUINS *can be made of cardboard*

Setting: *Subway car, horizontal view; seats facing audience are on either side of an open door (the only door the passengers use throughout the play), and are empty. Seated, with their backs to the audience, on either side of a closed door, are animal* MANNEQUINS: *a gorilla, a giraffe, any large bird, and three or four other animals (at the director's discretion), and a large human-type* MANNEQUIN *wearing a ten-gallon hat. There are two blackboard panels: stage front left and stage front right.*

Harold Jaffe, *Assassination: A Subway Ride in One Act*. Used by permission of the author.

The passengers—one or two at a time, except for BLACK 2 and
MODEL who are off stage—should walk through the audience to the edge
of stage left where each purchases from the NARRATOR (in his newspaper
vendor's outfit) a newspaper which reads on the outside in large black
letters: ASSASSINATION; passengers should then proceed off stage in
order to enter the subway car through the open door, take seats facing
the animals and the audience, open their newspapers, and read (com-
pulsively rather than attentively). Reading should continue throughout
the play unless character is directly involved in the action, or unless it is
otherwise specified in the stage directions. As soon as the passengers are
seated, the door closes. The RUSSIAN and YOUNG MAN sit together;
BLACK 1 and YOUNG WOMAN; RABBINICAL STUDENT and NUN; JUNIOR
EXECUTIVE and HIPPY (the EXEC occasionally looking up from his paper
to cast contemptuous glances at the HIPPY, and then looking around
for corroboration from the other passengers—which he does not get—
this should continue on and off throughout the play). The train begins
to move, and as it does the lights on stage should occasionally dim;
this too should continue throughout the play.

NARRATOR [Stage left, through a bullhorn to the audience, with mock
eloquence] Assassination: A Subway Ride in One Hack. [NARRATOR
puts on his conductor's cap, announces through bullhorn to the
audience] You are going uptown. Next stop Plastic.
[Train should continue for ten seconds or so]
RUSSIAN [Glancing at the Young Man a few times, as if about to say
something, he suddenly spreads his newspaper on the floor near his
seat and motions to it: YOUNG MAN looks up] She lays [He points to
the newspaper and spreads his legs provocatively in ludicrous imitation]
vith vun foot must ceiling holt, and then [Making jabbing motions
with his fist] Ah! Ah! Peez-da slot-kia. Sveet.
YOUNG MAN What do you call it? [Motioning to his crotch]
RUSSIAN Smoked meat——
YOUNG MAN I mean in your language, that word you said——
RUSSIAN Ah, pizda. [Licking his lips] I like. Sveet.
YOUNNG MAN What's her name, your girlfriend?
RUSSIAN Mary. [NUN looks up suddenly, then busies herself with her
newspaper again] You like smoked meat? [YOUNG MAN uncertain] Ech!
you don't know. Is goot, pizda. Sveet.
YOUNG MAN [As with sudden inspiration, imitating RUSSIAN's accent]
You old man, you can't do no more. [He shows RUSSIAN a bent
forefinger]

RUSSIAN [*With anger only partly feigned, putting his hand to the zipper of his fly*] Yeh! You vant see? [*YOUNG MAN doesn't take him up; RUSSIAN picks up newspaper, brings it very close to his face, licks his fingers, and reads*]

NARRATOR [*In Ku Klux Klan sheet, goes to panel, stage left, then to stage right, and in large letters chalks:* CONGO COONS RAPE NUNS. *He unhinges one of the panels, leeringly shows it to the audience, then to the passengers, and particularly to the* NUN, *all of whom look at it briefly and noncommitally.* NARRATOR *then hangs panel up and goes to his place at stage front left or right*] [*Train should continue for ten seconds*]

YOUNG WOMAN [*With serious mien, reaches into her shopping bag, takes out smaller bag, then slowly extracts chunk of watermelon, which she diffidently offers to* BLACK 1. *He looks at her with knowing irony. She takes a little bite, then offers it to him again*] Have some.

BLACK 1 [*Takes the watermelon, as if to taste it, then suddenly forces it into the young woman's mouth and face. She is puzzled but dutifully obedient*] Suck it! Here's some kazoo for you, bitch. Suck it. [*She eats watermelon until train, which is slowing down, stops and a single passenger—*BLACK 2*—gets on, at which point all look up at him briefly, then go back to their papers.* YOUNG WOMAN *places watermelon into bag and bag into shopping bag*]

BLACK 2 [*In beggar's garb, apparently blind, with dark glasses, cane and coin box, the coin box held against his placard which reads "White." He makes his way to the end of the car and pauses*]

NARRATOR [*In conductor's cap, through the bullhorn to the audience*] You are going uptown. Next stop Pox-Box and Fifty thoid. [*Then slyly*] Better nose up if you wanna be hoid.

BLACK 2 [*Begins to sing a doleful, darky ballad and walks slowly and rhythmically through the car, pausing at each passenger. He picks up some coins which are at the ten-gallon hat mannequin's feet, and he is given change by the* NUN, *the* YOUNG WOMAN, *and—with a flourish—by the* JUNIOR EXEC. *When he is finished, the beggar, obviously not blind, counts his coins, puts them into his pocket, takes off his glasses, puts them into his pocket, and turns to the audience*] Look-a-here! [*He turns his placard over to where it reads "Black," and points to it in an exaggerated manner. Then he turns to the passengers and does the same. They lift their heads briefly, and are visibly nonplussed, but go back to their newspapers—except for the* YOUNG WOMAN *and* BLACK 1: *she has a concerned look in her eyes,* BLACK 1 *is smiling.* BLACK 2 *strides jauntily over to* BLACK 2] Wha's happening, brother? [*He gives him skin, motions the* YOUNG WOMAN *out of the way, sits down, and is suddenly involved in intense-eyed conversation with* BLACK 1. *This should continue for ten or fifteen seconds, until*]

MODEL [*Clearly neanderthal—she has a bone in her teeth and is naked —enters from adjacent car, and does a showroom prance through the car in time to a primitive rendition of "America the Beautiful." She manages to attract attention, particularly from the* RUSSIAN. *When she gets to the end of the car and the music stops, she yells to the* NARRATOR] One more time! [*Music starts again, and she prances back. Passengers all go back to their newspapers*]

NARRATOR [*Through the bullhorn to the audience, and sounding like a carnival barker*] No, folks, she ain't much of a wrassler, but you ought to see her box! [*Then winking intimately*] Thought you'd like this bitty.

[*Train continues for ten seconds, then slows and stops*]

NARRATOR [*As conductor, through bullhorn to the audience*] You are going uptown. Buick Lane next. [*Then, mockingly*] Money today, manna mañana.

[*Train continues for ten seconds*]

RABBINICAL STUDENT [*Suddenly jumping up, obviously distraught, as he shuffles from one passenger to another*] Fletboosh? Is this Fletboosh? I vant to go to Fletboosh.

NUN [*Sanctimoniously*] You are on the wrong course.

EXEC You want to go to Brooklyn. We're going uptown. [STUDENT *doesn't seem to understand*] Where do you want to go in Flatbush?

RABBINICAL STUDENT Fletboosh, Fletboosh.

EXEC [*Places his attache case on his knees, takes out a pen and a sheet of paper, motions to the* STUDENT, *and begins to draw a diagram*] We've just left Pox and Fifty-third. Buick's next. [*Enunciating very carefully*] We are going up. You, naturally, want to go down. Downtown. [*He looks at* STUDENT] You want to go to Flatbush, right, Izzie?

RABBINICAL STUDENT Fletboosh, Fletboosh.

EXEC You cannot get to Flatbush by going up. [*He draws a straight line to the top of the page*] You have to go down, damn it! [*He draws a straight line to the bottom of the page*]

HIPPY [*Explosively*] Man, down *is* up.

EXEC [*Angrily*] Shut up you. [*Tauntingly*] If you know so much why don't you wash your skin. [*To the* STUDENT] Don't listen to *him.* You have to go *back*—where you came from. Do you understand?

YOUNG WOMAN [*Motioning to the* STUDENT, *who shuffles over to her*] Where do you want to go, sir?

RABBINICAL STUDENT Fletboosh.

YOUNG WOMAN [*Enunciating carefully*] I'm sorry, you are on the wrong train. The next stop is Buick Lane. The stop after that is High-Speed Douche——

RABBINICAL STUDENT [*Nodding his head*] Fletboosh, Fletboosh——

YOUNG WOMAN Not boosh, Douche, High-Speed Douche. It's a square— actually a triangle. I don't think you want to go there——

NUN [*Suddenly lifting her habit, displaying long underwear and chastity belt, and shrieking*] We are *here* [*Pointing to her thigh*], and we are going *here* [*Pointing to her heart*], you have to get off *here*, Yankel [*Grabbing her crotch. Then she straightens her habit, crosses herself, and fastidiously busies herself with the newspaper*]

YOUNG WOMAN [*Infinitely patient*] Sir, two [*Holds two fingers up*] more stops, then get out. That's High-Speed Douche—get out, go up the stairs to the other side, the downtown side [*She points to stage front left*], then ask the conductor of the downtown train how to get to Flatbush.

RABBINICAL STUDENT [*Seeming to understand*] Thank you, thank you very much. [*He sits down on the edge of his seat, next to the nun, picks up his newspaper, but doesn't read it*]
[*Train continues for ten seconds or so*]

NARRATOR [*Wearing a swastika armband, erases previous writing from panels, chalking instead:* CANCER IS A ZIONIST PLOT. *He shows one of the panels to the audience, then to the passengers who look at it briefly and noncommitally, then to the* RABBINICAL STUDENT, *who searches for his eye-glasses, but cannot find them, and apologetically motions to the* NARRATOR *that he cannot read the sign*]

WOMAN FROM THE AUDIENCE [*Exasperated*] What's going on here?

NARRATOR [*To the* WOMAN FROM THE AUDIENCE] Madam, you must pay attention.
[*Train continues for ten seconds, the passengers—except for the* RABBINICAL STUDENT—*reading their newspapers*]

MODEL [*In Sumerian-Egyptian flimsiness, does her showroom prance through the car in time to a middle-eastern rendition of "America the Beautiful." She pauses in front of* BLACK 1, *does a few extra gyrations, hands him a piece of paper, which he reads, apparently understands, and pockets; then she greets him provocatively*] Salaam.

BLACK 1 Salaam, sister.

EXEC [*To the* MODEL] Miss? [MODEL *prances over to him*] Miss, what's your name?

MODEL Rona Paradise.

EXEC Are you related to Robert Paradise?

MODEL I *am* Robert Paradise—that is, I was.

EXEC [*Startled*] Remember *me?* I'm Stuart—we went to high school together.

MODEL [*Looks at* EXEC *ironically, throws her head back, and continues her prance through the car*]

EXEC I don't understand that! [*He goes back to his newspaper*]
[*Train continues for ten seconds or so and then slows down and stops. A large* BEAR *alights and looks around the car for a place to sit. The* RUSSIAN *gets up, and with an ingratiating smile, approaches the* BEAR *with his hand extended. The* BEAR *growls at him, brushes the hand aside, and sits down with the animals*]

NARRATOR [*As conductor, through the bullhorn, to the audience*] You are going uptown. High-Speed Douche Square next, recently the site of the celebrated Douche-In.

HIPPY [*As if awakened*] Hey, man, what he say?

YOUNG MAN Duchin——

YOUNG WOMAN High-Speed Douche—where they had the Douche-In. Were you there? [*She gets up and shuffles over to him*]

HIPPY Yeah, wow.

YOUNG WOMAN Are you with one of the groups?

HIPPY Ma'am?

YOUNG WOMAN You look like this cat, Richard Pastramiano—he's the lead in Stiff Dick and the Cucumbers—that Sicilian hard rock group.

HIPPY Naw.

YOUNG WOMAN You look just like him. He has this beard—like yours—and these like finely molded Italian features. He looks just like you.

HIPPY Naw, I'm just me.

YOUNG WOMAN Do *you* play—do you *blow* anything, you know, like guitar?

HIPPY I'm like into the East—the tabla—

YOUNG WOMAN Tabla's drums, right?

HIPPY Yeah.

YOUNG WOMAN [*As if intoning*] Brahma, Vishnu, Siva—what is it—Brahma is creator, Vishnu destroyer and Siva Preserver—or is Vishnu the preserver?

HIPPY [*shrugs*]

YOUNG WOMAN Yes, I think that's it. [*After a pause*] You *know* what the sound of two hands clapping is. [HIPPY *looks at her*] What is the sound of one hand clapping?

BLACK 2 [*looking at* YOUNG WOMAN, *he suddenly claps his hands; she*

turns toward him as he begins to sing to her] Ah'm just sittin' heah
waitin' awn/some o' that stuff you' sittin' awn/ Glory Hal-le-lu-jah!
[*He laughs*]

YOUNG WOMAN [*Excuses herself—minimal response from* HIPPY—*and
at the invitation from* BLACK 2, *sits down between him and* BLACK 1;
jocularly] You two finished rappin'?

BLACK 1 Look-a-here, mama, brother is coming back to the pad. You call
Emily, hear, and we all do something tonight.

YOUNG WOMAN [*Thinking*] Emily? She got back from the march
yesterday—or early this morning. Yes, she's probably free. [*To* BLACK
2] I'm sure you'll dig Emily, brother.

BLACK 2 [*Tapping* BLACK 1, *who smiles knowingly*] I be plannin' to do
just that, baby.

[*Train continues for some ten seconds*]

MODEL [*Enters in something obviously medieval, does her showroom
prance to a medieval rendition of "America the Beautiful." She stops
suddenly before the* NUN, *lifts her skirts, and shows her flagellation
scars; the* NUN *crosses herself*] Have you ever heard of the In-qui-si-
tion, ba-by? I got it bad, but *your* ass is a fucking grape, and I ain't
a-kiddin'! [NUN *is visibly annoyed, though she tries hard to bury herself in her paper.* MODEL, *after staring at her, drops her dress, and
continues ambling through the car. As she reaches the end and
the music stops, she shouts to the* NARRATOR] One more once! [*She
goes through it again, playfully patting the* RUSSIAN's *head and winking at him*]

WOMAN FROM THE AUDIENCE [*Whining*] I don't under*stand* this.

NARRATOR [*Giving her a hard stare*] Madam, may I suggest that you
try listening with your stomach. Or if that doesn't work, try watching
with the third eye—you will find yours where your navel used to be.
[*Narrator puts on a policeman's riot helmet, erases previous writing
from panels, and attaches to each an identical blowup of the advertisement for Dean Martin's "The Silencers," in which Dino, as
detective Matt Helm, is straddling a giant pistol, from which emanate
semen-like stars, joyfully carried by a covey of scantily-clad Hollywood beauties. If this prop cannot be arranged, something similar
might be improvised.* NARRATOR *shows one of the panels to the
audience, then to the passengers—they don't react—and particularly
to the* JUNIOR EXEC, *who gestures a good deal with his arms, indicating that he does not see the advertisement's relevance to him*]
[*The train is slowing down; it stops, and the* RABBINICAL STUDENT
scurries off, dropping his newspaper. Ten seconds or so later he

emerges at stage left, where he addresses the NARRATOR (*in conductor's garb*): *they confer for a while, the conductor apparently giving the* STUDENT *much information, and finally pointing off stage. The* STUDENT *hurries in that direction and some seconds later ends up entering the same subway car, whose door has remained open. Door now closes. The* STUDENT, *not recognizing where he is, sits next to the* HIPPY, *looks around, then asks*] Fletboosh, this is Fletboosh?

HIPPY Who?

RABBINICAL STUDENT I vant to go to Fletboosh, Fletboosh.

HIPPY Right.

RABBINICAL STUDENT Is this Fletboosh?

HIPPY Man, it's where you want it to be. [*The* STUDENT *more or less accepts this information, but is still uneasy. He sees the newspaper he dropped, picks it up, and begins to read from right to left*]

NARRATOR [*As conductor, through bullhorn to the audience*] You are going uptown. We will soon be entering the tunnel. Meat Street next stop.

NUN [*Suddenly lifting her skirts, displaying long underwear and chastity belt, she screams—apparently to the black men, who look up at her*] You're just sitting there waiting on/some of that stuff I'm sitting on./You'll go to hell with a hardon/glory hallelujah! [*She drops her habit, crosses herself, and goes back to her newspaper. The black men laugh ironically, then go back to their papers*]

NARRATOR [*Has gone off stage, and is now seen entering the subway car from the adjacent car, wearing a policeman's riot helmet, carrying a "service" revolver, and swinging a night stick flamboyantly. He struts over to where the black men and the* YOUNG WOMAN *are sitting, and stares at them with obvious suspicion. When* BLACK 2 *crosses his legs, the* NARRATOR *taps his leg with the club*] No, boy!

BLACK 2 Watchchoo mean, man? I'm crossin' my legs.

YOUNG WOMAN He's just crossing his legs, officer.

NARRATOR Where you people heading? [*To the* YOUNG WOMAN, *pointing to the shopping bag*] What do you have in there?

YOUNG WOMAN [*Incredulously*] What?

NARRATOR Do you have any leaflets in there?

YOUNG WOMAN What kind of leaflets?

NARRATOR [*Angrily*] Perverted commie leaflets. [*At this point the* JUNIOR EXEC *looks over, smiles as if to say: they're finally getting theirs; then goes back to his paper*] Do you know *him*? [*Pointing with his night stick to the* RUSSIAN] Is he part of your tribe?

YOUNG WOMAN What the hell do you mean—

NARRATOR [*Loudly*] Lemme see the bag. [*He puts his night stick inside and pokes it around. Then he puts his hand inside, pulls out the watermelon in its bag*] What's in *here*?

YOUNG WOMAN Look for yourself.

NARRATOR [*Extracts watermelon from its bag, scrutinizes it, then hands it to* BLACK 2. *He puts his hand in again, this time taking out a diaphragm case, which he holds out in front of him*] What's this?

YOUNG WOMAN What?

NARRATOR Open it.

YOUNG WOMAN [*Angrily opens it and shows it to him*] It's a goddam diaphragm. [*At this point the* NUN *suddenly looks up, is promptly shocked, crosses herself, and puts her head into her newspaper*] What the hell do you want?

NARRATOR [*Looks at her, and then at the black men, with obvious contempt. He hands her the shopping bag, and continues strutting through the car*]

YOUNG WOMAN [*Loudly*] Fascist pig!

NARRATOR [*Turns around angrily, but then places his night stick on his breast, and turning to the audience, declaims*] In Chicago they call me the Prince of Peace. [*The* NARRATOR *emerges stage front left or right, picks up his bullhorn and addresses the audience with a sly wink*] I thought you'd like this bitty.

[*Train should continue for ten seconds or so*]

MODEL [*Enters in Victorian costume to "America the Beautiful," with overtones of "God Save the Queen," or something similar. She pauses before the* RUSSIAN, *suddenly envelops him with her skirts, wiggles provocatively, disencumbers herself, and continues her prance through the car*]

RUSSIAN [*Licking his lips, to* YOUNG MAN] Smoked meat!

YOUNG MAN No, dummy.

RUSSIAN Ah, yes. Sveet pizda.

YOUNG MAN [*Mockingly*] You like blurrup, blurrup? [*Cunnilingual movements with his tongue*]

RUSSIAN [*With exaggerated disgust*] No, I vant ah! ah! ah! [*Making jabbing motions with his fist*]

YOUNG MAN Is that what you do with—what's her name?

RUSSIAN Mary, yeh.

YOUNG MAN [*Pretending innocence*] What does she do with her feet?

RUSSIAN [*With broad smile*] Ah, you clever boy. She vun foot like . . . ah. [*He spreads his leg in ludicrous imitation*] Other foot must ceiling holt, and then ah! ah! [*Jabbing motions*] So sveet

YOUNG MAN [*Imitating* RUSSIAN'S *accent*] Ah, you old man. You can't do no more. [*He shows the* RUSSIAN *a bent forefinger*]

RUSSIAN [*With anger only partly feigned, putting his hand to the zipper of his fly*] Yeh! You vant see? [YOUNG MAN *doesn't take him up.* RUSSIAN *picks up newspaper, brings it close to his face, licks his finger, and reads*]

[*Train continues for ten seconds or so*]

EXEC [*Whose patience with the* HIPPY'S *imperviousness to his contempt has come to an end, places his attache case on his knees, and erupts*] Scum! Why don't you wash your skin?

HIPPY [*Plenty cool, looks at him through one eye, and smiles*] What?

EXEC [*Breathlessly*] You stinking bastard. You smell like swine. [*He looks to the other passengers for confirmation—they all continue to read. He motions his head to the* RABBINICAL STUDENT] At least he has a reason for his filth. It's part of his religion. You ain't got— you got no religion. You don't believe in anything but that filthy hair of yours. Do you? Do you believe in any principle or right, any ethic? Do you believe in *anything*?

HIPPY [*Quietly, without lifting his head*] Yeah.

EXEC What—what do you believe in? Tell me. Tell me one thing you believe in.

HIPPY [*Looking up at him*] I believe in you, Mr. Jones.

EXEC What? Me? Goddamn you. [*Flustered, he goes back to his paper*] [*Train continues for ten seconds*]

BLACK 2 [*To* YOUNG WOMAN] Where that watermelon at?

YOUNG WOMAN It's in the shopping bag. Would you like some?

BLACK 2 Yeah, give it yere. [*She gives it to him; he looks at watermelon for a long time, turning it around in his hands—then looks at* YOUNG WOMAN *with one eye raised*] Have you been sucking on this yere?

YOUNG WOMAN I had only a little bit.

BLACK 2 [*Shouting*] It stinks of she-pig. [*He tosses it on the floor, dons his dark glasses, takes out his blind-man's cup, turns around his placard, picks up his cane, and goes to the end of the car, from whence he begins to sing a doleful darky ballad and to walk slowly and rhythmically through the car, pausing at each passenger. The* BEAR *waves a threatening fist, but the* NUN, *the* YOUNG WOMAN, *and —with a flourish—the* JUNIOR EXEC *shell out. When he is finished, the beggar counts his coins, goes through the car and off stage, from where is heard the sound of coins being dropped into a vending machine. Beggar emerges as* BLACK 2, *except that he has forgotten to*

turn his placard to "Black"; he has a large slice of watermelon in
his hands as he strides jauntily to his previous seat. BLACK 1 *looks at*
him, reminds him to reverse his placard, then gives him skin. As
BLACK 2 *eats his watermelon, the* YOUNG WOMAN *gestures that she*
would like some, but is refused]
[*Train continues for some ten seconds*]
MODEL [*Emerges in a 1920s flapper outfit, to a Charleston beat of*
"*America the Beautiful." She pauses before the* RABBINICAL STUDENT,
looking him up and down appraisingly, then, loudly] Let's go Ikey!
[RABBINICAL STUDENT *gets up, takes off his large black hat, revealing*
a snappy little yarmulkah; he attempts to hand his hat to the NUN
but she refuses with visible disgust. He places it on his seat, then
joins in a frantic Charleston with the MODEL. *After a minute or so,*
the MODEL *stops dancing, looks contemptuously at the* STUDENT, *who*
with awkwardness and embarrassment pulls himself together, puts on
his large hat, and sits down to his paper. MODEL *continues her prance*
through the car]
WOMAN FROM THE AUDIENCE [*Petulantly*] Would somebody please tell
me what's going on?
NARRATOR Madam, you want sense. You refuse to be led. Listen to me:
the poet must bleed through his abstract head. [*Then through his*
bullhorn to the audience, with exaggerated articulation] Ad-just
trusses! Prepare for coives!
[*The train commences to give off shrieking noises. The passengers*
fall against each other, and seem somewhat troubled, but only briefly,
as the train apparently straightens out]
NARRATOR [*Goes to panels and on each chalks this diptych:* DIAL
A PRAYER/YOU MAY BE IT IN THE LOTTERY. *He shows*
one of the panels to the audience, but not to the passengers]
BLACK 2 [*Addressing* BLACK 1, *with some uneasiness*] Where Meat
Street at? [BLACK 1 *looks at him and shrugs*]
YOUNG WOMAN It's very odd. We should have been there already.
YOUNG MAN [*To* RUSSIAN] Did we *pass* Meat already?
RUSSIAN [*Not understanding*] Smoked meat——
YOUNG MAN Aw, you idiot——
EXEC This is probably a different route. Didn't the conductor say some-
thing about a tunnel?
YOUNG WOMAN There shouldn't be a tunnel around here, should there?
EXEC [*Looking around the car*] There's not even a darn map in the car.
HIPPY [*Ironically, to* JUNIOR EXEC] Hey, is this your *first* trip?
EXEC Shut up scum!

HIPPY [*Somewhat more aggressively*] You're pretty uptight. This *must* be your first trip. Where did you think you were going, Mr. Jones?

EXEC [*Really rattled, loudly*] I said shut up you filthy scum you!

BLACK 2 [*To Black 1*] Where that man at?

YOUNG WOMAN I think he's in the first car.

[*Train begins to shriek again and the passengers fall against each other. They are getting more uneasy*]

YOUNG WOMAN I don't remember there being so many curves here.

NUN It's very high for curves.

EXEC If only there was a map.

NUN We should be elevated soon.

EXEC [*Looking at* RABBINICAL STUDENT, *addressing the* NUN] Isn't he the same Jew, Sister—the one from before—who wanted to go to Flatbush?

NUN [*Looks at* STUDENT *carefully*] I can't tell.

EXEC [*To* STUDENT] Hey. Hey you [STUDENT *looks up*]—are you the one who wanted to go to Flatbush?

RABBINICAL STUDENT Fletboosh. Is Fletboosh?

EXEC [*Exasperated*] No, no——

YOUNG WOMAN [*To the* STUDENT] Did you speak to the conductor?

RABBINICAL STUDENT [*Apparently not understanding*] Speak?

YOUNG WOMAN [*Goes over to him*] The conductor. Remember, I told you to speak to the conductor on the downtown side. To ask him how to get to Flatbush. [*Enunciating very carefully*] Did you speak to the conductor on the downtown side?

RABBINICAL STUDENT Ah, yeh. Conductor. I speak.

EXEC [*Angry, more frightened than the others*] Then what are you doing here? We're going uptown. You want to go downtown. [STUDENT *smiles at him uncomprehendingly*] What the hell are you doing on this train. You're not going to see any of your kind where we're going. Do you understand me? There are no shuls up here.

NUN [*Loudly*] Synagogue of Satan!

YOUNG WOMAN I don't understand this. [*She goes back to her seat*]

EXEC I'm going to see if I could find the conductor, or a least a darn map. [*He gets up, leaving his attache case behind, and goes through the car into the adjacent car*]

[*Train continues for fifteen seconds or so, more or less evenly. Passengers are not as uneasy now: most of them are reading their papers. Suddenly there is a scream—then another—from off stage, and the lights go out for five or ten seconds. When they come on*]

the BEAR *is seen to be sitting in the* JUNIOR EXEC'S *seat with the*
EXEC'S *attache case on his lap*]

YOUNG WOMAN What was that scream? [BLACK 1 *shrugs*]

MODEL [*Enters in a very contemporary mini-outfit, but all in black.
She wears a placard around her neck which reads: "End Soon." She
does a rather solemn prance to a solemn version of "America the
Beautiful." She pauses before the* BEAR, *laughs knowingly, and continues through the car*]

[*Train continues for some ten seconds, everybody reading his paper,
except the* BEAR *who is looking straight ahead*]

YOUNG MAN [*To* RUSSIAN] Where the hell did he go?

RUSSIAN What?

YOUNG MAN The guy with the case. He went to find the conductor.

NUN I'm surprised he is not back.

YOUNG MAN [*Getting up*] I'll see if I could find the conductor, Sister.

NUN Young man, are you Catholic?

YOUNG MAN Yes, Sister.

[*Train continues for ten seconds or so, the passengers reading their
papers uneasily*]

NARRATOR [*To the* WOMAN FROM THE AUDIENCE] Madam? Madam,
what do you think of our entertainment? Is it making more *sense*
to you? [*Pause*] Did you buy your lottery ticket, Madam? [*Pause*]
You haven't *won* yet? You must be patient. I am sure that you will
get your chance.

[*Train commences to shriek again; the lights go out for five or ten
seconds. When they come on, one of the animal mannequins, perhaps the gorilla, is sitting in the* YOUNG MAN'S *seat*]

RUSSIAN [*Glancing up from his paper uneasily at the animal next to
him, finally looks at animal squarely, slowly spreads his newspaper
on the floor and addresses animal*] Smoked meat? You like? [*Pause,
more tentatively*] I got voman, Mary. [*Pause*] I like ven she lays
[*Motions to the newspaper*]—vun foot up [*He lifts his leg*] must
ceiling holt . . . you like smoked . . . [*His words trail off; uneasily
he picks up his newspaper, brings it close to his face, licks his fingers,
tries to read*]

YOUNG WOMAN [*To animal sitting next to* RUSSIAN] Sir, why did you
change your seat? [*No answer—she looks at* BLACK 1] That other
man went to find the conductor—what the hell happened to him?
[*Black 1 shrugs uneasily, goes back to his paper, as does* YOUNG
WOMAN]

[*Train continues for ten seconds or so, then the lights go out for five seconds, and when they come on, the* NARRATOR *is standing in the middle of the car in a Marine Drill Sergeant's uniform, holding a gig-pad, and with a swagger stick under his arm*]

NARRATOR [*To the passengers, loudly*] All right, we're just about there. [*Passengers look at him questioningly. The train is in fact slowing down, and as it prepares to stop, some of the passengers look through the windows—only dark outside—others get up and go towards the door. Train stops but the door does not open.* NARRATOR *addresses the passengers*] This is it, Meat Street.

BLACK 1 [*Angrily, but to nobody in particular*] Open the motherfuckin' door.

YOUNG WOMAN This doesn't look like Meat. What the hell is going on——

NARRATOR [*Peremptorily*] Shut up and sit down. Everybody. This is the last stop. [*Passengers sit down*]

RABBINICAL STUDENT [*Getting up*] Fletboosh?

NARRATOR [*Goes up to* RABBINICAL STUDENT, *looks at him contemptuously*] Yussel, you could fuck up a wet dream. [*He removes* STUDENT's *placard and puts it around his own neck, then pushes student to the end of the car and off stage. He comes back alone; the other passengers look uneasily at each other, but keep their seats. After fifteen seconds or so the* STUDENT *is seen standing in the audience with a basket of pretzels*]

RABBINICAL STUDENT [*To the audience, anxiety in his voice*] Fresh hot petzels. Get your fresh hot petzels. [*He hands pretzels to various people in the audience—This should go on for ten or fifteen seconds —then he goes off stage and emerges in the same car. He takes his seat*]

NARRATOR [*In the middle of the car, to the passengers, in peremptory drill-sergeant tone*] All Right, all you swinging' dicks FALL IN! [*Passengers look at each other in amazement*] Fall in rightchere! [*They all get up, taking their newspapers with them;* NARRATOR *looks squarely at the* NUN *and the* YOUNG WOMAN *who have also gotten up*] I said swingin' dicks—y'all got *dicks*? [*He pokes* NUN's *habit with his swagger stick. She and* YOUNG WOMAN *sit down. The men are lined up in front of him*] 'TENSHUN! [*They don't know quite how to respond*] I said 'TENSHUN! [*They come to attention*] All right tits—fall in. [*YOUNG WOMAN and* NUN *get up and line up next to men, all facing the audience.* NARRATOR *struts back and forth, looking at each of the passengers, then to the* RUSSIAN] Name?

RUSSIAN [*Frightened*] Misha——

NARRATOR I said name! [*He pokes* RUSSIAN's *placard with his swagger stick*]

RUSSIAN [*Looks at it as if for the first time—painfully tries to read it*] Som-oke Me-at——

NARRATOR [*To* YOUNG WOMAN] You, name!

YOUNG WOMAN I——

NARRATOR [*Hitting her with stick, pointing to her placard*] Name!

YOUNG WOMAN [*Noticing her placard with surprise—then slowly, incredulously*] Suck for Peace.

NARRATOR [*To Black 1*] You, name!

BLACK 1 [*Surprised to notice his placard—loudly*] Black.

NARRATOR [*To* NUN] You, name!

NUN [*Flustered, frightened, looks at her breast, smiles in relief, crosses herself, and says richly, defiantly*] God.

NARRATOR [*Ironically*] What all's God, Miss?

NUN [*As if from memory*] God is our Father. God is His Son, Jesus——

NARRATOR Where's he at now? Is he *here?* Is he in this shere subway, Miss?

NUN God is here. [*Pointing to her breast*]

NARRATOR [*To* RABBINICAL STUDENT] Where's God at, troop?

RABBINICAL STUDENT God?

NARRATOR Where's he at, God?

RABBINICAL STUDENT [*Not comprehending*] Fletboosh? This Fletboosh?

NARRATOR [*To* BLACK 2] You, name!

BLACK 2 [*Has turned his placard around*] Mah name's white, suh——

NARRATOR [*To* HIPPY] You, name!

HIPPY [*Disoriented*] Edgar——

NARRATOR [*Hits him with swagger stick, points to his placard*] Name!

HIPPY [*Looking at placard*] I guess . . . Love.

NARRATOR [*With menacing folksiness*] Now People. Folks. I want you all to listen up. I'm plannin' on holdin' a contest—a lottery. And I'm gonna select a winner in this shere lottery from among you all. But I'm not gonna' tell you what the prize is. I want that to be a surprise to you. If you want to speed this all up you could pick a winner yourself. Understand? Anybody want to win? [*No response*] Nobody wants to *win?* Now that's funny. But I sorta expected it. I'm gonna have to pick a winner myself. But I'm gonna do it fair and square—dontcha worry none. [*To the* WOMAN FROM THE AUDIENCE] Madam? Madam, I wonder if you'd help me here. I think getting closer to the entertainment here will help you to understand it better. Would you come up, Madam? Come into the subway car.

WOMAN FROM THE AUDIENCE [*As she walks toward the stage*] I'm going to do it, so that all of this will make more sense.

NARRATOR Madam, I would like you to collect the newspapers these people are holding. These newspapers they have been reading all through this subway ride. [*After she collects them*] Put those papers on one of the seats. [*She does*] Madam, now I want you to get in line.

WOMAN FROM THE AUDIENCE What——

NARRATOR [*Peremptorily*] I say fall in! With the rest of them. [*She falls in; then he addresses all the passengers*] I'm gonna ask y'all some questions, the answers of which you should definitely know. If you *don't* know these answers you will be a winner in this shere lottery I'm holdin'. Now [*To the* WOMAN FROM THE AUDIENCE], Madam, where are you?

WOMAN FROM THE AUDIENCE What do you *mean*?

NARRATOR Where are you right at this minute?

WOMAN FROM THE AUDIENCE Why I'm *here*, on this stage.

NARRATOR And who died?

WOMAN FROM THE AUDIENCE [*Definitely*] Reason!

NARRATOR [*Licks his pencil, makes a mark in his gig-pad; stands in front of the* RUSSIAN, *addresses him*] Your woman's name is Mary. She has a sweet pizda. [*Quickly*] Who died?

RUSSIAN [*Forlornly, lifts a bent forefinger*] No goot.

NARRATOR [*Licks his pencil, makes a mark in his gig-pad; stands in front of* YOUNG WOMAN] When did you become an ecumaniac?

YOUNG WOMAN What——

NARRATOR I said [*Enunciating carefully*] when did you become an ecu-maniac?

YOUNG WOMAN I——

NARRATOR Who died?

YOUNG WOMAN [*With feeling*] The world of the heart.

NARRATOR [*Licks his pencil, makes a mark in his gig-pad; stands in front of the* RABBINICAL STUDENT] You want to gō to *Flatbush*?

RABBINICAL STUDENT [*Nodding his head*] Fletboosh——

NARRATOR To the synagogue? To doven? To pray—who died?

RABBINICAL STUDENT Goy——

NARRATOR [*Licks his pencil, makes a mark in his gig-pad; stands in front of* HIPPY] Pick up your hair.

HIPPY [*Looks at him, then lifts his hair over one ear*]

NARRATOR [*Looks into* HIPPY'S *ear for ten seconds or so, then at* HIPPY] Let it fall. [HIPPY *lets his hair fall*] Mr. Love, who died?

HIPPY [*Haltingly*] Love . . . is dead.

NARRATOR [*Licks his pencil, makes a mark in his gig-pad; stands in front of* BLACK 1] When did you go Afro, brother?

BLACK 1 [*Defiantly*] You're not my brother——

NARRATOR Who died, brother?

BLACK 1 [*As if suddenly realizing*] The goddamn pig-white power structure!

NARRATOR [*Licks his pencil, makes a mark in his gig-pad; stands in front of* NUN, *points to the* RABBINICAL STUDENT] He offered you his hat, Miss. Why didn't you hold it for him?

NUN He——

NARRATOR Who died?

NUN [*Angrily motioning her head to the* RABBINICAL STUDENT] He and his kind killed my God——

NARRATOR [*Licks his pencil, makes a mark in his gig-pad; stands in front of* BLACK 2: *he pokes his placard with his swagger stick*] What are you—black or white?

BLACK 2 Ah don't want no trouble, suh, and ah don't think nobody's gonna die a'tall.

NARRATOR [*Licks his pencil, makes a mark in his gig-pad, looks at his pad for a long time, then looks at the passengers*] Guess what, folks? Would you believe it? I have more than one winner. Yes sir, I have [*He counts from his gig-pad*] two . . . three . . . six . . . seven . . . eight winners. Folks, you're all winners in this shere lottery. And like I promised, I'm gonna give you all prizes. First I want you to turn around . . . face your seats [*They slowly turn around*] I wanch'all to bend down . . . put your left hand over your eyes [*They do it—slowly*], that's right. Maybe you men'd better put your other hand—your right hand—over your family jewels, too, just in case . . . [*The men cup their genitals. The* NARRATOR *turns to the audience, loudly*] ALL RIGHT! [*Lights go off, eight loud thumps are heard. Lights remain off for at least ten seconds; when they come on the subway door facing the audience is open, but on the seats facing the audience are the animal mannequins, the ten-gallon hat dummy, and the* BEAR: *they are all looking straight ahead. Seated across from them, are the previous passengers, including the lady from the audience: they are very still and are looking straight ahead*]

NARRATOR [*As conductor, in his place at stage front left or right, addresses the audience through his bullhorn*] You are going down-town. Next stop Prairie. [*Door closes*]

MODEL [*With the head of a lion, or a bird, and naked, emerges from the adjacent car. She does a spirited prance through the car to the beat of "Abba-dabba-dabba . . ." or some other quick-moving animal song, and disappears into the next car*]

NARRATOR [*Goes to one panel, removes previous sign, and chalks:* THE BEGINNING. *He shows this panel to the animals, then hangs it up. He goes to the other panel, removes previous sign, chalks:* THE END. *He shows this panel to the audience*]

BLACKOUT

WHITHER

That we are living in a harrowing present is only too clear, but what of the future—what lies ahead? Tom Hayden, in his sober and reasoned essay, "The Ability to Face Whatever Comes," calls for a broadly based movement of organized radicals to work together with the various disenfranchised elements of the American community, such as the poor, the war protesters, the student dissenters, and others. Hayden admits that this alliance promises little hope of "building a utopian community in the here and now," but it is perhaps our only hope for restructuring the society. Paul Goodman, in his serious spoof, "1984," paints a vivid picture of an American "dystopia," a species of society which could result if this country continues on its present course. In "Buddhism and the Coming Revolution," Gary Snyder proclaims the need for an assimilation of the finest qualities of East and West: the social revolution of the West and the "individual insight into the basic self/void" of the East. According to Snyder, both are contained in the "traditional three aspects of the Dharma path: wisdom, meditation, and morality." We end the volume with Dr. Martin Luther King's "I Have a Dream," which like the selection that precedes it, is an eloquent plea for brotherhood and love.

The Ability to Face Whatever Comes

Most people think this is a healthy country, with a few isolated ailments. But the difficulties encountered in trying to cure those ailments persuade some of us that an epidemic has spread over America. Signs of it are everywhere. Three current ones are the Vietnam war, the reluctance of authorities to meet the needs of Negroes and poor people, and the furore over free speech in universities. In each case, the pattern is the same.

1. *People have little active control over decisions and institutions.* The Vietnam war is run from the LBJ ranch, the Pentagon and the US Mission in Saigon, without any real participation by representatives of the American and Vietnamese people. In the same way, the Administration decided that the Mississippi Freedom Democrats, in their present radical form, have no "legal" right to a place in the Democratic Party and the Congress. So, too, are poor people kept out of the poverty program unless they behave properly. University students as well are excluded from decisions about the kind of education they pay for and need.

2. *When trouble breaks out, Americans blame frustrated minorities of agitators; the mainstream of America is accepted as good for everyone except psychological misfits and outside enemies.* It is unthinkable to most people that the Vietnamese peasantry is the backbone of the anti-colonial movement. In much the same way Southern Negroes are seen as the tools of SNCC, in fact this view is held by reputable Northern liberals almost as much as by diehard segregationists. Critics of the Berkeley Free Speech Movement attacked a "Maoist" fringe for the trouble, even though actual polls showed that a majority of students favored the civil disobedience tactics.

3. *Those actually responsible for the Vietnam war, segregation, poverty and university paternalism are not Birchite generals, Southern rednecks and old-fashioned college alumni. Instead they are powerful and respectable men whose type is now dominant throughout society.* The war is a product of Johnson, McNamara, Rusk and their glamorous National Club. The destiny of Mississippi's political economy is in the hands of national Democratic bureaucrats, bankers and policymakers. Life and labor are most exploited in the very cities which are centers of

Democratic power and affluent liberalism. Berkeley is the most "advanced" public university; its administration is heralded widely for its application of industrial-relations concepts to organized education.

A civil rights worker in Mississippi can at least count on some Northern support; but what do you do if the whole country sees the Viet Cong guerrillas in the way white Mississippians see the civil rights movement? There is very little in American experience that would foster an identity between our people and the Vietnamese; there is at least a domestic tradition of support for racial equality and due process. There is no group in America which can directly press the case of the Vietnamese in the way that Negroes have pressed their case on white America. On the contrary, those Americans who stand for the Vietnamese have their message weakened or disqualified because they are students, professors or housewives. And people outside America who oppose the war are disqualified as Communists, narrow nationalists or both. The protest against the war almost seems to create a stronger patriotic current in the country. Where only the official versions of reality are generally accepted, how can a new reality break through the taboos? How can what is silenced by the established order make itself truly heard?

Yet even with this apparent perfection of social control, an uneasiness remains widespread. National consensus did not save Kennedy from violence, nor did it fully crush skepticism about the official stories of the murder. The civil rights bills did not prevent the ghetto rebellions of the last two summers. Neither did the poverty program, although it moved some of the rioting to Job Corps camps. Even LBJ's "guidelines" could not pacify the auto and steel workers during the last grievance negotiations. All our generals and counterguerrilla experts, plus our brute strength, can't teach those Asian peasants the American Way.

A Managed Society

The cause of this uneasiness traditionally has been the working class, more recently the Negroes, and nowadays it seems to be the youth. It is not simply the poor youth, those whom Labor Secretary Wirtz calls "the outlaws." The news from Darien is that the sons and daughters of chief executives are smoking pot. From Bronx High School of Science we hear that the college-bound kids tend to cheat the most. And, of course, there are those protest marchers everywhere. A decent citizen can't escape them by watching television; they're being interviewed as they burn draft cards. Nor the radio; all you get is Dylan, folk rock, protest songs. From the clubhouse at Augusta comes word that the General shares the distress of all parents; and down at Lake LBJ, the President, himself a family man, registers his surprise at this disinterest in the Great Society.

The cost of managing these conflicts is very high. A managed society is a paralyzed one, in which humane promises go unrealized, dreams die, people stop hoping for anything beyond the necessary evil. Depending on their social position, people act in variously impotent and damaging ways: delinquency, crime, narcotics, psychological failure, sexual insecurity, cheating, suicide.

Instead of workers driven into motion by class dynamics, the "proletarians" spawned in the paralyzed society are the various outcasts whose sense of reality cannot be adjusted completely to the dominant myths and given roles.

Many Negroes are outcasts in white society. Many working people are outcasts from business society, and most from union society as well. Many young people are outcasts because, if they are poor, they have no future within the existing system; and, if they are affluent, they cannot be fulfilled by endless striving for more of what they inherited at birth. Many professionals are outcasts because their talents are wasted by the Great Society. Housewives too.

These outcasts do not form an economic class; they share a common status. They are not unified by common places of work or living; they are isolated. They have no common set of immediate needs; their views of the world often clash. They seem to want only a modest freedom for themselves within a system they have no hope of changing. They flare into revolt now and then, but individually and indirectly; they appear more to be evading, perhaps mocking, the system while going along with its routines. The strain upon them comes from living with what they cannot accept but cannot change.

If neither a class crisis nor a genuine division of social opinion seems in the making, what can turn outcasts toward effective rebellion?

The problem is partially one of strategy and tactics, or building a movement; partially personal and existential, or finding a basis for radical work when there is very little hope for positive change within a lifetime. I offer only the most tentative and general ways to look at these problems, because I believe they will be settled, if at all, more by feel than theory and mostly in immediate specific situations.

"Building a movement" means that however alienated new radicals might be, they somehow work in existing American communities. If only to prevent the total closing of society, or to take real steps that create change, there must be community controversy inspired by an organized left. Without developing a human base, clearheaded about the way its needs are denied, the new radicalism will have neither leverage nor growth.

Points of departure for community work are nearly endless: organizing strong independent movements of the poor through protests, community centers and cooperatives, union organizing among low-income workers, and insurgent political campaigns; threading such neighborhood movements in coalition with similar forces around the country so that national movement and pressure is generated; connecting with the fresh radicalism on campuses, in the peace movement, and in professions wherever possible, so as to give all a broader vision, the reinforcement that comes with new energy, and a great popular base; deepening the work always to move new people out of silence and into active discovery of their own talents; going always below the existing leadership to keep insurgency growing at its root; keeping the issue of exclusion from the power structure in the fore always as the link between parts of the movement.

A Five Point Program

Real accomplishments are possible. First, the movement can make modest gains which mean something to individuals and neighborhoods: rent control, play streets, apartment repairs, higher welfare payments, jobs. Second, democratic movements appear, giving people opportunities for decision-making, protest and program which are not available now. Third, existing coalitions begin to support the new movements, or are challenged by them, thus changing the focus of community controversy. Fourth, radical ideas become more visible, especially attacks on poverty and civil rights policy, because the ideas flow from an organized movement that can challenge local power. Fifth, the work is a crucial learning experience that can be used in many ways by the people who are participating.

Acting as a radical means far more than overcoming the orthodox pressures to conform, great as those are. It means, at this time, working with little belief in Utopia. There simply is no active agency of radical change—no race, class or nation—in which radicals can invest high hopes as they have in previous times. Nor is there much possibility, so damaged are we, of building a utopian community in the here and now, from which to gather strength, go forth and change the world. That "the people" often are brilliant and resourceful should not blind us to faults. At least some of the time, people fight each other when their "interest" is in uniting; respond fearfully when they should stand up; vote "wrong" when radical alternatives are put forward; lose spirit in the final rounds of battle; remain attracted privately to the system of manipulated authority they condemn in public. But if radicalism is unable to bank fully on history or morality, what is available?

This problem, however it is stated, is wearing down the strength of many people in the new movements. It causes students to withdraw into fatalism after one or two years in the field, and it causes equally heavy forms of weariness among community people, North and South, at the grass roots of the civil rights, peace and labor movements. The same crisis, I imagine, has withered past movements and led radicals, such as the current labor leadership, into sorry marriages with the system they once tried to overthrow.

Then is the only value in rebellion itself, in the countless momentary times when people transcend their pettiness to commit themselves to great purposes? If so, then radicalism is doomed to be extraordinary, erupting only during those rare times of crisis and upsurge which American elites seem able to ride.

The alternative, if there is one, might be for radicalism to make itself ordinary, patiently taking up work that has only the virtue of facing and becoming part of the realities which are society's secret and its disgrace. Radicals then would identify with all the scorned, the illegitimate and the hurt, organizing people whose visible protest creates basic issues: who *is* criminal? who *is* representative? who *is* delinquent? Radicals then would ask of the conventional majority: at what cost have we laid down these lines and rules? Who is victimized, enslaved, freed? What have we won and what have we lost as a people who, long seeking a Christian commonwealth, put our best talents into the extermination of redskins, wops, micks, krauts, nips, niggers, gooks and red revolutionaries?

Radicalism then would give itself to, and become part of, the energy that is kept restless and active under the clamps of a paralyzed imperial society. Radicalism then would go beyond the concepts of optimism and pessimism as guides to work, finding itself in working despite odds. Its realism and sanity would be grounded in nothing more than the ability to face whatever comes.

1984

I. Socio-Psychological Factors

There were two main movements toward rural reconstruction in the early
'70s. The first was the social decision to stop harassing the radical
young, and rather to treat them kindly like Indians and underwrite their
reservations. This humane policy—instead of raids of Treasury agents
on the colleges, horrendous sentences for draft card burning, cracking
children's skulls on the Sunset Strip—was the idea of social engineer
Donald Michael, of the Institute for Policy Studies. Michael argued that,
if the serious aim of society was to increase the GNP, it was more efficient to treat the non-conformists like Indians. Naturally, this was
difficult when their reservations were in the middle of metropolitan areas,
like the Haight-Ashbury or East Greenwich Village, or on the big university campuses. But this plan became much more feasible when an
inventive tribe, the Diggers, suddenly remembered the peasant and
Taoist origins of their ideology and began to forage in the country.

The second wave of ruralism was the amazing multiplication of hermits
and monks who began to set up places in the depopulated areas for
their meditations and services to mankind. There had always been
individuals who felt that the mechanized urban areas were ugly and
unhygienic and who therefore fled to the country, at first only for the
summers. (I remember a nest of these in the '50s around Wardsboro,
members of the Congress for Cultural Freedom supported by the CIA.)
But it was not until the early '70s that humanists began to realize that
society had indeed reverted to Byzantine or Late Imperial times, and
who therefore withdrew to save their souls.

These two kinds of emigration sufficiently explain, I think, the present
patchquilt of settlement in Vermont. On the one hand, where the
Diggers settled, there are square-dance communes with their unauthentic
mountain music and the extraordinary effort to develop a late-frost hemp,
something like the inept taro culture in Micronesia. The Diggers have
been called lawless, but their simple code—(1) Live and Let Live, and
(2) the Golden Rule—is probably adequate for their simple lives. Except
for the ceremonial hemp, their agriculture is strictly for subsistence;
many of them live like pigs anyway. On the other hand, the hermits and
the religious, with their synods according to Roberts' "Rules of Order"

Paul Goodman, "1984," from *Ramparts* Magazine, September, 1967.
Reprinted by permission of *Ramparts*.

and their Finnish-style wooden architecture, perform social services by running Summerhill-type schools and rest homes for the retired. And their beautiful intensive and glasshouse farming, copied from the Dutch, provides the only tasty urban food now available. Besides these, there are the gurus like Goodman, who lives across the Connecticut and is terribly old.

The two distinct types coexist peaceably and of course are peaceable people. Indeed, it was during the Vietnam troubles that society first began to encourage their exodus, to get them out of the Pentagon's hair. It happened this way: Diggers and many other youths were burning draft cards in embarrassing numbers. In desperation, to get them away from settled places, the *agents provocateurs* began to schedule the be-ins and T-groups further and further out in the sticks, with transportation paid by the CIA. To the government's surprise, this caught on. The urban young suddenly decided it was groovy to dig up carrots right from the ground, to shake down apples, and to fuck the sheep; they began to camp out, and then to squat and settle. They also imagined they would grow hemp. Many professors, meantime, after signing several hundred anti-war protests in the Times (for which, by some slip-up, they could *not* get a CIA subsidy), finally became conscience-stricken about working for M.I.T., Columbia and Berkeley, and quit and set up little colleges in the hills. The rest is history. But it was not until the Kennedy-Wallace administration that the official policy of land grants and rural subsidies began. (As we shall see, this was after the Seven Plagues.)

At present there is plenty of mixing between Digger types and professor types, though at the beginning they hardly communicated. When some authentic music comes to Vermont, from Tanzania or Cambodia, it is common to find beatniks with their matted hair and lice sprawled on a professor's maple floor; and there is intermarriage. I do not mean to imply that Diggers are unattractive. Some are unkempt in a becoming way, some are diamonds in the rough, a few are real barbaric dandies. On the whole, they are sweet and serviceable people, are glad to serve as school aides, pull weeds, etc. The professors, in turn, are democratic and would like to teach them something, but unfortunately there was the break in the cultural tradition that occurred at the time of "Don't trust anybody over 30." Since the young wouldn't trust anybody—justifiably —they couldn't learn anything. And now their own children have an unbreakable apperceptive block, impervious to Head Start programs.

Common elements in the Vermont culture are fresh food, good hi-fi and much playing of musical instruments, jalopies of all vintages, disregard of moral legislation and low taxes. At some level, all are good citizens. Public services are cheap, roads are good enough, because every-body pitches in. It is touching to see Diggers who won't wash their faces carefully depositing their beer cans in litterbaskets. Another common element is, of course, Senator Aiken, who is now 100.

II. *Ecological and Economic Factors*

Generally speaking, emigration and rural reconstruction were unexpected consequences of the Great Enclosure policy which was supposed to get most people *off* the land and speed up urbanization. This is another example of the rule that, if people survive, inept social engineering will produce a contrary effect.

The American Enclosure of the 20th century consisted of subsidizing chain grocers and agrindustrial plantations, giving high profits to processors and packagers, befuddling the public with brand names, destroying fertile land for suburban sprawl and aircraft companies, destroying water supplies and importing expensive water, preventing rural cooperation by monopoly tactics, destroying country schools, farmers' markets and small food stores by urban renewal, destroying villages by highways and supermarkets. By the '60s only six per cent of the popula-tion was rural. Vast beautiful areas had been depopulated and were returning to swamp, as in the later Roman empire.

Meantime there were obvious signs of urban over-population. Urban costs mounted geometrically, for utilities, sanitation, policing, housing, schooling, welfare, transit, etc. To live in a densely populated area, in however degraded a condition, was itself a luxury; yet the inhabitants were becoming poorer and poorer. The middle classes, who had options, fled to the periphery to avoid taxes and the lower classes. Despite the agricultural technology, the price of food did not diminish, since the economics of scale went to the middlemen; and once the possibility of small competition was destroyed, the chains went to town. One could no longer buy an edible tomato. When Southern sharecropping was de-stroyed by mechanization, no effort was made to give subsistence to the Negroes; they were forced to come to northern urban areas, even though the worst public housing cost $20,000 a dwelling unit to provide. (I say "urban areas" because there were no longer such things as "cities." I say "dwelling unit" because there were no longer such things as "homes.") A psychiatric survey of midtown New York in the '60s showed that 75 per cent of the people were neurotic and 25 per cent needed immediate treatment. There were 70,000 heroin addicts in New York.

Since the structure was economically unviable, there were frequent riots, school boycotts, rent strikes and strikes of municipal services. To these, the government responded with noble speech, confused programs and enough actual money to finance several reports by sociologists. Departments of urban affairs were opened at several universities. In 1966, the mayor of New York said that it would cost $50 billion to make New York City alone "livable."

Thus, the Summer of Seven Plagues was entirely predictable, and was indeed predicted. It is still not clear, however, how many of the disasters occurred in a chain reaction, and how many were just "bad luck." It started with a transit strike in one of the big urban areas. For a couple of weeks many people couldn't get to work, and every available motor vehicle in the region crammed the streets. Then finally occurred what we had been expecting for years: the traffic got so thick that it did not move at all. Unfortunately, instead of just giving up and abandoning the cars for a time, the drivers kept edging back and forth to extricate themselves. And during this crisis there occurred a serious temperature inversion and a wind from the factories to the west. That night, 40,000 people died from the smog. The shock of this tragedy ended the transit strike. But unluckily, on the next night occurred the power failure that lasted two days and cost $2 billion, more than the cost of a month of the Vietnam war. This seems to have had some connection with the previous troubles. Some double agents paid by the CIA to do studies in sabotage had decided that it was a bully time for fun and games. This was one of the CIA's bigger booboos.

All spring and summer there had been a drought, and now a week after the blackout came the climax of the water famine, when the outmoded pipes sprang some fatal leaks that were not patched up in time. In an urban area of ten million people, this caused untold suffering and perhaps another 20,000 deaths. And this in turn led directly to the great riot, for it *was* a long hot summer. And a few days later the new SST, returning from its maiden voyage, overshot and plunged into the skyscrapers. But this too had been in the cards and had been foretold. It is now more than a decade since the Seven Plagues, yet we still cannot calculate the mental breakdowns.

It was at this time that one of the junkies among the Diggers was heard to say, "Zap! This urban area has put the whammies on me!" "But man," said his friend, "like how you gonna score up there in that mountain where a stream runs?" "Zap! I say Zap!" A coed said, "I am tired of having premarital intercourse in urban areas. Who loves to lie with me under the greenwood tree, come hither! come hither!" As in a dream, an economist remembered Borsodi's "Prosperity and Security" which he had read as a boy. And a humanist wrote a paper pointing out that Michelangelo's Florence numbered 100,000 and Goethe's Weimar perhaps 25,000.

A finite number of years later, after several million people had already emigrated to the land, Lurleen Wallace—Bobby had had the usual Kennedy luck—signed the Land Grant and Rural Subsistence Act. Mildred Loomis, the grand lady of the Green Revolution, was named administrator; but since she was a kind of Henry George anarchist, her phone was bugged.

III. Rural Reconstruction

The tendency of efficient technology since 1900—electrification, automobiles, power tools, distant communication—was toward dispersal and decentralization. Only promoters and self-aggrandizers had pushed the urbanization. Thus some kind of rural reconstruction was bound to occur. When cybernation made possible the absolute concentration of a whole industry in a small area with a small labor force, the vast agglomerations of factory towns became obsolete; and there was no technical reason why decentralized teams of designers and programmers should not tend their gardens or go fishing. Nevertheless, it has been a gradual process, full of serendipity and hang-ups, for rural life to find its present shape.

The present rural reconstruction, such as it is, is not "pastoral" withdrawal. The Diggers and the humanist professors wanted to get out of the urban areas, but they certainly did not intend to quit the mainstream of social problems; if anything, both groups were more socially committed than the average, though they did not have the "politics" of liberal reformers. In any case, they created a framework of social service, and the immense number who have come since the Plagues and the government grants have fitted into it. It is a peculiar post-urban kind of ruralism.

(As of 1983, the "rural" population was 12 per cent and the United States as a whole was already more livable. Perhaps most important, there has been a lively revival of regional towns, instead of the idiotic "new towns" and dormitory towns conceived during the '60s.)

The Diggers and professors were pacifists. They took ecological problems seriously and were, of course, the chief agents, as workers, pressure groups and by nonviolent resistance, in cleaning the rivers, diminishing the insecticides, stopping the despoiling and the motels. And finally, they adopted the principle, each group in its own competence, to use the country to help solve urban problems that were insoluble or too difficult or expensive in urban settings. Following this principle, they were able to channel back to the country a portion of the enormous urban budget, e.g. for education, welfare and psychiatry. Let me give a few examples.

Back in the '60s, it had become not uncommon for Diggers and other young people to go insane and be hospitalized for a short spell, whether because of LSD or just life in America. This brought them into contact with the appalling reality of harmless loonies rotting away untreated in asylums. Now, when they took to the country, they prevailed on the doctors to release many such people to their own easy-going custody; and this resulted in the spectacular increase in remissions that has revolutionized therapy. A similar process occurred with tens of thousands of runaway adolescents who used to end up in reformatories. And also, a surprising number of adult derelicts managed to settle down among the Diggers and begin to farm and feed themselves. That is, just as the Students for a Democratic Society developed into a kind of Franciscans among the urban poor, many of the Diggers soon came to be running Catholic Worker type farms in the country.

Ironically, when the professors, using institutional and political means, tried to initiate similar programs, they met with far less success. For instance, they proposed country schooling and farm life for a certain number of slum children, in order to open their minds and give them some options. Likewise, they tried to encourage people on welfare to get out of the urban areas to where they would get more for their money. These proposals required administrative changes so that the urban money could be allotted to the country, and naturally the urban administrators resisted. But astoundingly, the poor also resisted, saying, "You're sending us back to the sticks!"—they were thinking of their own parents in Mississippi. It was not until 1978, when the government finally came around to the Guaranteed Income, that the poor could make rational choices because they could make their own choices. And almost at once 10,000 Negro families came to Vermont, took the land grant, and bought jalopies like everybody else.

As a cultural force, the hermits and monks were more adept. During the middle of the century, of course, the universities became totally corrupted by the industrial-military; apparently Western culture was done for. But *yang* and *yin*, just at this moment the humanists reappeared in the woods, to Xerox the manuscripts and carry on the tradition. And soon come hordes of eager students, apparently from nowhere, since they had lain low during the brainwashing. Indeed, it is only now, in the last terrible year or two, that we can begin to appreciate what a tremendous brain drain from society their defection has been. A vastly disproportionate share of the imaginative emigrated to the country. The dull were left behind to manage things. But since the social machine was mainly run by computer, its ineptitude did not show up, until . . .

But to end on a merrier note, let me mention the beginnings of specialist farming, where I happen to know the inside story, entirely typical of our human arrangements, alas. M., the mayor of a rather large urban area in the middle west, was the brother-in-law of L., who owned one of the hotels. L. thought he could steal a march on his competitors if he could revive the novelty of edible food. He got M. reelected and M. rammed through the quixotic reestablishment of a farmers' market, where L. signed the prime contracts. But to everybody's consternation, this tipped off the national fad of Quality that boomed in the middle '70s. Luckily it happened overnight. By the time the chain grocers tried to have fresh food banned under the Food and Drug law, it was too late.

IV. 1984

And now?

"God works in many ways His wonders to perform." But He's not a skillful mechanic. A man drives over a cliff and "by a miracle" he only breaks his back. It would be more divine if he were a better driver and stayed on the road.

An H-bomb "accidentally" fell on Akron, wiped it out, and blasted or poisoned two million people. To be sure, it was the fourth "accident," though two of the bombs exploded at sea and one killed only a few score Eskimos.

What stupid fuck-ups men are! No, they are probably not stupid by nature. By working in rigid institutions with crooked purposes even an intelligent animal must make a moron of himself. McNamara set the standard for them all.

What *is* miraculous, however, is that even the Americans have now joined the universal revulsion. It looks as though the industrial-military is finished. But of course, then, the entire fabric of society is in shreds, since they have no other method of organization. It isn't even a "revolutionary situation." With the fall of the CIA, every left group has lost a third of its members and 100 per cent of its funds. And since the Air Force couldn't get a ship off the ground today, every right group is impotent. I suppose the universities will have to close. What will become of the CIA? What will become of the National Merit Scholarships?

It is already clear that we here in Vermont are going to be inundated. These people are running back and forth like chickens without heads, and naturally a lot of them run to us, since we have developed some kind of rudimentary structure of community. But what? In the country at large, a rural-urban ratio of 20-80 per cent or even 30-70 per cent is thinkable, it even makes sense. But this present flood is chaos.

Well, we'll do our duty as we always have. We're braced for it. And—thank God—at whatever cost—is there *really* a possibility of peace? Can we *live* without the nightmare of those bombs always in the back of our minds, or will we all flip?

Buddhism and the Coming Revolution

Buddhism holds that the universe and all creatures in it are intrinsically in a state of complete wisdom, love and compassion; acting in natural response and mutual interdependence. The personal realization of this from-the-beginning state cannot be had for and by one-"self"—because it is not fully realized unless one has given the self up; and away.

In the Buddhist view, that which obstructs the effortless manifestation of this is Ignorance, which projects into fear and needless craving. Historically, Buddhist philosophers have failed to analyze out the degree to which ignorance and suffering are caused or encouraged by social factors, considering fear-and-desire to be given facts of the human condition. Consequently the major concern of Buddhist philosophy is epistemology and "psychology" with no attention paid to historical or sociological problems. Although Mahayana Buddhism has a grand vision of universal salvation, the *actual* achievement of Buddhism has been the development of practical systems of meditation toward the end of liberating a few dedicated individuals from psychological hangups and cultural conditionings. Institutional Buddhism has been conspicuously ready to accept or ignore the inequalities and tyrannies of whatever political system it found itself under. This can be death to Buddhism, because it is death to any meaningful function of compassion. Wisdom without compassion feels no pain.

No one today can afford to be innocent, or indulge himself in ignorance of the nature of contemporary governments, politics and social orders. The national politics of the modern world maintain their existence by deliberately fostered craving and fear: monstrous protection rackets. The "free world" has become economically dependent on a fantastic system of stimulation of greed which cannot be fulfilled, sexual desire which cannot be satiated and hatred which has no outlet except against oneself, the persons one is supposed to love, or the revolutionary aspirations of pitiful, poverty-stricken marginal societies like Cuba or Vietnam. The conditions of the Cold War have turned all modern societies—Communist included—into vicious distorters of man's true potential. They create populations of "preta"—hungry ghosts, with giant appetites and throats no bigger than needles. The soil, the forests and all animal life are being consumed by these cancerous collectivities; the air and water of the planet is being fouled by them.

There is nothing in human nature or the requirements of human social organization which intrinsically requires that a culture be contradictory, repressive and productive of violent and frustrated personalities. Recent findings in anthropology and psychology make this more and more evident. One can prove it for himself by taking a good look at his own nature through meditation. Once a person has this much faith and insight, he must be led to a deep concern with the need for radical social change through a variety of hopefully non-violent means.

The joyous and voluntary poverty of Buddhism becomes a positive force. The traditional harmlessness and refusal to take life in any form has nation-shaking implications. The practice of meditation, for which one needs only "the ground beneath one's feet" wipes out mountains of junk being pumped into the mind by the mass media and supermarket universities. The belief in a serene and generous fulfillment of natural loving desires destroys ideologists which blind, maim and repress—and points the way to a kind of community which would amaze "moralists" and transform armies of men who are fighters because they cannot be lovers.

Avatamsaka (Kegon) Buddhist philosophy sees the world as a vast interrelated network in which all objects and creatures are necessary and illuminated. From one standpoint, governments, wars, or all that we consider "evil" are uncompromisingly contained in this totalistic realm. The hawk, the swoop and the hare are one. From the "human" standpoint we cannot live in those terms unless all beings see with the same enlightened eye. The Bodhisattva lives by the sufferer's standard, and he must be effective in aiding those who suffer.

The mercy of the West has been social revolution; the mercy of the East has been individual insight into the basic self/void. We need both. They are both contained in the traditional three aspects of the Dharma path: wisdom (prajña), meditation (dhyãna), and morality (sīla). Wisdom is intuitive knowledge of the mind of love and clarity that lies beneath one's ego-driven anxieties and aggressions. Meditation is going into the mind to see this for yourself—over and over again, until it becomes the mind you live in. Morality is bringing it back out in the way you live, through personal example and responsible action, ultimately toward the true community (sangha) of "all beings." This last aspect means, for me, supporting any cultural and economic revolution that moves clearly toward a free, international, classless world. It means using such means as civil disobedience, outspoken criticism, protest, pacifism, voluntary poverty and even gentle violence if it comes to a matter of restraining some impetuous redneck. It means affirming the widest possible spectrum of non-harmful individual behavior—defending the right of individuals to smoke hemp, eat peyote, be polygynous, polyandrous or homosexual. Worlds of behavior and custom long banned by the Judaeo-Capitalist-Christian-Marxist West. It means respecting intelligence and learning, but not as greed or means to personal power. Working on one's own responsibility, but willing to work with a group. "Forming the new society within the shell of the old"—the I.W.W. slogan of fifty years ago.

The traditional cultures are in any case doomed, and rather than cling to their good aspects hopelessly it should be remembered that whatever is or ever was in any other culture can be reconstructed from the unconscious, through meditation. In fact, it is my own view that the coming revolution will close the circle and link us in many ways with the most creative aspects of our archaic past. If we are lucky we may eventually arrive at a totally integrated world culture with matrilineal descent, free-form marriage, natural-credit communist economy, less industry, far less population and lots more national parks.

I Have a Dream

Five score years ago, a great American, in whose symbolic shadow we stand, signed the Emancipation Proclamation. This momentous decree came as a great beacon light of hope to millions of Negro slaves who had been seared in the flames of withering injustice. It came as a joyous daybreak to end the long night of captivity.

But one hundred years later, we must face the tragic fact that the Negro is still not free. One hundred years later, the life of the Negro is still sadly crippled by the manacles of segregation and the chains of discrimination. One hundred years later, the Negro lives on a lonely island of poverty in the midst of a vast ocean of material prosperity. One hundred years later, the Negro is still languished in the corners of American society and finds himself an exile in his own land. So we have come here today to dramatize an appalling condition.

In a sense we have come to our nation's Capital to cash a check. When the architects of our republic wrote the magnificent words of the Constitution and the Declaration of Independence, they were signing a promissory note to which every American was to fall heir. This note was a promise that all men would be guaranteed the unalienable rights of life, liberty, and the pursuit of happiness.

It is obvious today that America has defaulted on this promissory note insofar as her citizens of color are concerned. Instead of honoring this sacred obligation, America has given the Negro people a bad check; a check which has come back marked "insufficient funds." But we refuse to believe that the bank of justice is bankrupt. We refuse to believe that there are insufficient funds in the great vaults of opportunity of this nation. So we have come to cash this check—a check that will give us upon demand the riches of freedom and the security of justice. We have also come to this hallowed spot to remind America of the fierce urgency of *now*. This is no time to engage in the luxury of cooling off or to take the tranquilizing drug of gradualism. *Now* is the time to make real the promises of Democracy. *Now* is the time to rise from the dark and desolate valley of segregation to the sunlit path of racial justice. *Now* is the time to open the doors of opportunity to all of God's children. *Now* is the time to lift our nation from the quicksands of racial injustice to the solid rock of brotherhood.

It would be fatal for the nation to overlook the urgency of the moment and to underestimate the determination of the Negro. This sweltering summer of the Negro's legitimate discontent will not pass until there is an invigorating autumn of freedom and equality. 1963 is not an end, but a beginning. Those who hope that the Negro needed to blow off steam and will now be content will have a rude awakening if the nation returns to business as usual. There will be neither rest nor tranquillity in America until the Negro is granted his citizenship rights. The whirlwinds of revolt will continue to shake the foundations of our nation until the bright day of justice emerges.

But there is something that I must say to my people who stand on the warm threshold which leads into the palace of justice. In the process of gaining our rightful place we must not be guilty of wrongful deeds. Let us not seek to satisfy our thirst for freedom by drinking from the cup of bitterness and hatred. We must forever conduct our struggle on the high plane of dignity and discipline. We must not allow our creative protest to degenerate into physical violence. Again and again we must rise to the majestic heights of meeting physical force with soul force. The marvelous new militancy which has engulfed the Negro community must not lead us to a distrust of all white people, for many of our white brothers, as evidenced by their presence here today, have come to realize that their destiny and their freedom is inextricably bound to our freedom. We cannot walk alone.

And as we walk, we must make the pledge that we shall march ahead. We cannot turn back. There are those who are asking the devotees of civil rights, "When will you be satisfied?" We can never be satisfied as long as the Negro is the victim of the unspeakable horrors of police brutality. We can never be satisfied as long as our bodies, heavy with the fatigue of travel, cannot gain lodging in the motels of the highways and the hotels of the cities. We cannot be satisfied as long as the Negro's basic mobility is from a smaller ghetto to a larger one. We can never be satisfied as long as a Negro in Mississippi cannot vote and a Negro in New York believes he has nothing for which to vote. No, no, we are not satisfied, and we will not be satisfied until justice rolls down like waters and righteousness like a mighty stream.

I am not unmindful that some of you have come here out of great trials and tribulations. Some of you have come fresh from narrow jail cells. Some of you have come from areas where your quest for freedom left you battered by the storms of persecution and staggered by the winds of police brutality. You have been the veterans of creative suffering. Continue to work with the faith that unearned suffering is redemptive.

Go back to Mississippi, go back to Alabama, go back to South Carolina, go back to Georgia, go back to Louisiana, go back to the slums and ghettos of our northern cities, knowing that somehow this situation can and will be changed. Let us not wallow in the valley of despair.

I say to you today, my friends, that in spite of the difficulties and frustrations of the moment I still have a dream. It is a dream deeply rooted in the American dream.

I have a dream that one day this nation will rise up and live out the true meaning of its creed: "We hold these truths to be self-evident; that all men are created equal."

I have a dream that one day on the red hills of Georgia the sons of former slaves and the sons of former slaveowners will be able to sit down together at the table of brotherhood.

I have a dream that one day even the state of Mississippi, a desert state sweltering with the heat of injustice and oppression, will be transformed into an oasis of freedom and justice.

I have a dream that my four little children will one day live in a nation where they will not be judged by the color of their skin but by the content of their character.

I have a dream today.

I have a dream that one day the state of Alabama, whose governor's lips are presently dripping with the words of interposition and nullification, will be transformed into a situation where little black boys and black girls will be able to join hands with little white boys and white girls and walk together as sisters and brothers.

I have a dream today.

I have a dream that one day every valley shall be exalted, every hill and mountain shall be made low, the rough places will be made plain, and the crooked places will be made straight, and the glory of the Lord shall be revealed, and all flesh shall see it together.

This is our hope. This is the faith with which I return to the South. With this faith we will be able to hew out of the mountain of despair a stone of hope. With this faith we will be able to transform the jangling discords of our nation into a beautiful symphony of brotherhood. With this faith we will be able to work together, to pray together, to struggle together, to go to jail together, to stand up for freedom together, knowing that we will be free one day.

This will be the day when all of God's children will be able to sing with new meaning

> My country, 'tis of thee,
> Sweet land of liberty,
>   Of thee I sing:
> Land where my fathers died,
> Land of the pilgrims' pride,
> From every mountain side
>   Let freedom ring.

And if America is to be a great nation this must become true. So let freedom ring from the prodigious hilltops of New Hampshire. Let freedom ring from the mighty mountains of New York. Let freedom ring from the heightening Alleghenies of Pennsylvania!

Let freedom ring from the snowcapped Rockies of Colorado!

Let freedom ring from the curvacious peaks of California!

But not only that; let freedom ring from Stone Mountain of Georgia!

Let freedom ring from Lookout Mountain of Tennessee!

Let freedom ring from every hill and molehill of Mississippi. From every mountainside, let freedom ring.

When we let freedom ring, when we let it ring from every village and every hamlet, from every state and every city, we will be able to speed up that day when all of God's children, black men and white men, Jews and Gentiles, Protestants and Catholics, will be able to join hands and sing in the words of the old Negro spiritual, "Free at last! free at last! thank God almighty, we are free at last!"

AUTHOR AND
TITLE INDEX

E 1345